Lotus Notes and Domino 4.5

Architecture, Administration, and Security

Scott L. Thomas

Brad J. Hoyt

McGraw-Hill

New York   San Francisco   Washington, D.C
Auckland   Bogotá   Caracas   Lisbon   London
Madrid   Mexico City   Milan   Montreal   New Delhi
San Juan   Singapore   Sydney   Tokyo   Toronto

Library of Congress Cataloging-in-Publication Data

Thomas, Scott L.
    Lotus Notes and Domino 4.5 architecture, administration, and security /
Scott L. Thomas, Bradley Hoyt.
        p.   cm.
    Includes index.
    ISBN 0-07-064562-0
    1. Lotus Notes for Windows.   2. Lotus Domino.   3. Business—Computer programs.
4. Groupware (Computer software)   5. Database management—Computer programs.
6. Electronic mail systems.   7. Web servers—Software.   8. Computer networks—
Security measures.
I. Hoyt, Bradley.   II. Title.
HF5548.4.L692T47   1997
005.369—dc21   97-23410
                                                                              CIP

McGraw-Hill

*A Division of The **McGraw-Hill** Companies*

The views expressed in this book are solely those of the author, and do not
represent the views of any other party or parties.

1 2 3 4 5 6 7 8 9 0   DOC/DOC   9 0 2 1 0 9 8 7

ISBN   0-07-064562-0

*The sponsoring editor for this book was Judy Brief. It was set in New Century Schoolbook
by E. D. Evans, freelance designer for McGraw-Hill's Professional Book Group composition
unit. The Chapter opener art and icons were created by David Evans, freelance designer
for McGraw-Hill's Professional Book Group composition unit.*

Printed and bound by R.R. Donnelley & Sons Company.

*McGraw-Hill books are available at special quantity discounts to use as premiums and
sales promotions, or for use in corporate training programs. For more information, please
write to the Director of Special Sales, McGraw-Hill, 11 West 19th Street, New York, NY
10011. Or contact your local bookstore.*

*Product or brand names used in this book may be trade names or trademarks. Where we believe that
there may be proprietary claims to such trade names or trademarks, the name has been used with an
initial capital or it has been capitalized in the style used by the name claimant. Regardless of the capi-
talization used, all such names have been used in an editorial manner without any intent to convey
endorsement of or other affiliation with the name claimant. Neither the author nor the publisher
intends to express any judgement as to the validity or legal status of any such proprietary claims.*

    This book is printed on recycled, acid-free paper containing
a minimum of 50% recycled de-inked fiber.

To my Grandfather Jones, who always taught me
hard work is the key to success.

— Scott L. Thomas

To Cheri, Preston, Heidi, Spencer, and Claire,
who define and drive me.

—Brad J. Hoyt

Table of Contents

✓ Chapter 9   Windows NT Integration 277

✓ Chapter 10   Replication 307

Acknowledgments

Writing a book is an incredible undertaking, especially if you have never done it before. A book such as this that is intended to provide detailed insight and how-to information based on the author's knowledge should be easy, right? Wrong. It takes more than years of experience to create a compelling, engaging and practical book that is usable by more than the recyclers. It takes capable, competent, and willing reviewers, editors, and, of course readers like you.

We would like to thank our technical reviewers: Roger Pegler of Intranet Systems Pty Limited (rpegler@ntranet.com.au), Amy Peasley of Whittman-Hart, and David Marshak from the Patricia Seybold Group. Thanks also to James Gold of Lotus Development Corporation.

We also thank Sheldon Laube, co-founder Executive Vice President and Chief Technology Officer of US Web, former CTO of Novell, and former National Director of Information Technology at Price Waterhouse LLC for indirectly getting us into Notes, providing us with insight, and writing the foreword to this book.

Additional thanks go to Judy Brief, our editor at McGraw-Hill, Edie Evans, design and production manager, Gwynne Jackson, copyeditor, and the other members of the McGraw-Hill staff who made this book possible.

And finally, thanks go out to our families and friends who listened to us when we thought we would never leave the computer.

Scott L. Thomas
Brad J. Hoyt

Foreword

In December of 1989 Lotus Development Corporation announced Lotus Notes 1.0 in a small press conference in Boston and once again changed the technology industry. Lotus Notes introduced the mainstream business community to the power of GroupWare, an obscure technology aimed at helping groups of people work more effectively together. Within two years, virtually every major corporation in the world was evaluating how the power of Notes could be used to improve organization effectiveness.

At the December product launch I was privileged to announce that Price Waterhouse (my employer at the time) had purchased 10,000 copies of Notes. Purchasing Notes however was the easiest part of the process at that time. Implementing and administering the world's largest Notes implementation (at the time) was an incredible challenge for Price Waterhouse and other early adopters of the Notes product. There were no education courses, books, or even consultants with real world experience with Notes. Each implementation was a new adventure and the IT executives were responsible for breaking new ground. Today there is a wide range of Notes experience to draw upon in new implementations.

The authors of this work have a vast body of experience in Notes architecture and administration. This book is a must-read guide for any organization planning a Notes implementation. Their practical advice and guidance lead Notes administrators through the most difficult parts of the deployment process and helps them insure a successful implementation.

Since 1989 Notes has released increasingly powerful versions of Notes to deliver powerful new capabilities. With the release of Lotus Domino, based on Notes, Lotus has embraced the Internet and the World Wide Web and made Notes into one of the premier Web development platforms. Lotus has shown their ability to evolve Notes to meet the ever-changing needs of their customers now and into the future.

Sheldon Laube
Executive Vice President, Chief Technology Officer
USWeb Corporation

Introduction

Purpose and Objective

What we will discuss within this book is how to effectively architect, administer, and secure a new or existing Notes and Domino network within your enterprise. We will cover topics that directly relate to 100% Notes networks, and Internet and Intranet implementations using both the Notes client and a Web browser.

The book you are reading has been a work in progress for over three years. We initially started writing it as a white paper detailing best practices for Notes 3.0 architecture, administration, and security. Through numerous Notes consulting engagements we have gathered and gained deep experience and assisted in the successful deployment of Notes networks in many Fortune 1000 organizations. What you will find within this book is not only our initial white paper started in 1993, but the combined experiences and knowledge we have acquired in the interim.

The implementation of Notes in most organizations has typically followed a bottom-up pattern. The power of Notes was traditionally embraced at the departmental level, and moved horizontally across the organization. This was essentially a grassroots movement driven by innovative departments with a clear idea of the value of collaboration. As departments started to link their disparate Notes systems, the Information Systems groups started to take notice. As organizations realized the collective value of Notes as a business tool, it became necessary to create an organizational vision for its use and growth. This book is the starting point for helping an organization unleash the power of Lotus Notes.

There is a method to the madness, and even organizations that consciously deploy Notes one department or application at a time have a need for a comprehensive road map. This roadmap includes an architecture for deployment, a strategy for implementation and management (administration), a robust security model, and an understanding of the effort needed to achieve specific business objectives.

In every software genre, you will find one defining product. That product may have been the first, the best, or simply the one that gained the best reputation for available features and functionality. In the groupware genre, Lotus Notes has become the defining product. Many competitors have billed themselves as the "Notes killer," but none have succeeded nor come close. With the release of Lotus Notes 4.5 and the *Lotus Domino server,* powered by Lotus Notes, Lotus has raised the bar to an even higher level. In this the age of the Internet and World Wide Web, Lotus Notes was said to be on its deathbed and is still sometimes referred to as a "legacy application." This couldn't be further from the truth. In fact, many Fortune 1000 companies use Notes to communicate, collaborate, and coordinate their activities throughout their enterprises, and are also using Notes as a platform for extranet applications as well.

Our experience with Notes seems like a career-long endeavor that has stretched from before Notes 1.0 to Notes/Domino 4.6. We have moved away from Notes at times, but always seem to find our way back. Our collective experience spans over 10 years, and includes the creation of applications, deployment and management of application suites and departmental systems, as well as architecting enterprise Notes systems.

An area much neglected in the Notes world is the area of Notes systems architecture, administration, and security. Most books concerning Lotus Notes focus on Notes application development. This book fills the missing void for Notes literature. We do not intend to educate you on what groupware is—that would be a book in itself— we expect you to have a basic understanding of the fundamentals of groupware and Lotus Notes. We will try to educate you on the finer points of architecting, administering, and securing an enterprise system based on the Notes platform. While it is important to develop compelling applications—unless there is a manageable and scaleable architecture—and plan for growth, even awesome applications will fail. We will also, where appropriate, discuss some of the history of Notes, its core components, how they have evolved, and our experience implementing systems that use them. As we discuss the issues, we will provide *Tips* and *Traps* to further emphasize important points.

Groupware Defined

Arguably, Lotus Notes can be considered the best groupware package on the market today. Many people try to define exactly what groupware and Lotus Notes are. In order to gain a better understanding of the issues surrounding Notes architecture, administration, and security, we must have a common definition of groupware. For those people familiar with the products that market themselves as groupware no definition may be necessary, but for those unfamiliar with the groupware genre, we will put forth a simple definition.

Our basic definition of groupware is as follows: *groupware* is an integrated application development and deployment platform that meets an organization's information-sharing needs. The basic components of groupware are:

- A data store which stores and manages access to structured, semi-structured, and unstructured data—for example, text, rich-text, images, audio, and video.

- A communications infrastructure to support messaging, mail routing, content replication, and mobile users.

- An environment that provides for secure storage, transmission, and usage of applications.

- An application development environment, which allows for the customization of applications using the previous components.

With all of these discrete components combined in one package, Notes offers organizations a means to easily share information, effectively communicate, collaborate, and coordinate key business processes. Teamwork now takes on a whole new definition as users are able to share all types of information in one information store, including e-mail, wordprocessing documents, faxes, discussion databases, and even data pulled from legacy systems. All of this information sharing can take place regardless of location, networks, platforms, or time zones. This is the real power of groupware product like Lotus Notes.

Lotus Notes is not a panacea. There are obvious tradeoffs in any integrated platform, but Notes skillfully integrates its core components in a way that provides maximum functionality with a minimum number of tradeoffs. If each individual component were compared with competitors in that application class they would perhaps be found wanting. But when combined into an integrated platform, they hum like a finely tuned automobile.

History

Lotus Notes was created by Ray Ozzie and the engineers at Iris Associates in the late eighties. The first version of Lotus Notes was released in beta form in late 1989, with the official release in 1990. Ozzie's idea of collaborative computing was sparked from his days at the University of Illinois while using a simple educational program named "Plato," used by faculty and students to share information pertaining to classes taught at the institution. Ironically, Marc Andreesen, co-founder of Netscape Communications, attended the University of Illinois as well and has been humorously accused of finding Ray's old class notes left behind in a school locker at the university.

What Ray and his team developed with version 1.0 of Lotus Notes was the industry's first generally accepted example of groupware: a package that enabled users to quickly develop and share information, thoughts, and ideas seamlessly across the office or the world regardless of platform, network protocol, or location.

Many other products have tried to imitate and compete with Notes, such as Novell Groupwise, Microsoft Exchange, Collabra Share (now owned by Netscape), and Netscape themselves. They have all claimed to be a better Notes than Notes. Some certainly provide a richer function set in certain discrete components, but Notes' overall power is in its support of integrated components. Microsoft Exchange, for example, tried to position itself to compete with Notes. What developers found was just how complex it is to develop a package like Lotus Notes. Microsoft now has repositioned Exchange as the messaging component of its suite of products.

The year 1996 was heralded as the year that would bring the demise of Lotus Notes. The Notes "killer" had materialized, and it was the World Wide Web. Many people before this time had also predicted the end of Lotus Notes, and when IBM purchased Lotus in 1995, the technology gliterati decried IBM and Lou Gerstner as buffoons for the purchase. In the year and a half since IBM purchased Lotus, Lotus/IBM quickly responded to the threat against Notes with Domino. Marketers renamed the Notes server to the Domino server. The development teams cranked out the code, the quality assurance people cranked up the testing machine, and outcame the reborn Notes. It is an Intranet-in-a-box application, which not only includes the core (historical) Notes functionality, but also adds fully integrated Internet standard protocols in a single package.

From a technical standpoint, it still is a Notes server, which now supports the most widely available Internet standards-based protocols. One of the most important additions is the server add-on task, HTTP, which simply runs on the desired Notes server and enables Web browsers to access Notes applications transparently. The process translates Notes applications from the native Notes format to HTML format. The industry has responded overwhelmingly to the new "openness" of the Notes architecture. Issues surround the use of a Web browser instead of a Notes client to access a Notes (Domino) server, and will be addressed throughout this book.

Notes

Throughout this book, Domino and Notes will be used inter-changeably to address the server. A Domino server is a Notes server, and as mentioned before, it is a marketing plan to position Notes as a more open architecture specifically tailored to the Web. The client still remains a Notes client, in its various forms.

Now that you have a brief understanding of the evolution of Lotus Notes and its definition, we will help guide you through proper planning and administration of a Notes network. Each chapter details the issues you should consider in properly designing, configuring, deploying, and securing your Notes/Domino environment. The information is based on our experience with Notes throughout the years and intends to help you avoid the potential pitfalls that many organizations experience. Each chapter is structured to be a handy resource for both new and existing Notes/Domino installations. With this said, let's talk Notes!

Lotus Notes in Your Organization

What are the issues that you need to consider before deploying or redeploying Notes in your organization? This chapter will provide you with the answer to that question by discussing the key success factors, the creation and staffing of deployment teams, and the available Notes server offerings and client types.

Many not familiar with Lotus Notes would at first glance consider it just another simple program installed on a user's desktop. Lotus Notes by design is very simple to adapt to and use not only from a functionality standpoint, but also from a developer standpoint. The concept of rapid application development/deployment certainly holds true with Notes. The average user can quickly develop an application to suit his or her needs in a matter of minutes, either from scratch or from a derivative of the numerous sample Notes sample applications. This has been one of the major strengths of Notes in terms of use and rapid acceptance.

This ease of adaptation on the desktop level often turns into a sinkhole for many IT (*Information Technology*) organizations. Most overburdened IT organizations rarely have the time or the training to properly deploy Notes in the enterprise. End users see Notes as a simple application and demand IT organizations to install a Notes server for their department to support their Notes application. Word then spreads, and several more departments within the organization demand Notes servers for their applications. Before long, there are several pockets of Notes servers throughout the organization.

The next phase in this growing Notes web within an organization is the request for different departments to share their applications. To the end user, this should be a simple task. To the overburdened and often undertrained administrator, it turns into hours of work. In many organizations, users start to use the integrated mail capabilities of Notes rather than the corporate standard, adding fuel to the fire.

It is this back-end world of Lotus Notes that we will help prepare you for. It cannot be stressed enough to administrators and to IT managers that if Notes is to be adopted within an organization, it must be treated as if it were an infrastructure component or operating system such as Novell, Windows NT, or UNIX. Proper time, planning, and support is needed to support a Notes infrastructure. A Notes network cannot be simply "put up."

Traps

Proper time and consideration before installing Lotus Notes within an enterprise, even if a small installation is essential. Rearchitecting a Notes infrastructure is a very difficult task, especially in larger installations. Lotus Notes is very complex to reengineer as a homogenous environment when faced with multiple unique Notes installations.

This chapter will discuss topics and considerations that should be addressed when deploying Lotus Notes. Again, it cannot be stressed enough that proper planning of the infrastructure and naming standards must be done up front with all the involved departments of your organization.

Topics you should consider are naming standards, hardware requirements, application standards, security, mail routing, replication service levels, and administration responsibilities, just to name a few. Lotus Notes has been labeled in the industry as a highly administrative application from the back end, and rightfully so (although with the latest release of Notes, the administrative requirements have been significantly reduced). We will cover all these topics with advice and experience to help you successfully deploy, administer, and secure your Notes network.

Key Success Factors

There is no single key to a successful Notes implementation, but there are several factors that will contribute to a successful deployment. These factors are:

- **Management buy-in and acceptance of Lotus Notes.** Lotus Notes is most successful when its use is driven from the top of an organization. There must be buy-in at all levels, but unless management is behind its implementation, it is destined to be marginally successful at best. Management must provide visionary applications and then require their use. Such examples might be human resource information or specific department information contained within a Notes application. Once users realize the power and ease of Notes, other applications quickly take form.

  It is when Notes is driven by small groups or departments that Notes enterprise implementations prove unsuccessful. That's not to say those departmental implementations will not be successful: many are. But in order for the organization as a whole to benefit, the vision needs to encompass the entire organization. If upper-level management does not see the advantages of using Notes and apply the proper resources, success will be elusive. Also, if "killer applications" are never developed, users may never be compelled to use Notes.

- **Proper planning up front.** An enterprise-wide Notes implementation does require a significant amount of administration on the back end. If a Notes system is not properly designed and architected from day one, administrators will be overburdened and will struggle to keep the Notes network running to sufficiently support the Notes user community. This design must include naming standards, hardware requirements, and infrastructure planning. Any of these issues not properly addressed up front may prove disastrous to the system once the Notes network is supporting hundreds of users.

● **Policies and procedures for Notes application development.** Although Notes application development is not discussed in this book, appropriate development policies and procedures are essential for a successful Notes network. Management of how Notes applications are designed and by whom is essential for a healthy Notes network. An incorrectly designed Notes application or an excessive number of Notes applications can easily bring down a Notes server.

These policies and procedures should not be onerous, but should be designed to provide the maximum amount of flexibility, while providing the greatest level of manageability.

● **Development of a Notes killer application.** The Notes development team needs to design a few simple but highly effective applications to attract users to Notes. They should be applications that surround business processes used every day by the majority of individuals in the organization. The applications should be simple so as not to confuse the novice Notes user. Applications can be modified after the community becomes comfortable with Notes.

By providing simple yet compelling applications that simplify some basic tasks, you can create excitement around Notes.

● **Proper Notes administration personnel.** Again, Notes should not be treated like just another desktop application. Rather, it should be treated as another network operating system. In order to effectively support a Notes infrastructure, properly trained Notes personnel should be put into place to manage the Notes environment.

Deployment Teams

Our experience has shown that a very effective way to implement Notes in an organization is to form *deployment* teams. These teams are focused on different aspects of the implementation, but with obviously complementary objectives. In smaller implementations or organizations, team members may have roles on multiple teams.

- **Notes Architecture and Administration Team.** Initially, this team is responsible for the overall design of the Notes infrastructure within your organization. This includes all naming standards, platforms, hardware, security, and other Notes specifics. This team is also responsible for the ongoing administration of the infrastructure. This team guides the installation team for the rollout of Notes to your organization, and also takes care of any upgrades once the Notes environment is established.

  It cannot be stated enough that the Notes administration team must be properly trained for Notes system administration. Notes needs to be treated as if it were an infrastructure and or operating system component, and requires much attention and administration once it is in place. Also, another very important consideration is detailed planning in regards to designing a Notes infrastructure. Proper planning of naming, server capacity, Notes application development, and personnel is essential to a successful Notes installation. These points will be stressed numerous times throughout this book.

  The Notes administration team is the heart of the Notes network. If you are the CIO of your organization and planning a Notes rollout in your firm, you should understand the importance of a qualified Notes staff. Proper training for this team is essential and bringing in an outside consulting organization, at least for the initial rollout, is highly recommended.

- **Notes Installation Team.** This team is particularly important in organizations where Lotus Notes does not yet exist. The installation team works closely with the Notes administration team to roll out and or upgrade Notes to all desktops as well as the server line. This team should consist of a group of individuals familiar with your environment, including the network infrastructure, all equipment Notes will be associated with, and the business elements of the organization.

This team will be responsible for all logistical planning on how to effectively roll out Notes in the organization. There are a number of different methods and tools available to assist with rolling out Notes to end users, which is discussed later in this book. This team may have to physically touch machines in order to install and configure Notes. Also, many organizations link end-user training responsibilities to this group.

The installation team may choose to only roll out Notes initially to a pilot user group. This approach is recommended especially for larger organizations. From this pilot group, the team can learn from the experience and receive user feedback so they can more effectively roll out Notes to the entire firm.

● **Notes Development Team.** The Notes development team will be responsible initially for identifying, developing, deploying, and maintaining the initial seed applications. These seed applications will hopefully be the "killer applications" that will be part of the initial rollout to users, and generate user and management awareness of Notes. This team closely coordinates their activities with the project and business leads within the organization to fully exploit Notes and receive the maximum return on investment.

The Notes development team is also responsible for developing a set of policies and procedures for developing and maintaining Notes applications. These policies and procedures include standard form layouts, data dictionary, security constructs, and a basic development methodology. Once the first few Notes applications are rolled out to the organization, the development team is responsible for upgrading and maintaining those applications. The team is also responsible for developing new Notes applications; if development rights are granted to end users, the team is responsible for reviewing the custom applications as well. Similar to Notes administration, it is beneficial to an organization to provide developers with proper training and to consider bringing in an outside Notes development consulting organization especially for the initial Notes applications. This initial guidance will be both a timesaver and cost saver down the road. This team is also responsible for testing Notes applications with newer releases of Lotus Notes to certify existing applications will perform properly.

Tips

The use of consultants and/or packaged applications should be used to jumpstart your application development efforts. This not only allows you to accomplish more in a shorter amount of time, but provides a mechanism for transferring knowledge from third parties to your own staff.

- **Notes Training Team.** The Notes training team is very important for an initial Notes rollout within an organization. They are responsible for training endusers on how to effectively utilize Lotus Notes within your organization. This includes the use of all new Notes applications as well as the basic functionality of Lotus Notes. If Notes mail is going to be used, the team is responsible for teaching the community the differences between the current mail system and Notes mail. It is highly recommended that an organization provide Notes training to the end user community no matter how simple it may be. It could range from a two-day class to a simple one hour video. This training will decrease costs immensely in terms of help desk calls that will be received if no training at all is offered.

- **Notes Help Desk.** It is inevitable that no matter how well the system is architected, and how much Notes training is offered, users will have questions and problems with Notes on their desktops. It is very important that a support mechanism—namely a help desk—be put in place before the initial rollout. The help desk team will be expected to answer questions concerning basic Notes functionality, specific procedural issues, and issues surrounding e-mail and Notes application functionality specific to the organization. During the initial rollout of Notes, the help desk can expect to field many functional and procedural calls. Once the rollout is complete and the organization and users are comfortable with Notes, the help desk can be scaled back in regards to personnel.

Notes (Domino) Server Offerings

With the release of Notes 4.5, a server may now serve applications for either a Notes client or a Web browser on a user's desktop. If a Notes administrator wishes to use Notes 4.5 only to act as a server to Notes clients, then installation and configuration is the same as earlier releases of Lotus Notes. If a Notes administrator wishes to make Notes applications available to Web browsers as well as Notes clients, then the administrator simply loads an HTTP process on the Notes server. The HTTP process is free of charge and installs during the server install or upgrade process. The HTTP process is also available from the Lotus Web site and will work on earlier releases of Notes version 4 servers. It is recommended that you upgrade your Notes server to at least version 4.5 if it is going to act as a server for Web browsers in production mode. The process to enable Web browser access to Notes applications is explained thoroughly in Chapter 13, *Internet and Web Application Servers.*

Notes server licensing is explained in the following section. For the most part, it is based on the number of processors in the machine where the Notes server is running. Again, to clarify, Lotus/IBM has renamed the Notes server as the Domino server powered by Lotus Notes. The terms "Notes servers" and "Domino servers" can be used interchangeably to explain the same machine.

Tips

It should be noted that for the entire server classes and services listed that the actual code for all types exists within the software shipment. It is up to the administrator to decide whether or not to install the services or add multiple processors to the machine. If the choice is made, it is up to the organization to responsibly purchase the required license types.

Domino 4.5 Single Processor License

This is the standard Notes license for a Notes (Domino) 4.5 server. It provides the standard Notes functionality to support workgroup collaborative computing using either a Notes client or Web browser. The Notes 4.5 server now supports SMTP, X.400, Java, Netscape Plugins, ActiveX, POP3, HTTP, HTML, MAPI, SNMP, and SSL, to name a few standards.

Domino 4.5 Multi-Processor License

The Notes (Domino) server code is not any different for a single-processor or multiprocessor machine. Lotus does not ship a different version of Lotus Notes for a multiprocessor Notes server. It is simply a licensing issue set by Lotus/IBM. Multiprocessing is actually handled by the operating system itself rather than the application. For example, if a second processor were added to a Windows NT server running Lotus Notes, Windows NT would handle the multiprocessing processes (not Lotus Notes). The organization would still be responsible for purchasing a multiprocessor license from Lotus.

Domino 4.5 Advanced Services License

Advanced Services are new add-ons that ship with Notes version 4.5. The services include the following:

- **Clustering.** Clustering includes fail-over and load balancing to enable administrators to configure servers to automatically switch over to backup servers in the event of failure. Domino servers can also be configured to help balance server loads; this prevents specific servers from being overloaded.

- **Partitioning.** Partitioning enables administrators to set up and configure several Notes servers on a single physical machine. To the Notes user, each virtual server on the machine appears as a separate Notes server retaining its own unique security and naming configurations.

- **Usage Tracking and Billing.** This provides detailed system utilization of each of the Notes servers within the Notes environment. This includes a billing process which tracks, records, and stores information about Notes activities. Specific Notes activities which can be tracked include session and mail activity, replication, and database and document access and use.

The advanced services license must be purchased separately based on the number of Domino servers in your organization. The advanced services are shipped on the installation CD, but you are responsible for purchasing the license for the product from Lotus/IBM if you decide to implement them. The advanced services are explained in greater detail in Chapter 7, *Installation Guidelines.*

Notes Client Types

There a several client types that can be used to access applications and information on Domino servers. These clients are the traditional Notes clients, Web browsers, and POP3 mail programs.

Lotus Notes License

This is the full-featured Notes license type. It enables users to perform all of the Notes functionality including server and user administration, Notes application development, and all end-user functions including Notes application and mail usage. The version 4.5 Notes client incorporates the 3-pane window format similar to the cc:Mail interface look and feel. With Notes 4.5, calendars and schedules are integrated directly into users' mail files making it easier to perform those functions even for remote users.

A Web browser is also incorporated within the client to enable users to access Web servers directly without having to switch to another product. Browsers like Microsoft Internet Explorer and Netscape Communicator can also replace the Notes browser. The ability still exists for users to access Web servers through an Inter-Notes server as well.

Lotus Notes Desktop License

The Lotus Notes Desktop license gives users the same functionality as the Lotus Notes license, minus the administration tools and Notes database application development functionality. Users are able to access and use all Notes applications, including custom Notes applications. The license can easily be upgraded to the full-featured Notes license should the need arise.

Like the full-featured version, Web server access can be performed from the built-in Web browser, other browsers, or through an Lotus Notes Mail License

Lotus Notes Mail License

The Notes mail client license enables users to use Notes e-mail which also includes all the functionality of group scheduling and calendaring. Users with this license type are unable to access any Notes applications or perform any Notes administration tasks. Like the Notes desktop license, users can be easily upgraded to the Desktop or full-featured Lotus Notes license if the need arises.

Domino Mail Access License

This license is similar to the Notes mail license in that it enables users to use a Web browser to access Notes mail files. Also, any POP3-compliant mail client may access Notes mail databases as well (this includes products such as Eudora). Web browsers may also be used to access Notes applications.

Web Browser Access

Domino 4.5 supports direct access to Notes databases, with some limitations on functionality. No charge is associated for Web browser access to Notes applications. Only Notes mail access requires a license.

Table 1.1 shows the functionality capabilities of each type of license.

Table 1.1
Notes Client
License Features

Support	Domino Mail Access	Notes Mail	Notes Desktop	Notes
Send and Receive E-Mail	X	X	X	X
Mobile Configurations		X	X	X
Calendaring and Scheduling		X	X	X
Support for Rich Text		X	X	X
Run Custom Developed Notes Applications			X	X
Perform System Administration Functions				X
Develop New Notes Applications				X

Chapter 2

System Considerations

This chapter identifies the platform and operating system issues you need to address with respect to both your server and client machines. The intent is to provide you with a basic understanding of the issues and choices. We will also discuss an approach to server classifications as part of our implementation methodology.

Hardware Standards

Selecting proper hardware and operating systems for both your Domino servers and clients is essential to successfully deploy Notes within your organization. Lotus provides basic recommendations for both hardware and operating systems; however, in order to provide vendor independence, Lotus/IBM will not make a direct recommendation. What we provide is a description of all hardware and operating system standards currently offered by Notes. Some provide better functionality than others and those elements will be shown. However, it is up to your organization to understand how each platform will fit into your environment and to best pick what is right for your Notes deployment. In most cases there is no right or best answer and ultimately a choice must be made that best suits your IT department's needs for a Notes infrastructure.

Server Hardware Selections

It can be stated that you can never have enough power for any given server. The more power, the better performance realized. This saying certainly now holds true for version 4.5 of Lotus Notes. Before version 4.0, a Notes server would only support in the area of 100 concurrent users. Large infrastructures were forced to support dozens of Notes servers to handle users' Notes applications and mail files. Since the release of Lotus Notes version 4.0, the number of simultaneous working users supported on a single server is in the area of 1500 or more on an Intel Pentium platform using a multi-processor machine with 500 or greater megabytes of RAM.

This fact by no means makes it necessary for administrators to go out and buy this powerful a machine to support their users. Hardware requirements should be tailored to the environment the administrator supports. Continuous monitoring of the Notes servers will tell administrators when resources begin to struggle and when an upgrade to the hardware may be necessary.

Lotus states the following as the minimum hardware requirements for a Notes server on the following platforms:

Table 2.1
Domino Server
Hardware
Requirements

Platform	RAM (Megabytes)	Disk space (Megabytes)
Hewlett-Packard; HP-UX 10.01	64 minimum, 96 or more recommended.	300 minimum, 500 or more recommended.
IBM OS/2 Warp and Warp Connect; OS/2 2.11 SMP	32 minimum, 48 or more recommended.	300 minimum, 500 or more recommended.
IBM AIX 4.1.3 and 4.1.4	64 minimum, 96 or more recommended.	300 minimum, 500 or more recommended.
Microsoft Windows NT 3.51 4.0 (Intel, Alpha)	48 minimum, 64 or more recommended.	300 minimum, 500 or more recommended.
Microsoft Windows 95	16 minimum, 24 or more recommended.	150 minimum, 300 or more recommended.
Novell NetWare 3.12, 4.1	644 minimum, 96 or more recommended.	300 minimum, 500 or more recommended.
Sun Solaris 2.4 and 2.5/SPARC	24 minimum, 32 or more recommended.	300 minimum, 500 or more recommended.
Sun Solaris 2.5/x86	24 minimum, 32 or more recommended.	300 minimum, 500 or more recommended.

Server Classes

Our experience has shown that large and small Notes networks benefit from a segregation of servers into 5 classes. These server classes are *application* (including Web Servers), *mail*, *hub*, *development*, and *gateway*. By segregating servers into classes, you can create a scaleable and maintainable environment. Each class of server has differing hardware and management requirements. On the following pages we discuss the five classes of servers and the associated hardware requirements.

- **Application Server** Application servers house the production Notes applications accessed by all users. Disk requirements, RAM capacity, and processor capacity can be quite demanding, depending on the number and types of Notes applications. Every time a document is added to a Notes application, the Notes server must perform a number of tasks. These activities could include providing disk storage, indexing the document, full-text indexing the document, performing actions on the document through Notes agents or APIs, as well as several other Notes-related activities. While attending to those Notes application-related tasks, Notes application servers may also be performing other Notes server processes including replication, mail routing, and supporting concurrent user access.

Determining hardware requirements for an application Notes server becomes dynamic within a Notes environment. Usually demands grow in size based on the number of concurrent users, the design and functionality of the applications being used, and general server load. For this reason it is very important for Notes administrators to proactively monitor application Notes servers to provide a stable environment. These monitoring techniques are discussed later within this book. It is also important for administrators to communicate with Notes application developers regarding design parameters for Notes applications. Developers should understand the implications of their applications within a Notes environment. A single intense Notes application could very easily bring a Notes server to its knees (even with no users accessing that application). Developers may want to consider incorporating archiving and purging functions to control database sizes.

The absolute maximum size of a Notes database is 4 gigabytes. The default size for a Notes application is 1 gigabyte. The variables that must be determined when scoping hardware requirements for an application Notes server then include:

- Number Notes applications residing on the Notes server.

- Number of documents per Notes database, plus turnover (new and deleted documents)—5000 in and out each day can be more important than the 10,000 total.

- Potential size of each document.

- Number of concurrent users per database.

- The number of views the application will contain. Each view can add additional resources to a Notes server, including processor time and disk requirements.

- Any other additional requirements for the Notes application such as full text indexes, or connectivity to other data resources such as DB2 applications through NotesPump.

With these numbers determined, we can better estimate the requirements for an application Notes server. Let us take an example of the ACME company that is planning on rolling out 3 initial Notes applications to its user community. The company currently has 400 Notes users, which will be accessing the application Notes server. ACME has decided to go with the Windows NT platform as its operating system for Lotus Notes using the Intel Pentium platform.

- **Application A** is going to be a discussion type Notes application with users reading and writing to it periodically. All 400 Notes users will access the application with peak usage in the morning and right after lunch.

- **Application B** will be a repository with numerous file attachments to many documents. The database will begin with around 1000 documents; as many as 20 documents may be added, deleted, or modified per day.

- **Application C** will be a bulletin board-type application posting ACME's current news and informational items. Users will read the database periodically. Only a handful of documents will be added and deleted each day.

With this information, ACME's Notes administrators can begin to determine the hardware requirements needed to support these applications. It can be determined that ACME will be able to support these initial requirements with a single Lotus Notes application server. Let's look at the numbers on how we decided this requirement.

From the numbers for each application, it can be determined that the initial disk space requirements to support the applications will be around 50 megabytes for Application A, 1.5 gigabytes for Application B, and around 50 megabytes for Application C.

Approximate Notes application sizes are based largely on our experiences with these types of databases. For example, on average, a Notes discussion database without file attachments can grow to a size of 50 megabytes. After this threshold, many Notes administrators begin to purge a database of this type. To illustrate Notes application disk requirements for Application B, we offer the following table based on past consulting experiences:

Table 2.2
Application B
Requirements

Initial documents	1,000
Avg. document size	250,000 bytes (250kb)
Total initial space requirements	250,000,000 bytes (250mb)
Additions (est. 260 business days times 20 adds per day)	5,200
Total adds size requirement	1,300,000,000 megabytes (1.3gb)
Total space needs	1,550,000,000 megabytes (1.55 gb)

Just from this disk space sampling, it can be determined that the Lotus recommendation of 500 megabytes will not suffice for this application server. A minimum of 2 gigabytes of Notes server disk space will be needed to support these Notes applications, Notes server process, and Windows NT operating system code. This too only represents 3 new Notes applications for the ACME company. As more applications and documents are added to the environment, more disk space will be needed.

It should be noted that additional disk capacity would be needed as more views are added to a Notes application and if full text indexes will be incorporated. Table 2.2 does not take these factors into consideration. These issues are discussed in greater detail in Chapter 12, *Notes Application and Security Issues*.

Minimum recommended memory requirements are listed from Lotus at 64 megabytes of RAM. With this handful of applications along with the potential number of concurrent users, 64 megabytes may not return the desired level of performance. Much of this depends on the time of day as well. In most organizations, Notes activity is seen in peaks of morning, afternoon, and the end of business day. Server performance will obviously be lower at these times of day. More than likely, 128 megabytes of RAM would offer a better level of performance. More memory may be necessary as the infrastructure grows, along with the additional Intel Pentium processors.

Tips

It is important for Notes administrators to continually monitor application Notes servers with the included monitoring tools and any third party tools to determine performance and resource levels of the application Notes servers. With this information, administrators then can determine when it may be necessary to add hardware, implement Notes clustering for load-balancing, or add another application Notes server to offer manual load-balancing.

- **Mail Server** Hardware requirements vary between organizations for Notes mail servers. Mostly they are based upon an organization's policies regarding user mail files. Some organizations have strict settings in regards to mail file sizes. Other organizations take the view that the administration costs associated with policing mail files does not outweigh the cost of additional disk space. Rather, adding disk space is cheaper than policing.

Notes mail servers certainly do not need the amount of hardware power that a Notes application server would need. Most users only access their own mail files and do not perform any intensive Notes database activities like a public Notes application might be performing.

Again let us take the ACME example of 400 Notes users. Let us say as well that ACME has set limits that user mail files are not to exceed 10 megabytes of disk space without using shared mail. From this number we can determine that the maximum size of all Notes mail applications will have a maximum value of 4 gigabytes. This can be housed on a single Notes server. To be on the safe side, the ACME Notes administrators should configure the Notes server with at least 5 gigabytes of disk space for overhead, as well as for the Windows NT operating system and Notes server code.

Processor and memory requirements will not be as intensive here as on the application Notes server. It can be estimated that all users will not be accessing their mail files at the same time at any given moment, although there will more than likely be the standard 3 peaks within a day—morning, midday, and late afternoon. For this reason, on ACME's Notes mail server, a single Pentium processor machine and 64 megabytes of RAM will suffice. Certainly 128 megabytes of RAM would be better for faster performance.

Tips

Notes administors need to monitor Notes mail servers closely for disk space usage. If a mail Notes server runs out of space, users will not be able to send or receive electronic mail. Administrators should consider using quotas or archives either through mandatory or voluntary measures (quotas and archives are explained later within the book). Also, administrators may want to consider placing user mail files on a separate drive from where the Notes mail router resides (MAIL.BOX). This way, the mail router can still continue even if the user mail files can't grow.

- **Hub Server** Hub servers are responsible for replication and mail routing between spoke Notes servers. They are the hearts of a hub-and- spoke replication environment. This type of architecture is explained in greater detail later within the book.

Like Notes mail servers, disk space requirements will be the main hardware resource. Notes users will not be accessing Hub Notes servers; therefore, indexing will not be as intense. This reduces the need for greater processor and memory requirements. The amount of disk space needed depends on the number and size of applications the Hub server has to replicate to other Notes servers with a Notes network.

If ACME's application Notes server was going to replicate all 3 of its applications in full to its hub server and then ultimately to other

ACME application servers throughout the organization, the hub Notes server would need at least enough disk space to replicate the Notes applications between ACME application servers. The hub server would also need additional disk space to house electronic mail messages in transit between mail servers within the environment.

- **Development Server** A development Notes server is usually configured to match the production environment. It is dedicated to application developers for programming and testing new applications. For this reason, not much attention is given to this type of machine. Unless otherwise specified by developers, the minimum server requirements are usually given to a machine of this type.

It is important to make provisions for these types of machines when architecting your Notes network—you do not want applications development taking place on or in the production network.

- **Gateway Server** Gateway Notes servers run the Lotus MTAs (Message Transfer Agents), fax gateways, pager gateways, and any other third-party gateway products. They are never directly accessed by Notes users and are only responsible for processes such as translating Notes mail messages to and from Notes format to other mail protocols. Disk requirements are normally fairly low. Memory requirements, though, are usually greater than those of standard Notes servers. Processing power can also be intensive at times, as the MTAs and gateways may need to perform high-speed translations of different types of electronic formats. Usually a single processor machine with 64 megabytes of RAM is enough to support such machines. The actual system and memory requirements depend on the volume of traffic being handled by the machines. Significantly more memory is needed where high volumes of electronic mail are passed. Notes administrators need to monitor performance daily to proactively avoid potential problems. If additional MTAs will be added to a machine, it is recommended that you also add 16 additional megabytes per MTA.

Other Hardware Considerations

Notes infrastructure design and server placement also has a bearing upon the hardware requirements. Some organizations take the approach of consolidating servers into a handful of large Notes servers and utilizing their current wide area network infrastructure rather than using a separate server for each of the above classes. Hub, mail, and gateway servers are combined into 1 or 2 large Notes servers. The necessary hardware requirements in this scenario involve multi-processor, high-powered machines with large amounts of RAM and disk space. Using this scenario with an Intel Pentium solution, administrators should design the servers with the maximum amount of hardware available to the machine if supporting more than 1500 users per machine. Server clustering should certainly be considered if your organization is contemplating using this method of server placement. Infrastructure design and server placement is discussed later in this book.

Considerations that apply to all scenarios and server classes involve configuring and purchasing the proper hardware. Such examples include using reputable server brands such as IBM, Compaq, or Hewlett-Packard when using the Intel platform. Off-brands many times have compatibility problems with the operating systems they are running. Any cost savings then realized are many times lost due to unforeseen downtime. It is also recommended that the organization always purchase the machine with a proper service agreement in place. These companies have proven themselves industry leaders in the server environment for Intel systems. Numerous benchmarking tests have been done on these companies' machines and have proven themselves not only in testing environments, but in the field as well.

A hot spare machine is always a good idea if cost models within your organization support them. SCSI drives are a preferable option over IDE drives when designing a Notes server. SCSI drive systems give the administrator greater flexibility and performance.

Drive configurations are also another important factor when considering hardware standards. It is highly recommended that drive arrays are configured where applicable using hardware level RAID 0, 1, or 5 (*RAID* stands for *Redundant Array of Inexpensive Disks*). RAID level 5 provides block striping where parity blocks are distributed over multiple drives. In the event of a drive failure, an administrator simply needs to pull the drive and replace the faulty drive without downing the Notes server. RAID 5 not only enhances performance, but also provides another layer of fault tolerance for Notes servers.

RAID 1, known as disk mirroring, can be used instead of RAID 5 if this is the corporate standard. RAID 1 provides disk mirroring along with striping. An exact mirror of each disk exists. If using RAID 1, it is recommended that each disk is attached to separate disk controller cards (defined as *disk duplexing*); the server will attain better performance than if each drive is attached to the same controller card.

Some operating systems, such as Windows NT, also support fault tolerance within the operating system itself. However, it is recommended that hardware level RAID is used, thus taking the burden off of the operating system and letting the hardware BIOS of the machine itself handle this work. The hardware level option will offer better performance and let the operating system attend to running the Notes server code. Most organizations choose to use RAID level 5 for their Notes servers.

Which ever RAID level option is determined best for your organization's Notes servers is certainly better than not deploying RAID technology at all. If RAID technology is not being used within your environment, you should certainly investigate upgrading your current hardware to improve performance and provide a layer of data redundancy.

Network card requirements are based upon the number of potential concurrent users accessing the Notes server at any given time. For most Notes servers, a single network card provides ample bandwidth for supporting user access. In the event that a Notes server is to support more than 500 concurrent users, additional network cards may be necessary. In this type of scenario, a network card can be installed in the server; each card then could serve a different segment or ring depending on whether the network environment is Token Ring or Ethernet. The Notes servers will not route packets between networks and the operating system should not be configured to route between networks—this will take system resources away from running the Notes server code.

Another solution to ease network bottlenecks on Notes servers on Ethernet networks is to install the Notes server on a 100-megabit segment or, even better, directly into an Ethernet switch. The Ethernet switch and card can be configured to run in what is called *full duplex mode*, which supports a full 100-megabit data stream in both directions. It is this type of solution that should be seriously considered for Notes servers expected to support over 1500 concurrent

Notes users. Network architecture requirements should be defined and reviewed by the organization's network architecture team.

Dial-up solutions for remote Notes users present another hardware concern for administrators deploying Notes servers within an organization. Dial-up solutions are discussed later with this book. Dial-up hardware needs to be ordered and configured based on what type of solution is determined best for the organization.

Client Hardware Selections

Client hardware requirements will mostly be determined by the operating system running on the Notes client. For the average Notes user, no additional requirements are necessary to run Notes on any supported platform. For example, on a machine running Windows 95, Notes will run adequately with 16 megabytes of RAM. Similar to the Notes server requirements, the more hardware that is available to Notes, the better the performance.

This point holds especially true when replicating Notes applications to local Notes client machines. When a Notes application exists on a Notes server and is accessed by a client workstation, the Notes server does the indexing of a Notes application. Notes utilizes true client/server technology. However, when users replicate Notes applications to their local desktops, the Notes client itself performs the Notes indexing process when using the local replica copy. Also, if the local copy of the application is full-text indexed, then the client again must update this index. For this reason, greater hardware may be needed to support users utilizing local database replication.

Greater processor power and more RAM may be needed for the indexing process for local database copies as well. In addition, more disk space will be required for machines that replicate locally. Disk requirements are based upon the amount of data replicated and the size of the Notes application itself.

For remote users, a modem will be needed for remote access.

Operating System Platforms

One of the greatest strengths of Lotus Notes is its ability to deploy applications across almost any computing platform without any change in the data's format and content. For this reason, Notes developers can create applications for deployment across multiple platforms without worrying about the operating system or protocol the system is running. There are some functional differences between platforms that developers need to be cognizant of. For example, certain fonts are not always available on non-Windows platforms.

On the Notes server, the following platforms and protocols are supported (protocols are discussed in Chapter 3, *Network Protocols*):

Table 2.3
Supported Notes
Server Platforms

Notes Server Platforms	Protocols
Microsoft Windows NT (3.51, 4.0)	AppleTalk, Banyan VINES, NetBIOS, NetBEUI, Novell SPX/SPXII, TCP/IP, X.25, X.PC, SNA
Microsoft Windows 95	NetBIOS, NetBEUI, Novell SPX, TCP/IP, X.PC
Sun Solaris (Solaris 2.4, 2.51)	TCP/IP, Novell SPX/SPXII, X.PC
Hewlett-Packard HP-UNIX (10.01)	CP/IP, Novell SPX/SPXII, X.PC
IBM AIX-UNIX (4.1.4)	TCP/IP, Novell SPX/SPXII, X.PC
Novell NetWare NLM (3.12, 4.1)	AppleTalk, Novell SPX/SPXII, TCP/IP, X.PC
IBM OS/2 Warp and Warp Connect; OS/2 2.11 SMP	AppleTalk, Banyan VINES, NetBIOS, NetBEUI, Novell SPX, TCP/IP, X.PC, X.25, SNA

On the Notes client the following platforms and protocols are supported:

Table 2.4
Supported Notes
Client Platforms

Platforms	Protocols
Microsoft Windows NT (3.51, 4.0)	Banyan VINES, NetBIOS, NetBEUI, Novell SPX/SPXII, TCP/IP, X.25, X.PC
Microsoft Windows 95	Banyan VINES, NetBIOS, NetBEUI, Novell SPX, TCP/IP, X.PC
Microsoft Windows 3.1	Novell SPX, NetBIOS, NetBEUI, TCP/IP, X.PC
Sun SolarisUNIX (Solaris 2.4, 2.51)	Novell SPXII, TCP/IP, X.PC
Hewlett-Packard HP-UNIX (10.01)	Novell SPX, TCP/IP, X.PC
IBM AIX-UNIX (4.1.4)	Novell SPX, TCP/IP, X.PC
IBM OS/2 Warp and Warp Connect	Banyan VINES, Novell SPX, NetBIOS, NetBEUI, X.PC
Apple Macintosh (7.5)	AppleTalk, TCP/IP, X.PC, MacTCP

Before discussing each operating system that Notes will operate, it should be noted that in order to support Web browser access to a Notes application, the HTTP process must be loaded on the Notes server. The HTTP process enables a Notes server to act as a world-class Web server by serving all Notes applications to standard Web browsers. The HTTP process translates Notes applications transparently into HTML format for Web browser access. Proper configurations must be set for Web users to effectively and efficiently access the Notes server. The entire configuration for the HTTP process is explained in depth in Chapter 13, *Internet and Web Application Servers*. The HTTP process is not available on all operating systems, or may not be released in the latest version. If administrators are considering a platform for the Notes server to run the HTTP process, Windows NT or UNIX are the only two options available as of the print date of this book. Also, as with all Web products, TCP/IP must be enabled on the Domino server to grant access to the HTTP process for Web browsers. There are similar restrictions as to which server platforms support ODBC calls in LotusScript.

Tips

The Lotus Notes server actually does not require a server to use the "classic" server definition. Using a network definition, the Notes server in reality only appears as another workstation node on a network where clients connect to the Notes server. A Notes server does not provide file and print services. An operating system such as Windows NT or Novell NetWare running the Domino server simply acts as a host.

Even though an administrator does not have to configure and administer the operating system a Notes server runs on in the manner it was designed for, this does not mean an administrator does not have to be familiar with the operating system itself. For instance, if an administrator is installing a Notes server running on Windows NT, the person still must have a good understanding of the operating system. File and print services that are available on the machine do not need to be configured, but most other processes will need attention and understanding. Examples for the Windows NT platform include items such as basic Windows NT configurations, service pack updates, RAS configurations, and basic Windows NT domain configurations, to name a few. As with any operating system administrators choose to run their Notes servers on, knowledge of the platform must be realized.

Lotus will not publish preferred operating systems or protocols in terms of performance in order not to favor one vendor over another. They leave the decision as to what operating system to use to the organizations themselves. However, it can determined that some operating systems running Lotus Notes have performance and administration advantages over others.

NotesBench, a benchmarking program, can be obtained from Lotus to perform Notes benchmark testing. Normally, it is only given to Premier Lotus Business Partners after organizations have attended proper training on the product. For the average company, this program is unattainable. However, many hardware vendors have used the program to provide NotesBench results on their own systems using different operating systems. This information may often be obtained by contacting the hardware vendors.

Besides performance, organizations must look at the cost of training administrators when contemplating a new operating system to run Lotus Notes. For example, a Novell NetWare shop where the administrators have never run Windows NT are faced with a learning curve if Windows NT is the platform chosen to run Lotus Notes. Although Windows NT will only be used as an application server to house Lotus Notes, it is still a new operating system that administrators must become accustomed to. This is a cost that must be weighed when considering new operating system platforms to house Domino servers powered by Notes.

From the earliest versions of Lotus Notes, the only platform the server would run was IBM's OS/2 (it actually supported Microsoft Windows 3.0, but performance was unacceptable with more than 3 users). With the introduction of version 3 of Lotus Notes, Iris began porting the server code to support other platforms. Since the release of version 4 of Lotus Notes, IT shops may choose virtually any platform they desire to run Notes servers. Although Lotus will not publicly admit it, every platform is not equal for running Notes.

Windows NT

Windows NT is quickly becoming a preferred application server in most IT departments not only for Lotus Notes but for many other applications. In some cases, it is taking over the responsibility from UNIX servers in many applications. The case holds true as well with Lotus Notes. Certainly, the most popular platform for a Lotus Notes server is currently Windows NT. The Wintel (Windows/Intel industry acronym) platform is now Lotus' choice for primary development for Lotus Notes. Windows NT now is the preferred operating system for Notes in terms of customer base as well. Most Notes server add-ons such as the pager, fax, cc:Mail, and SMTP gateways are developed on the NT platform first; for some products, they will *only* exist on the Windows NT platform. This trend especially holds true for third-party add-on Notes products. This development point also is valid for the HTTP process that now opens the Notes architecture up to standard Web browsers. It is only available for the Windows NT or UNIX platforms.

Most organizations will agree that from a Notes server standpoint, Windows NT running TCP/IP is the preferred operating environment. Most Notes benchmarking results will test environments running this operating system and protocol. A majority of Notes sites across the world now run Notes on Windows NT so potential bugs and fixes are far more likely to surface on NT over any other platform. As mentioned earlier in this book, Windows NT running Notes 4.5 can now be scaled to support over 1500 simultaneous working users if need be.

If desired, Lotus Notes can run on Windows NT running on an Alpha machine rather than an Intel machine. This option is more costly. Unless in-house expertise exists for Alpha machines, most organizations would benefit running Notes on a Windows NT Intel machine.

It is highly recommended that the Notes server not be run on a Windows NT machine that is supporting users for file and print operations. The same holds true especially for Primary and Backup Windows NT domain controllers. Lotus Notes should be installed on a dedicated Windows NT server due to the resources the Notes server demands and the unique configuration needed to the Windows NT server itself (see configuring Windows NT in Chapter 9, *Windows NT Integration*).

Tips

It is also important not to share the Notes and any associated directories on Windows NT. Users should never access Notes databases directly from the file system on a shared network drive. If a user accesses a Notes application directly from a mapped network drive by bypassing the Notes server, all Notes security is circumvented. Also, if multiple users access Notes applications in the same manner, the risk of Notes database corruption exists.

It is highly recommended that the latest Windows NT Service Packs are applied to the Windows NT machine housing your Lotus Notes servers.

For corporations using Windows NT Workstation, Lotus Notes has a 32-bit client that is supported. The code is the same Notes client code that is run on Windows 95 workstations.

Tips

If there is no driving reason to install Notes on a specific operating system platform and all things are equal within an IT shop in terms of decision criteria, it is recommended that Lotus Notes servers be installed on the Windows NT platform.

UNIX

UNIX is also another popular option for running Lotus Notes servers, especially for supporting large numbers of users on a single machine. However, UNIX machines fully dedicated for Lotus Notes servers are far more expensive than their Intel counterparts. UNIX does not provide the flexibility in terms of protocols supported for client access. UNIX also is somewhat more difficult for administrators to learn than most of the other operating systems

Lotus Notes supports. Obviously, if UNIX knowledge exists in-house, this is not an issue.

UNIX is the only other operating system besides Windows NT that currently supports the HTTP process on Notes servers to enable Notes application access from Web browsers.

In terms of platforms, it can be argued that UNIX may be a more powerful OS, which in many cases is true. However, when weighing the administration learning curve for the operating system, protocol flexibility, and Notes server companion products, UNIX tends to be a more expensive option. For running Lotus Notes, UNIX servers do not offer much more performance gains, thus giving a Windows NT solution a significant cost advantage.

Novell NetWare—NLM

Before the release of the NetWare NLM version of Lotus Notes, much of the industry thought that this platform would become the choice of Lotus N otes shops. Performance and scalability was supposed to be dramatically improved. Most IT shops already had numerous Novell file and print servers in house and the matched expertise to manage the servers. It was to be a perfect match.

However, most people were disappointed with the release, as it did not provide the promised performance. It also was quite resource-intensive, bringing some underpowered Novell file and print servers to their knees. The reality was that most Novell administrators thought they could simply run the Notes server on an existing Net-Ware server without having to dedicate a machine to this task. They quickly found out otherwise.

With release 4 of Lotus Notes, the NLM version of Notes is somewhat better. However, some disadvantages still exist. For instance, the Notes server process is still quite intensive on this platform. It is not recommended that a Notes server run on a Novell server that is being used for file and print operations. Both the Notes server and the file and print operations would be competing for resources, resulting in the degradation of both processes. Also, in the event of a Notes server failure, the failed Notes server could potentially bring down the Novell server itself. Also, the Notes server often needs to be restarted, thus disrupting all file and print activity that the Novell server is performing.

Administering a Novell Notes server is somewhat more difficult as well. Unlike other systems, the Novell server console does not support a GUI (*graphical user interface*). For this reason, administration of the Notes server must be done only from a workstation. Normally, this is the preferred method of administering any Notes server on any platform, but in case of an emergency, administration cannot be done from the server console.

Lotus Notes add-ons are almost non-existent on the Novell NetWare Notes server platform. In order for code to be ported to Novell, it must exist as an NLM (NetWare Loadable Module). Novell NLMs are much more difficult to write and port and for this reason, developers tend to shy from using Novell as a development standard for Lotus Notes server add-on processes.

Lotus Notes supports both NDS and bindery lookups when using Novell's SPX and SPXII protocols for connecting between Notes servers and for connecting between Notes servers and clients.

Neither Novell SFTIII (system fault tolerance) nor NASI (Novell's dial-in/out server) is supported with Lotus Notes.

IBM OS/2 Warp

OS/2 Warp can yield superior performance, especially when armed with SMP (*symmetrical multi-processor*) machines. OS/2 was the first true operating system Lotus Notes supported for servers in the earlier versions of the product. With release 3 of Notes, other platforms were made available.

Today, more and more IT shops are fading from OS/2 as an application server and a file and print server. Organizations are beginning to migrate to Microsoft's Windows NT to house their application and file and print needs.

OS/2 is still a good option to house Lotus Notes servers and will provide adequate performance for large Lotus Notes installations. Many organizations shy away from OS/2, as it is viewed as an additional operating system to support and the industry as a whole is not embracing OS/2.

The latest OS/2 patches should be applied to OS/2 servers for supporting Lotus Notes servers.

Windows 95

Windows 95 supports both the Notes client and server code. The server code for Windows 95 is the same 32-bit code that runs on the Windows NT platform. The major difference is that Notes servers running on Windows 95 will not support the same number of users that Windows NT will support. If you are going to use Windows 95 as your operating system to support a Notes server, it should only be used to support a workgroup in the area of 15 people or less.

Windows 95 as an operating system to support the Notes client is quickly becoming the standard for the desktop in many organizations. As more organizations migrate from Windows 3.1 to either Windows 95 or Windows NT, Notes clients will also be migrated to the 32-bit version of the client.

Windows 3.1

The server version of Notes for Windows 3.1 was phased out in version 4 of Lotus Notes. Currently, only the 16-bit version of the Notes client is available in version 4 of Lotus Notes. Eventually, the 16-bit version of the Notes client may be phased out as well, depending on the availability of Windows 3.1 in corporate America. As more corporations migrate from Windows 3.1 to either Windows 95 or Windows NT, the support levels for the 16-bit Windows 3.1 client will diminish. In fact, Microsoft has announced that support for the Windows 3.1 operating system will no longer exist after this year.

Macintosh

The Macintosh version of Notes is only supported on the client; no server version exists. Lotus Notes makes it very simple to develop applications that can exist on multiple platforms including Macintosh without loss of functionality or the look and feel of the application. This is especially important where a mixture of platforms exist within an organization. Lotus Notes can bring users together by letting users share information easily and efficiently through a common interface, regardless of platform.

Network Protocols

The interconnection of computer systems is one of the cornerstones of Lotus Notes. If computers could not be connected there would be no reason to use collaborative technologies like Notes. For this very reason, a discussion and understanding of network protocols is one of the cornerstones of this book.

By definition, a network protocol represents the mechanism that enables systems on a network to communicate with one another. Knowledge of protocols is important in order to configure and troubleshoot networks effectively. Most protocol vendors and engineers compare protocols to a protocol reference model known as the Open System Interconnection (OSI) model. The framework was developed in 1978 by the International Organizations of Standards (ISO) in order to compare different communication systems and to enable developers to follow a basic guideline when developing open systems. Not all protocols follow the model specifically, but the model does provide a good framework when comparing different types of protocols. Many protocols map directly to the model only with certain layers.

The OSI reference model contains the following 7 layers:

Table 3.1
OSI Layers

Application	Layer 7
Presentation	Layer 6
Session	Layer 5
Transport	Layer 4
Network	Layer 3
Data Link	Layer 2
Physical	Layer 1

Each layer has a specific responsibility, and after performing its specific function passes information to the next layer. Below is a brief description of the responsibility of each layer.

- **Physical Layer.** The physical layer of the OSI model is the communication channel dealing with the mechanical, electrical, and procedural interfaces over a physical medium. The physical layer is responsible for transmitting the actual bits of data represented as either a 1 or 0 (binary). Examples include the cabling infrastructure of a network.

- **Data Link Layer.** The data link layer is responsible for grouping the bits from the physical layers into what are called *frames*. The format of a frame contains different fields responsible for passing data on a LAN or WAN environment. In terms of a LAN infrastructure there are two popular frame formats, one being a Token Ring frame and the other an Ethernet frame.

    A typical data link frame contains 4 main fields including an address field, control field, data field, and an error control field (see Figure 3-1).

Figure 3-1
Typical Data Link
Layer Frame

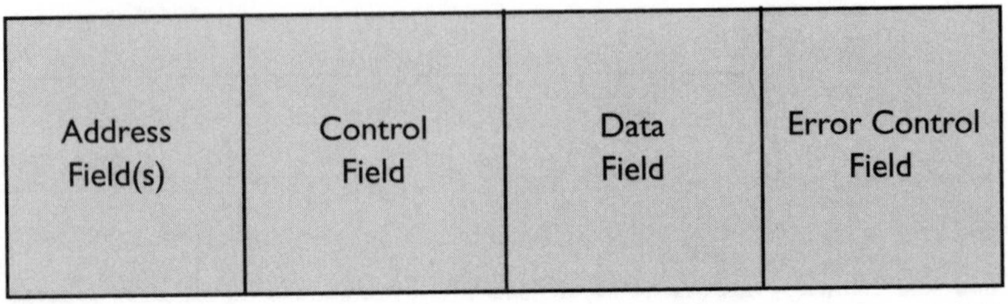

Address Field(s)	Control Field	Data Field	Error Control Field

The address field(s) contain the addresses of the sending and receiving node. The control field differentiates between types of data link frames. The data field is actually the payload of the frame. In the case of Lotus Notes, it is the actual data that is passed between the Notes client and a Notes server. The error control field usually uses some sort of checksum algorithm to check for any possible errors within the frame during transit. It is this layer that a bridge or switch utilizes to pass data.

- **Network Layer.** The network layer of the OSI model builds on the data link layer. It provides transport between two different networks, either physical or logical. The networking component responsible for this transportation between networks is known fittingly enough as a *router*. The network layer of a protocol can be responsible for routing packets between two like topologies such as two ethernet LAN segments, or two different topologies such as Token Ring and Ethernet networks.

    It is this layer that directs packets on the Internet to the proper networks throughout the world. By definition, the Internet is simply a series of interconnected TCP/IP networks. These connections are made over high speed phone lines supplied by phone companies and Internet service providers. The network layer protocol responsible for the Internet is IP (Internet Protocol), this is the IP part of the TCP/IP name. In Novell environments, the IPX protocol resembles the network layer of the OSI model. Likewise for Notes networks, this layer is responsible for transporting packets of data to servers and clients on different networks depending on which protocol is chosen.

- **Transport Layer.** The transport layer provides enhancements to the network layer of the OSI model. It ensures reliable data delivery and end-to-end data integrity. The transport layer can provide the means for multiple logical connections over a single network connection. This process is known as *multiplexing*. In order to keep track of these addresses, a naming scheme is used, as transport addresses are associated with the layer. These names are sometimes referred to in different operating systems and protocols as *sockets* and *port numbers*.

Examples in this layer would be SPX in the Novell environment and TCP for a TCP/IP network. *TCP* stands for Transmission Control Protocol.

- **Session Layer.** The session layer of the OSI model builds on the transport layer. This layer allows application communication between two machines either in half or full duplex modes. For example, on a Windows NT server, the server can be configured to use NetBIOS (Network Basic Input/Output System) over the native NetBEUI (Network BIOS Extended User Interface) protocols or over TCP/IP. NetBIOS can be defined as a session layer protocol. Session layer protocols such as NetBIOS and NetBEUI are known as *unroutable protocols* and are limited for use on only one network, unless encapsulated within a routable protocol such as TCP/IP.

- **Presentation Layer.** The presentation layer takes the information passed to it from the session layer; it manages the way data is presented. Such examples would be ASCII and EBCDIC formats for text files. If NotesView were used to manage Notes servers within a Notes network using SNMP (Simple Network Management Protocol), this would be an example of a presentation layer protocol.

- **Application Layer.** The application layer contains all protocols and functions necessary for server and user applications to communicate effectively. This is where most Lotus Notes client and server code operates in the OSI model. The application layer uses information passed up from all the lower layers to communicate and operate. Many applications, including Lotus Notes, allow the application layer services to be accessed by other programs. To enable this, Lotus Notes (along with many other applications) provides Application Programming Interfaces (APIs).

As stated earlier, most protocols do not map directly to the model. The OSI model only provides a framework for protocol developers to engineer and compare protocols.

Notes servers and clients can be configured with one or more protocols per machine. Table 3.2 shows which protocols are supported per operating system platform:

Table 3.2
Supported Notes
Server Protocols

Protocol	Notes Server Platform
AppleTalk	Microsoft Windows NT, Novell NetWare NLM, IBM OS/2 Warp
Banyan VINES	Microsoft Windows NT, IBM OS/2 Warp
NetBIOS	Microsoft Windows NT, Microsoft Windows 95, IBM OS/2 Warp
SPX	Microsoft Windows NT, Microsoft Windows 95, Sun Solaris, HP-UNIX, IBM-AIX, Novell NetWare NLM, IBM OS/2 Warp
SPXII	Microsoft Windows NT, Sun Solaris, HP-UNIX, IBM-AIX, Novell NetWare NLM
SNA	Microsoft Windows NT, IBM OS/2 Warp
TCP/IP	Microsoft Windows NT, Microsoft Windows 95, Sun Solaris, HP-UNIX, IBM-AIX, Novell NetWare NLM, IBM OS/2 Warp
X.25	Microsoft Windows NT, IBM OS/2 Warp
X.PC	Microsoft Windows NT, Microsoft Windows 95, Sun Solaris, HP-UNIX, IBM-AIX, Novell NetWare NLM, IBM OS/2 Warp

On the Notes client the following platforms and protocols are supported:

Table 3.3
Supported Notes
Client Protocols

Platforms	Protocols
Microsoft Windows NT (3.51, 4.0)	Banyan VINES, NetBIOS, NetBEUI, Novell SPX/SPXII, TCP/IP, X.PC
Microsoft Windows 95	Banyan VINES, NetBIOS, NetBEUI, Novell SPX, TCP/IP, X.PC
Microsoft Windows 3.1	Novell SPX, NetBIOS, NetBEUI, TCP/IP, X.PC
Sun Solaris-UNIX (Solaris 2.4, 2.5, 2.51)	Novell SPX II, TCP/IP, X.PC
Hewlett-Packard HP-UNIX (10.01)	Novell SPX, TCP/IP, X.PC
IBM AIX-UNIX (4.1.4)	Novell SPX, TCP/IP, X.PC
IBM OS/2 Warp and Warp Connect	Banyan VINES, Novell SPX, NetBIOS, NetBEUI, X.PC
Apple Macintosh (7.5)	AppleTalk, TCP/IP, X.PC, MacTCP

Many times, Notes servers must be configured with multiple protocols in order to support all types of Notes clients. This is certainly possible, but some caution should be exercised when deploying servers with multiple protocols. Many operating systems support different numbers of active connections per protocol. For example, some operating systems support many more active connections using TCP/IP than NetBIOS. This consideration should be understood before determining how a particular Notes server will be housing its Notes clients within a network.

This issue of scalability in regards to protocols should be considered when selecting a protocol for a Notes server. Table 3.4 lists the number of active sessions a particular protocol can support in regards to an operating system platform:

Table 3.4
Concurrent Session Limitations per Protocol and OS

OS/Protocol	TCP/IP	IPX/SPX	NetBIOS	VINES	AppleTalk	X.PC	X.25
OS/2	Hardware dependent	Hardware dependent	100	50	50	64 ports	64
Windows NT	Hardware dependent	Hardware dependent	252	Hardware dependent	255	64 ports	64
Solaris	Hardware dependent	Hardware dependent	N/A	N/A	N/A	64 ports	N/A
HP-UX	Hardware dependent	Hardware dependent	N/A	N/A	N/A	64 ports	N/A
AIX	Hardware dependent	Hardware dependent	N/A	N/A	N/A	64 ports	N/A
NLM	Hardware dependent	Hardware dependent	N/A	N/A	120	64 ports	N/A
Windows 95	Hardware dependent	Hardware dependent	N/A	N/A	N/A	64 ports	N/A

Another important point is that multiple protocols require more administration per server and do somewhat decrease Notes server performance. Many times, administrators are forced to use multiple protocols on a Notes server as some Notes clients are not capable of running a preferred protocol. For instance, many Novell organizations wish to run TCP/IP as the default Notes protocol. Because of memory and processor constraints on the desktop, some machines are incapable of running TCP/IP (for Notes access) and IPX/SPX (for Novell file and print access) simultaneously. For this reason, the Notes server must be configured with both TCP/IP and IPX/SPX to support all Notes clients.

TCP/IP

TCP/IP is quickly becoming the protocol of choice for many Local Area Networks (LANs) and Wide Area Networks (WANs). Organizations are trying to consolidate protocols in order to better administer and control their networks. Other protocols are beginning to be phased out in place of TCP/IP. With Intranet and Internet Web applications quickly becoming popular across industry lines, this protocol migration is becoming even more apparent.

By definition, the Internet is actually many TCP/IP networks interconnected to one another. Practically speaking, if a machine is not running TCP/IP, that machine cannot really be connected to the Internet. If an organization is running TCP/IP on its internal network and does not have connectivity to any other TCP/IP network, then by definition they have an *Intranet*. Web servers, Web browsers, FTP applications, Telnet applications, Lotus Notes servers, and Lotus Notes clients running TCP/IP are simply applications existing on either an Internet or Intranet. Many organizations with TCP/IP connectivity to other networks place a device called a *firewall* to protect their internal TCP/IP network (Intranet) from users from the outside world (Internet). This is a highly recommended device if your firm is contemplating using the Domino server to house applications for access on the Internet. This topic is discussed more thoroughly in Chapter 13, *Internet and Web Application Servers*.

Notes

We want to differentiate our use of the term Intranet from the current meaning associated with the term. We use the term Intranet to mean a TCP/IP network in use within an organization. The term Intranet is often used to describe the applications in use behind a firewall and running on a network that uses Internet based standards to interoperate (HTML, SMTP, etc.).

TCP/IP attracts networking administrators because it is a better-behaved protocol when compared to others such as NetBIOS and IPX. NetBIOS, for example, is based on what are called *broadcasts* in order to resolve networking addresses. This means for one machine to contact and communicate with one another, the calling machine must send out a packet of data to all machines in search of the receiver. On large networks, this can become an immense problem—especially in WAN environments where bandwidth is lower and costs associated with the links are high. TCP/IP can be configured on networks to minimize broadcasts and not congest networking environments.

TCP/IP does have its drawbacks, mostly in administrating and configuring the protocol. Unlike most protocols, network addresses and host addresses must be manually configured on each machine and each network. The addresses are assumed *static*, meaning that a machine is tied to a particular address and many times to a specific physical location on a network. If a machine is to move physical locations within an organization to a new network segment or ring, then the administrator must assign the machine a new address, keeping in mind not to duplicate another machine's address, which would create severe problems.

Tips

DHCP can be used to overcome static TCP/IP workstation addressing. DHCP is discussed in detail later in this chapter.

As mentioned above, a TCP/IP address consists of a host address (address assigned to a machine running the TCP/IP protocol) and a network address (address assigned to the network segment running the TCP/IP protocol). The current version of TCP/IP (version 4) has the following classes and available number of host and network addresses:

Table 3.5
TCP/IP Address
Classes

Address Class	Number of Networks	Number of Hosts (Nodes) per Network	Address Numbers (First Octet)	Default Subnet Mask
A	126	16,777,214	001-126	255.0.0.0
B	16,384	65,534	128-191	255.255.0.0
C	2,097,151	254	192-223	255.255.255.0

It should be noted the network address of 127 cannot be used; it is reserved for loopback testing and interprocess communication on the local computer and therefore is not a valid network address. Also, network numbers greater than 224 cannot be used as they are reserved for special protocols such as IGMP multicast. They also cannot be used as network addresses.

Class A addresses are for very large organizations. There are only 126 types of these networks. Class B networks are for large- to medium-type networks. Class C addresses are for smaller organizations. For example, for a class C network, only 254 machines (nodes) can exist.

Tips

TCP/IP address translations can be used so that an organization can use a "borrowed" registered TCP/IP address within its networks. The borrowed address then can be translated into a legitimate TCP/IP address belonging to the organization itself (a smaller class C address) or to the organization's Internet service provider for access to the Internet. Most firewall products provide this type of TCP/IP address translations.

TCP/IP address spaces are currently becoming scarce. For this reason, next generation TCP/IP is being standardized and will begin its deployment within the next few years. It will be version 6 of TCP/IP and is coined as *next generation IP*. (Version 5 of TCP/IP has already been assigned and is only experimental).

Normally for readability, the 32-bit TCP/IP address is represented in decimal format. An example of a TCP/IP address in decimal (base 10) notation would be:

```
142.20.75.101
```

In its native binary notation, the same address would be:

```
10001110 00010100 01001011 01100101
```

What distinguishes which part of the above address is considered a network address or a host address is called a *subnet mask*. A subnet mask is what also must be configured on a machine or network device along with its assigned TCP/IP address. Subnet masks are assigned upon the design of an IP network. Once set, all machines on the same network segment should use the same subnet mask.

Using the above class B TCP/IP network address example of 142.20.75.101, the mandatory subnet mask is 255.255.0.0. With this subnet mask only one network is available, 142.20.0.0 (142.20.xxx.xxx) with 65,534 available hosts (machines). However, if the third octet is masked, 254 networks now become available (255 is reserved for broadcasts) with 254 hosts (machines) on each network. An assigned subnet mask of 255.255.255.0 yields an IP network number of 142.20.75.0 (or 142.20.75.xxx) and a host (machine) number of 101. The network numbers now available are 142.20.1–142.20.254 with 254 hosts per network. In binary format, the 147.20.75.101 with subnet mask 255.255.255.0 shows:

```
IP Address =  10001110 00010100 01001011 01100101

IP Subnet Mask =  11111111 11111111 11111111 00000000
```

Class A addresses have by mandatory default a subnet mask of 255.0.0.0. Class B has by mandatory default subnet mask 255.255.0.0. Finally, Class C addresses have by mandatory default subnet mask 255.255.255.0. Administrators may choose to further subnet from the mandatory subnet mask for the respective address classes. This will give administrators additional TCP/IP subnetworks, but will reduce the number of hosts (nodes) on each subnet.

TCP/IP networks commonly resolve these IP addresses assigned to machines to actual MAC (Media Access Control) addresses by using ARP (Address Resolution Protocol). Every network card has a unique MAC number hard coded into it from the manufacturer (some network cards enable administrators to change this number; however, this should be avoided). Network card manufacturers are required to register their cards in order to prevent duplication of this number. When a machine needs to resolve an IP address, the machine looks within an ARP table on the network to resolve the IP address to an actual MAC address. If the machine knows the MAC address of the recipient, the IP packet is delivered to the correct machine. If the machine does not know the MAC address, it sends an ARP request to determine the MAC address of the desired IP recipient.

Another administration headache of TCP/IP involves the problem of resolving IP addresses into actual machines names. A common example of this involves the resolution of a Web server address for a web client. This resolution is commonly done in two ways, either through the use of local HOST files on a local machine, or more commonly through the use of a Domain Name Server (DNS). For an example, when a Web client requests to connect to a Web site—let's say *www.acme.com*—the machine requests the IP address of *www.acme.com* from the network's domain name server if the machine is configured to use DNS. The DNS then returns to the Web client the actual IP address of the Web server, and the Web browser then connects to the site.

When configuring Lotus Notes servers and clients to use TCP/IP, the same issues face administrators. Proper planning and configuration are necessary on a TCP/IP network to support a Notes infrastructure efficiently.

To ease administration of a Notes network using TCP/IP, it is suggested that administrators should work directly with the organization's networking/telecommunications team to discuss the use of DNS and DHCP.

Again, DNS stands for a *Domain Name Server*, which resolves IP addresses into actual machine names. If DNS is not implemented on a TCP/IP network where Notes servers will exists, administrators have to add and maintain HOST files on each local machine. A HOST file is simply a text file that has IP address entries and corresponding server names. A sample entry within a HOST file would be:

```
192.5.5.118  Chicago-Notes01 ;Chicago Notes Application Server
192.5.5.120  Chicago-Notes02 ;Chicago Notes Mail Server
```

The local machine without DNS looks in its local HOST file any time a Notes client wants to connect to either of the above Notes servers, in order to resolve the Notes server name into the corresponding IP address. Any time additional Notes servers are added to the network or the IP address or server name changes, administrators have to edit each HOST file on each machine. If DNS is used, administrators simply need to edit the domain name once on the domain name server. All clients then connecting using DNS resolve the new changes.

Tips

Administrators considering using TCP/IP as the transport protocol for their Notes network should consider using DNS to resolve Notes server IP addresses.

It should be noted that in Windows NT environments the use of WINS (Windows Internet Name Service) is not used by Notes servers or clients. Similar to DNS, WINS resolves machine names (in Window NT a machine name=NetBIOS name) of Windows machines running TCP/IP to the corresponding IP address. WINS is a proprietary Microsoft naming standard providing similar functionality to that of DNS; however, it is used only on Windows NT and Windows 95 networks. With the release of Windows NT 4.0, the WINS database can be configured to communicate with a DNS database to pass machine information.

Another administration headache concerning TCP/IP deals with manually assigning and tracking IP addresses of machines. This becomes increasingly difficult for mobile users who could potentially move their machines around on the network. What many organizations are now taking advantage of is DHCP (Dynamic Host Configuration Protocol). This protocol automatically assigns an IP address to a machine upon boot-up. This enables users to physically move their machines without the administrator having to configure the machine each time. IP address leases can be configured to automatically obtain DNS, WINS, and default gateway/router addresses as well. The leases can also expire, which gets the loaned address back from a machine at a specific time.

In order to use DHCP, network administrators must set up and configure DHCP servers on each network segment. Routers can be configured to forward DHCP requests (called *BOOTP forwarding*) so that each segment does not need a DHCP server, but this router configuration is not recommended in most cases. Also, client machines must be configured to use DHCP. Windows 95 and Windows NT workstations, for example, both support DHCP. Notes servers should *not* be configured to use DHCP. A static TCP/IP address should be assigned to all Notes servers as DNS entries, and HOST files need a constant TCP/IP address.

Tips

Administrators considering using TCP/IP as the transport protocol for their Notes network should consider using DHCP to assign and maintain TCP/IP addresses for their Notes clients.

If administrators plan on using the HTTP process on the Notes servers, administrators will have to configure the operating system of the Notes server to use TCP/IP as well as the Notes server itself. It would also be beneficial to add another entry to DNS for the HTTP process (Domino process). Let us take for an example a Notes server at ACME. The server would require the following DNS entry for Notes client connectivity to the Notes server using TCP/IP:

```
Chicago-Notes01
```

Note that only the CN (Common Name) of the Notes server is entered in the DNS database. The fully distinguished name (Chicago-Notes01/ACME) should not be used.

The second entry within DNS should be:

```
www.acme.com
```

Notes clients and servers use the common name of a server for connectivity. For example, server Chicago-Notes01/ACME is resolved by using only Chicago-Notes01. The fully distinguished name of the Notes server should not be placed in HOST files of DNS.

This entry will resolve the IP address so that Web browser may access the Domino server and all of its Notes applications. The complete entry would then appear in DNS or a local HOST file as follows:

```
192.5.5.118    Chicago-Notes01    www.acme.com   ;Chicago Notes Server
```

Both entries would resolve the same IP address to the same network card. The difference would be the port number the client is requesting as explained in the Transport Layer of this section. The Lotus Notes server uses TCP port number 1352 for Notes clients. The HTTP process, like all web servers, uses the default port number of 80 for Web browser access.

Tips

If administrators are considering using the HTTP process on a Notes server to enable hosting Notes applications to Web browsers, TCP/IP must be installed and enabled on the Notes server operating system and on the Notes server itself.

TCP/IP offers some of the best performance over WAN environments, and is one of the top two choices for protocols in LAN environments. The TCP/IP protocol by design is a *sliding window protocol,* which means the size of each packet can adjust dynamically depending on the sender and receiver and the condition of the pipe between them. Most other protocols are fixed sized packets. TCP/IP also enables more simultaneous sessions (also called *sockets,* depending on the protocol) on most operating system environments. NetBIOS, for instance, is only able to support around 100 concurrent sessions on most operating systems.

Tips

For security reasons, telnet and FTP services should be disabled on the machine housing the Lotus Notes server. This also applies to NFS mounts as well. These processes pose a security breach in that an intruder could possibly access data, circumventing the Notes server process and its security model.

The IP address or host address of a Notes server should appear in the server record of the public Name and Address book in the Net Address field, as shown in Figure 3-2:

Figure 3-2

Net Address
Field for TCP/IP

▼ **Network Configuration**

Port	Notes Network	Net Address	Enabled	
☞ TCPIP ☐	☞ Chicago-TCPIP ☐	☞ 155.201.55.106 ☐	⦿ ENABLED	○ DISABLED
☞ ☐	☞ ☐	☞ Chicago-Notes01 ☐	○ ENABLED	⦿ DISABLED
☞ ☐	☞ ☐	☞ Chicago-Notes01 ☐	○ ENABLED	⦿ DISABLED
☞ ☐	☞ ☐	☞ Chicago-Notes01 ☐	○ ENABLED	⦿ DISABLED
☞ ☐	☞ ☐	☞ Chicago-Notes01 ☐	○ ENABLED	⦿ DISABLED

This field in the Notes server document enables other Notes servers to connect to the Notes server running TCP/IP by looking up the server address within the public Name and Address book. If the IP address is used (such as 155.201.55.106) and DNS is inaccessible, then Notes servers can still connect. If the host name is used (such as Chicago-Notes01.acme.com) then DNS must be running or a HOST file entry must exist on the requesting machine.

On a Notes client running TCP/IP, users and administrators can configure what Lotus calls a *secondary name server*. The secondary name server is used when the following conditions occur:

● The Notes user's Notes e-mail server is not responding

● The Notes user's Notes home server is not running TCP/IP

● The Notes user's Notes home server's TCP/IP address is not being resolved

The use of this field is recommended in larger Notes environments where multiple Notes servers are used. For smaller environments where only one Notes server exists, this setting will be useless.

The settings for configuring the Notes secondary name server is found by clicking:

1. **File**

2. **Mobile**

3. **Locations**

The user then selects which location to edit and opens that location. Within the advanced section of this document, the screen shown in Figure 3-3 appears:

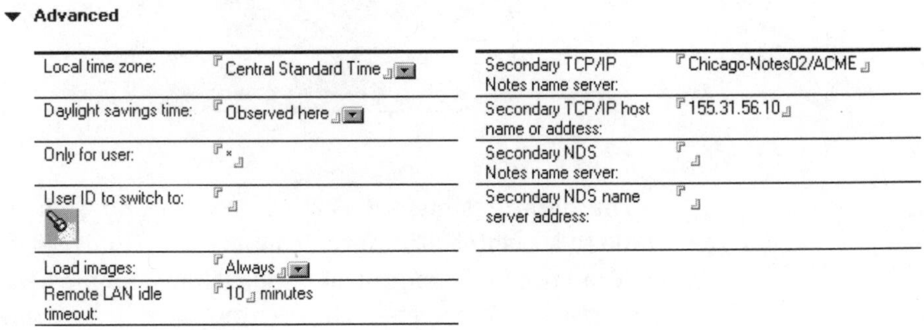

Figure 3-3

Secondary Name
Server Fields
for TCP/IP

▼ Advanced			
Local time zone:	Central Standard Time	Secondary TCP/IP Notes name server:	Chicago-Notes02/ACME
Daylight savings time:	Observed here	Secondary TCP/IP host name or address:	155.31.56.10
Only for user:	*	Secondary NDS Notes name server:	
User ID to switch to:		Secondary NDS name server address:	
Load images:	Always		
Remote LAN idle timeout:	10 minutes		

Within the secondary TCP/IP Notes server name field, enter the name of a Notes server running TCP/IP other than the home or e-mail Notes server. The field contains the actual IP address of the secondary Notes server name or the DNS host name of the Notes server. If only an IP address is listed, then the name will not have to be resolved via a HOST file or DNS. This is helpful in the event of a DNS failure. However, if this field is hard coded with the actual IP address (for example, 155.31.56.10), and the Notes server's IP address changes, then each machine will have to be edited to change this entry. It is recommended that you use the host name of the server rather than hard coding the address.

A time-out value can also be set for TCP/IP. This setting can be found by clicking:

1. **File**

2. **Tools**

3. **User preferences...**

4. Then select **Port**

5. Then select **TCP/IP Options**

The screen shown in Figure 3-4 will appear:

Figure 3-4
TCP/IP
Options Field

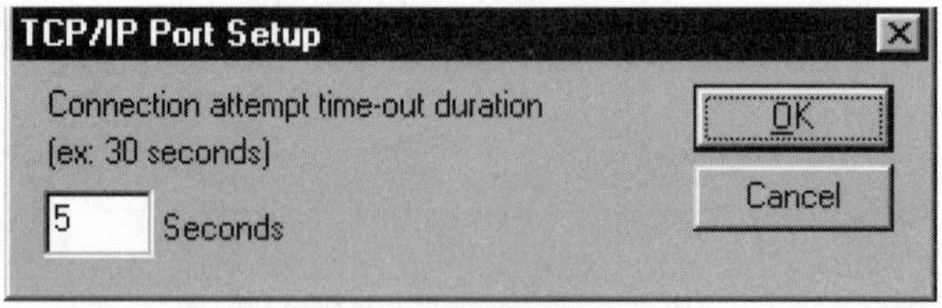

The default time-out setting is 5 seconds; users can change this value to let Notes attempt to connect to a Notes server running TCP/IP for the specified amount of time. It only applies to the first time the user tries to connect—other attempts will not use this value. This value also applies between servers that replicate with each other. In the case of server-to-server communications it determines the amount of time before an error message is issued to a Notes server console.

This setting is also useful for remote users using a PPP connection. This setting can be adjusted to avoid long connection wait periods upon initial connection to a Notes server.

Tips

PING.EXE, a program that usually comes with most TCP/IP stacks, is a very useful tool for troubleshooting and testing connectivity between two TCP/IP machines. For example, on a Windows 95 workstation at a DOS prompt, a user can test TCP/IP connectivity by typing:

```
ping Chicago-Notes01
```

If there is a response from the target machine using the ping utility, then connectivity can be assumed. This does not mean the Notes server code is running and responding to the ping request, only that the machine itself is running and TCP/IP is responding. If the user sees no response, then it can be assumed that there are connectivity problems with the network itself and not Notes.

SPX

SPX stands for *sequenced packet exchange* and is the primary protocol of a Novell NetWare file and print environment. Notes servers and clients support SPX as well as Novell's NetBIOS over SPX.

The Notes SPX port driver uses what is called *dynamic sockets*. The range of sockets a Notes server may use with SPX is 0x4000–0x7FFF. When a Notes server starts, it is assigned a socket number from the IPX/SPX operating system driver. Because it is dynamic, it is guaranteed not to use a socket number used by another application.

It is important to note that if SPX is going to be used to provide connectivity for Notes servers and clients that a Novell file server must exist on the network. Notes servers and clients obtain Notes server addresses from Novell file servers.

Traps

If administrators are considering using SPX for Notes client and server connectivity, a Novell file server must exist on the network.

SPX address resolution can be compared to DNS and ARP resolutions in the TCP/IP world. However, no manual user or administrator intervention is necessary to assign host numbers to local machines as the host number is actually the MAC address of its network card. SPX network numbers are assigned to each segment at the time the Novell server is initially configured.

Notes server SPX addresses are obtained in two manners when using the SPX protocol. With Novell 3.x servers, addresses are obtained from the bindery of the Novell server. This is a database (similar to DNS) of all registered servers. Registration is done through a Novell protocol known as a *SAP* (Service Advertising Protocol).

The other method of resolving SPX addressing is through *NDS* (NetWare Directory Services). NDS is used on Novell 4.x file and print servers and is a x.500-compliant naming structure. This NDS database is maintained and replicated among Novell 4.x servers. The NDS database can be configured to add Notes servers to its inventory.

Notes clients can be configured to use either NDS or bindery services or even both. The settings can be found by clicking:

1. **File**

2. **Tools**

3. **User preferences...**

4. Then clicking **Ports**

5. Then clicking **SPX Options...**

The following screen will appear:

Figure 3-5
SPX Options Fields

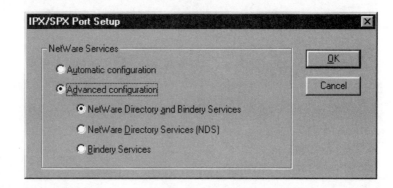

Within this screen, NDS or Bindery Services can be selected.

If NDS is used, a user must be logged into the Novell NDS tree with sufficient privileges to traverse the tree. If sufficient privileges are not granted, a Notes client will not be able to look up the properties and connect to a Notes server.

A simple NDS tree structure may look something like Figure 3-6:

Figure 3-6
Sample NDS Tree

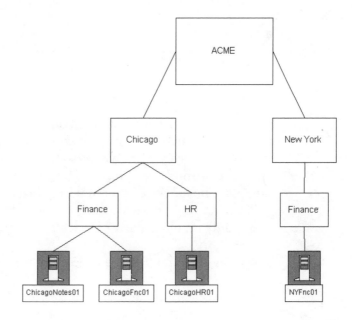

In this example, HR users that work on the ChicagoHR01 Novell file server will need privileges to traverse the NDS tree in order to access the ChicagoNotes01 Notes server, located under the Finance object.

Similar to TCP/IP, the SPX NDS option has settings for a fallback Notes server in the case a Notes user's home server is not responding. The settings can be found by clicking:

1. **File**

2. **Mobile**

3. **Locations**

The user then selects which location to edit and opens that location document. Within the advanced section of the document, the following screen shown in Figure 3-7 appears:

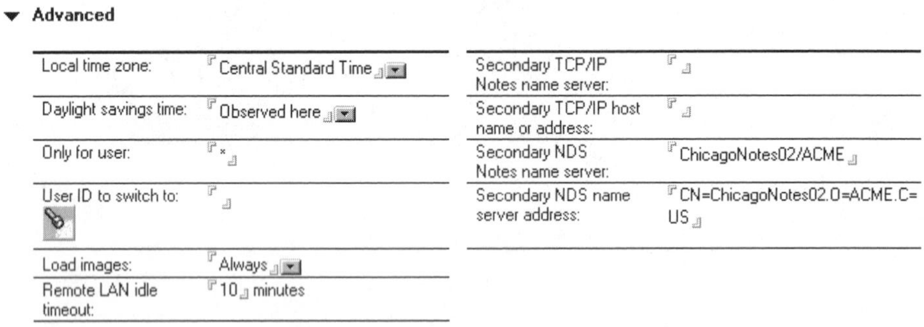

Figure 3-7

Secondary Name Server Fields for SPX using NDS

▼ **Advanced**

Local time zone:	Central Standard Time	Secondary TCP/IP Notes name server:	
Daylight savings time:	Observed here	Secondary TCP/IP host name or address:	
Only for user:	*	Secondary NDS Notes name server:	ChicagoNotes02/ACME
User ID to switch to:		Secondary NDS name server address:	CN=ChicagoNotes02.O=ACME.C= US
Load images:	Always		
Remote LAN idle timeout:	10 minutes		

SPX has some limitations that must be considered when naming servers. The maximum size the common name (CN) of a Notes server may be is 48 characters when using the Novell bindery. Notes server names also must be unique. The following lists some other items that must be followed when naming a Notes server using SPX:

● Only alphanumeric characters are allowed.

● Leading and trailing spaces are removed.

● Spaces are condensed and converted to the underscore.

- Names are upper case, as the Novell bindery is case sensitive.

- The following characters are not allowed:

/ slash

\ backslash

: colon

; semicolon

+ plus

- minus

, comma

* asterisk

? question mark

Different operating system platforms have different requirements and settings for the SPX protocol. For instance, OS/2 requires the NetWare requester to be installed on the machine to provide connectivity to the NetWare environment. The latest version can be obtained from Novell on their Web site at www.novell.com.

For Windows NT and Windows 95, the Microsoft NWLINK protocol may be used along with the Windows NT SAP (Service Advertising Protocol) Agent. NWLINK is Microsoft's version of IPX/SPX. Microsoft has rewritten it for connecting Microsoft products to a NetWare network. NWLINK will communicate with Notes clients and servers running SPX. If NDS and NWLINK are going to be used to resolve SPX addresses rather than bindery services, then the appropriate network service must be installed on Windows 95 and Windows NT machines. The NWLINK protocol and NDS service ship with Windows 95 and Windows NT free of charge.

Tips

If Microsoft's NWLINK protocol is going to be used for Notes server and client connectivity on a Windows NT server, both the Gateway Service for Novell and the Windows NT SAP agent must be installed within Windows NT services.

If desired, Novell also has its own Windows NT and Windows 95 requester and can be used instead of Microsoft's NWLINK. The requester can be obtained free of charge at Novell's Web site at *www.novell.com*. The Novell requester for Windows 95 and Windows NT has NDS functionality automatically installed.

If SPX is going to be used on Windows 3.1, then the following files are necessary on the Notes client workstation:

- NWCALLS.DLL

- NWIPXSPX.DLL

- NWNET.DLL (for NDS support)

- NWLOCALE.DLL (for NDS support)

If SPX is going to be run on UNIX systems running Notes, it should be noted that SPX would only be able to use bindery operations. NDS SPX address resolutions are not supported.

SPXII

SPXII is an improvement over SPX offering better performance on most systems. It is available on Notes Servers running on the UNIX, Novell, and Windows NT platforms. Specifically, it offers the following improvements:

- **Window Flow Control** This means that the protocol allows additional packets to be sent without waiting for an acknowledgment of reception by the receiver.

- **Larger Packet Sizes** The original SPX protocol only accepts a fixed packet size of 576 bytes. This is somewhat small and degrades performance on most networks. SPXII, however, accepts packet sizes that are negotiated between the sender and receiver. Sizes of whatever each machine and the medium the packets are traversing are accepted.

- **Safer methods of closing connections** SPXII unlike SPX ensures that data is not lost when a connection from one machine to another is closed.

Tips

SPXII should be considered by administrators; it offers improved performance between Notes servers and Notes clients.

Banyan VINES

For Banyan file and print environments, Lotus Notes servers and clients can communicate through the use of the Banyan VINES protocol. VINES, similar to Novell NetWare, provides file and print resources to local machines. Lotus does not have a Notes server product for the VINES file and print server; the Lotus Notes server and VINES server must exist on different machines. Only the VINES protocol may be utilized by Lotus Notes. The VINES protocol can only be used on VINES networks. Administrators should consult their Banyan VINES documentation for proper configuration of the protocol within the network. Although performance is adequate using this protocol, it is recommended that you migrate to the TCP/IP protocol if possible for use with Lotus Notes.

Banyan has its own proprietary e-mail system, which can be used with all Banyan clients. In order for e-mail messages to traverse from Notes mail to Banyan Mail, a gateway product such as V-Bridge for Notes must be installed.

NetBIOS

NetBIOS stands for *Network Basic Input Output System*. Lotus Notes supports the following operating system NetBIOS standards:

- DEC PATHWORKS

- IBM LAN Server

- Novell NetBIOS

- Microsoft NetBEUI (Network Basic Extended User Interface—Microsoft's implementation of NetBIOS)

NetBIOS offers superior performance in LAN environments and requires very little administration. The reason for the performance NetBIOS enjoys is that it does not contain much overhead within the design of its protocol frame. It is a session layer protocol containing far less information within the packet frame about traversing a network than a protocol such as TCP/IP.

NetBIOS name resolutions are handled through network broadcasts on LAN segments. A Notes client announces to all machines on an Ethernet segment (or ring) that it is looking for a particular Notes server. The Notes server (or router) then responds with the proper address of the Notes server. This does cause some network traffic issues. For this reason, NetBIOS is not usually the protocol of choice. However, for smaller network installations, NetBIOS works very well.

NetBIOS is also known as an *unroutable protocol*. This means that most router configurations will not pass NetBIOS packets to other network segments or rings. It also creates problems for bridged network environments in that NetBIOS requests can easily flood other rings or segments if bridges are not properly configured to filter such broadcasts.

Lotus Notes does have some configuration details an administrator may need to address if NetBIOS will be used for connectivity. One such detail is configuring Notes to use the correct LANA number of the machine. LANA numbers are used by the operating system to determine which NetBIOS driver to use where multiple instances of NetBIOS are loaded. For instance, a user may be using both Novell's NetBIOS and Microsoft's NetBIOS (NetBEUI) on the same network card on a Windows NT machine. Upon bootup, the operating system assigns a LANA number to each instance starting at 0. This LANA number may be configured and changed within Windows NT.

To direct Notes to use the correct NetBIOS instance, Notes must be configured to use the proper LANA number. This number may be configured in Notes by clicking:

1. **File**

2. **Tools**

3. **User Preferences...**

4. Then click **Ports**

5. Then click **LAN0 Options...**

The following screen, shown in Figure 3-8, will appear:

Figure 3-8
LANA Number
Configuration

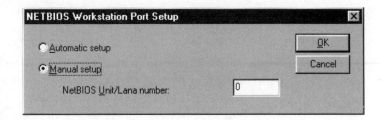

Within this box you can assign the appropriate LANA number for Notes to use.

With NetBIOS like most other protocols other than TCP/IP, the number of active sessions are limited by the operating system. For example, when running NetBIOS on an OS/2 Notes server, the maximum number of sessions supported is 100. After 100 concurrent users establish connections on the Notes server, subsequent users will be dropped. For larger organizations this number may not be sufficient.

AppleTalk

The AppleTalk protocol can be installed to support OS/2 Notes servers, Windows NT Notes server, and Macintosh Notes clients. Installation and configuration, like many Macintosh products, is fairly easy and straightforward. Administrators should consult their respective product manuals (OS/2, Windows NT, and Macintosh) to properly install AppleTalk on the machines. Once configured on the operating system, Notes will use the protocol. Configuration also must be established on Notes as well within the ports section of the Notes user interface select (**File**, **Tools**, **User Preferences**, **Ports**).

X.PC

X.PC is the protocol Notes uses to communicate directly from a Notes server to another Notes server or from a Notes server to a Notes client. The protocol has its roots in the telecommunications company Tymnet, and is the protocol responsible for connecting Notes users and servers directly via analog connections. It also can be used when users dial into a PAD (Packet Assembler/Dissembler) when connecting into an X.25 network (see the section X.25 later in this chapter).

Lotus has improved performance of the X.PC protocol throughout the evolution of Notes. One of the most important factors in dealing with a successful analog connection using the X.PC protocol involves using the correct modem driver. Lotus and many modem manufactures continually update and add to the long list of modems supported by Lotus Notes. It is important for users to ensure they are using the proper and most updated Notes modem driver. Complete listings can be found on Lotus Web home page, *www.lotus.com*.

Tips

Many unreliable connections are caused when the incorrect Notes modem driver has been used.

To select a modem for Notes to use to directly connect to a Notes server, click:

1. **File**

2. **Tools**

3. **User Preferences...**

4. Then click **Ports**

5. Then click **COM1 Options...** (or **COMx**, depending on your modem port)

The screen shown in Figure 3-9 will appear:

Figure 3-9
COM port Options

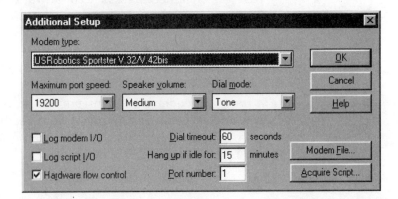

If your modem is still not listed, you may select **Auto Configure.** This will often work with your modem.

- **Log modem I/O** should only be selected if you are experiencing modem connectivity problems. With this option selected, the AT commands and responses will be recorded to the Notes log on the local machine.

- **Log script I/O** when checked, will log script information to the local Notes log. Script information is only recorded when connecting to a server via an acquire script, such as when connecting through a X.25 PAD.

- **Hardware flow control** is normally always checked on machines to enable the machine to control the buffering of data to the COM port(s).

- **Dial timeout** and **Hang up if idle for** fields may be changed if necessary and are self-explanatory.

- The **Port number box** signifies the COM port number the modem will be using, for example, COM1 or COM2.

- The **Modem File...** box should only be accessed if you are experiencing connectivity problems and you are accustomed to AT connect scripts for modems. Normally there is no need to modify this file.

- The **Acquire Script...** box lets you edit an acquire script for use when connecting to a x.25 network via a PAD.

Notes users connecting to a Notes server through a PPP or RAS connection do not use the X.PC protocol. A PPP or RAS connection actually encapsulates networking protocols such as TCP/IP and SPX within its own header and then connects a user as if he or she was recognized as a node on the network. Specifics concerning remote connectivity including PPP and RAS connections are discussed in Chapter 11, *Electronic Mail*.

Some issues and tips surrounding modems with the use of Lotus Notes include:

- The modem drivers are stored in the modems directory relative to the Notes data directory. Once a modem is working, the unneeded drivers may be deleted.

- Modem standards are different around the world. Many modems support the setting of an S-Register to get the modem to behave properly in local conditions.

- The speed setting in the dial box is the port rate, not the carrier rate. Slowing this rate down in situations of poor line conditions does not change the modem's carrier speed. You have to change the AT commands for this.

- The speed setting should always be quicker than the maximum modem carrier rate.

- The most common problem when getting a carrier but no Notes connection is that the responses from the modem are not listed nor able to be matched to those in the modem driver.

- Many drivers do not configure the modem accurately to report the carrier and port speeds to Notes. Notes can report a carrier speed instead of the port speed or vice versa.

- X.PC can also be used for null modem cable connections.

SNA

The SNA protocol can be used on networks where it is the prevalent protocol. It can only be used to connect Notes servers; Notes client connectivity with SNA is not supported. SNA also is an add-on protocol. It must be purchased separately from Lotus, and is not part of the core package of Lotus Notes.

Most organizations do not use this protocol unless a current SNA environment already exists and it is the only protocol that can be used, especially in wide area networks.

X.25

Like the SNA protocol, the X.25 protocol is an add-on product that must be purchased separately. It can only be used to connect Notes servers. Notes clients do not support the use of the product.

The X.25 protocol can be used on X.25 networks and Notes clients may use the X.PC protocol to dial into a PAD (Packet Assembler/Dissembler), where the packets can then be routed on the X.25 network directly into a Notes server.

Tracing Connections

With Notes version 4.0 and higher, Notes users and administrators can trace network connections to ensure they are working properly. This is done by clicking:

1. **File**

2. **Tools**

3. **User Preferences...**

4. Then click **Ports**

5. Then click **Trace Connection** while highlighting the protocol you wish to trace.

The following screen will appear (see Figure 3-10):

Figure 3-10
Tracing Port
Connections

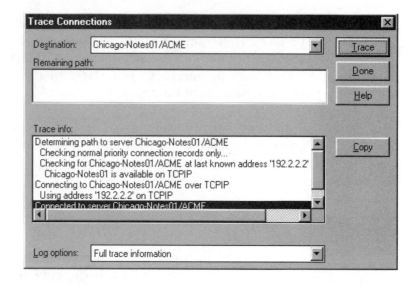

There are 5 log options to choose from:

- **Nothing** No information is logged to the user screen, even if there are errors.

- **Errors Only** Once TRACE is clicked, only error messages that the Notes server or client encounters are reported to the user.

- **Summary progress information** This setting not only reports errors like the Errors Only setting, but also reports to the user all major comments in connecting to the target Notes server.

- **Detailed progress information** This is the default setting for tracing a connection. It reports all information that the summary progress information setting reports with additional information concerning the connection process.

- **Full trace information** This setting returns very detailed information concerning the entire process of connecting to the target Notes server.

Tracing a connection is very helpful in determining problematic connections. All ports that are enabled on the server or client will be traced and returned until a successful connection is accomplished. If a failure occurs, this will also be reported to the user.

Other Port Settings

Within the Port screen of User Preferences, several options are available to the Notes user and administrator. To reference the Port User Preferences screen, click:

1. **File**

2. **Tools**

3. **User Preferences...**

4. Then click **Ports**

The following screen shown in Figure 3-11 will appear:

Figure 3-11
User Preferences
for Notes Ports

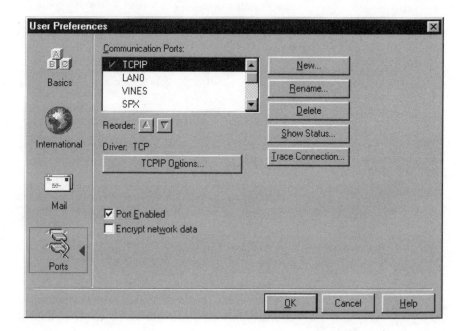

● **Port Reorder** This button will reorder the port drivers listed within the port listings box. To reorder the ports on a Notes server or client, highlight the first desired protocol and then click the **up arrow** of the reorder port button, as shown in the figure above. Continue to click the **up arrow** until the desired protocol appears in the order you wish Notes servers and clients to connect. In other words, a Notes server with a listing of TCPIP then SPX, assuming both ports are enabled, will connect with other Notes servers first using TCPIP and then SPX if TCP/IP fails.

This procedure will also reorder the port listing order in the NOTES.INI file of the machine. In prior releases of Lotus Notes, the port order needed to be configured through the NOTES.INI file or directly on the Notes server console by using the **SET CONFIG** command.

This setting is only valid on machines where more than one port driver is enabled for use.

● **New Port** This enables a user to add a new port to the Notes server or client. The screen shown in Figure 3-12 appears after the NEW button is clicked:

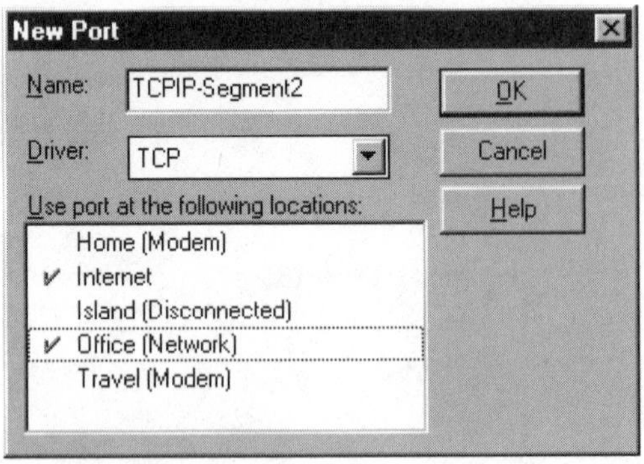

Figure 3-12
New Notes Port
Configuration

The user then should fill in the name of the port. This can be any name that the user wishes. It should be descriptive, associating to the driver that will be used. In other words, the name of the port should not be *SPX-Ring5* if the port will be using the TCP/IP driver.

In the driver box, select the driver for Notes to use.

In the **Use port in the following locations** box, select the locations which you wish to use this port driver. They will appear within the locations forms of the name and address book of that machine.

It should be noted that for the COM ports, the number at the end of the name should directly coincide with the actual COM port used; *Port name COM1* should use COM1 of the operating system.

- **Rename Port** As stated above in the new port section, the name of a port is for descriptive purposes only. The driver selected for the port is the factor that decides what protocol Lotus Notes will use.

  By clicking the **Rename** button of the Port User Preferences screen, the user can rename the port. Again, it does not affect what type of protocol Notes will use.

- **Delete Port** The delete port does simply what its name says: it removes the port from the Notes server or client.

Tips

For a Notes server, once a port is deleted, the corresponding port should be removed from any server and connection records of the public Name and Address book for that particular server.

- **Show Status** The **Show Status** button will show the status of the highlighted, active port. Network statistics for the port driver will be provided, as shown in Figure 3-13 (from sample screen of TCP/IP):

Figure 3-13
Notes Port
Status

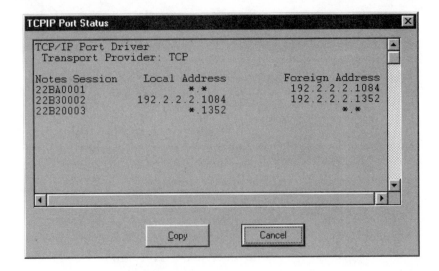

Note that for TCP/IP, the local and foreign TCP/IP addresses are shown with the port number of the application appended. Notes uses TCP/IP port number 1352, unless otherwise configured within the SERVICES file of the operating system.

Tips

If you have multiple protocols configured on your Notes machine, you may force the use of a protocol when connecting to a Notes server by typing 3 exclamation (!!!) marks between the port name and server name within the SERVER field when performing a File, Database, Open as shown below:

```
TCPIP!!!Chicago-Notes01
```

This will force the Notes user interface to connect to the Notes server using the TCP/IP port.

Naming Conventions

As with any system that an organization plans to implement, the creation of naming standards from the onset is a very important issue to address before ever undertaking deployment. This is especially true for a Lotus Notes network. When compared to earlier releases of Notes, the current version makes the process of renaming certain components of the Notes networks far easier with less impact on the network. However, many issues still exist that can cause hours of headaches for Notes administrators if naming standards are not planned before a rollout. For this reason, it is highly recommended that administrators pay very close attention when developing naming standards for all Notes components. Notes administrators should meet with all key business departments to understand the business hierarchy of the company. The naming standards Notes uses will directly reflect this business hierarchy as well as geographic location.

Tips

Even the most ill-conceived naming scheme is better than none. You should also keep in mind that organizations change over time, so a flexible and extensible scheme is desirable.

Component naming is crucial to the successful implementation of Lotus Notes. The key components of a Notes network from a naming standpoint are Certifiers, Servers, Domains, and Users. It is crucial to determine the overall naming conventions for servers, users, and certifiers before implementing Lotus Notes. An ad hoc Notes implementation will only lead to confusion and problems as the infrastructure grows across company divisions. If current organizational standards for naming systems and networking infrastructure components exist, it is strongly recommended that they be adopted for your Lotus Notes environment as well.

Traps

Once you have started down a given naming path, it becomes increasingly difficult to change direction. That is not to say that it's impossible to change direction, but it becomes more costly in terms of downtime and resources required to make the change.

Certifiers—Flat and Hierarchical

Lotus Notes uses two different methods for what Lotus calls certification. The two manners are defined as either a *flat naming model* or a *hierarchical naming model* (also called *fully distinguished naming*). Every user and server within a Notes environment must be created by one of these two types of certifiers. It is with a certifier that a Notes server and user validate their identity.

Before explaining the differences between flat and hierarchical certifiers, basic guidelines of how Lotus Notes handles certification must be explained. All Notes user and server names, passwords, license numbers, and certificates are stored in a file called a *Notes ID file*. Unlike other systems where this information is stored in a central database on the server itself, each user and server retains its information locally in this ID file. This file must be accessed every time a Notes client or server is started, and many times while the server and client are in operation. Without this ID file, a Notes client or server will not function. It is very important that ID files be maintained and secured properly. Maintenance of these ID files are explained in Chapter 8, *Administration Issues*.

A Notes user or server ID file must contain at least one certificate in common with the target Notes server in order to properly authenticate. A certificate can be thought of as a "stamp." For a Notes server to authenticate with another Notes server or user, the two Lotus Notes ID files must have a certificate in common; each ID file must share the same "stamp." User and server ID files are created by an administrator with a certifier ID file. This certifier ID file can be thought of as the "stamper." It is this file that gives a Notes user and server files their certificate and identity. This is actually a form of public key cryptography, licensed by Lotus from RSA.

Authentication is the process used to validate that a server or user ID can access a given Notes server. This process occurs as a challenge and response between a workstation and a server, or between two servers. When a client attempts to establish a connection with a server, the ID information is sent to the server, as well as a list of certificates that are used to validate its right to connect to the server.

Creation of the certifier files is explained in Chapter 8, *Administration Issues*.

With this basic definition of certification, we now can discuss flat and hierarchical naming.

Flat Certificate Naming

This method of certification is simply the common name of a Notes server or user. For a Notes user, this is normally the user's first and last name. This is a flat naming standard, and can be compared to the naming standard in a Novell 3.x environment. The flat naming standard was the original and only naming standard with the first release through version 2 of Lotus Notes.

In this method, an ID file may contain many certificates ("stamps"). For example, let us take the example of the ACME company with a Notes server located in the New York office and another

Notes server in the Chicago office. All New York Notes servers may have a certificate in common, say the New York certifier. All users and servers in the New York office would then have this certifier applied to their Notes ID files.

Still another office, say in Chicago, may share another flat certifier in common called the Chicago certifier. All Notes servers and users in Chicago would share this certificate.

For the two Notes servers in Chicago and New York to communicate, the Notes administrator would need to do one of two things. The administrator would need to apply one of the certifiers from the other office to their local Notes server ID file, or more commonly create a new, third certifier—say the Notes Server certificate—to each of the server ID files.

Tips

In the unlikely event flat certificates are going to be used within your organization, you should create classes of flat certificates based on location and access types. This would provide you with server-to-server certificates and user-to-server certificates.

In this latter example, the Chicago Notes server would have the Chicago certificate and Notes Server certificate applied to its ID file. The New York Notes server ID file would hold the New York certificate and the Notes Server certificate. Users in Chicago could not authenticate to the New York Notes server because they would not have a certificate in common (Chicago Notes users only have the Chicago certificate; the New York Notes server only has the New York certificate and the Notes Server certificate).

As discussed before, a flat user or server ID only contains a common name. An example would be:

```
Server: Chicago-Notes01
Users:  Scott Thomas
        Brad Hoyt
```

With this example, if another user within the organization were to have the name Scott Thomas, the second Scott would not be acceptable. The Notes administrator would have to create the second Scott Thomas with a middle initial in order to create the user. This can lead to quite a bit of confusion for administrators and users alike. For example, if Brad were to e-mail Scott and there was a Scott Thomas and a Scott L. Thomas within the Notes network, Brad would have to know which user was which. Most people would not know for sure, leading e-mail to be delivered to the incorrect recipient. Hierarchical naming, discussed below, helps alleviate this problem.

Hierarchical Certificate Naming

The second (and recommended) approach in creating and naming Notes users and servers is referred to as *hierarchical naming* or *fully distinguished naming*, which was introduced with release 3 of Lotus Notes. Hierarchical naming closely follows x.500 naming standards and can be compared to Novell's NDS naming format in Novell version 4.x environments. Unlike flat user and server ID files, a hierarchically created ID file may only contain one hierarchical certificate ("stamp").

Since the release of version 3 of Lotus Notes, hierarchical naming is the default naming standard for registering Notes users and servers. Flat user and server names are still supported, but must be created separately. Most organizations have converted or are in the process of converting from flat certifiers, user, and server names to the default hierarchical naming standard. With the release of version 4 of Lotus Notes, built-in conversion utilities exist to automate much of the conversion process.

Tips

If you have an existing Notes network currently using flat naming standards, it is recommended that you convert all users and servers to a hierarchical naming structure to take advantage of what hierarchical naming offers. Also, in order to connect to some other Notes networks, including Lotus, your Notes server must be a hierarchically named Notes server.

Hierarchical naming has the following advantages over flat naming standards:

● **Reduction of duplicate server and user names.** This holds true especially for larger companies where two or more users have the same name. Because of the format of a hierarchical name, users and servers may share the same common name as long as they have different organizational units within their fully qualified name.

● **More specific security entries.** Although not inherently designed to improve security, fully distinguished names provide a higher level of security by enabling administrators to enter fully qualified names in database access control lists and server access lists. In a flat naming structure, a user within or outside the company has a higher chance of using a user ID with the same name of another person to fraudulently access a Notes application or server.

● **Faster user and server authentication.** By design, in order for two IDs to authenticate (either Notes server-to-server or Notes server-to-Notes client) the IDs must have a certificate in common. Hierarchical IDs can only contain one certificate and require cross-certificates in order to authenticate outside of their hierarchy. In a flat naming scheme, a user or server ID may contain multiple certificates in order to authenticate. As more flat certifiers are added to an ID file, the authentication process slows.

● **Decentralization of registering new users and servers.** In a flat naming environment, a single Notes administrator does most of the registering of new users and servers. With hierarchical naming, organizational unit certifiers may be distributed to local offices, where a local administrator may handle certification of local users and servers at that specific office.

● **Use of the Administration Process.** The administration process that runs on Notes version 4 servers will only recognize hierarchical users and servers.

Lotus Notes uses the following structure for hierarchical naming:

```
CN/OU/OU/OU/OU/O/C
```

where:

- CN = Common Name

- OU = Organizational Unit (can be up to four levels deep)

- O = Organization

- C = Country Code (optional)

for example

```
CN=Scott Thomas/OU=Marketing/OU=Chicago/O=ACME/C=US
```

```
CN=Chicago-Notes01/O=ACME/C=US
```

As you can see from this naming structure, users and servers can have the same name as long as the OU format is different. In other words, another user named Scott Thomas could exist in the Finance group in Chicago as well as in the Marketing group, and Notes would treat each as a unique user. The second Scott's fully distinguished name would be:

```
CN=Scott Thomas/OU=Finance/OU=Chicago/O=ACME/C=US
```

Each of the above layers of a hierarchical name will now be explained.

Country Code

The two-letter country code is optional in terms of the hierarchical naming scheme. All country codes are defined by the CCITT. It is recommended that this be used only if your company has locations outside the country of the installed base. It is also used to distinguish a company from another in the event a company of the same name exists in a different country. The country code will appear on all e-mail messages and is necessary in all documents in terms of naming. In other words, when a user receives an e-mail message from another user, the country code (US in our example) will appear appended at the end of his or her name.

Tips

Country codes are not normally used, except to distinguish companies of the same name in different countries. Even then, a variation on the company name may be preferable. In the example of various locations, the country code can be a problem.

Organization

The organization is the top level of the hierarchy and is required for all Notes server and user ID files. The organization name appears on all server and user names, including e-mails, unless otherwise specified by Notes applications designers. The organization certifer name is usually the name of the company. In our example, the organization would be ACME. The length of the organization name may be from 3 to 64 characters. The Organization (O) is created when the first Notes server is created, and is saved on the first Notes server with a file name of CERT.ID. The registration of the organization certifier is also recorded in the public Name and Address book of the Notes server. With this certifier file, Notes users and servers may be created as well as additional Organizational Units (OUs), explained below. It is one of the most important files in a Notes infrastructure, and should be password-protected and maintained by only one or two Notes administrators.

Another Organizational certifier file may be created after the first Notes server is created, but proper planning must be considered in performing this task. An example where a Notes administrator may create a new Organizational certifier would be an instance where a company was changing its name. The administrator would then have to recertify all user and server Notes ID files. Another example where a Notes administrator would create another Organizational certifier would be when the administrator wishes to connect to another set of Notes servers,perhaps for external connectivity to another third-party Notes network.

Organizational Units

Organizational Units are optional and are used to further distinguish a user or server within an company. OUs appear directly underneath an Organization or another Organizational Unit in the naming hierarchy. They usually represent a division or geographical location within a company.

You may have up to 4 such division levels (OUs); however, it is recommended that you implement no more than 2 or 3 layers. The length of each Organizational Unit may be up to 32 characters. You may, however, have as many OUs as you wish at a given level, such as in our example, as many city locations at the first level as you wish:

```
CN=Scott Thomas/OU=Marketing/OU=NewYork/O=ACME/C=US

CN=Scott Thomas/OU=Marketing/OU=Chicago/O=ACME/C=US

CN=Scott Thomas/OU=Marketing/OU=Dallas/O=ACME/C=US
```

The more levels deep you do go, the more administration is likely to be involved. Let's say if users transfer divisions—in our example, from Chicago to Dallas—the person must be recertified. If the organization did not have any OUs defined, as in CN=Scott Thomas/O=ACME/C=US, the user would not have to be recertified.

The use of OU certifiers can help ease the burden of administration especially when creating new users. For example, if administration of ACME is done from the Chicago office, the OU certifier file of /OU=Marketing/OU=NewYork/O=ACME/C=US could be sent to New York and the Notes administrator in that location could be responsible for certifying and creating new users, thus reducing the burden to the central Chicago Notes IS staff.

When registering Notes servers, it is recommended that in environments where organizational units are used, proper consideration be attended to when determining where to place the Notes server. Many times multiple departments will be accessing a Notes server. Let us take a look again at our examples at ACME:

User:

```
CN=Scott Thomas/OU=Marketing/OU=Chicago/O=ACME/C=US
```

Server:

```
CN=Chicago-Notes01/O=ACME/C=US
```

The ACME Notes administration team decided to place the Notes server under the /ACME certifier. The Notes server could be placed anywhere in the hierarchy, but to keep things simple and to avoid confusion, this is where the ACME teams decided to place all Notes servers within the company. Different departments and geographic locations of ACME will be accessing the Notes server. Because of this, it does not make sense to place the server at the department level, such as /Marketing/Chicago/ACME. This leads to confusion for other departments that may be using the Notes server.

Actual placement of the Notes server in the hierarchy of a company's fully distinguished naming scheme is not important in terms of performance. However, whichever level is decided upon by your Notes administration team should be followed. This provides consistency and avoids confusion both to the Notes administration team and the Notes user community.

Tips

If you are considering using Organizational Units in your hierarchical naming scheme, it is recommended to keep the number of levels to a minimum. A single Organizational Unit usually suffices for most organizations. Two Organizational Units is usually the recommended maximum number of levels.

"Fake" Organizational Units

"Fake" Organizational Units are used in the event that two people have the SAME name at the SAME level of the hierarchy. In our example, the possibility exists that two users named Scott Thomas could exist within the same hierarchy:

```
CN=Scott Thomas/OU=Marketing/OU=Chicago/O=ACME/C=US
```

In such an event, a "fake" organizational unit could be used to distinguish this person from the other Scott Thomas. This OU would be counted as another level in the hierarchy. The "fake" level would not be used for security checks within the Notes security model. An example could look something like this for the two users named Scott Thomas:

```
CN=Scott Thomas/Manager/OU=Marketing/OU=Chicago/O=ACME/C=US

CN=Scott Thomas/Operations/OU=Marketing/OU=Chicago/O=ACME/C=US
```

The "fake" organizational unit provides a way for Notes users to easily distinguish between the two Scott Thomases.

Most companies, instead of incorporating a fake organizational unit, simply use the user's middle initial. This method of the middle initial proves less confusing and simplifies the naming format.

Common Name

The common name (CN) represents a Notes user or server name. It may be up to 80 characters in length, depending on which protocol is used (different protocols support different common name lengths). The common name of an ID can be compared to the format a Flat user or server ID would have.

Normally, for company installations that are not too large, only a CN (Common Name) and an O (Organization) are used. Adding additional OUs puts further administration burden and complexity on the environment and usually is not necessary.

For larger Notes installations, one or two organizational units are necessary to provide detail of a user's location and/or department as well as avoiding the possibility of duplicate user names. If OUs are going to be used, it is recommended that it only go one or two levels deep. Most of the time, one OU is the preferred level of complexity within a hierarchical naming scheme.

Each level in the fully distinguished naming scheme except the Common Name and Country Code of Notes is represented as a certifier ID File. In other words, the O level is a certifier ID file, and for each OU, they too represent separate certifier ID files. These are some of the most important files in the Notes environment and must be password protected, stored securely, and only accessed by a handful of Notes administrators.

Traps

If an unauthorized user were to get a hold of a Organization or Organizational Unit certifier ID file, he or she could create any new or existing Notes user or server and gain access to Notes applications and servers within the Notes infrastructure.

Let us look again at our examples of a fully distinguished Notes user and server:

```
CN=Scott Thomas/OU=Marketing/OU=Chicago/O=ACME/C=US

CN=Chicago-Notes01/O=ACME/C=US
```

In this example, Marketing and Chicago both represent Organizational Units. Each Organizational Unit is a certifier ID file. The Organization /ACME is also a certifier ID file.

Chronologically, the /ACME certifier was created first. This was done initially when the first Notes server of the company was created. It was saved on this Notes server as the file name CERT.ID. The Notes administrators at ACME then decided the first level organizational units for the Notes network would be geographically based. From the /ACME certifier, the OU certifier /Chicago was created by the Notes administrator from his Notes workstation. Other 2nd level OU certifiers could also be created from the /ACME certifier to represent other geographic locations.

From the /Chicago certifier OU, the Notes administrator of ACME created the /Marketing OU certifier. Any number of 3rd level OU certifiers could be created from the /Chicago OU certifier to represent different departments within the company at each location. Take note that if the Notes administrator of ACME could have created a /Marketing OU certifier from a /NewYork/ACME certifier, this would be a separate file from the /Marketing/Chicago/ACME certifier.

Finally, in our example, the user Scott Thomas was created from the /Marketing OU certifier. Any number of users or servers could be created from the /Marketing OU certifier ID file. As stated before, another Scott Thomas could exist as long as the ID file was created with a different OU certifier.

As in our Notes server example above, it is also important to point out that Notes users don't necessarily have to be created from the second level OU certifier. A server or user could have been created from the first level OU certifier or even from the O certifier itself. Such examples would be:

```
CN=Scott Thomas/OU=Chicago/O=ACME/C=US
```

or

```
CN=Scott Thomas/O=ACME/C=US
```

Tips

Although possible, the registering of Notes users in the high levels of a hierarchical naming scheme is not recommended. If a procedure is set by the Notes administration team to register users and servers at the same level of hierarchy, then it should be followed to avoid confusion.

As mentioned before, in order for a hierarchical Notes user ID and server ID to authenticate, they must share a certificate in common or obtain a cross-certificate (cross-certification is explained in Chapter 5, *Public Name and Address Book Domain Structure*). In ACME's case, all server and user IDs share a common certificate ancestor of /ACME. Because of this, all ID files within the company are able to authenticate with one another.

It should be noted that in mixed flat and hierarchical naming environments, authentication might still take place. As stated before, a hierarchical user ID may only contain 1 hierarchical certificate. However, it may have several flat certificates. In other words, the only way for a flat ID file to authenticate with a hierarchical ID file is if the two ID files share in common a flat certificate. Take note though; two hierarchical ID files not sharing a hierarchical certificate but sharing a flat certificate *cannot* authenticate.

Notes Servers

In naming Notes servers, most organizations take one of two approaches. In the first, the Notes administration team follows a strict server-naming standard where each character in the server name is significant. For example, the first three characters of a server name may represent location, the fourth through sixth may represent a department, the seventh character a server type, and the eighth through the last character represent the Notes server name. Such a convention might look something like this:

```
CHIMKTMNOTES01
```

Where:

- Characters 1– 3 = Location Code (CHI, NYC, etc.)

- Characters 4–6 = Department (MKT, FIN, etc.)

- Character 7 = Server Type (M = Mail, H = Hub, etc.)

- Characters 8–end = Server Name (Notes01)

This method of server naming certainly proves very beneficial to Notes administrators. Administrators are able to easily determine location and server type by simply looking at the Common Name (CN) of the Notes server. However, this server naming standard sometimes proves confusing to end users, as the Notes server name is harder to remember. Many times much of what the naming procedures are providing duplicate what the hierarchical naming standards are accomplishing. Using the same server name from above with our ACME hierarchical example yields:

```
CHIMKTMNOTES01/OU=Chicago/O=ACME/C=US
```

In this example, both the department and the location are provided in the hierarchical name of the server, as well as the common name.

Many companies choose to use a more practical naming standard based on location, department, and Notes server class. The fully distinguished name then handles issues such as Notes server type and location.

Such examples include the following:

```
Chicago-Hub01

Chicago-Mkt01

Chicago-Notes01
```

Using the ACME example, the fully distinguished names would then be:

```
CN=Chicago-Hub01/O=ACME/C=US

CN=Chicago-Mkt01/O=ACME/C=US

CN=Chicago-Notes01/O=ACME/C=US
```

The use of location naming within the CN for Notes servers in general proves effective for giving Notes users and administrators a way to keep track of Notes servers. It is also beneficial to include the word NOTES within the server name to distinguish that the server is indeed a Notes server. The end of the common name of the server should end in a 2-digit number to maintain continuity.

It should be noted again that TCP/IP, SPX, and NetBIOS all support different lengths for a Notes server common (CN) name. Also, certain characters must be avoided, as different protocols do not support all characters. Spaces are usually avoided, since they lead to confusion.

The names of servers are used by Notes itself, and also by users to access server resources. Again, if current organizational standards exist, they should be followed. If no standards exist or the development of new standards is desirable, the above recommendations can be followed.

Tips

Whichever Notes server naming standard is adopted should be applied organization-wide to minimize confusion to both Notes administrators and end users.

Domain Names

A *domain* in Lotus Notes is one or more Notes servers that share a common name and address book. Domain naming standards refer to the creation of naming standards for these Domains. The Lotus Notes public Name and Address book, its uses, and forms are explained thoroughly in Chapter 5, *Public Name and Address Book Domain Structures*. A Notes domain should not be confused with other domain structures on other systems such as a Windows NT domain.

Notes

With Notes release 4.5, a Windows NT domain may now be configured to add and remove users to a Notes public Name and Address book providing directory synchronization. Refer to Chapter 9, Windows NT Integration *for more details.*

For most organizations, the Lotus Notes domain name is the same name used for the organization (O) certifier of the company. The Notes domain name is almost always the name of the company. In our continuing example for ACME, the organization certifier name is /ACME. The domain name for the company would also be ACME. The name of the domain is defined when the first Lotus Notes server is configured within the company.

The domain name of your Notes network is appended to a user's name when Notes mail is sent. Normally, within the same domain, the domain does not appear in users' e-mails. When Notes mail is sent from the user's home Lotus Notes domain to Notes user at another company, the user's home domain is appended to the user's name along with any other Notes domains the e-mail traversed while in transit. Also, for addressing Notes mail to another Notes user outside of the company, the other company's domain name must be appended to the recipient's name.

For example, let us assume the ACME company has a Notes connection from their Notes mail server to the ABC company's Notes mail server. If a Notes user from ACME sent an e-mail to a Notes user at ABC Company, the Notes recipient would see the following in the FROM and TO fields of the e-mail message:

```
TO: Brad Hoyt/ABC@ABC
FROM: Scott Thomas/Marketing/Chicago/ACME@ACME
```

Scott had to manually append @ABC to Brad's fully distinguished name in order for the e-mail message to be successfully delivered to an external Notes domain. Since the e-mail originated from another Notes domain (another Notes network), Scott's home domain shows appended on the e-mail.

Some larger companies choose to have multiple domains (see Chapter 5 for more explanation) within their Notes network. This situation usually only applies to very large Notes installations. The names of the domains then are usually the company name with a further description of what purpose the domain serves. Many times it is broken down by geographical location or department. Examples of different Notes domain names include:

```
ACME-West, ACME-East, ACME-South, etc.

ACME-US, ACME-Europe, ACME-Asia, etc.

ACME-Mktg, ACME-Fin, ACME-HR, etc.
```

Other Notes domains are often set up for other Notes-related purposes. For example, many times companies set up test Notes domains where users and administrators develop and test new Notes applications. By doing this, any applications, procedures or add-ons that are being used in the test domain will not affect the company's production Notes domain. Names for name for this type of domain would be:

```
ACME-Development

ACME-Test
```

Also, as explained in Chapter 5, *Public Name and Address Book Domain Structure* within the "External Connectivity" section, a separate Notes domain is created to pose as a Notes firewall. This protects the Notes domain within an organization from outside Notes domains. Many times these domains are named to reflect their purpose. For ACME an example external domain name would be:

```
ACME-Ext or ACME-External
```

Other third party add-ons may need a unique domain name as well, even though they may not be a traditional Notes domain housing users and servers. Such examples include many gateway products including SMTP, FAX, and Pager gateways. Many organizations name these types of domains as:

```
INTERNET = SMTP gateway

FAX = Fax Gateway

PAGER = Pager Gateway
```

A Notes user then simply appends the domain name to send a message to a specific gateway. For example, if a Notes user at ACME wishes to send a page to the Notes pager gateway, the format would look like this in the TO field of an e-mail message:

```
TO: 3170247 @ Pager

(Pager PIN#)
```

Notes User Names

User names are actually one of the easier and more obvious structures to create. You know your users and their names. The gotcha with creating users is whether to include the middle initial. Many organizations choose not to use the middle initial as it can be confusing to both the end user and administrators. The use of middle initials can be especially confusing when addressing electronic mail. Most people do not know an individual's middle initial, which leads to addressing problems. This holds especially true for remote users where many times the remote user does not have access to an address book containing the recipient's address. If administrators create Notes users with middle initials, then e-mail messages must contain the middle initial as well, unless an alias is being used. Electronic mail will not be successfully delivered if this case does not hold true.

The Notes administrator can choose to use a period following the middle initial. If the period is going to be used, it should always be used. Do not create some duplicate user names with middle initial with a period and others without a period.

With this situation explained, it is recommended that the only time a middle initial be used when creating Notes users is when the instance of duplicate names occurs at the same level of hierarchy in the fully distinguished name. As discussed earlier, hierarchical naming avoids many of the potential duplicate names as the same name can exist as long as the fully distinguished name is different.

Also discussed before, fake OUs can be used which simply puts another OU in the fully distinguished name. This fake OU will not affect the name in terms of access control. This functionality is rarely used; middle initials are used instead when facing duplicate name entries.

Tips

If two Notes users have the same name and appear at the same level of hierarchy in a fully distinguished naming scheme, Notes administrators should use the middle initials of the users to differentiate them.

The following example shows when a middle initial or fake OU is *not* necessary:

Two users both named Scott Thomas exist in the ACME company. One works in the Finance department and the other in Human Resources. The Notes administration team of ACME designed a hierarchical naming structure where each department and location are separate OU certifiers. The result is that both users can exist without a middle initial:

```
Scott Thomas/Finance/Chicago/ACME
Scott Thomas/HR/Chicago/ACME
```

However, if both Scotts existed in Chicago and worked in the Finance department, then the Notes administrator would be forced to use a middle initial for one or both users:

```
Scott L. Thomas/Finance/Chicago/ACME
Scott A. Thomas/Finance/Chicago/ACME
```

Aliases are allowed in the public Name and Address book in the individuals' personal records to allow other names, such as nicknames and entries without the middle initial. It should be noted, though, that database ACL entries only use the full name as listed. Aliases are ignored in this case.

Tips

The Domino HTTP process will use only the first entry listed in the full name field of a document for authentication through a Web browser. If a Notes user is also going to access a Notes server through a Web browser, then the user will have to use his or her fully distinguished name for authentication through a Web browser.

Group Names

This section discusses the value of—and need for—the creation of a Notes group naming structure.

Group names are used to logically group users for purposes of messaging, access to Notes servers, and security for Notes applications. Group names can also be nested within one another and can be up to 64 characters in length.

A group naming standard should be set by the Notes administration team of your organization and be consistently enforced. Most organizations let a number of people create groups in the public Name and Address book. Since release 4 of Lotus Notes, Lotus has roles tailored to letting a specific group of users create and/or modify group names in the public name and address book.

Similar to server naming standards (discussed earlier), some companies take a very specific approach to group naming, where each character representation within the group name actually has a specific meaning. For instance, the first three characters of a group name may represent a location, the fourth through sixth may represent a department, the remaining characters may represent the group's function. Such an example may look something like this:

```
CHIFINADMIN or Chi-Fin-Admin
```

Other companies take a less structured approach to group naming standards, where only a piece of the above methodology is taken. For example, many organizations only name a group for the function it serves. Such an example would be:

```
Finance Notes Editors
```

Whatever approach is taken, it should be adopted and enforced within the Notes environment. Confusion among the Notes community could surface, causing duplicate groups to be created.

A key concern with group names is that the numbers can explode as applications and mailing lists grow. The number of groups can then have an adverse impact on the Notes servers themselves. The more entries within a public Name and Address book, the more intensive the Notes server must work. It is recommended that individuals use personal Address Book group lists whenever possible on their local Notes client machines. Another solution is to create a separate cascaded address book from the public Address book for e-mail listings. However, groups for ACL entries in Notes applications are only recognized from the primary public Name and Address book and must exist there.

Lotus Notes has two default groups, *LocalDomainServers* and *OtherDomainServers*. We recommend that you use these default groups and not create unnecessary work for yourself by changing them. Every server created within a Notes domain is placed within the LocalDomainServers group. This group should also appear in every ACL of every database application to ensure proper replication. It is also recommended that this group have **Manager** access to ease the burden of administration. Some applications may not be designed to have such a setting, however. The OtherDomainServers group is used to list servers outside the current domain. It is often used to disallow servers access to other servers and/or applications.

Two other group names that are recommended within a Notes organization are a *Notes Admin* group and a *Notes Developers* group. The Notes Admin group should appear with **Manager** access to all Notes applications and all pertinent Notes server administration fields of the server documents in the public Name and Address Books. The Notes Developers group should appear with **Manager** access on all Notes applications. In larger organizations, sub-Notes Admin and Developer groups can be used. For server administration for the worldwide ACME company, there would be a central group Notes Admin, that would appear in all Notes applications and in all server documents. Each geographical location or department then would have a local Notes Admin group in each server document in the public Name and Address book—for example, Chicago-Notes Admin. In this way, the local Notes administrators would be able to administer their local Notes servers without gaining access to other Notes servers within the organization. The same sub-administration group concept could apply to the Notes Developer group.

Notes does not have a global administration or root account like many other systems with access privileges to all resources. Access rights are granted on a user ID and/or group basis. For this reason, a group like Notes Admin placed with **Manager** access on all Notes applications and server administration fields of server documents proves very beneficial to the Notes Administration team.

Tips

It is recommended that Notes administrators use the predefined server groups LocalDomainServers and OtherDomainServers. It is also recommended that Notes administrators create two groups named Notes Admin and Notes Developers to better manage your Notes infrastructure.

Some organizations set up group names to hold a listing of all Notes users. Such an example for ACME may be a group listing called:

`ACME Notes Users` or `ACME All`

Following this idea, companies also split divisions or geographical regions into groups for security and e-mail group listings. Such examples would include:

`NY ACME Notes Users` or `NY ACME All`

`Chicago ACME Notes Users` or `Chicago ACME All`

The following characters cannot or should not be used when naming Notes groups:

/	Reserved for hierarchical naming.
@	Reserved for domain names.
+	Reserved for hierarchical naming.
=	Reserved so that string that follows is treated as hierarchical.
;	Reserved so that each piece of text separated by semicolon is treated as separate list with all of the same members. Result is duplication of lists.
,	Reserved so that each piece of text separated by a period is treated as separate list with all of the same members. Result is duplication of lists.

Directory Schema

A *directory scheme* refers to the on-disk directory structure of the file system on the Notes server itself. When users access a Notes server, the location of databases should exist in the same types of directories. For instance, all mail databases by default appear under a directory named \MAIL. All firm-wide replicated databases should appear within the same name structure on all servers, such as \FIRMWIDE. This maintains continuity so that administrators and end users know exactly where to look for a specific database when accessing multiple Notes servers.

Directory links can be used to provide an easy way of increasing the amount of disk space a Notes server has available without any repartitioning or reinstallation. The administrator just makes a Notes directory link that points to another drive on the server. The link then appears as another directory on the Notes server. Directory links also provide another layer of security, allowing administrators to define which users or groups are allowed to access a specific directory. With Notes version 4.5, directory links can now be made from the administration console of an administrator's workstation rather than performing the operation at the Notes server. To create a directory link, consult Chapter 8, *Administration Issues*.

Tips

The key to directory schema is developing a logical structure that is scalable, and then to consistently apply it.

ID File Names

The naming of Notes ID files refers to the actual file name on the file system of a server or workstation. It is recommended that all Notes user ID files use the .ID extension so that users, administrators, and Notes clients and servers can recognize that they are Notes ID files. There are three different types of ID files. It is recommended that a naming approach be adopted to name the different classes.

- **Notes User ID files.** These files exist on a Notes user's workstation or a shared area on a LAN. We recommend that you use a first-initial-last-name approach. This method combines the first letter of the user's first name and the first 7 characters of the user's last name. If a user ID is initially created and stored in the public Name and Address book, the file name is set to USER.ID. This can be changed once the user has retrieved the ID, but can be difficult to enforce. This method can lead to confusion, especially if an administrator has to keep track of everyone's ID file.

Traps

For security reasons we do not recommend storing a user ID file in the public Name and Address book during registration.

- **Notes Server ID files** These files exist on the Notes server's machine. Initially, when the first Notes server is created, the file name is named SERVER.ID. As with Notes user ID files, this can lead to confusion. We recommend that the file name represent the server name. Such an example may be:

CHINOTE1.ID

As stated with Notes user ID files, administrators should not store Notes server ID files within the public Name and Address book for security reasons.

- **Notes Certifier ID Files** Notes certifier ID files are one of the most important files within a Notes infrastructure. Proper security measures should be taken so that only a few Notes administrators have access to the files. With a certifier ID file, any person could create a fraudulent Notes ID file thereby gaining unauthorized access to any Notes server or application.

There are three different types of Notes certifier ID files: organizational certifiers, organizational unit certifiers, and flat certifiers. Most companies will not have flat certifiers unless they have flat-named Notes servers within their company or they have a need to connect their hierarchically-named Notes server to another company's flat named Notes server.

Most companies name their certifiers per their name. In our ACME example, the /ACME certifier would be named:

```
ACME.ID
```

The `/CHICAGO/ACME` certifier would be named:

```
CHICAGO.ID
```

As with all other components within Notes, whatever standard is adopted should be followed with consistency to avoid confusion.

If your certificate files do not use the default extension of ID, they will not automatically show up in file selection dialog boxes.

Notes Named Network

By definition a Lotus Notes named network is a grouping of Notes servers on the same physical segment or ring that share a common network protocol. Sometimes a Notes named network can span multiple rings or segments, but the Notes servers must have a network protocol in common. For Notes servers running the X.PC protocol for remote connectivity, a Notes network name is not necessary. Notes servers grouped in the same Notes named network will appear in the server list for Notes users when they perform a **File**, **Database**, **Open**.

By default when a Notes server is first created, the name of the Notes network for that server is **Network1**. This is not descriptive in terms of location, network type, or protocol type the Notes server is running. When more Notes servers are added to a Notes infrastructure this type of generic naming can lead to confusion for Notes administrators.

It is recommended that in naming Notes networks that Notes administrators use a descriptive name addressing at least one or all of the following:

● Network protocol

● Network type

● Location

Some organizations take the approach where the first few letters describe the protocol being used, the second set describe the network type, and the final set describe the location. Samples include:

```
TCPIP-Ethernet-Chicago

SPX-TokenRing-NY

NetBIOS-Chicago

SPXII-LA
```

The location where Notes named networks are configured is the public Name and Address book within the server record.

If multiple protocols are configured, either on separate cards or the same card, then a separate Notes named network entry is necessary.

Exact Notes named network configuration guidelines are explained in Chapter 5, *Public Name and Address Book Domain Structure.*

Tips

While the use of spaces in naming standards in Notes do work, they can cause problems, especially when talking to other systems. Even performing commands on the Notes server becomes a task as you have to enclose the name in quotes.

Public Name and Address Book Domain Structure

In this chapter, we address the domain structure of the Notes public Name and Address Book. The database forms that comprise the public Name and Address book are the core of any Notes network. If the public Name and Address book is not managed and maintained properly, there will be serious consequences to your Notes infrastructure.

Definition

A Lotus Notes *domain* is defined as a collection of users, servers, and groups that share a common name and address book within a Notes environment. A Notes domain can encompass servers and users on the same as well as different physical networks.

The Lotus Notes infrastructure within a company must be designed to replicate this common Name and Address book to all Notes servers within the organization. This same copy must exist on every production Notes server within the company's Notes network. Any changes made to this database should then be replicated to all other Notes servers to keep the configuration of all components the same. It is also responsible for basic security and management of all users and servers. Although it is possible to have multiple domains (multiple Name and Address books) within a company, we recommend that a company only use one public Name and Address book—it makes it much easier to control the functions of servers, and users, and their security.

The public Name and Address book for a Notes infrastructure is the heart of the network. All Notes servers, users, groups and other configuration items are maintained within this Notes database. For this reason, proper security measures need to be put into place to prevent unauthorized access. Normally, all administration of the public Name and Address book is handled centrally by a select few people to avoid confusion. It is imperative that these select few Notes administrators only make additions or modifications to the public Name and Address book on *one* Notes server, preferably a Notes hub server. The additions and modifications will then be replicated to all other Notes servers within the infrastructure, through scheduled replication events. If this policy is not followed, Notes infrastructures run the risk of save and replication conflicts. This could happen when a Notes administrator in one location makes a modification to a document within the public Name and Address book, and another administrator in another location edits the same document. What occurs during the next replication is called a *replication conflict*.

Another common error occurs when a Notes administrator modifies the same document within the public Name and Address book on multiple Notes servers not realizing the Notes replication engine will carry the one modification to all replica copies of the database.

A Notes network holds a unique approach in replication of its public Name and Address book as to how it is configured and administered. This approach must be completely understood by all who are involved in supporting and administering the network. All too often, stories are heard of how Notes administrators mistakenly remove groups or servers from the public Name and Address book on their local Notes server thinking they are not needed. Then the deletions traverse to all the Notes servers within the Notes network through replication, bringing it to a screeching halt. A famous instance of this very scenario was played out at a Big Six Accounting firm where a Notes administrator did this very thing, bringing the 10,000-plus user Notes network to a standstill. Because the deletion stubs were sent to all replica copies of the Name and Address book, the Notes database had to be modified on each Notes server to re-enable the connections!

Traps

Administrators should only add or edit documents to the public Name and Address book on a single Notes server. Replication then moves the changes to all Notes servers within the infrastructure. All Notes administrators within your company must understand this concept, as any mistakes made to the public Name and Address book will replicate to all Notes servers in the organization.

Let us take for example the case of ACME corporation. They have Notes servers located in New York, Boston, Miami, Los Angeles, and Chicago. All Notes servers replicate with a hub Notes server in Chicago (see Figure 5-1).

Figure 5-1

Name and
Address Book
Server Replication

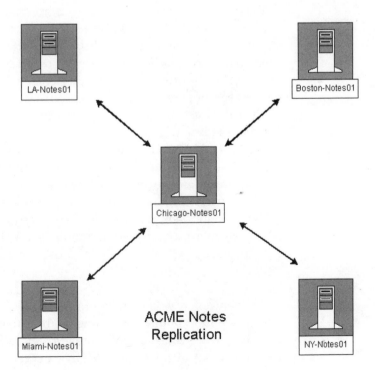

In this scenario, the Notes administration team should always make additions and modifications to the public Name and Address book on the hub Notes server in Chicago. This provides the quickest response to all Notes servers within the infrastructure. If, for instance, a Notes administrator edited a server record on the public Name and Address book on the Miami Notes server, the change would have to replicate from Miami to Chicago and then out to the other servers.

An exception to this procedure would be the case in which a local office needs a new person created or a group modified immediately. In this scenario, it makes sense for the Notes administration team or the local Notes administrator to make the addition or modification to the local Notes server. This will then provide immediate response for the local office, as the office will not have to wait for the next scheduled replication from the hub server for the change to take place.

When administrators do any administration to a Notes database application, including the public Name and Address book, all editing should always be done at the administrator's local workstation. Administration at the server through the Notes GUI (graphical user interface) should never be done unless absolutely necessary— the Notes server GUI circumvents the Notes security model. From the Notes user interface at the server, all Notes applications can be assumed local to the Notes client. A user from the Notes server has MANAGER equivalent access to a Notes application. Using the Notes user interface from a Notes server also causes performance degradation at the server. Editing a Notes application, such as the public Name and Address book from the Notes server does not provide a security audit trail to changes. All changes are registered as made by the Notes server rather than a Notes user.

As mentioned before, it is recommended that a company only utilize one central public Name and Address book (domain) for the organization. With release 4 of Notes, a single Name and Address book can house all of an organization's users and servers. Many times maximum numbers are limited to the hardware the Notes server is running. There also is a limit to the number of Notes servers that can exist within a single Notes named network within the public Name and Address book. Most organizations can easily operate with only a single Name and Address book. If multiple Name and Address books are used, administration as well as end user confusion may surface within the environment.

One problem that arises with large singular domain structures is directory listing access for remote users. Public Name and Address books grow into very large databases as more users and applications are added to the infrastructure. Unless remote users are connected to the Notes network, they have no access to the public Name and Address book for e-mail name resolutions. What many organizations put into place is a light Name and Address book that only replicates the person and group documents to the local desktops. This provides e-mail listings for remote users, so they don't have to be connected to the Notes network to resolve e-mail addresses. Cascaded address books may be utilized as well as Notes directory assistance (new with release 4.5 of Lotus Notes) to manage multiple domains. These topics are explained in greater detail later in this chapter.

Like any Notes applications, the database's forms and views can be modified. However, for the public Name and Address book, this is highly discouraged. Each form and view, along with fields within a Notes application, has a specific function for the operation of the Notes server as well as the Notes network. Deleting or modifying a view or form without proper understanding of the operation of the public Name and Address book can have massive effects to a Notes installation. It is also possible that by modifying the public Name and Address book, users without full Notes licenses will not be able to access the address book. Also, Lotus continually makes changes to the public Name and Address book template to add functionality. As newer versions of Notes are released, the design of the public Name and Address book often requires redesigning. If proprietary changes are made to the database, they may be lost when the Notes server upgrades to the next build.

Tips

Administrators are highly discouraged from making any design changes to the public Name and Address book. The public Name and Address book is the heart of a Notes network; any improper design changes to any forms or views could cause major problems with the Notes infrastructure.

Securing the Public Name and Address Book

By default, the ACL (access control list) setting for the public Name and Address book is set to Author. This setting lets individual users edit their own person records, enabling the users to update any personal information they wish to store within their record. Many organizations, however, choose not to let users modify their records, because a user's mail information and public keys are stored within their person record. If a user changes any of this important information, mail routing and encryption procedures will be disrupted. For these reasons, many companies choose to set the default access to READER. The decision you make within your company should be based on the comfort level you have with your users' understanding of the person record in the public Name and Address book, and whether or not you feel it is necessary for them to add additional information to their person records.

With the release of Notes 4, there are a number of new and improved items within the Notes public Name and Address book, particularly in the areas related to security and administration.

New are administration roles governing who can create and modify different parameters within the public Name and Address book. If you are upgrading your Notes server from release 3 to release 4, there is a macro (or *agent*—macros are called *agents* in release 4 of Notes) that adds these administration roles to the public Name and Address book. The agent is called *Add Admin Roles to Access Control List*. For upgrades from release 3 of Notes, it is imperative that this agent is run, or documents on the version 4 environment may not be able to be created. For new version 4 Notes servers that are not involved in an upgrade from version 3, the roles are automatically included in the public Name and Address book.

As with all Notes applications in all versions of Lotus Notes, a user must have at least AUTHOR access in order to create a Notes document with the **Create Documents** box checked. Within the public Name and Address book for version 4 Lotus Notes networks, additional roles now determine what a user can view, create, and edit within the database. Figure 5-2 shows what the configuration looks like:

Figure 5-2

Notes 4 Public Name and Address Book ACL and Role List

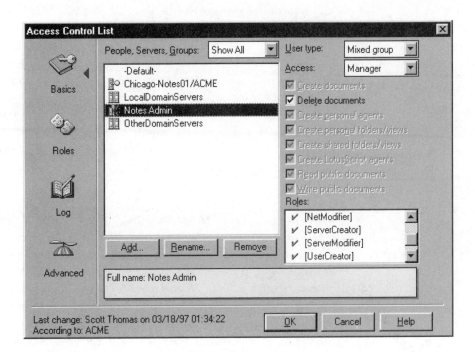

There are 2 sets of roles, *modifier* and *creator*. The creator role must be granted to any user or group to allow the creation of that type of document in the public Name and Address book. If a creator role is not granted, no user or group may create a document in the public Name and Address book, even if that user or group has MANAGER privileges to the database. For example, if the Notes Admin group of ACME has MANAGER access to the public Name and Address book and wishes to create a new person document, they will be denied access until the role *UserCreator* is granted.

The modifier set of roles will let a Notes user or group edit the specified type of document with only AUTHOR access privileges granted. This enables Notes administrators to grant certain users or groups the ability to modify certain types of Notes documents, while restricting modification access to other documents. For example, the ACME Notes administration team can grant the *GroupModifier* role to a Notes user or group, enabling the user or group to edit group documents in the public Name and Address book without granting them EDITOR access. However, since the other modifier roles are not granted, these users or groups will not be able to edit any other type of document, such as person or server records.

The roles can be selected for a user or group by highlighting the user or group in the ACL and then clicking the role you wish that user or group to perform. If a Notes user is not a member of the role, she will not be able to create a document in the public Name and Address book—it will not appear in the list under the Create menu of the Notes GUI. What these new roles provide is the ability of the core Notes administration team to distribute the Notes administration tasks.

Tips

It should be noted that, as with Notes version 3, anyone with EDITOR or higher privileges can still edit all documents in the public Name and Address book, regardless of whether or not they are a member of a modifier role. Users with EDITOR or higher ACL access to the public Name and Address book automatically have modifier role access. However, the creator roles must be granted to users in order to create documents in the public Name and Address book, even if the user or group has MANAGER access to the database.

Let us look at our example corporation, ACME. The ACME Notes administration team can grant a specific group of users—a Notes development team—the ability to only modify group listings within the public Name and Address book. This is done by granting the group GroupModifier privileges with AUTHOR access to the public Name and Address Book. The Notes development team would have the ability to add and delete users from groups, but would not be able to create new groups or perform any other task to the Name and Address book, as none of the other roles have been assigned.

The following lists the eight new roles in the version 4 Notes public Name and Address book:

- **GroupCreator.** This role enables users to create groups within the public Name and Address book. Normally, this role is only granted to a select few users to prevent an explosion of unauthorized groups from being created. This role must be assigned in order to create groups, regardless of ACL access to the database.

- **GroupModifier.** A user or group with this role assigned may modify groups, with only AUTHOR access granted. This includes all groups within the public Name and Address book, not just groups where owner access is granted.

- **NetCreator.** This role must be assigned, regardless of ACL access, in order to create Server Configuration documents, Connection documents, Domain documents, Mail-In Database documents, Program documents, or Setup Profile documents. The central Notes administration team is the only group within in a company that should have these privileges.

- **NetModifier.** This role is assigned to users who need to modify Server Configuration documents, Connection documents, Domain documents, Mail-In Database documents, Program documents, or Setup Profile documents. Again, this is normally the central Notes administration team, or in some instances, a remote Notes administration team.

- **ServerCreator.** Administrators who need to create new server documents within the public Name and Address book need to have the ServerCreator role assigned to them. This includes an instance when an administrator is registering a new Notes server from the administration console.

- **ServerModifier.** The ServerModifier role is assigned to administrators who need to modify all Notes server documents within the public Name and Address book. Again, users with EDITOR access or higher automatically assume this role. The role should only be granted to the core Notes Administration team, and possibly to those administrators in remote locations where multiple server administration is necessary.

- **UserCreator.** The UserCreator role is granted to those administrators who need to create person records in the public Name and Address book. This includes the instances when administrators create new user IDs when registering a new person from the administration console of the Notes GUI. Without this role, regardless of ACL access, a new Notes user cannot be created.

- **UserModifier.** The UserModifier role should be granted to those administrators with AUTHOR access in order to maintain and edit all person documents within the public Name and Address book.

Directory Assistance

Directory assistance is new with release 4.5 of Lotus Notes. It gives users the ability to select names from secondary Name and Address books, as well as resolving Notes mail recipients that may exist within another Name and Address book. Directory assistance has the following advantages for Notes administrators and users:

- Depending on the network link between Notes domains, replication of public Name and Address books may not be necessary with directory assistance.

- Users may select users from other public Name and Address books as well as resolving user names, greatly simplifying cross-domain e-mail addressing.

- Naming rules may be set per public Name and Address book so the Master Address book may efficiently search the databases.

- Directory assistance supports an unlimited number of domains (public Name and Address books).

- Directory assistance lets users utilize the type ahead feature when addressing e-mails to all public Name and Address books.

→ If directory assistance is going to be used, all Notes servers must have replica copies of the Master Name and Address book and replica copies of other domain Name and Address books. If there is a high-speed link between domains, a replica copy of that particular public Name and Address book is not necessary as the database may be accessed directly through the high-speed link.

If ACME corporation would like to use directory assistance to manage multiple domains, the Notes administrator must create a Master Name and Address book and create separate directory assistance documents for each domain within this database. This Master Name and Address book must then be replicated to all Notes servers in all Notes domains. An example of a directory assistance document within the Master Name and Address book for the ACME domain is shown in Figure 5-3:

Figure 5-3

Notes Directory Assistance Document within a Master Name and Address Book

Directory Assistance

Basics

Domain Type:	⌐Notes ⌐ ▼
Domain Name:	⌐ACME ⌐
Company Name:	⌐ACME ⌐

Rules

	OrgUnit4	OrgUnit3	OrgUnit2	OrgUnit1	Organization	Country	Enabled
Rule1:	⌐*⌐/	⌐*⌐/	⌐*⌐/	⌐Chicago⌐/	⌐ACME⌐/	⌐⌐	⌐ENABLED⌐▼
Rule2:	⌐*⌐/	⌐*⌐/	⌐*⌐/	⌐NY⌐/	⌐ACME⌐/	⌐⌐	⌐ENABLED⌐▼
Rule3:	⌐⌐/	⌐⌐/	⌐⌐/	⌐⌐/	⌐⌐/	⌐⌐	⌐DISABLED⌐▼
Rule4:	⌐⌐/	⌐⌐/	⌐⌐/	⌐⌐/	⌐⌐/	⌐⌐	⌐DISABLED⌐▼
Rule5:	⌐⌐/	⌐⌐/	⌐⌐/	⌐⌐/	⌐⌐/	⌐⌐	⌐DISABLED⌐▼

Replicas

	Server Name	Address Book Filename	Address Book Title	Enabled
Replica1:	⌐Chicago-Notes01/ACME⌐	⌐names.nsf⌐	⌐ACME's Address Book⌐	⌐ENABLED⌐▼
Replica2:	⌐NY-Notes01/ACME⌐	⌐names.nsf⌐	⌐ACME's Address Book⌐	⌐ENABLED⌐▼
Replica3:	⌐⌐	⌐⌐	⌐⌐	⌐DISABLED⌐▼
Replica4:	⌐⌐	⌐⌐	⌐⌐	⌐DISABLED⌐▼
Replica5:	⌐⌐	⌐⌐	⌐⌐	⌐DISABLED⌐▼

Once the necessary replica and links are configured, follow these steps to establish directory assistance:

1. Create the Master Name and Address book for the organization. This Notes database application needs to be based upon the Master Name and Address book template (**MAB45.NTF**).

2. Within the domain type, select **Notes.**

3. Enter the Notes domain name that this document will be configuring.

4. Within the Company Name field, enter the name of the company. This is for descriptive purposes only.

5. Within the Rules section, enter one or more rule sets that associate with users and servers existing within this domain. It is within the rules section that the Master Address book determines which public Name and Address book to search for a user.

6. Within the Replicas section, enter the server name(s) and the corresponding location of each public Name and Address book.

7. Save and close the document.

Once the above steps are completed, additional documents must be created for other Notes domains that will be used. Once all directory assistance documents are created for each domain, the Master Name and Address book should be replicated to all involved Notes servers in all Notes domains. ACL access for the Master Address book should be set to EDITOR or higher for all replicating Notes servers and READER access for all users.

Once these tasks are created, the Notes administrator may now enable directory assistance. To do so:

1. Select the view **Server\Servers** from the public Name and Address book.

2. Select the servers within this view that share the same filename and directory paths for the Master Address book.

3. From the menu, select **Actions, Set Master Address Book Information.**

4. The Notes administrator should then enter the file name and path that was given for the Master Name and Address book.

?

Once this procedure is completed, the Notes administration process will populate the Master address book name field within each server document selected.

Traps

It is possible to manually enter the Master Name and Address book information in each field of each server document rather than following the above procedure. This manual intervention is somewhat tedious, and could lead to replication conflicts if not performed properly.

Cascaded Name and Address Books

Multiple public Name and Address books may be cascaded upon a Notes server. This provides users the ability to search and resolve user and group names for e-mail purposes. Cascaded address books may be replica copies of other Notes domain address books that are replicated to a company's own domain. Non-replicating, departmental Name and Address books may also be developed to house additional user and group names. Cascaded Name and Address books have the following properties:

- Notes servers search cascaded Name and Address books in the order they are cascaded, following the public Name and Address book. This order is set within the **NAMES=** setting within the **NOTES.INI** file.

- The **NAMES=** setting may only have 256 characters, so the number of cascaded Name and Address books is limited.

- ACL security resolutions can not use user names or groups from secondary cascaded Name and Address books.

∴ *presumably directory assistance*
allows acl to use
user/groups from other
domains

In order to establish cascading Name and Address books, the Notes administrator must make a replica copy of each public Name and Address book from each domain on his or her home Notes server. The filename cannot be **names.nsf** if placed in the Notes data directory, as this is the filename used by the home Notes server. Once all replica copies are established on the target Notes server(s), the administrator can add a line to the target server's **NOTES.INI** file similar to the following:

```
NOTES=NAMES,WESTNAME,EASTNAME
```

This entry would cascade two additional public Name and Address books with database names of **WESTNAME.NSF** and **EAST-NAME.NSF**.

Tips

Although either directory assistance or cascaded name and address books may be used to manage multiple domains within a single company, we highly recommend you only use a single domain to house all users and server if sizing is not an issue.

Merging Multiple Domains

The *merging of domains* simply means the combination of two or more public Name and Address books into a single public Name and Address book that will be used by all Notes servers and users.

The main reasons for merging domains include:

● One company acquires another

● A company has multiple Notes installations within different departments and wishes to consolidate all installations into a single domain.

To merge multiple Notes domains, a Notes administrator needs to consider all domain references within public Name and Address book, including:

● Server documents

● Connection documents

● Domain documents

● Person documents

● Location documents

- Mail-In DB documents

- Group documents

A Notes administrator also needs to consider all domain references within Notes users' personal Name and Address books:

- Location documents

- Group documents

Finally a Notes administrator needs to consider all domain references within Notes applications and the **NOTES.INI** files, including:

- **CERTLOG.NSF**

- **ADMIN4.NSF**

- **EVENTS4.NSF**

- **STATREP.NSF**

- Notes Custom Applications with hard-coded entries containing the old domain name(s)

- **DOMAIN=** line within the **NOTES.INI** file.

The following list outlines the steps necessary to merge domains. The *winner* domain refers to the domain that will exist once the merge is complete. The *loser* domain(s) refer to those old domain(s) that will no longer be used.

1. Determine the domain winner and loser(s).

2. Identify all documents within the public Name and Address book that need to be modified.

3. Shut down all involved Notes servers and clients.

4. Back up the public Name and Address book in all domains.

5. Bring up all involved Notes servers and clients.

6. Modify all documents in public Name and Address book(s) of the loser domain(s) to reflect the winner domain name.

7. Delete any unneeded connection documents.

8. Delete any unneeded adjacent and non-adjacent domain documents.

9. Copy and paste modified documents from the loser domain(s) public Name and Address book(s) to the winner domain's Name and Address book.

10. Change **DOMAIN=** line in **NOTES.INI** file for loser domain Notes servers to reflect the winner domain name.

11. Test the new public Name and Address book.

12. Make replica copies of new winner public Name and Address book to all old loser domain Notes servers.

13. Remove loser domain public Name and Address books from the loser domain Notes servers.

Notes Named Network Structure

A Lotus Notes named network definition groups servers that share a common network protocol on the same physical LAN. Lotus Notes servers that exist on different LAN segments separated by a router should be housed on a different Lotus Notes named network. All Notes servers on the same Notes network appear in a user's server list when a Notes client performs a **File**, **Database**, **Open**.

A Notes named network is configured in the Public Name and Address book within each server document. A single Notes server may belong to multiple Lotus Notes named networks if the Notes server has multiple network cards attached to different physical segments, or if a single network card is running multiple protocols.

COM ports are not associated with Lotus Notes named networks and therefore are not defined within a Notes server document.

Figure 5-4 shows an example of the configuration of a Lotus Notes named network within a server document in the public Name and Address book:

Figure 5-4

Lotus Notes Named Network Configuration

▼ **Network Configuration**

Port	Notes Network	Net Address	Enabled	
⌜TCPIP⌟	⌜Chicago-TCPIP⌟	⌜192.2.2.2⌟	◉ ENABLED	○ DISABLED
⌜SPX⌟	⌜Chicago-SPX⌟	⌜Chicago-Notes01⌟	◉ ENABLED	○ DISABLED
⌜ ⌟	⌜ ⌟	⌜Chicago-Notes01⌟	○ ENABLED	◉ DISABLED
⌜ ⌟	⌜ ⌟	⌜Chicago-Notes01⌟	○ ENABLED	◉ DISABLED
⌜ ⌟	⌜ ⌟	⌜Chicago-Notes01⌟	○ ENABLED	◉ DISABLED

As can be seen within Figure 5-4, SPX and TCP/IP are running on the Notes server. Each protocol therefore needs to be established within its own Notes network. As explained in Chapter 4, *Naming Conventions*, it is helpful to give a Notes named network a descriptive name. Location and protocol are usually the preferred method.

An important point to understand is that Notes servers within the same Notes named network do not need mail connection records between them. The Notes mail router knows the existence of other Notes servers and e-mail is instantly delivered to Notes servers on the same Notes network. As stated before, Notes servers grouped in the same named Notes network will all appear in the server lists when Notes users perform a **File**, **Database**, **Open**.

With this point understood, it is possible by design to include Notes servers sharing the same protocol on a WAN within the same Notes network, assuming the network connections are capable of handling external connectivity. To illustrate, if ACME has three Notes servers on a WAN all running TCP/IP located in NY, Chicago, and Los Angeles, the administrator could setup the Notes named network to include all three servers. In this scenario, no mail connection records would be necessary between the servers, only replication connection records. Electronic mail would be delivered between the servers automatically. All three Notes servers would appear within server lists for users in all three locations enabling them to connect to other servers (assuming proper security standards).

This design, especially for slower WAN links, is not desired. The preferred method in the above scenario would be to create three separate Notes named networks.

Traps

By design, mail connection records between servers on the same Notes Network are not needed and only add confusion and complexity to connection records within public Name and Address books, as well as overhead to mail routing between those servers.

Figure 5-5 depicts five different Lotus Notes named networks all within a single Lotus Notes domain.

Figure 5-5

Lotus Notes Named Network Example

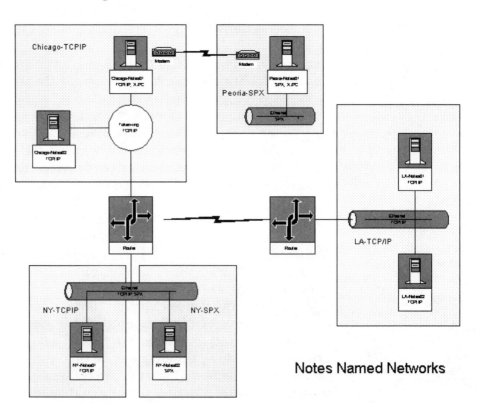

Within the Chicago location, both Notes servers are on the same Token Ring, running the same protocol, TCP/IP. Therefore these two servers are grouped on the same Lotus Notes named network and only need a replication connection record between them. An e-mail connection record is not necessary.

The NY location, however, is configured in two separate Notes named networks even though the two Notes servers reside on the same Ethernet segment. This is because the two Notes servers are running separate protocols. For this reason, the two servers will not be able to replicate or route mail between them. Replication and mail routing will have to be accomplished through a remote Notes server. This obviously is not an ideal design situation, and the Notes administrator should configure one of the Notes servers with an additional protocol shared by the other Notes server to avoid routing and replicating remotely.

External Connectivity

With many companies, there comes a time where the desire and/or need arises to connect your company's Notes environment with another company's Notes infrastructure. Lotus Notes was designed to enable a Notes administrator to perform this function very easily. The main concern that faces a Notes administrator is the manner in which an external Notes connection is established. There are several security concerns that must be addressed to keep your company's internal Notes infrastructure secure.

There are a number of ways from a physical standpoint to connect your organization's Notes server to another company's Notes server. These include the following:

- An analog connection using a Notes-supported analog modem. Connection speeds will be up to 33.6 Kbps.

- A digital ISDN connection using a Notes-supported ISDN modem. Connection speeds will be up to 128 Kbps, depending on the configuration of the modem and BRI ISDN line.

- A network connection through a private network that is connected to both your company and the target company (for example, CompuServe).

- A network connection through a public network such as the Internet. This type of connection is usually a dedicated phone link, such as a T1 or fractional T1.

All these instances require that proper configurations are set. Pay particular attention to the security issues surrounding opening up your Notes environment to other companies.

For direct private line connections such as modem connections, Notes takes control over the COM port, analog modem or ISDN modem upon server startup. For this reason, Notes will not allow any other type of connection except for that of a Notes client or server. Once a Notes client or server connects to a Notes server, all of the Notes security features are deployed. This includes authentication, port-access lists, server-access lists, database ACL settings, and any encryption mechanisms enabled on either the Notes server or client. If a Notes client or server does not pass any of these security mechanisms, the call will be dropped.

For Notes servers running on public networks such as the Internet, additional measures should be put into place. Like an analog connection, all of the security measures will be in place including server access lists and database ACL settings. However, two items should be highly considered when connecting a Notes server to another Notes server or client through a public network such as the Internet.

1. The internal Notes server should be behind what is called a *network firewall application*. A firewall application is a program that runs on a machine that sits between the internal network and the public network. It examines each packet of data that enters or leaves the internal network and based upon a set of predefined rules, determines whether or not that particular packet of data is allowed in or out of the network. Industry leaders of firewall applications include Raptor and Checkpoint. For a TCP/IP connection to an external Notes server, the main issue concerning a firewall application is that the predefined rule set should be set to only allow packets from the external Notes

server. Also, all Notes servers listen for TCP/IP packets on TCP/IP port 1352. The firewall application administrator should adjust the rule set on the firewall machine accordingly.

2. You should encrypt the data going over the network. Once this option is enabled on a Notes server or client, all data passing over that particular port will be encrypted regardless of the receiver's settings. If only the initiator is set to encrypt data over a network or COM port, the setting will force the receiver to encrypt data as well. It should be noted that encrypting data over a port will cause a minimal performance decrease. However, the benefit of encrypted data far outweighs the decrease.

As mentioned before, Lotus Notes supports direct connections from an internal Notes server to an external Notes server very easily. In terms of an ideal secure environment, this is not the best model. The following two sections explain security measures to consider when connecting to an external company. The two issues deal with creating a *Notes firewall domain* and cross-certification of Notes ID files.

Notes Firewall Domains

A Notes firewall domain is similar in concept to a network firewall application that restricts packets of data on a physical network. The Notes firewall domain consists of a separate Notes server or servers existing in a separate Notes domain from that of a company's internal Notes domain. Usually the name of this external domain represents its function, for example:

```
ACME-External
```

It is within this domain that Notes servers external to the company connect. This domain provides a buffer so that in the unlikely event a security breach occurs, the production Notes domain is not compromised. Sometimes, it may be necessary for external companies to view the public Name and Address book of the external Notes server. With a Notes firewall domain in place, all internal Notes users and groups cannot be seen by an external company. They exist only in the internal Notes domain, protected by the firewall Notes domain.

Cross-Certification

Another important item to consider when connecting your Notes network to an external Notes network is creating a separate Notes Organization certifier. This way, the external Notes connection will not be authenticating with your internal Notes certifier. Taking again our ACME example, the Notes administrator would create another organizational certifier. Its name would be something like:

```
/ACME-External
```

From this external Notes certifier ID file, the Notes administrator would create a new Notes server ID that exists in its own new external Notes domain. The Notes administrator then would cross-certify this new external Notes server with ACME's internal Notes server. The Notes administrator would then repeat the cross-certification process with the external company's Notes server using ACME's external Notes server. Connection records would then be set within the new external Notes domain to route e-mail and replicate to the external company. This procedure then would be repeated with the connection between the internal and external Notes domains within ACME. Figure 5-6 shows this type of external Notes configuration:

Figure 5-6

External Notes Connection Configuration

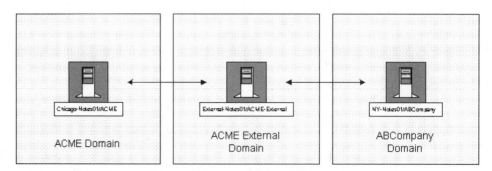

Chicago-Notes01/ACME

External-Notes01/ACME-External

NY-Notes01/ABCompany

ACME Domain

ACME External Domain

ABCompany Domain

Cross-certification applies to hierarchical ID files that do not share a certificate in common so that they may authenticate. If authentication is needed between a hierarchical and flat ID, cross-certification is not used. Most companies will only have one organization certifier ID, so cross-certification within a company is never needed.

Tips

Most companies will only need to cross-certify ID files in the event they wish to connect to an external Notes infrastructure to replicate Notes applications or route Notes mail.

As the name implies, cross-certification is a two way process. One company must certify an external ID file in which the result is stored within the certifying company's Name and Address book. The external company then must perform this process with the other company's ID file. Unless certification is done on both company's ID files, authentication between the two company's Notes servers will not take place. Unlike flat certificates, cross-certificates are stored within the public Name and Address book of each company. If the cross-certification document is ever deleted from either address book, authentication between the two Notes servers will not occur. This feature gives a Notes administrator control in the event he or she wishes to cease connectivity with an external company. Figure 5-7 shows a sample cross-certification document between /ACME and /ABCompany:

Figure 5-7

Notes Cross-
Certificate Record

CROSS CERTIFICATE:/ACME -/ABCompany

Basics

Certificate type:	Notes Cross-Certificate
Issued By:	/ACME
Issued To:	/ABCompany
Combined Name:	O=ACME:O=ABCompany
Comment:	
Organizations:	O=ACME:O=ABCompany

Administration

Owners:	Scott Thomas/Marketing/Chicago/ACME
Administrators:	Notes Admin

Traps

Within a Notes server document, if the Notes server is configured to allow anonymous access, authentication will not take place and cross-certification will not be necessary. From a security standpoint, this is not a desired method. Also, if the Notes server is running the HTTP process, Notes authentication does not take place; thus, cross-certification is not needed.

Cross-certification may occur between the following ID files:

- **Notes server ID to Notes server ID.** This is the most secure method of cross-certification (see Figure 5-8). It allows authentication only between two server ID files. For example, if ACME certifies ABCompany's server ID (NY-Notes01/ABCompany) and ABCompany certifies ACME's server ID (Chicago-Notes01/ACME), authentication can only take place between the two servers IDs. If another Notes server within the ABCompany tries to connect to an ACME Notes server, authentication will fail.

Figure 5-8

Cross-Certification—
Notes Server
to Notes Server

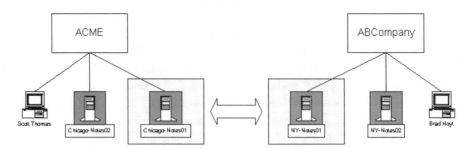

- **Notes server ID to Notes user ID.** This type of cross-certification (Figure 5-9) only allows authentication between a single Notes server and a single external Notes user. For example, a Notes administrator could certify an ABCompany's Notes user (Joe User/ABCompany), and Joe User/ABCompany could certify ACME's Notes server (Chicago-Notes01/ACME). In this manner Joe User from ABCompany would only be able to authenticate with `Chicago-Notes01/ACME`. The actual cross-certificate documents would exist in the public Name and Address book for the `Chicago-Notes01/ACME` Notes server and in the personal Name and Address book on the Joe User/ABCompany's machine.

Figure 5-9

Cross-Certification—
Notes Server
to Notes User

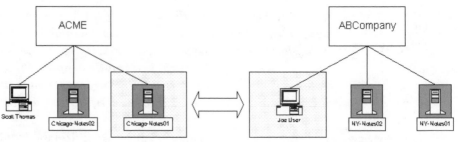

- **Notes organization ID to Notes organization ID.**
  This is the most wide-open certification model (see Figure
  5-10) and is not recommended unless used within a company,
  between two internal organization certifiers. With this type of
  cross-certification, all users and servers in both companies
  will be able to authenticate with one another regardless of
  position in the hierarchy tree. For example, if the ACME Notes
  administrator certifies the /ABCompany certifier and the
  ABCompany Notes administrator certifies the /ACME certifier,
  all Notes servers and users in both organizations will be able
  to authenticate with one another. If Notes server access lists
  and ACL lists on each Notes server permits, access to Notes
  applications can occur.

Figure 5-10

Cross-Certification—
Organization to
Organization

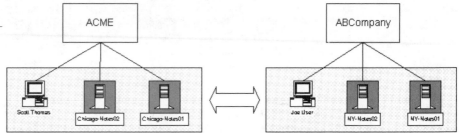

- **Notes organization ID to Notes organizational unit ID.**
  This is still a wide-open certification model and applies to one
  or both companies where certification occurs at an organizational unit level (Figure 5-11). In other words, a Notes administrator may have created a Notes ID hierarchy where there
  are 2 or more levels of a naming structure, for example, chica-
  go-Notes01/ACME. In this type of cross-certification, all users
  and servers within a given tree hierarchy will be able to
  authenticate on one end with all servers and users. On the
  other side, all servers and users will only be able to authenticate with servers and users at the organizational unit level or
  it's children.

To illustrate, the ACME Notes administrator certifies the
/ABCompany certifier and the ABCompany Notes administrator
certifies the /Finance/ACME certifier. With this scenario, all users
and servers within ACME's /Finance/ACME tree will be able to

authenticate with ALL users and servers within the ABCompany Notes infrastructure. All users and servers within the ABCompany organization will only be able to authenticate with users and servers within the `/Finance/ACME` tree. `Chicago-Notes02/ACME` would be inaccessible from users and servers in the ABCompany Notes infrastructure.

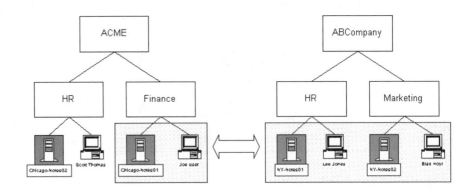

- **Notes organization ID to Notes server ID.** This type of cross-certification enables one company to authenticate with all users and servers within its organization. The other company, however, is only able to authenticate with the single Notes server. See Figure 5-12. To illustrate, the ACME Notes administrator certifies the `/ABCompany` certifier ID. The ABCompany Notes administrator certifies the `Chicago-Notes01/ACME` server ID file. In this example, all servers and users within ACME will be able to authenticate with all users and servers in the ABCompany Notes infrastructure. All users and servers in the ABCompany will only be able to authenticate with the `Chicago-Notes01/ACME` Notes server.

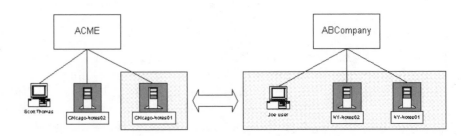

- **Notes organization ID to Notes user ID.** With this type of cross-certification, a single external Notes user will be able to authenticate with all Notes servers within the organization. However, because this is a cross-certification between a Notes user ID file, the other organization will not be able to authenticate with any other Notes server within the second company. As illustrated in Figure 5-13, the ACME Notes administrator certifies the `Joe User/ABCompany` user ID file. Joe User/ABCompany then certifies the `/ACME` certifier. Joe User/ABCompany then would be able to authenticate with all Notes servers within the ACME organization. However, because the other end of the cross-certification is with a single Notes user ID file, no server or user within ACME will be able to authenticate with Notes servers within ABCompany.

Figure 5-13

Cross-Certification—
Organization to User

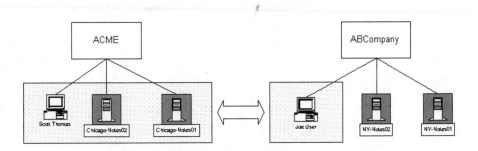

- **Notes organizational unit ID to Notes organizational unit ID.** Within this type of cross-certification, all Notes servers and users within both companies will be able to authenticate with Notes servers and users at the certified organizational unit level, or their children. As illustrated in Figure 5-14, the ACME Notes administrator certifies the `/HR/ABCompany` certifier ID file. The ABCompany Notes administrator certifies the `Finance/ACME` certifier. In this scenario, all ACME Notes users and servers within the `/Finance/ACME` tree will be able to authenticate with all Notes users and servers within ABCompany's `/HR/ABCompany` hierarchy tree and vice versa. Any users or servers outside of either hierarchy will not be able to authenticate.

Figure 5-14

Cross-Certification—
Organizational Unit to
Organizational Unit

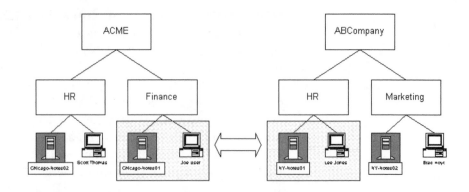

- **Notes organizational unit ID to Notes server ID.** This type of cross-certification (see Figure 5-15) enables all users and servers within a given level of hierarchy to authenticate with a single external Notes server. To illustrate, the ACME Notes administrator certifies the `NY-Notes01/HR/ABCompany` Notes server ID file. The ABCompany Notes administrator certifies the `/Finance/ACME` certifier ID file. In this scenario, the `NY-Notes01/HR/ABCompany` Notes server can authenticate with all ACME Notes servers and users within the `/Finance/ACME` tree hierarchy.

Figure 5-15

Cross-Certification—
Organizational Unit
to Notes Server

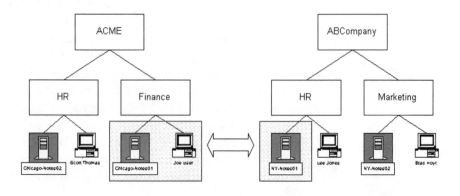

- **Notes organizational unit ID to Notes user ID.** This type of cross-certification enables a single external Notes user to authenticate with Notes servers within a given level of hierarchy (Figure 5-16). To illustrate, the ACME Notes administrator certifies the external Notes user `Lee Jones/HR/ABCompany`. The ABCompany Notes administrator certifies the `/Finance/ACME` certifier ID file. In this scenario, the Notes user `Lee Jones/HR/ABCompany` can authenticate with all ACME Notes servers and users within the `/Finance/ACME` tree hierarchy.

Figure 5-16

Cross-Certification—
Organizational Unit
to Notes User

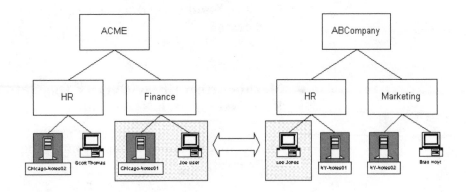

Notes

*Users and administrators should never send copies of their certifier, user, or server ID files to other companies. Users and administrators may create what is called a **safe copy** of an ID file, which cannot be used by anyone to perform Notes functions other than those necessary for cross-certification (see the "Create Safe Copy" section, later in this chapter).*

In order to cross-certify hierarchical ID files, Lotus Notes offers *four* different methods.

- **Method 1(a):** Through Notes Mail: **Send Safe Copy of ID File.** If a Notes mail connection exists either directly or through an intermediary Notes network, cross-certification of Notes ID's through Notes mail may be used. Each Notes administrator at each company must perform the following steps:

1. Click **File**, **Tools**, **User ID**.

2. Click the **Certificates** icon and then click the **Request Cross Certificate** button.

3. Select the ID file you wish to have cross-certified.

4. Once the ID file is selected, a dialog box appears in which you need to address the Notes mail message.

5. Click **Send** to send the safe copy to the other Notes administrator.

● **Method 1(b): Cross-Certify the Safe Copy of the ID Received through Notes Mail.**

1. Open the mail document containing the cross-certificate request.

2. Click **Actions**, **Cross Certify Attached ID File**.

3. Choose the certifier ID file you wish to use to certify the attached ID file and click **OK**.

4. Within the **Subject Name** field, select which level of cross-certification you desire for the external company. For example, if the ABCompany sends the ACME Notes administrator a safe copy of its server ID file, it will contain information for that Notes server as well as any higher level of hierarchy it belongs to. For Notes server NY-Test/ABCompany, the selections NY-Test/ABCompany and /ABCompany will appear. Care should be taken if /ABCompany is selected, as all users and servers within ABCompany will be able to authenticate. If only NY-Test/ABCompany is selected, then only that server will be able to authenticate.

5. Click the **Certifier** button to change the certifier that will be issuing the cross-certificate.

6. Click the **Server** button to change the registration server.

7. Within the expiration field, the date for expiration may be changed.

8. Once all is selected, the Notes administrator may click the **Cross Certify** button to perform certification.

Once certification is complete, the other Notes administrator at the other company must perform these same steps. Mailing back the safe copy of the ID file is not necessary, as the cross-certification information is stored within the public Name and Address book and not in the ID files itself.

- **Method 2: On Demand.** Cross-certification on demand enables users and administrators to certify with an external hierarchical Notes server on the fly when cross-certification has already been performed on the target Notes server. Cross-certification on demand also occurs when a user opens a signed mail message and the user is not cross-certified with the hierarchy of the sender.

But we are →
cross-certified with
sender's hierarchy

If you wish to cross-certify a Notes server of a different hierarchy (assuming cross-certification has already been performed on the other end), follow these steps:

1. Start the GUI on the Notes server running the process. For Notes user workstations, simply start Lotus Notes.

2. Select **File**, **Database**, **Open** and type the name of the Notes server in the server field.

3. Notes displays the name of the organization, its public key, and three buttons.

4. Click the **Yes** button to cross-certify the root certifier of the other company's hierarchy and put the cross-certificate in the public Name and Address book of the Notes server. For Notes users, the cross-certificate will be placed in their personal Name and Address books. This process is fine for Notes users; however, certifying the other company's root certifier on the Notes server may not be desired. The **Advanced Options** button lets you select to only certify the target Notes server—not the root certifier. Again, this process can only happen if the other company has performed certification on your company's ID file.

5. Click the **No** button to prevent a cross-certificate from being created.

6. Click the **Advanced Options** button to change cross-certification options. Within the **Subject Name** field, select which level of cross-certification you desire for the external company. For example, if the ACME Notes administrator is accessing the ABCompany Notes server, it will contain information for that Notes server as well as any higher level of hierarchy it belongs to. For Notes server, NY-Test/ABCompany, the selections NY-Test/ABCompany and /ABCompany will appear. Care should be taken if /ABCompany is selected, as all users and servers within ABCompany will be able to authenticate. If only NY-Test/ABCompany is selected, then only that server will be able to authenticate.

7. Click **Cross Certify** to cross-certify the ID File.

- **Method 3: Verbally over the phone.** Cross-certification can be performed over the phone between two Notes administrators by reading validation codes to each other. Both administrators must perform these actions on their respective Notes networks:

1. Click **File**, **Tools**, **Server Administration**.

2. Click **Certifiers** and choose **Cross Certify Key**.

3. Choose the certifier ID file of your organization that you will use to create the cross-certificate.

4. A cross-certify key dialog box will appear. Within the **Subject Name** field, select which level of cross-certification you desire for the external company. For example, if the ACME Notes administrator wishes to only cross-certify the NY-Test/ABCompany Notes server, he or she would type in that entry as given by the ABCompany's Notes administrator. If the Notes administrator types in /ABCompany, then cross-certification will happen at that level of the hierarchy. Care should be taken if /ABCompany is selected, as all users and servers within ABCompany will be able to authenticate.

5. Within the **Key** field, type in the public key of the ID file you are cross-certifying, including spaces. The Notes administrator of the other company will provide you with this number.

6. The **Certifier** button lets you change the certifier that will be issuing the cross-certificate.

7. The **Server** button is used to change the registration server.

8. Within the expiration field, change the date for expiration if so desired.

9. Once all is selected, click the **Cross Certify** button to perform certification.

Again, these steps must be performed on both sides (both companies) by Notes administrators for this procedure to work properly.

● **Method 4: Physically Mailing an ID File through Snail Mail (the Post Office).** Since the release of Notes version 4, this is the least desirable method in terms of speed considering the other 3 methods to cross-certify. However, if you wish to use this method of cross-certification, each Notes administrator must create a safe copy of his or her ID file (certifier, server, or user ID file depending on the desired level of access—see the earlier sections discussing cross-certification). A safe copy of an ID file cannot be used for accessing a Notes server; it only contains enough information to perform certification.

Once the safe copy of the ID file is made, each Notes administrator must copy the file to a diskette and mail it to the intended recipient.Once each Notes administrator receives the safe copy of the ID file, each administrator must certify that ID file. Again, this is a two-way process: if only one Notes administrator certifies the other's safe copy, authentication will not take place.

Create Safe Copy of Notes ID File

In order to create a safe-copy of an ID file, take the following steps:

1. Click **File**, **Tools**, **Server Administration.**

2. Click **Administration, ID File** and select the ID file you wish to make a safe copy of.

3. Click the **More Options** icon and then click **Create Safe Copy.**

4. Enter a filename and path to store the safe copy of the ID file. The default filename is **Safe.ID.**

5. Copy the safe copy of the file to a diskette and mail it to the other company's Notes administrator.

Again, a safe copy cannot be used to perform Notes activities. The file only contains enough information to perform certification procedures.

Cross-Certify Safe Copy ID File

Once you receive a safe copy of an ID file from a Notes administrator from another company, the following procedures should be followed to cross-certify the ID file:

1. Click **File**, **Tools**, **Server Administration.**

2. Click the **Certifiers** icon and click **Cross Certify ID File.**

3. Choose the certifier ID file of your organization that you will use.

4. Next, select the other company's safe copy ID file that was sent on diskette. The dialog box shown in Figure 5-17 appears:

Figure 5-17

Cross-Certification
Dialog Box

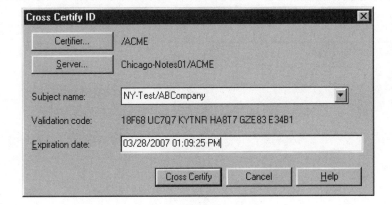

5. Within the **Subject Name** field, select which level of cross-certification you desire for the external company. For example, if the ABCompany sends the ACME Notes administrator a safe copy of its server ID file, it will contain information for that Notes server as well as any higher level of hierarchy it belongs to. For Notes server NY-Test/ABCompany, the selections NY-Test/ABCompany and /ABCompany will appear. Care should be taken if /ABCompany is selected, as all users and servers within ABCompany will be able to authenticate. If only NY-Test/ABCompany is selected, then only that server will be able to authenticate.

6. The **Certifier** button lets you change the certifier that will be issuing the cross-certificate.

7. The **Server** button is used to change the registration server.

8. Within the expiration field, you can change the date for expiration.

9. Once all is selected, the Notes administrator clicks the **Cross Certify** button to perform certification.

Once certification is complete, the other Notes administrator at the other company must perform these same steps. Mailing back the safe copy of the ID file is not necessary, as the cross-certification information is stored within the public Name and Address book and not in the ID file itself.

Chapter 6

Public Name and Address Book Forms and Views

There are many different forms and views within the Notes public Name and Address book. Each is equally important within the infrastructure: proper planning and configuration of every document created using these forms is essential for a healthy Notes network. This chapter describes each form and view within the public Name and Address book and the function the documents created using them serves.

Group Records

Lotus Notes group records serve two purposes. One is to provide group e-mail listings for electronic mail users. The other is to provide group listings for access control for Notes database and server access. Groups can be *nested* (a group appearing within another group) up to six levels deep within Lotus Notes.

When using group records for electronic mail purposes, the records may exist in three different locations. The primary location for a group record for e-mail lists can be created in the public Name and Address book. The second location exists in any cascaded Name and Address book on the Notes user's home mail server. The final place is in any Notes user's personal Name and Address book.

Groups can be created so that users do not have to enter every recipient's name in the **To** field of an e-mail message. When a Notes user is addressing an electronic mail message and the type ahead feature is enabled on the client, Notes first checks the personal, then the public Name and Address book for any group matches.

For group records to control access to Notes applications and for access privileges to Notes servers themselves, the group record must exist in the primary public Name and Address book.

With Notes release 4 and higher, four new attributes exists for group records in controlling their functionality. One of the main concerns addressed by their creation was security issues. The following list covers these different types:

- **Multi-Purpose Group.** This is the default type when creating a new group. When set to a multi-purpose type of group, the group may resolve e-mail lists as well as provide ACL access to Notes servers and applications.

- **Access Control List Only.** This group will only be used to control access to Notes servers and access to Notes database applications through access control lists (ACLs). The group is not used to resolve names for e-mail purposes. Users will not see this group listed when addressing e-mail messages. Often, administrators want groups for security reasons only and do not want people using them for e-mail. Also, a group of this type will not tax the server much, since Notes servers for e-mail purposes will not access it.

- **Mail Only.** A Mail Only type group will only provide e-mail listing functionality. No Access Control List (ACL) resolution for Notes application or server access can be performed with groups of this type. If this type of group is added to the ACL of a Notes application, it will be ignored and the **Default** level of access will be granted, unless there is another listing within the database ACL that pertains to the user.

- **Deny Access List.** This group type is used to deny access in the Deny Access List within a Notes server document.

Two hidden views, within the public Name and Address book— $Users and $ServerAccess—select group documents that match specific groups types. $Users is used to resolve Mail Only and Mutli-Purpose group documents. The $ServerAccess hidden view selects Access Control List Only, Multi-Purpose, and Deny List Only group documents. By using these different types of groups, the Notes server will not be as burdened; the hidden views will not have to re-index groups not included within them.

When a Notes administrator adds or edits a group record in the public Name and Address book, the record for electronic mailing purposes will be available within one minute. For access control to Notes applications, however, the Notes user must log off (restart Notes or press **F5**) and then log in again before the change becomes available. This is because group information is cached upon login to the Notes server.

An example of a group record within the public Name and Address book is shown in Figure 6-1:

Figure 6-1

Notes Group
Record Document

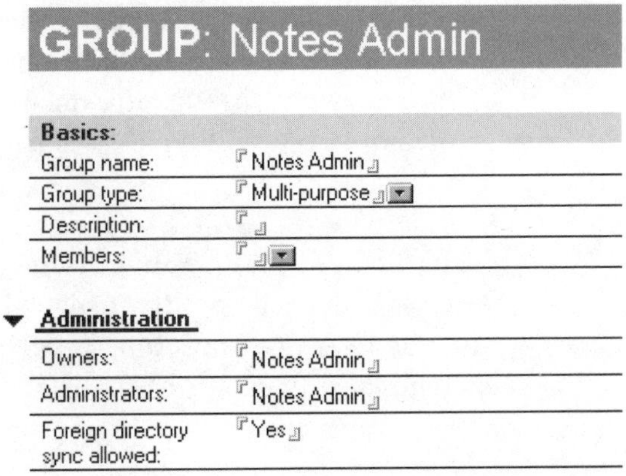

- **Group Name Field:** Within this field you should type in the name of the group as it will appear for ACL access and/or e-mail listings. Proper naming considerations should be employed as explained in Chapter 4, *Naming Conventions*.

● **Group Type:** The type of group should be either Multi-Purpose (for access control and mailing list), Access Control List Only (for server and database access control), Mail Only (for e-mail mailing lists), or Deny List Only (to deny access to servers and databases), as described earlier within this chapter.

● **Description:** This field is for descriptive purposes only and provides no functionality to Notes server processes. It appears within the Group view of the public Name and Address book.

You should always enter a description for each group to indicate its intended purpose to users and other administrators.

Tips

● **Members:** This is the field where user, servers, and other group names appear. A user's fully distinguished name or common name may be used. The pulldown button may be used to search the public Name and Address book and select any members to be added to the group.

● **Owners:** The owner(s) of the group is responsible for maintaining and editing the group document. It is in this field that the AUTHOR level ACL access is assumed. If a user or group has AUTHOR access to the public Name and Address book and appears within a group document within this field, the user or group listed will be able to modify the document.

It should be noted, as explained in Chapter 5, that if a user has AUTHOR access to the public Name and Address book and has the role GroupModifier assigned, the user will be able to edit a group document even if the user does not appear within this field. This same point also holds true for any user granted EDITOR or higher ACL access.

Use of this field will allow you to have a single owner or group of owners for all groups in the Name and Address book, and then delegate day-to-day management of those groups to others.

Tips

- **Administrators:** This field also enables any listed users or groups with the ability to edit the entire group document. This is usually reserved for administrators of the Notes infrastructure.

- **Foreign directory sync allowed:** This field is responsible for allowing synchronization of the group name to other foreign mail and directories, such as to cc:Mail environments using the cc:Mail MTA.

Group records are sorted within the public Name and Address book by the Notes **Groups** view. Figure 6-2 below shows the Notes view.

Figure 6-2
A Lotus Notes
Group View

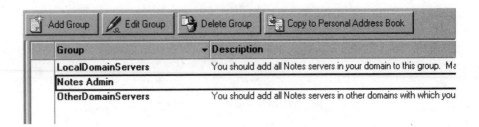

Notice within the **Group** view that buttons exist to add, edit, or delete a group. These buttons provide the same functionality as the pulldown options in the Create menu with the exception that when using the buttons, some functions are associated with the administration process. The **Copy to Personal Address Book** button enables a user to copy the group along with the member list, if so desired, to the user's personal Name and Address book.

Person Records

Person records contain user and mail information for every user within a Notes infrastructure, including users that access servers and databases with a Web browser. The record includes items such as Notes user name, aliases, HTTP password, e-mail information, work-related information, public key, Notes license types, and password change intervals.

Once a person record is added or modified within the public Name and Address book, it becomes available for electronic mail within one minute of its modification or addition.

Figure 6-3 shows an example of the first section of a person record.

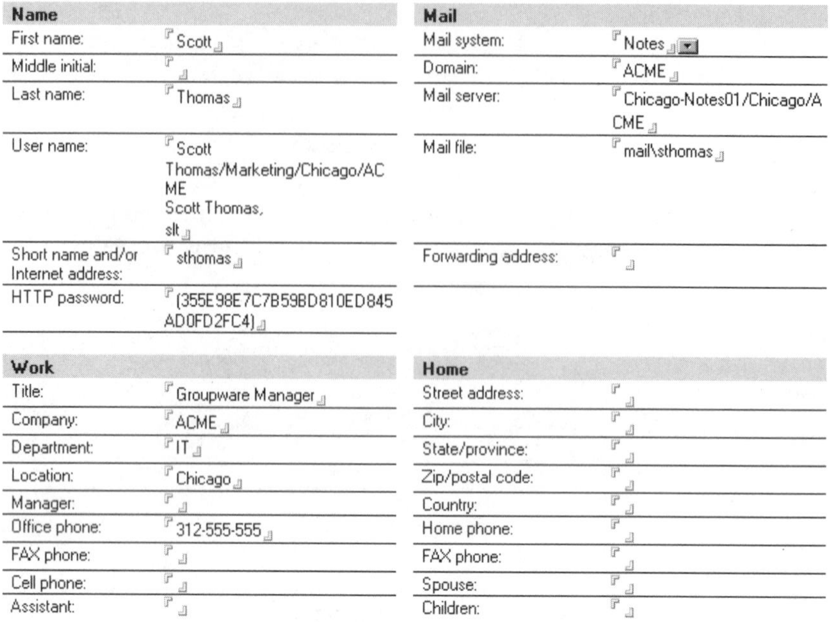

Figure 6-3

Notes Person
Record (First
Section)

Name		Mail	
First name:	Scott	Mail system:	Notes
Middle initial:		Domain:	ACME
Last name:	Thomas	Mail server:	Chicago-Notes01/Chicago/ACME
User name:	Scott Thomas/Marketing/Chicago/ACME Scott Thomas, slt	Mail file:	mail\sthomas
Short name and/or Internet address:	sthomas	Forwarding address:	
HTTP password:	(355E98E7C7B59BD810ED845 AD0FD2FC4)		

Work		Home	
Title:	Groupware Manager	Street address:	
Company:	ACME	City:	
Department:	IT	State/province:	
Location:	Chicago	Zip/postal code:	
Manager:		Country:	
Office phone:	312-555-555	Home phone:	
FAX phone:		FAX phone:	
Cell phone:		Spouse:	
Assistant:		Children:	

- **First Name:** This is the first name of the Notes user. The field is filled upon user creation and should never be changed within this document.

- **Middle Initial:** Like the First Name field, this field is filled upon user creation and also should never be modified from within this Notes document. Normally, most administrators never use this field unless there are two people within the company with the same name.

- **Last Name:** Again, this field is filled at user creation and should not be modified from within this record.

- **User Name:** This field is also filled upon user creation and will contain the user's fully distinguished name, followed by the user's common name. The first entry containing the user's fully distinguished name is where all ACL resolutions for Notes database and server access is performed. For this reason, it is essential that this first entry within the field never be changed. If it is changed, users will not be able to access any Notes applications or servers. It is this first entry within the user name that is also used as the user name when connecting from a Web browser to the Domino server. When accessing a Notes application with a Web browser, the entire fully distinguished name must be used when prompted for user name and password.

Interesting

→ Any other entries following this first entry are assumed aliases of that person. Any name can follow this initial entry: all aliases will only be used for e-mail resolutions. None of the aliases will be used for ACL access to Notes applications and Notes server access. Alias entries should be entered followed by semi-colons. When the document is saved, the field will be parsed and semi-colons will be removed.

(Comma in example)

- **Short name and/or Internet address:** The short name is commonly used by foreign e-mail systems such as PROFS, or the Internet using products such as the Lotus SMTP MTA. This field is also filled at user creation and shouldn't be modified by users. Administrators may need to modify this field if an external mail system needs to access this field and two users within the Notes infrastructure both have the same short name.

- **HTTP password:** This field is new with release 4.5 of Notes. It should be filled by a Notes administrator or by the users themselves. This field provides password access to Notes applications from Web browsers and for POP3 Mail clients.

Once the password is entered, the administrator or user can press **F9** (refresh) or save the document. The password will be encrypted within the field to prevent other users from reading it.

- **Mail System:** Within this field is where the mail system is determined. Selections include **Notes mail, cc:Mail, Internet mail (SMTP), POP3 mail, X.400 mail, Other,** and **None. Notes mail** is the default selection. The cc:Mail, Internet mail, POP3 mail, and X.400 mail systems require that the appropriate add-ons be installed within the Notes infrastructure. The cc:Mail and SMTP (Internet Mail) MTA's (Message Transfer Agents) are free of charge from Lotus. The POP3 mail program is also free of charge and ships with the Notes server code, providing a message store for POP3 mail clients such as Eudora and Netscape. The X.400 MTA is an additional product that must be purchased separately and installed within the Notes network.

If this entry is changed to a value other than Notes mail, then many of the following described fields will not appear within a person record, or the names of the fields may be different.

Again, this field should only be modified by the Notes administrator or by a knowledgeable Notes user.

- **Domain:** The domain field is filled upon creation of the Notes user assuming Notes mail is used. This field contains the domain name to which the Notes user belongs. The Notes administration team creates the domain name when the Notes network is first architected. A Notes user should not modify this field.

- **Mail Server:** For Notes mail users, this signifies the user's home mail server where his or her mail database application resides. The field is filled initially when the Notes mail user is created. It is from this field that the Notes mail router decides how to route mail to the correct Notes mail server within a network. This field should never be modified except by a knowledgeable Notes administrator. Incorrect information will result in undeliverable mail.

- **Mail File:** The Notes mail file field is filled upon creation of the Notes mail user. The field directs where the Notes mail router delivers a Notes mail message. The contents should contain the path of a Notes user's mail file, starting from where the Notes data directory exists on the Notes server. If the Notes server code is installed in the directory "c:\notes\data," then this is assumed to be the root. Most mail files are stored in "c:\notes\data\mail," so the entry for a user would be "mail\sthomas." The **.nsf** extension is assumed and is not needed. This field should never be modified except by a Notes administrator. Incorrect information will result in undeliverable mail.

- **Forwarding Address:** This field is by default left blank and should only be used in the event a user wishes to have his or her mail forwarded to another e-mail address. If this field is filled, e-mail will not be delivered to the user's Notes mail address. Users often fill this field when they are going to be in a location where Notes mail is inaccessible, but where they have an external Internet account. When they return, the field is then cleared. Another use of the field is by Notes administrators to create "dummy" person records for specific needs to direct community mail to a Notes application. A Mail-In Database record can be used instead.

- **Work and Home Information Sections:** These sections are for informational purposes only and provide no functionality to a Notes network. A Notes user can fill these fields in a manner they wish.

Figure 6-4 shows the second half of a Notes person record in the public Name and Address book.

Figure 6-4

Notes Person Record (Second Section)

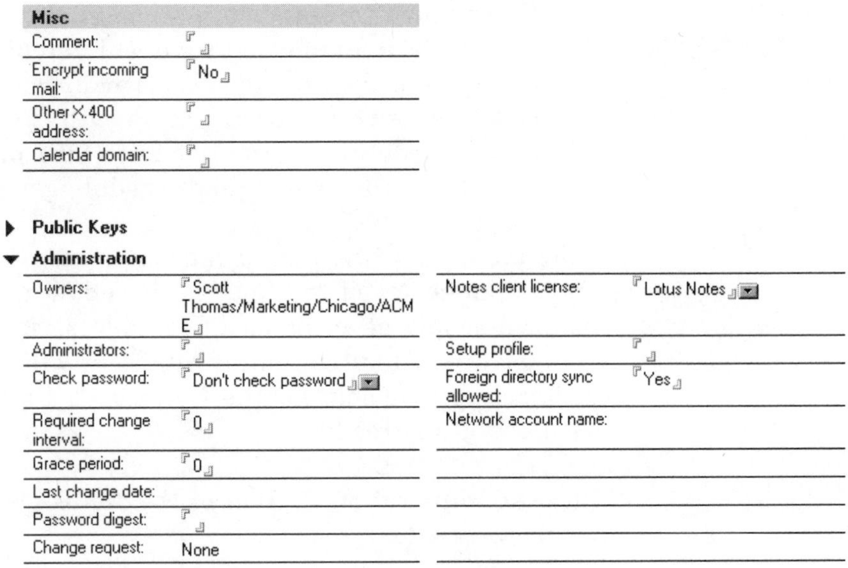

Misc

Comment:	
Encrypt incoming mail:	No
Other X.400 address:	
Calendar domain:	

▶ **Public Keys**

▼ **Administration**

Owners:	Scott Thomas/Marketing/Chicago/ACME	Notes client license:	Lotus Notes
Administrators:		Setup profile:	
Check password:	Don't check password	Foreign directory sync allowed:	Yes
Required change interval:	0	Network account name:	
Grace period:	0		
Last change date:			
Password digest:			
Change request:	None		

The Miscellaneous Section contains the following fields:

- **Comment:** This field is for descriptive purposes only. It can be modified and filled by either the Notes administrator or user.

- **Encrypt incoming mail:** This field instructs the Notes mail router to encrypt all incoming mail to the specified Notes mail user. If this selection is set to **yes**, only the recipient will be able to read his or her mail messages in the respective Notes mail file. Not even a Notes administrator with MANAGER access to the user's Notes mail file or even from the Notes server itself will be able to read the encrypted mail. Some organizations forbid their Notes mail users from using this field, as the mail system is owned by the company itself and the Notes mail users do not have a right to privacy for their company-based e-mail system. This can be overridden by setting the NOTES.INI variable, **MailEncryptIncoming=0**, on the Notes mail server.

Useful? *#*

Do this —

- **Other X.400 address:** This field is used to resolve other X.400 addresses a user may have if an X.400 e-mail system is being used within the organization.

- **Calendar domain:** This optional field is used so that a user may direct free time queries to a different Notes domain other than where they receive Notes mail. Such an example would be for Lotus Organizer 2.x users with Notes mail who are still using scheduling information in an OR2 file, rather than using the built in calendaring and scheduling within Notes 4.5.

The Public Keys Section of the Notes person record contains the certified public key of the Notes user and is in hexadecimal format. This field should never be modified, unless intentionally by a Notes administrator. Modification of this field will corrupt the private/public key relationship for the Notes user. Encrypting mail will no longer operate correctly.

The Administration Section of the Notes person record contains the following fields:

- **Owners:** This field signifies who may modify this document with AUTHOR ACL access. This is the name of the person themselves.

- **Administrators:** This field enables any listed users or groups with the ability to edit the entire person record. This is usually reserved for administrators of the Notes infrastructure. It should be noted that this field is irrelevant if a potential modifier has EDITOR access or higher to the public Name and Address book, or if a user or group other then the owner of the document has AUTHOR access with the UserModifier Role granted.

- **Check password:** This field is used to check passwords of user ID files or to lock out a user ID file completely. This functionality is new with release 4.5 of Notes, and the Notes workstation as well as the server must be running at least release 4.5. Once password checking is enabled, the user's ID file is modified and cannot be used with earlier versions of Notes. In order to be enabled password checking must be set within this field of the person document as well as in the server document of the user's Notes mail server. The Notes Administration Process running on the mail server can actually modify this field. It is triggered by the Notes administrator using the Notes administration console, which is the recommended method for using the checking password feature. This process is described in greater detail in Chapter 8, *Administration Issues*.

V. Useful →

- **Required change interval:** This field contains the number of days after which the user is required to change his or password. As with other operating systems, every 30 to 60 days is a standard change interval. Like the Check password field, this field should be filled by the Notes Administration Process triggered from an administrator using the Notes administration console.

Sync with NT ?
Any default ?

- **Grace period:** This field contains the number of days the user has to change his or her password once a change password request occurs. Again, the Notes Administration process should handle this field.

- **Last change date:** This is a computed field listing when the Notes user last changed the password.

- **Password digest:** The password digest field keeps track of all passwords used by Notes users, up to 50 entries. This repository prevents obsolete Notes user IDs from accessing Notes resources.

50

- **Notes Client License:** This field is used to signify what type of Notes license the Notes user is utilizing. If an upgrade is desired, the administrator should change the license type as described in Chapter 8, *Administration Issues.*

- **Setup profile:** This field is used when a Notes user is set up for the first time. The administrator populates it upon user creation.

- **Foreign directory sync allowed:** This field is responsible for allowing synchronization of the person record information to other foreign mail and directories. Such an example would be to cc:Mail environments using the cc:Mail MTA.

Person records are sorted in the public Name and Address book by last name of the Notes users. In order to view this sort, a Notes user may go into the public Address book and select the **People** view. An example of this view is shown in Figure 6-5:

Figure 6-5

Lotus Notes
People View

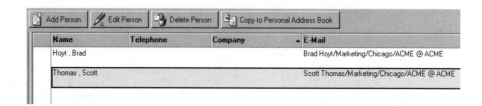

Similar to the **Group** view, buttons exist to add, edit, and delete a person record. These buttons will only work assuming proper ACL access and roles to the public Name and Address book, and are associated with the administration process of the Notes server.

Notes users should be created from the Notes server administration tool rather than from the button from the **People** view. Simply creating a person record within this view will not create a Notes user ID, which is necessary for client access to a Notes server. Person information for people accessing Notes servers and applications from a Web browser can be created using the **Create** button in the public Name and Address book.

The **Copy to Personal Address Book** button in this view will copy a person record from the public Name and Address book to a Notes user's personal Name and Address book.

Certifier Records

Whenever a Notes administrator registers a flat organization or a hierarchical certifier ID from the Notes server administration tool, the information concerning the file is stored within a Certifier record in the Notes public Name and Address book. Also, cross-certificates to other organizations are stored within this type of document. The contents of the record are shown in Figure 6-6:

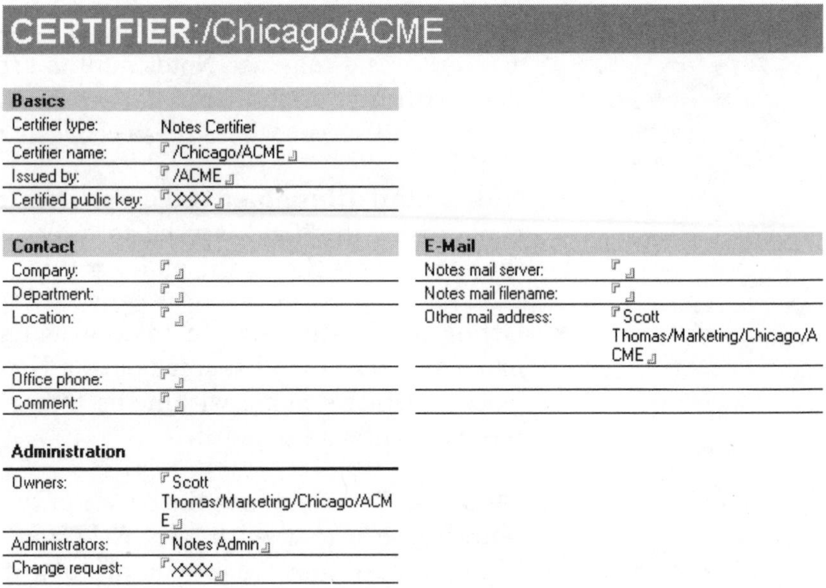

Figure 6-6

Notes Certifier Record

CERTIFIER:/Chicago/ACME

Basics
Certifier type:	Notes Certifier
Certifier name:	/Chicago/ACME
Issued by:	/ACME
Certified public key:	XXXX

Contact
Company:	
Department:	
Location:	
Office phone:	
Comment:	

E-Mail
Notes mail server:	
Notes mail filename:	
Other mail address:	Scott Thomas/Marketing/Chicago/ACME

▼ **Administration**
Owners:	Scott Thomas/Marketing/Chicago/ACME
Administrators:	Notes Admin
Change request:	XXXX

Listed below are the different fields within the Notes certifier record, along with their description:

- **Certifier type:** This computed field is populated when either a certifier ID or cross-certificate is created by a Notes administrator. The field entry is either a certifier or cross-certificate entry.

- **Certifier name:** This field contains the distinguished name of the certifier. It is filled upon creation of the certifier ID. It should not be modified except by a knowledgeable Notes administrator.

- **Issued by:** This field is also filled upon creation and contains the higher level of the fully distinguished name that created the certifier. In other words, it is the father of this hierarchical ID in x.500 format.

- **Certified public key:** This is the public key of the certifier ID and should never be modified, except by a knowledgeable Notes administrator.

- **Contact Info:** The fields within this section have no functionality in terms of operating a Notes infrastructure. The fields are for informational purposes only.

- **Notes mail server:** When a user or server ID's certificate expires, a user may use Notes mail to send a request to renew the certificate. Within this field, a Notes administrator may place a mail server where these requests would reside.

- **Notes mail filename:** Like the item concerning the Notes mail server, this field is used to direct certificate requests to the appropriate file on the mail server.

- **Other mail address:** Instead of using the Notes mail filename and Notes mail server fields, a Notes administrator may place a person's name within the Other mail address field to receive certificate requests.

- **Owners:** This field lists the owner of the document and represents those people with only AUTHOR access to the public Name and Address book who are able to edit the document. Users or groups with EDITOR or higher access, or with AUTHOR access and the NetModifier Role, may still edit the document without exiting from within this field.

- **Administrators:** This field should be filled with any Notes administrators or groups in charge of administrating this document. The entire document can be edited by these people and/or groups.

- **Change Request:** This field should contain the public key for the Notes administrator's in charge of handling certificate requests. The field is only pertinent if encryption will be used for Notes mail certificate requests to the recipient listed within the E-mail section of this document.

The Notes view that sorts the different Notes certificates and cross-certificates is called the **Server/Certificates** view. An example of this view is shown in Figure 6-7:

Figure 6-7

Lotus Notes Certificates View

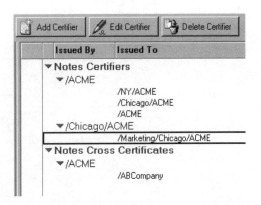

Buttons exist to add, edit, and delete a certificate or cross-certificate, assuming proper ACL access to the public Name and Address book. It is highly advisable, though, that all creations are done from the Notes administration tool. As with creating user IDs, this button will only create the document and not the actual certifier ID file.

Configuration Records

With release 4.0 of Lotus Notes, Notes administrators may configure a single or multiple Notes servers from within the public Name and Address book. These settings are stored and configured from configuration records within the public Name and Address book.

Configuration settings for Notes servers may be done at the Notes server console through a series of **Set Config** commands, editing the Notes server's **Notes.INI** file, or by configuring them within the public Name and Address book configuration records. The configuration records in the public Name and Address book take precedence over any settings in the **Notes.INI** file and once set in the public Name and Address book take affect almost immediately. There is no need to shut down or restart the Notes server. The settings will then be written to the Notes server's **Notes.INI** file as well.

Figure 6-8 shows what a Notes configuration record looks like:

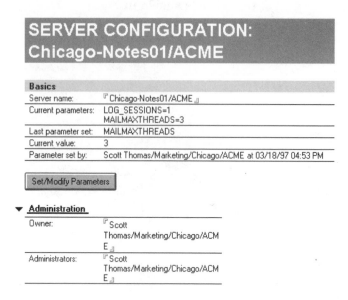

Listed below are the fields that are found within a Lotus Notes configuration record, along with an explanation of each field:

- **Server name**: This field represents which server(s) the parameters within the current document will be applied to. An asterisk (*) means that all Notes servers within the domain will be affected by the configuration settings. A group of servers may also be listed within the field.

- **Current parameters**: The current parameters field shows any settings within the configuration document. The included button within the document can be used to populate the field with the appropriate settings.

As shown in Figure 6-8, the ACME Notes administrator has set LOG_SESSIONS=1 which will log all user sessions to the Notes log. A complete list of parameters are shown in Table 6.1.

- **Current value:** This shows the current value of the last parameter set.

- **Last parameter set:** This lists the last parameter that was set within the configuration document.

- **Parameter set by:** The Parameter set by field shows the person that last set a configuration setting within the document.

- **Set/Modify Parameters:** This button can be used within the document while in edit mode to add or change configuration settings for a particular Notes server or group of Notes servers.

- **Owner:** This field lists the owner of the document. It represents those people with only AUTHOR access to the public Name and Address book who are able to edit the document. Users or groups with EDITOR or higher access or with AUTHOR access and the NetModifier Role may still edit the document, however, without exiting from within this field.

- **Administrator:** This field should be populated with any Notes administrators or groups in charge of administrating this document.

The view that can be used to sort all configuration documents within the public Name and Address book is the **Server\Configurations** view. An example of this view is shown in Figure 6-9:

Figure 6-9

Lotus Notes
Configuration View

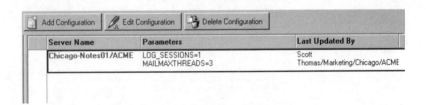

A Notes administration may add, edit, or delete a configuration document from within this view, assuming proper ACL and role access to the public Name and Address book, using the included buttons. From within the Lotus Notes server administration tool, the administrator can traverse to this view in order to configure Notes server configuration documents as well.

Tips

Most configurations can be changed without restarting the Notes server. However, the following variables require a Notes server restart: `ServerTasks, ServerTasks At, NSF_Buffere_Pool_Size, Domain, ModemFileDirectory, ServerKeyFileName,` *and* `Ports.`

Table 6.1 shows configuration settings available via the configuration documents.

Table 6.1
Configuration Parameters

A5

NOTES.INI Variable	Description
ADMINPINTERVAL	The interval in which the administration process on a Notes server looks for any administration requests to perform.
ADMINPMODIFYPERSONDOCUMENTSAT	Determines when the person documents will be modified within the public Name and Address book by the administration process.
AMGR_DOCUPDATEAGENTMININTERVAL	Determines the minimum amount of time between the executions of the same document update triggered agent.
AMGR_DOCUPDATEEVENTDELAY	Determines the delay time that the Agent Manager schedules a document update triggered agent after a document update event.
AMGR_NEWMAILAGENTMININTERVAL	The minimum amount of time in minutes between the execution of the same new mail triggered agent.
AMGR_NEWMAILEVENTDELAY	The time in minutes that Agent Manager schedules a new mail triggered agent after a new mail message is delivered.
AMGR_WEEKENDAYS	Represents values for the **Don't run on Weekends** checkbox option in the **Agent Run on Schedule Options** box.
DEFAULT_INDEX_LIFETIME_DAYS	Set the time in days before the view index for Notes applications are discarded. The default setting is 45 days.
LOG_AGENTMANAGER	Specifies whether or not agent executions are logged to the Notes server Notes log file.
LOG_MAILROUTING	Represents the level of reporting to the Notes log file of a Notes server for mail events.
LOG_REPLICATION	Specifies whether or not replication events are logged to the Notes server's log file.
LOG_SESSIONS	Specifies whether or not a user's sessions (user accesses a Notes server) are logged to the Notes log file.
LOG_TASKS	Specifies whether or not information is displayed and logged when a Notes server polls configuration documents and server records.
LOG_VIEW_EVENTS	Species whether or not information is logged to the Notes log and to the console when Notes applications' views are rebuilt.
MAIL_LOG_TO_MISCEVENTS	Specifies whether or not all mail router events are logged to the Notes log under the Miscellaneous view instead of the Mail Routing Events view.
MAILDISABLEPRIORITY	Forces the mail router on the Notes server to ignore Notes mail message priorities.
MAILLOWPRIORITY	Sets the time that Low priority mail messages will be delivered.
MAILMAXTHREADS	Determines the number of mail threads a Notes server will use to route mail to other Notes servers.
MAILTIMEOUT	Determines the number of days the Notes mail router will hold undelivered mail until it is sent back to the sender.

Table 6.1

Configuration
Parameters, Cont'd.

NOTES.INI Variable	Description
MEMORY_QUOTA	Used only on OS/2 servers; responsible for the maximum amount of virtual memory the Notes server may use.
NAME_CHANGE_EXPIRATION_DAYS	Sets the number of days a change request may remain active.
NETWARENDSNAME	Sets the NetWare Directory Services Object Name for the Notes server to *known* within an NDS tree. This setting is used with the SPX driver in Novell 4.1 environments.
NO_FORCE_ACTIVITY_LOGGING	Used to control activity logging for each Notes application.
NSF_BUFFER_POOL_SIZE	Notes views that are in use are kept within the NSF buffer pool. The size of this variable is automatically determined upon server startup. Once this value is changed, a Notes server restart is necessary.
NWNDSPASSWORD	Automatically logs a Notes server into a Novell NDS tree. Intended for unattended operations.
NWNDSUSERID	Sets the user name to use in order to log into a Novell NDS tree.
PHONELOG	Determines whether or not phone calls are logged to the Notes log file.
REPL_ERROR_TOLERANCE	Determines the number of accepted replication errors of the same type between a Notes application before replication is terminated.
REPL_PUSH_RETRIES	Determines the number of times a push replication will be tried by the calling Notes server.
REPLICATORS	Determines the number of replication server tasks that will run on a Notes server.
REPORTUSEMAIL	Determines whether or not the Notes mail router will be used to pass Notes server statistics to another server.
SERVER_MAXSESSIONS	This setting determines the number of maximum sessions that will be supported on the Notes server. Once this value is reached, the user or server that is the least recently connected will be dropped.
SERVER_SESSION_TIMEOUT	Determines the maximum number of minutes a user or server can remain idle before the connection is dropped.
SERVER_SHOW_PERFORMANCE	Shows the number of users and transactions each minute on the Notes server console.
SERVERPULLREPLIACTION	Forces the Notes server to use Pull-Pull replication, and overrides any connection documents within the public Name and Address book.
SHARED_MAIL	Determines whether the Notes server will use shared mail for Notes mail users.
SHOW_TASK_DETAILS	Determines whether the name of the current transaction is displayed with the session message.
SWAPPATH	This value is used with OS/2 servers and sets the location of the swapper file.
UPDATE_NO_FULLTEXT	Determines whether the creation of full text indexes are allowed on the Notes server.
UPDATE_SUPPRESION_LIMIT	Overrides the UPDATE_SUPPRESSION_TIME setting if the specified number of duplicate requests to update indexes and views are received.
UPDATE_SUPPRESSION_TIME	Specifies the delay time between Notes application view updates and full text index updates.
UPDATERS	Specifies the number of indexer processes that may run simultaneously on a Notes server.

Connection Records

Notes server connection records within the public Name and Address book control replication and Notes mail routing between Notes servers within a single domain, as well as connections to other domains. Connection records can control when replication and Notes mail routing occurs, along with what databases are replicated.

Tips

A Notes mail connection record is not necessary for Notes servers within the same Notes named network. Only replication connection records are necessary. The Notes mail routers will automatically deliver mail to the appropriate Notes server within the same Notes network.

Connection records should be created by Notes administrators from their personal workstations within the public Name and Address book. Figure 6-10 shows what a Notes connection document looks like:

Figure 6-10
Lotus Notes
Connection
Record

SERVER CONNECTION

Basics

Connection type:	Local Area Network	Usage priority:	Normal
Source server:	Chicago-Notes01/ACME	Destination server:	Chicago-Notes02/ACME
Source domain:	ACME	Destination domain:	ACME
Use the port(s):	TCPIP	Optional network address:	192.22.554.36

[Choose ports]

Scheduled Connection		**Routing and Replication**	
Schedule:	ENABLED	Tasks:	Replication, Mail Routing
Call at times:	08:00 AM - 10:00 PM each day	Route at once if:	1 messages pending
Repeat interval of:	60 minutes	Routing cost:	1
Days of week:	Sun, Mon, Tue, Wed, Thu, Fri, Sat	Replicate databases of:	Low & Medium & High priority
		Replication Type:	Pull Push
		Files/Directories to Replicate:	(all if none specified)
		Replication Time Limit:	minutes

Many of the fields listed below deal with configuring the connection record in terms of establishing mail routing and replication between Notes servers. For more explanation on these two issues, refer to Chapter 10, *Replication* and Chapter 11, *Electronic Mail*. The following fields exist within the Notes connection record:

- **Connection type:** Select which type of server connection record you wish to use to connect to the target server. Choices include: Local Area Network, Dialup Modem, Passthru Server, Remote LAN Service, X.25, SMTP, X.400, cc:Mail, and SNA.

- **Source server:** Select the source Notes server that will be initiating the replication or e-mail connection.

- **Source domain:** Select the domain of the Notes server that is initiating the replication or e-mail connection.

- **Use the port(s):** Select the port(s) that the initiating Notes server will use. The initiating and target Notes server must be running at least one protocol in common in order to transfer e-mail or replicate Notes applications. If this field is left blank when Local Area Network is selected within the connection document, then Notes will use all available information, including all enabled ports and all enabled and disabled connections records, to try to make a connection to the target server.

- **Choose ports** Button: This button lets you select the network ports available on the Notes server. Once you select the desired ports, the selections will populate into the **Use the port(s)** field.

- **Usage priority:** If the **Normal** selection is set, then Notes will use this connection document. If the **Low** setting is set, then Notes will look at this connection record last.

Tips

You can create connection records with a Low usage priority to provide a backup connection in case the Normal priority connection is unavailable. For example, if the Normal priority connection is via TCP/IP across the Internet, and your Internet connection is down, you could have a backup connection via dial-up modem to the target server.

- **Destination server:** Select the target Notes server that the initiating Notes server will be replicating and/or routing e-mail to.

- **Destination domain:** Enter the destination domain of the target Notes server.

- **Optional network address:** Enter the optional network address of the target Notes server. For TCP/IP networks, this is the IP address of the target Notes server.

- **Schedule:** This field is used to enable or disable the connection document.

- **Call at times:** This field lists the times the initiating Notes server will replicate with the target Notes server, as well as connect to deliver mail if the mail waiting threshold is not reached. Replication and/or mail routing must appear in the task field of this connection document for this field to operate for replication and/or mail routing to occur. For a more detailed description on this field, consult Chapters 10 and 11.

- **Repeat interval of:** Enter the interval for the replication event to repeat in minutes.

- **Days of week:** Enter the days of the week when the replication schedule should operate.

- **Tasks:** Enter the task(s) this connection record will be performing, including replication and/or any e-mail routing.

- **Route at once if:** This field tells Notes how often to force a call or connection to route e-mail. If this number is set to a number such as five, then Notes will not route e-mail to the target Notes server until 5 e-mail messages exist within the router mail box or until the next scheduled connection to the target Notes server. This excludes servers on the same Notes named network. This field is ignored for High priority mail messages.

- **Routing cost:** This is the relative cost of the connection that the Notes servers use to determine the best path for Notes to connect. This number can have values in the range of 1–10 and should not be modified unless there is a specific reason.

- **Replicate databases of XXX Priority:** Notes database applications can be set to a priority of High, Medium, or Low. This field within the connection record specifies what databases will replicate, based on the priority of the connection record. Each database in a Notes network can have a priority assigned to it by administrators or designers.

- **Replication type:** This specifies in what manner and direction the initiating Notes server will replicate. The replication types are push-pull, pull-pull, pull-push, push-push. The various replication types are explained in more detail in Chapter 10, *Replication*.

- **Files/Directories to replicate:** If this field is left empty, all replica databases in common will be replicated assuming proper ACL access. If this field contains entries, then only those Notes applications will be replicated by this connection record.

- **Replication Time Limit:** This is the time limit that a scheduled replication may use. If the limit is surpassed, replication for the connection will be halted.

- **Comments:** This field is for informational purposes only.

- **Owners:** This field lists the owner of the document and represents those people with only AUTHOR access to the public Name and Address book who are able to edit the document. Users or groups with EDITOR or higher access or with AUTHOR access and the NetModifier Role may still edit the document, however, without exiting from within this field.

- **Administrators:** This field should be filled with any Notes administrators or groups in charge of administrating this document.

The view in the public Name and Address book that sorts all connection records is the **Server\Connections** view. An example of this view is shown in Figure 6-11.

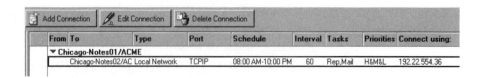

This view contains three buttons to add, edit, and delete connection records it assumes proper ACL access to the public Name and Address book and that proper roles are assigned to the user and group.

Once a Notes administrator makes an addition or modification to a connection record in the public Name and Address book, it *usually* becomes available within one minute. Circumstances may exist where this may not be true. For instance, if a Notes administrator runs a Notes agent on the public Name and Address book where all connection records are modified, and there are many of them, the view will need to be rebuilt. While the view is being built, the server uses the old information in the Notes server cache. Once though the Notes server completes the rebuild of the index for the server connection's view, the new modifications or additions are put into place.

Domain Records

Domain records within the public Name and Address book define name, location, and access to adjacent and non-adjacent Notes domains and non-Notes domains.

A sample of a Foreign Notes domain record is shown in Figure 6-12.

Figure 6-12

Lotus Notes
Foreign Domain
Record

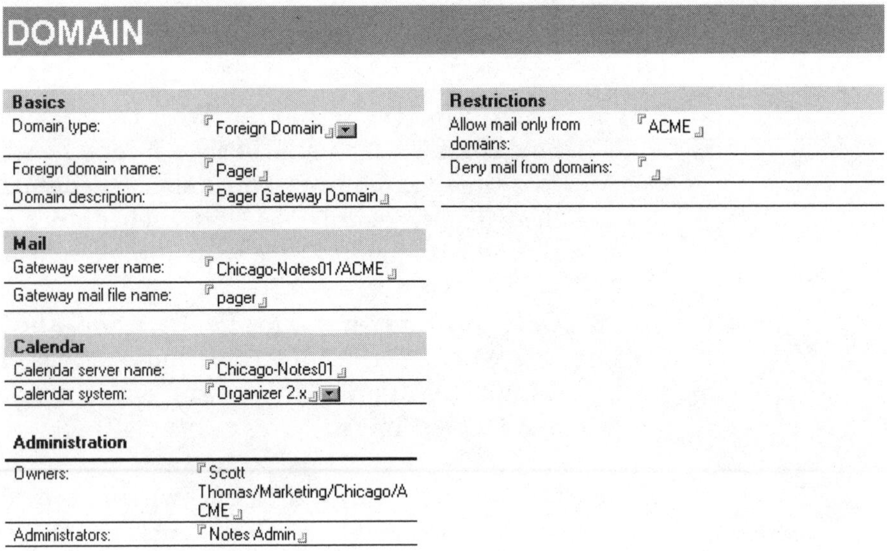

DOMAIN

Basics

		Restrictions	
Domain type:	Foreign Domain	Allow mail only from domains:	ACME
Foreign domain name:	Pager	Deny mail from domains:	
Domain description:	Pager Gateway Domain		

Mail

Gateway server name:	Chicago-Notes01/ACME
Gateway mail file name:	pager

Calendar

Calendar server name:	Chicago-Notes01
Calendar system:	Organizer 2.x

Administration

Owners:	Scott Thomas/Marketing/Chicago/ACME
Administrators:	Notes Admin

The following fields exist within a Notes foreign domain record:

- **Domain type:** This setting specifies which type of domain the record will be. Choices for domains include: foreign, non-adjacent, adjacent, foreign x.400, foreign SMTP, foreign cc:Mail, and Global. Foreign domains are used for gateway add-ons. Non-adjacent and adjacent domain records are used to control access for e-mail to other domains. Also, a non-adjacent domain record directs Notes mail to the appropriate target domain without users knowing the intermediary domain between the two domains. Foreign cc:Mail, SMTP, and Global domains control other e-mail functions.

- **Foreign domain name:** This field contains the name of the foreign domain.

- **Domain description:** This field is for informational purposes and describes the domain record.

- **Gateway server name:** This field contains the name of the Notes server where the server gateway product is installed.

- **Gateway mail file name:** This field contains the name of the gateway's mailbox database file.

- **Calendar server name:** With the release of Notes 4.5, this field contains the name of the server where an add-in performs free time searches on non-Notes scheduling applications. The field is only required if Notes scheduling information will be shared with a non-Notes scheduling application.

- **Calendar system:** This field specifies the name of the add-in that will be performing free time searches on non-Notes scheduling applications. The two current choices are **Organizer 2.x** and **OfficeVision.**

- **Owners:** This field lists the owner of the document and represents those people with only AUTHOR access to the public Name and Address book who are able to edit the document. Users or groups with EDITOR or higher access or with AUTHOR access and the NetModifier Role may still edit the document, however, without exiting from within this field.

- **Administrators:** This field should be filled with any Notes administrators or groups in charge of administrating this document.

- **Allow mail only from domains:** This field will allow e-mail only from the specified domain(s). An example for populating this field would be the case where a pager gateway existed and external users should not be allowed to use the gateway, tying up the resource and thus costing the company more money.

- **Deny mail from domains:** Similar to **Allow mail only from domains**, this field restricts who may mail documents to the domain.

The view within the public Name and Address book that sorts domain records is the **Server\Domains** view. An example of this view is shown in Figure 6-13:

Add Domain
Edit Domain
Delete Domain
Domain
Next Domain
Foreign Domain

Figure 6-13
Lotus Notes Domain View

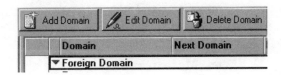

The Lotus Notes domain view includes buttons to create, edit, and delete domain documents from within the public Name and Address book, assuming proper ACL rights and roles.

Mail-In Database Records

Similar to person records within the public Name and Address book, Mail-In database records provide a means for receiving e-mails directly into a Notes application. A Notes application developer may create applications where users may need to mail documents into that application. These types of applications are generally referred to as *mail enabled applications.*

Both Notes mail and non-Note mail clients can send messages to a mail enabled application.

Figure 6-14 shows a Notes Mail-In database record:

MAIL-IN DATABASE
Basics
Mail-in name: HR Application
Description: Mail-In Database Record for ACME HR Notes Application
Location
Domain: ACME
Server: Chicago-Notes01/ACME
Filename: firmwide/hr
Administration
Owners: Scott Thomas/Marketing/Chicago/ACME
Administrators: Notes Admin
Foreign directory sync allowed: Yes

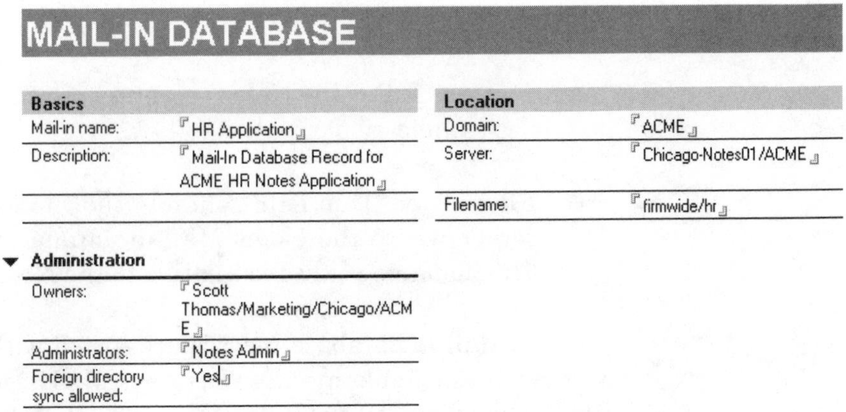

Figure 6-14
Lotus Notes Mail-In Database Record

The following fields can be found in the Lotus Notes Mail-In Database Record:

- **Mail-in name:** This is the name that will be used to direct Notes mail to the Notes database application. Within a Notes e-mail memo, this is the name that will be placed by users in the **To** field.

- **Description:** This is for informational purposes only and describes the purpose of the Mail-In database record.

- **Owners:** This field lists the owner of the document and represents those people with only AUTHOR access to the public Name and Address book who are able to edit the document. Users or groups with EDITOR or higher access or with AUTHOR access and the NetModifier Role may still edit the document without exiting from within this field.

- **Administrators:** This field should be filled with any Notes administrators or groups in charge of administrating this document.

- **Foreign directory sync allowed:** This field is responsible for allowing synchronization of the record to other foreign mail and directories. Such an example would be to cc:Mail environments using the cc:Mail MTA.

- **Domain:** Enter the domain where the Notes Mail-In database application exists.

- **Server:** Enter the Notes server where the Notes Mail-In database application exists.

- **Filename:** This field contains the file location on the Notes server where the Notes Mail-in database application resides. The filename is always relative to the Notes data directory.

Notes Mail-in database records are sorted within the public Name and Address book by the **Server\Mail-In Databases and Resources** view. An example of this view is shown in Figure 6-15:

Figure 6-15

Lotus Notes Mail
In Database View

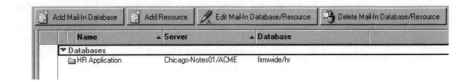

The Mail-In Database view also contains the buttons **Add Mail-In Database**, **Add Resource**, **Edit Mail-In Database/Resource**, and **Delete Mail-In Database/Resource**. Assuming proper ACL access and applied roles, an administrator may use these buttons to perform those actions. It should be noted that resources are for calendaring and scheduling so that resources and meeting rooms may be established for use with the system.

Program Records

Program records in the public Name and Address book enable Notes administrators to run server programs at specified times. Server program documents may run UNIX shell scripts or programs, a Notes server add-in program, or an API program.

Figure 6-16 shows a sample program record in the public Name and Address book.

Figure 6-16

Lotus Notes
Program Record

PROGRAM: ncompact.exe

Basics		Schedule	
Program name:	ncompact.exe	Enabled/disabled:	ENABLED
Command line:		Run at times:	11:00 PM each day
Server to run on:	Chicago-Notes01/ACME	Repeat interval of:	0 minutes
Comments:	Notes Compaction Program	Days of week:	Sun, Mon, Tue, Wed, Thu, Fri, Sat

▼ Administration

Owners:	Scott Thomas/Marketing/Chicago/ACME
Administrators:	Notes Admin

The following fields exist within the Lotus Notes program record:

- **Program name:** This field contains the name of the actual program to run on the Notes server. It should be noted that if the program is a Notes server program, it will have a prefix. For instance, the Notes server program **compact.exe**, if run on a Windows NT server, will be named **ncompact.exe** and must be entered as **ncompact.exe** within the program name field of a program document.

- **Command line:** If any commands or parameters are needed to execute the program, they should be entered in this field.

- **Server to run on:** This field should contain the Notes server(s) that the program will run on.

- **Comments:** This field is for description purposes only.

- **Owners:** This field lists the owner of the document and represents those people with only AUTHOR access to the public Name and Address book who are able to edit the document. Users or groups with EDITOR or higher access or with AUTHOR access and the NetModifier Role may still edit the document, however, without exiting from within this field.

- **Administrators:** This field should be filled with any Notes administrators or groups in charge of administrating this document.

- **Enabled/disabled:** This field determines whether or not the program is DISABLED or ENABLED. The third setting, STARTUP ONLY, will only run the program when the Notes server is first started.

- **Run at times:** This field specifies the time of day the program will run.

- **Repeat interval of XXX minutes:** This field specifies how often the program will repeat. A value of zero will only run the program once.

- **Days of week:** The days of week field specifies on which days of the week this program will run.

Notes program records are sorted within the public Name and Address book by the **Server\Programs** view. An example of this view is shown in Figure 6-17:

Figure 6-17

Lotus Notes
Program View

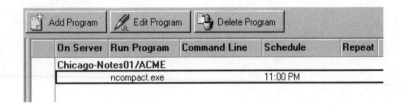

The Lotus Notes program view includes buttons to create, edit, and delete program documents from within the public Name and Address book, assuming proper ACL rights and roles.

Server Records

The server record in the public Name and Address book contains information for every Notes server including the server name, domain, notes named network, cluster name, Master Address Book name, and security and server administration information. Server records are created within the public Name and Address book when a Notes administrator registers a Notes server.

Traps

If you make a change to a server document, you must restart the server for the change to take place.

There are several sections within a Notes server record. Figure 6-18 shows is a sample of the first section of a Notes server record:

SERVER: Chicago-Notes01/ACME

Basics

Server name:	Chicago-Notes01/ACME
Server title:	Chicago Notes Mail Server
Domain name:	ACME
Cluster name:	
Master address book name:	

Server build number:	Release 4.5a
Administrators:	Notes Admin
Routing tasks:	Mail Routing
Server's phone number(s):	

▼ **Server Location Information**

Phone Dialing

Prefix for outside line:	
International prefix:	
Country code at this location:	
Long distance prefix:	1
Area code at this location:	

Calling card access number:	
Calling card number:	
Dialing Rules...	
Remote LAN idle timeout:	minutes

The following fields exis within this first part of the Notes server record:

- **Server name:** This field is populated when the Notes administrator creates a new server within the organization. This field should never be modified.

- **Server title:** This field is for descriptive purposes only and does not have any operational purposes for the Notes server.

- **Domain name:** This field is filled upon the creation of the Notes server. The field is normally never modified, unless the Notes server is moved from one Notes domain to another.

- **Cluster name:** This calculated field is populated when the Notes server is added to a Notes cluster.

- **Master address book name:** If directory assistance is going to be used to manage multiple Notes domains, this field contains the name of the master address book.

- **Server build number:** This calculated field is populated by the administration process running on the Notes server.

- **Administrators:** This field should be populated with the Notes administrators in charge of administering the server. It gives the proper authority to manage the Notes server and provides access to items such as remote console.

Tips

It is recommended that you use group names in this field instead of individual administrator names.

- **Routing tasks:** This field specifies the type of e-mail routing that will be performed on the Notes server.

- **Server's phone number(s):** If the Notes server will be permitting dial-in access to the Notes server itself, then the administrators should enter those dial-in numbers. The field is for descriptive purposes only.

- **Prefix for outside line:** If the Notes server will be dialing out through a modem and there is a prefix required, then this field should contain that number.

- **International prefix:** If the Notes server requires an international prefix to dial out, then this field should contain that number.

- **Country code at this location:** If the Notes server requires a country code, enter it in this field.

- **Long distance prefix:** If there is a long distance prefix, then this field should be filled.

- **Area code at this location:** Enter the area code at the Notes server's.

- **Calling card access number:** If a phone calling card is going to be used, enter the access number for the service.

- **Calling card number:** If a calling card is going to be used, enter the calling card number.

- **Dialing Rules** Button: If the dial-out procedure requires additional procedures, press this button to add the procedures.

- **Remote LAN idle timeout:** Enter a number in minutes to force the Notes server to hang up the line in the event of inactivity.

Figure 6-19 shows the second section of the Notes server record.

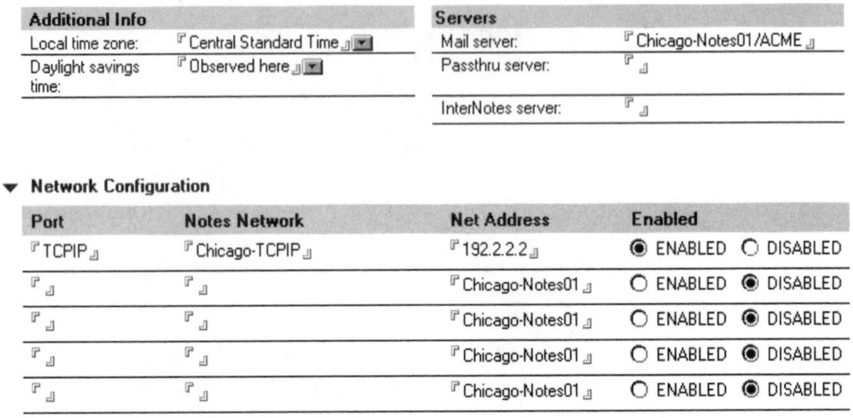

Figure 6-19

Lotus Notes
Server Record,
Section 2

Port	Notes Network	Net Address	Enabled
˹TCPIP˺	˹Chicago-TCPIP˺	˹192.2.2.2˺	◉ ENABLED ○ DISABLED
˹ ˺	˹ ˺	˹Chicago-Notes01˺	○ ENABLED ◉ DISABLED
˹ ˺	˹ ˺	˹Chicago-Notes01˺	○ ENABLED ◉ DISABLED
˹ ˺	˹ ˺	˹Chicago-Notes01˺	○ ENABLED ◉ DISABLED
˹ ˺	˹ ˺	˹Chicago-Notes01˺	○ ENABLED ◉ DISABLED

- **Local time zone:** opulate this field with the proper time zone.

- **Daylight savings time:** Specify whether or not daylight savings time is observed at this location.

- **Mail server:** Enter the name of the Notes mail server. This field is important if the Notes server is a mail server and will be e-mailing documents to users. Normally, this field is not used by Notes servers.

- **Passthru server:** If this Notes server will be using another server via pass through to access other Notes servers, enter the name of that Notes pass through server.

- **InterNotes server:** If this Notes server will be using an InterNotes server, enter the name of that server. This field is rarely used on Notes servers.

- **Port:** All the enabled network ports of the Notes server need to be entered within the Ports fields. COM ports do not need to be entered.

- **Notes Network:** This field should contain the name of the Notes network the server and port belong to. All Notes servers that share the same protocol and exist within the same LAN segment or ring should be included within the same Notes network.

- **Net Address:** This should be the address of the Notes server's network port. For IP networks, this should be the IP address or the DNS entry of the server.

- **Enabled/Disabled:** This field signifies whether the port is enabled or disabled.

Figure 6-20 shows the third part of the Notes server record.

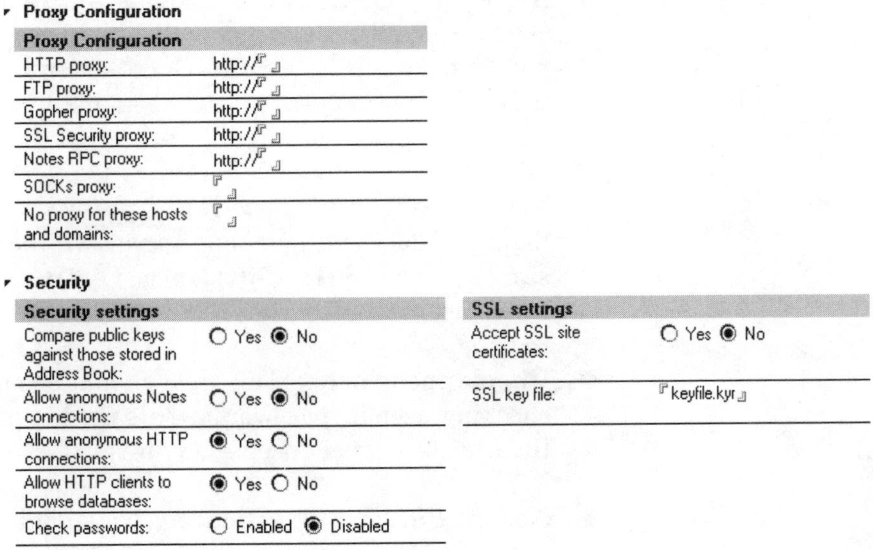

▸ Proxy Configuration

Proxy Configuration	
HTTP proxy:	http://
FTP proxy:	http://
Gopher proxy:	http://
SSL Security proxy:	http://
Notes RPC proxy:	http://
SOCKs proxy:	
No proxy for these hosts and domains:	

▸ Security

Security settings	
Compare public keys against those stored in Address Book:	○ Yes ◉ No
Allow anonymous Notes connections:	○ Yes ◉ No
Allow anonymous HTTP connections:	◉ Yes ○ No
Allow HTTP clients to browse databases:	◉ Yes ○ No
Check passwords:	○ Enabled ◉ Disabled

SSL settings	
Accept SSL site certificates:	○ Yes ◉ No
SSL key file:	keyfile.kyr

Figure 6-20 Lotus Notes Server Record, Section 3

- **Proxy Addresses:** If a proxy will be used to allow HTTP, FTP, Gopher, SSL, or Notes RPC, then enter the address(es) of that proxy machine.

- **Compare public keys:** This field will compare the public key of the user ID with the entry of the user's public key in the public Name and Address book during authentication. If they do not match, access will not be granted. This field protects against the prospect of a fake user ID. This field normally is not used unless the prospect of a false ID file is expected.

- **Allow anonymous Notes connections:** Enabling this field will enable all Notes ID files to authenticate with the Notes servers, regardless of certificates held. This field is not recommended for use, especially where critical data is an issue.

- **Allow anonymous HTTP connections:** If this entry is set to **No**, then the Notes server will override the individual database access control list setting regarding anonymous users. All anonymous Web users will need a name and password when trying to access the Notes server from a Web browser. When set to **Yes**, anonymous access will be granted to any database that has the default access of Reader or above in the ACL.

- **Allow HTTP clients to browse databases:** If this field is set to **Yes**, Web browsers will be able to see a list of Notes databases when issuing an OpenServer URL command. If set to **No**, Web browsers will not see a list but will be able to open a Notes application directly if the URL is known. An example URL used to browse a server is `http://ACME`. ACME is the Notes server running the HTTP process. Listed within DNS, a listing of databases on that server will be listed in a manner similar to the **File**, **Database, Open** command within the Notes user interface.

- **Check passwords:** This field should be enabled if you will be checking user ID passwords. This field must also be enabled in the user(s)' person documents for this feature to work.

- **Accept SSL site certificates:** This field determines whether or not the Notes server will accept SSL site certificates.

- **SSL Key file:** This is the file name for the SSL key ring used by Domino for encryption activities.

Figure 6-21 shows the fourth part of the Notes server record.

Figure 6-21

Lotus Notes Server
Record, Section 4

▼ **Restrictions**

Server Access	Who can -		Passthru Use	Who can -
Only allow server access to users listed in this Address Book:	⌜No⌟▾		Access this server:	⌜Chicago-Notes01 Passthru⌟▾
Access server:	⌜Allow Chicago-Notes01⌟▾		Route through:	⌜Chicago-Notes01 Passthru⌟▾
Not access server:	⌜Deny Chicago-Notes01⌟▾		Cause calling:	⌜Chicago-Notes01 Passthru⌟▾
Create new databases:	⌜Notes Admin⌟▾		Destinations allowed:	⌜⌟▾
Create replica databases:	⌜Notes Admin⌟▾			

▼ **Agent Manager**

Agent Restrictions	Who can -	Parameters	
Run personal agents:	⌜⌟▾	Refresh agent cache:	⌜12:00 AM⌟
Run restricted LotusScript agents:	⌜Notes Develop Admin⌟▾		
Run unrestricted LotusScript agents:	⌜Notes Develop Admin⌟▾		

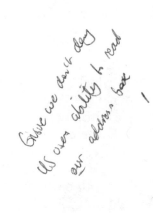

- **Only allow server access to users listed in this address book:** When set to **Yes**, this field will only allow users with person records in the public Name and Address book to access the Notes server. Note that with this field set to **Yes**, other Notes servers will not be able to access the Notes server unless it is listed in the Access Server field or is a member of a group within the Access Server field. This field is not used for Web browser access.

- **Access server:** This field contains those users, servers, and groups that are allowed access to the Notes server. If this field is left blank, then all Notes users, servers, and groups will be allowed access. This field is only used for Notes clients; Web browser access is not controlled by this field.

- **Not access server:** Enter servers, groups, or users that you wish to deny access to the Notes servers. It is beneficial to populate a group such as "Deny Access" with users who have left the company, and then to place this group within this field. This field is not used for Web browser access.

- **Create new databases:** Only enter users or groups you wish to grant the ability to create new Notes database applications on the server. If the field is left blank, all Notes users will be able to create new Notes database applications. This field is not used for Web browser access.

- **Create replica databases:** Enter users or groups you wish to be able to create new replica Notes applications within this field. If this field is left blank, no one will be able to create new replica database applications unless done at the Notes server interface. This field is not used for Web browser access.

- **Access this server through Passthru:** This field allows users, groups, and servers to access this server as a passthru destination. If this field is left blank then no users or servers can access this Notes server as a passthru destination.

- **Passthru route through:** This field should be populated with users, servers, or groups you wish to access the Notes server for passthru to another Notes server destination. If this field is left blank, then no user or server will be able to use this Notes server as a passthru server.

- **Passthru cause calling:** This field designates which servers, groups, or users may force the Notes server to "call" or contact another server and act as an intermediary (passthru) contact to another Notes server. If this field is left blank, the no destinations are allowed to be called.

- **Passthru destinations allowed:** This field lists all destination Notes servers that are allowed. If this field is left blank, all Notes servers are possible destinations via passthru.

- **Run personal agents:** This field designates which people and groups are allowed to run personal agents on a Notes server. If this field is left blank, all people and groups are allowed to run personal agents.

- **Run restricted LotusScript agents:** This field signifies those users and groups who are able to run restricted Lotus-Script agents. If this field is left blank, no one is allowed to run restricted LotusScript agents.

- **Run unrestricted LotusScript agents:** This field signifies those users and groups who are able to run unrestricted LotusScript agents. If this field is left blank, no one is allowed to run unrestricted LotusScript agents.

- **Refresh agent cache:** This field contains the time the Agent Manager's agent cache will be updated.

Figure 6-22 shows the fifth section of the Notes server record.

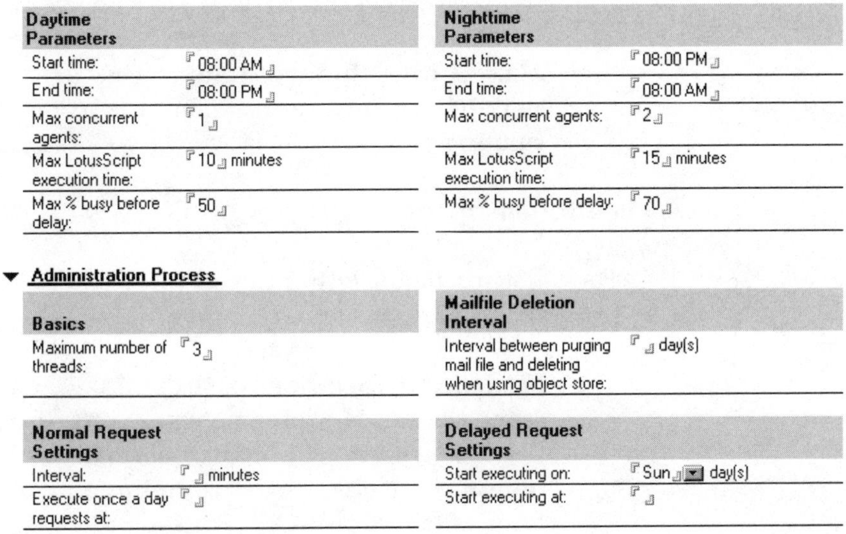

Figure 6-22

Lotus Notes
Server Record,
Section 5

Daytime Parameters		Nighttime Parameters	
Start time:	08:00 AM	Start time:	08:00 PM
End time:	08:00 PM	End time:	08:00 AM
Max concurrent agents:	1	Max concurrent agents:	2
Max LotusScript execution time:	10 minutes	Max LotusScript execution time:	15 minutes
Max % busy before delay:	50	Max % busy before delay:	70

▼ **Administration Process**

Basics		Mailfile Deletion Interval	
Maximum number of threads:	3	Interval between purging mail file and deleting when using object store:	day(s)

Normal Request Settings		Delayed Request Settings	
Interval:	minutes	Start executing on:	Sun ▾ day(s)
Execute once a day requests at:		Start executing at:	

Daytime and Nightime Parameters

The agent manager can be configured to run differently during the day and in the evening. Each section (daytime and nighttime) has the following fields:

- **Start time:** This field lists the time of day or night to start agent executions.

- **End time:** This field sets the time of day to end agent executions.

- **Max concurrent agents:** This field contains the maximum number of agents that may be run at any given time. It should be noted that only one agent can run on a Notes database application at a time. However, other agents can run on other Notes applications at the same time. Multiple agents will take resources that could be used by other Notes processes, so care should be taken when increasing this value.

- **Max LotusScript execution time:** This field contains the maximum number of minutes an agent is able to run. If the agent has not completed in the allotted time, it will be halted. If the value is set too high, it could consume too many resources; care should be taken when setting this value.

- **Max % busy before delay:** This field represents as a percentage the maximum amount of time a server may spend running an agent.

Administration Process

The following fields within the server document control the administration process on the specific Notes server:

- **Maximum number of threads:** This field controls how many threads the administration process will use on the specified Notes server. This value normally should not be increased unless the Notes server is running on a SMP machine with large amounts of RAM.

- **Interval:** This field signifies how often the administration process will carry out administration requests.

- **Execute once a day requests at:** This field contains the time of day the administration process will update person documents in the public Name and Address book.

Once user deleted ? ?

- **Interval between purging mail file...** This field details the number of days the Object Collect task waits until it runs against users' mail files that use shared mail, and when the users' mail files are deleted.

- **Start executing on:** This field signifies on what day(s) of the week delayed requests are carried out on the Notes server.

- **Start executing at:** This field details what time of day delayed requests are carried out.

Figure 6-23 shows the sixth section of the Notes server record.

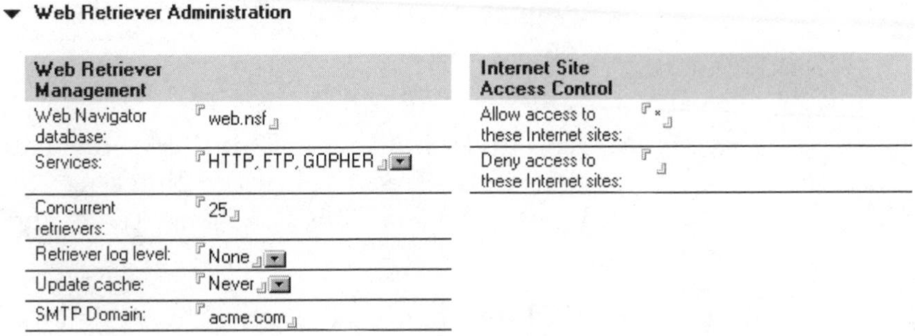

Figure 6-23

Lotus Notes
Server Record,
Section 6

▼ **Web Retriever Administration**

Web Retriever Management		Internet Site Access Control	
Web Navigator database:	web.nsf	Allow access to these Internet sites:	*
Services:	HTTP, FTP, GOPHER ▼	Deny access to these Internet sites:	
Concurrent retrievers:	25		
Retriever log level:	None ▼		
Update cache:	Never ▼		
SMTP Domain:	acme.com		

Figure 6-23 contains the fields that control and configure the InterNotes process on the Notes server. The InterNotes process enables Notes clients to access Web servers through a Notes server without the need for a Web browser or TCP/IP on the desktop. Web sites are pulled by the InterNotes server into an InterNotes, Notes database application. This database in turn presents the data from the remote Web site to the Notes clients within this application. For Notes clients to use the InterNotes process on a Domino (Notes) server, the WEB process must be loaded on the Notes server. This is done by typing in the following line at the Notes server console:

```
Load Web
```

Within the **Notes.INI** file of the Notes server on the **SERVER-TASKS=** line, the task may be appended so that it will automatically load upon Notes server startup. A more detailed discussion of the InterNotes server is found in Chapter 13, *Internet and Web Application Servers.*

- **Web Navigator database:** This field represents the Notes database application that will host all remote Web site pages.

- **Services:** This field controls what services are allowed from the InterNotes server. These include FTP, GOPHER, HTTP, HTTPS, and FINGER.

- **Concurrent retrievers:** This field represents the maximum number of processes or threads that are permitted to access remote Web sites.

- **Retriever log level:** This field represents the level of logging that will be recorded to the Notes log database on the Notes server. The levels include None, Terse, and Verbose.

- **Update cache:** This entry controls how often the document within the Web Notes application is updated.

- **SMTP Domain:** This field represents the domain used to route SMTP mail.

- **Allow access to these Internet sites:** This field controls what sites users are able to connect to. Wildcards (*) may be used if desired. For example, ***.com** allows users to connect to any site ending with **.com.**

- **Deny access to these Internet sites:** This field controls what sites users are not allowed to connect to. Like the allow access field, wildcards may be used. ***.acme.com** would prevent users from connecting to any server within **.acme.com.**

Figure 6-24 shows the seventh section of the Notes server record.

Figure 6-24

Lotus Notes
Server Record,
Section 7

Basics		Operational Information	
TCP/IP port number:	80	Cache directory (for GIFs and file attachments):	domino\cache
TCP/IP port status:	Enabled	Garbage collection:	Enabled
SSL port number:	443	Garbage collection interval:	60 minutes
SSL port status:	Enabled	Maximum cache size:	50 (MB)
Host name:	www.acme.com	Delete cache on shutdown:	Disabled
DNS lookup:	Disabled	Image conversion format:	JPEG
Default home page:		Progressive rendering:	Enabled
Maximum active threads:	40	JPEG image quality	75
Minimum active threads:	20	Default lines per view:	30
		Default character set group:	Western

Mapping		Logging	
HTML directory:	domino\html	Access log:	domino\logs\access
Home URL:	/?Open	Error log:	domino\logs\errors
CGI URL path:	/cgi-bin	Time stamp:	LocalTime
CGI directory:	domino\cgi-bin	No log:	www.acme.com
Icon URL path:	/icons		
Path to icons:	domino\icons		

Figure 6-24 lists the configurations for the HTTP process that enables a Notes server to present Notes applications to Web browsers. Complete details on the HTTP process are explained in Chapter 13, *Internet and Web Application Servers.*

- **TCP/IP port number:** This field represents the port number of the HTTP process to listen for HTTP requests. Port 80 is the default used by all HTTP Web servers and clients. Other than port 80, no port below 1024 should ever be used. If another port is going to be used for the HTTP process, clients must specify the port used. For instance, another popular port to use to listen for HTTP requests is port 8008. For a Web browser to access a Domino server running the HTTP process, the user would have to specify the server name and port number, e.g. **http://www.acme.com:8008/.**

If the port number is changed, the Domino server must be restarted.

● **TCP/IP port status:** This field specifies the status of the TCP/IP port. Either this port and/or the SSL port must be enabled to use the HTTP process.

● **SSL port number:** Similar to the TCP/IP port number, the SSL port number is the number that is set for the HTTP process to listen for HTTPS requests (Secure Sockets). The default in the industry for the port number is 443 and should not be changed.

● **SSL port status:** This field must be enabled for the HTTP process to accept SSL requests. It may be enabled along with the TCP/IP port if desired. If this port is enabled while the Domino server is operating, the server must be restarted.

● **Host name:** This field contains the fully qualified host name for the Notes server. This should be the address as defined in DNS. If the Notes server is not registered within DNS, the IP address should be used. If the field is left blank, then the Notes server will use the address defined in the operating system's TCP/IP configuration.

● **DNS lookup:** This field determines whether or not the HTTP process will look up the qualified host name of Web browsers contacting the server. If it is enabled, the Notes server will lose some performance in order to process each lookup. Also, if the field is enabled and logging is enabled, then the actual machine (host) names of clients will be logged rather than the IP addresses of the requesting machines.

● **Default home page:** This field represents the name of the HTML page to use for the server's home page. If you decide to use an HTML home page, the file must be placed within the Domino HTML directory and the **Home URL** field must be blank.

If a Notes database application is going to be used for the home page, then this field should be left blank.

- **Maximum active threads:** This specifies the maximum number of threads that can be used to answer browser requests. The more hardware the Notes server contains (processors, RAM, etc.), the higher the number of threads the Notes server running the HTTP process will be able to handle.

- **Minimum active threads:** This is the minimum number of active threads the Notes server will keep open, even if the threads are idle. Like the maximum number of active threads field, the more hardware that is available to the server, the higher this number may be set.

- **HTML directory:** This field specifies the directory in which to place HTML files that will be hosted by the Domino server. A Domino server can host either Notes applications and/or HTML files to any standard Web browser.

- **Home URL:** Within this field, enter the about document, navigator, or Notes database application for users to access when a Web browser first contacts the Notes server. If an HTML document is going to be used for the server for the home page instead, leave this field blank. The default setting of **/?Open** will list all Notes applications available on the Notes server, assuming this security option is enabled. To specify a database to act as the Domino home page, an entry such as **/home.nsf** may be used.

- **CGI URL path:** This field contains the URL path for CGI programs. This is *not* the path as related to the file system of the Notes server.

- **CGI directory:** This field specifies the directory location of the CGI program files. The path is relative to the data directory of the installed Notes server.

- **Icon URL path:** This field contains the URL path for icons. Note that this field does not represent the operating system path.

- **Path to icons:** This field represents the directory location of the icons. This field is also relative to the data directory of the Notes installation.

- **Cache directory:** This directory stores images and file attachments. When a Web browser requests an image or file attachment, it is stored within this directory. If the item is requested again, the image is displayed from this directory, which improves performance. This directory is located below the Notes data directory.

- **Garbage collection/interval:** These fields specify if garbage collection is enabled and, if so, at what interval to run. Files that are no longer needed will be deleted, beginning with the least-accessed files.

- **Maximum cache size:** This field specifies the upper size limit for the cache directory. Once this size is reached, the Domino server will automatically delete unnecessary files. If more disk space is available, this size may be adjusted accordingly.

- **Delete cache on shutdown:** If this field is enabled, the Domino server will clear the contents of the cache directory when the server is shut down.

- **Image conversion format:** This field determines what format to convert images to. The choice is either JPEG or GIF.

- **Progressive rendering:** If JPEG format is enabled, progressive rendering enables images to be loaded to Web browsers progressively.

- **JPEG image quality:** If JPEG format is enabled, the image quality may be selected from a range of 5 to 100, with 100 being the best quality and largest size of an image.

- **Default lines per view:** This setting sets the number of lines the HTTP process will use to display a Notes database application view. This setting will affect all Notes applications on the Notes server.

- **Default character set group:** This field represents which character set to use when Web browsers access the Domino server.

- **Access log:** This field represents the path and/or filename of the access log for HTTP access statistics. If you do not wish to have Web client requests logged, leave the field blank. The log information can be logged to either a Notes database or the NCSA standard log file format.

- **Error log:** This field represents the path and/or filename of the error log for HTTP errors. If you do not want to log errors, leave the field blank.

- **Time stamp:** This field specifies if the logs are recorded using the local time of the Notes server or Greenwich Mean Time (GMT).

- **No log:** This field is used to not log certain clients within the access log. For example, you may not wish to log users internal to your company, but still wish to log all hits from external clients. Such an example within this field may look like: ***.acme.com.**

The final section of the Notes server document is shown in Figure 6-25.

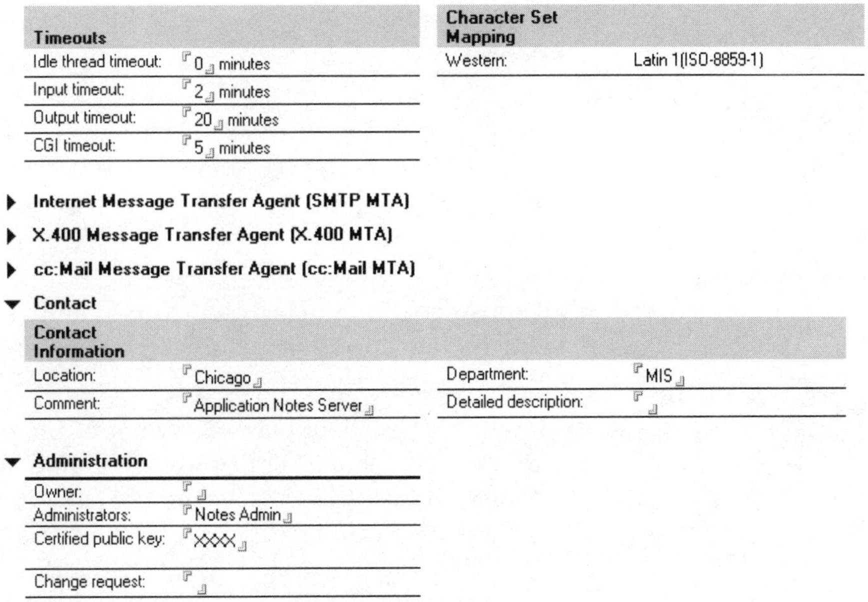

Figure 6-25

Lotus Notes
Server Record,
Section 8

Timeouts		Character Set Mapping	
Idle thread timeout:	0 minutes	Western:	Latin 1 (ISO-8859-1)
Input timeout:	2 minutes		
Output timeout:	20 minutes		
CGI timeout:	5 minutes		

▶ **Internet Message Transfer Agent (SMTP MTA)**

▶ **X.400 Message Transfer Agent (X.400 MTA)**

▶ **cc:Mail Message Transfer Agent (cc:Mail MTA)**

▼ **Contact**

Contact Information			
Location:	Chicago	Department:	MIS
Comment:	Application Notes Server	Detailed description:	

▼ **Administration**

Owner:	
Administrators:	Notes Admin
Certified public key:	XXXX
Change request:	

The following fields are including within this section:

- **Idle thread timeout:** This field specifies the number of minutes the HTTP process should keep a thread available before dropping it. If you do not wish the server to drop an idle thread, set the value for this field to zero.

- **Input timeout:** This is the time in minutes the Web browser has to send a request to the server. If the client does not send a request within the specified time, the connection is dropped.

- **Output timeout:** This is the amount of time in minutes the server has to send a request to a Web browser. This value does not apply to CGI programs. The connection is dropped if this value is reached by the server.

- **CGI timeout:** This value is the maximum amount of time in minutes after a CGI program starts that it is allowed to run. If the time elapses without completion of the program, the task is terminated.

- **Western:** Western is the default character set used by the HTTP process. Other sets may be necessary for international access.

- **MTA Sections:** If an MTA such as cc:Mail, x.400, or SMTP is installed on the Notes server, these sections will be available. Within these sections, the corresponding MTAs may be configured.

- **Contact Information Section:** The fields appearing within this section are for descriptive purposes only.

- **Owner:** This field lists the owner of the document and represents those people with only AUTHOR access to the public Name and Address book who are able to edit the document. Users or groups with EDITOR or higher access or with AUTHOR access and the ServerModifier Role may still edit the document, however, without exiting from within this field.

- **Administrators:** This field should be filled with any Notes administrators or groups in charge of administrating this document.

- **Certified Public Key:** This field contains the certified public key for the Notes server. The field should never be modified except on purpose by a knowledgeable Notes administrator.

- **Change request:** The administration process of a Notes server uses this field if a change is requested on the Notes server. The contents of the field expire after 21 days unless otherwise set by the **Name_Change_Expiration_Days** setting in the **Notes.INI** file.

Notes servers within the public Name and Address book are sorted by the view **Server\Servers**. Figure 6-26 shows a sample of this view:

Figure 6-26

Lotus Notes
Server View

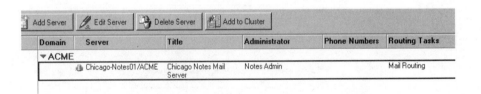

Domain	Server	Title	Administrator	Phone Numbers	Routing Tasks
▼ ACME					
	Chicago-Notes01/ACME	Chicago Notes Mail Server	Notes Admin		Mail Routing

The Lotus Notes server view includes buttons to add, edit, and delete server documents from within the public Name and Address book, assuming proper ACL rights and applied roles. It should be noted though that new Notes servers should be registered through the server administration panel in order to generate a new Notes server ID. The **Add to Cluster** button will add a specific Notes server to a Notes cluster.

Setup Profile Records

Setup profiles can be created by Notes administrators within the public Name and Address book to pre-configure several settings before creating the Notes user. Such settings include specifics regarding Internet settings, passthru options, and Notes database icons that appear on users' workspaces. Figure 6-27 shows the first part of a setup profile record within the public Name and Address book.

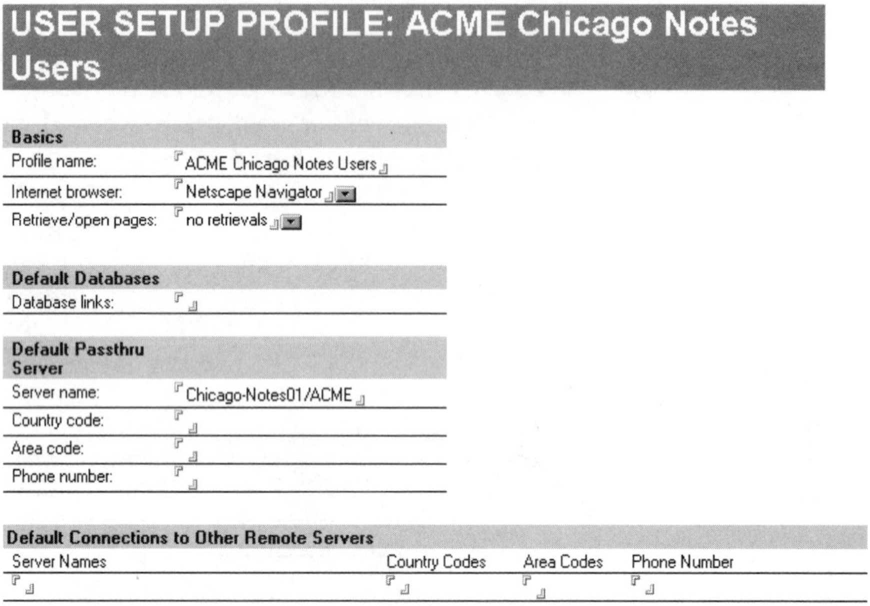

Figure 6-27

Lotus Notes Setup Profile Record, Part 1

USER SETUP PROFILE: ACME Chicago Notes Users

Basics

Profile name:	ACME Chicago Notes Users
Internet browser:	Netscape Navigator
Retrieve/open pages:	no retrievals

Default Databases

Database links:	

Default Passthru Server

Server name:	Chicago-Notes01/ACME
Country code:	
Area code:	
Phone number:	

Default Connections to Other Remote Servers

Server Names	Country Codes	Area Codes	Phone Number

- **Profile name:** Enter the name of the profile for descriptive purposes.

- **Internet browser:** Select the browser that you wish this group to use. Choices include the built-in Notes browser, Netscape Navigator, Microsoft Internet Explorer, and others.

- **Retrieve/open pages:** This field represents the location from which to retrieve Web pages.

- **Database links:** Within this field, place database links of Notes applications you wish to appear on a user's Notes desktop upon initial user setup.

- **Server name:** Within this field, place the Notes server name you wish users to use for Notes passthru operation.

- **Country code/Area code/Phone number:** Within these fields, place the phone number of the Notes server performing passthru.

- **Server Names:** Within this field, place Notes server(s) name(s) of other Notes servers with which you wish to have connection records.

- **Country codes/Area Codes/Phone Number:** Within this field, enter the phone number(s) of the other Notes servers.

Figure 6-28 shows the second part of the Notes Setup Profile Record.

Figure 6-28

Lotus Notes
Setup Profile
Record, Part 2

Secondary TCP/IP Notes name server:	Chicago-Notes02/ACME
Secondary TCP/IP host name or address:	chicago-notes02.acme.com
Secondary NDS Notes name server:	
Secondary NDS name server address:	

Default Java Applet Security			**Default Proxy Configuration**	
Trusted hosts:			HTTP proxy:	http://
Network access for trusted hosts:	Allow access only to originating host		Use HTTP proxy for all Internet protocols:	Yes
Network access for untrusted hosts:	No access allowed		FTP proxy:	http://
			Gopher proxy:	http://
			Security proxy:	http://
			Notes RPC proxy:	http://
			SOCKS proxy:	
			No proxy for these hosts and domains:	

Administration

| Owners: | Scott Thomas/Marketing/Chicago/ACME |
| Administrators: | Notes Admin |

- **Default Secondary Name Servers:** Within this section, place secondary Notes server settings for the Notes workstations. Explanation of these fields may be found earlier in this chapter.

- **Default Java Applet Security:** Enter the Java security options for a Notes workstation.

- **Default Proxy Configuration:** Within this field, enter any proxy information if one is used within your organization.

- **Owners:** This field lists the owner of the document and represents those people with only AUTHOR access to the public Name and Address book who are able to edit the document. Users or groups with EDITOR or higher access or with AUTHOR access and the NetModifier Role may still edit the document without exiting from within this field.

- **Administrators:** This field should be filled with any Notes administrators or groups in charge of administrating this document.

Notes Setup Profile records are sorted within the public Name and Address book by the view **Server\Setup Profiles**. Figure 6-29 shows a sample of this view.

Figure 6-29
Lotus Notes
Setup Profile View

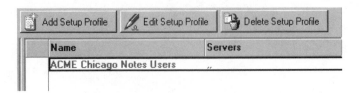

The Lotus Notes setup profile view includes buttons to add, edit, and delete setup profile documents from within the public Name and Address book, assuming proper ACL rights and roles.

We have just detailed all Notes server documents within the public Name and Address book and directly associated Notes views. There are other Notes views that sort server records that serve specific purposes. These other views in the public Name and Address book include: **Server\Clusters, Server\Deny Access Groups, Server\Licenses, Server\Mail Users, Server\Networks,** and **Server\V3 Stats & Events.**

- The **Server\Clusters** view sorts all Notes servers in the domain by what cluster they belong to—if they have been configured to use Notes clustering. The view includes buttons to edit a Notes server and to remove a Notes server from a cluster.

- The **Server\Deny Access Groups** view sorts all groups that have been defined as Deny Access Groups. Like the **Groups** view, this view includes buttons to add, edit, and delete groups, assuming proper ACL access to the public Name and Address book.

- The **Server\Licenses** view sorts all person and server documents by license type. This view gives administrators a quick snapshot of how many Notes licenses the organization holds. The view also includes a button to add a person, assuming proper ACL rights to the public Name and Address book. It should be noted that new Notes users should be created from the Notes administration panel in order to create a new Notes user ID file.

- The **Server\Mail Users** view sorts all mail users within the public Name and Address book. This view is used when a Notes administrator wishes to send Notes client workstation upgrades to users through Notes mail. A Notes administrator may select one or more users and then select the button to send an upgrade notification. The view also includes buttons to add, edit, and delete person records, assuming proper ACL access to the public Name and Address book.

- The **Server\Network** view sorts all Notes servers within the domain by the Notes network name(s). The view includes buttons to add, edit, and delete server documents within the public Name and Address book, assuming proper ACL access.

- The **Server\V3 Statistics & Events** view sorts all statistics and events that are held over for any version 3.x Notes servers within the domain. These documents and view are no longer needed once all Notes servers within the company are upgraded to version 4.0 or higher.

Installation Guidelines

The stage has been set, and now it is time to put your planning to the test. Before any hardware or software is installed on a new server machine, it is important to set the naming standards per guidelines set by Notes Administration Team. Items such as server names, protocols, type of server (mail, hub, etc.), replication schedules, mail routing schedules, and such need to be defined before the actually installation proceeds.

Server Installation Guidelines

The following items list the main steps on how to install and deploy Notes servers efficiently and effectively within a Notes environment. We will follow the steps to install a Notes server in a Windows NT environment. We use Windows NT as our example installation environment because it is currently the most popular operating system platform for a Notes server. To install a Notes server on a different operating system, consult your Notes documentation. (Generally speaking, these Notes installation guidelines hold true for most operating systems, but the specifics are for Windows NT.)

Define Naming Standards for Notes Servers

Before the first piece of hardware is ever assembled, a set of well-defined naming standards (explained in Chapter 4) for the Notes infrastructure is essential for a healthy Notes network. It is far easier for a Notes administration team to develop and adhere to naming standards from the onset than to install Notes in an ad hoc fashion, later having to reconfigure the entire Notes infrastructure.

Assemble the Hardware

This includes all items such as network card(s), hard drives, keyboard, mouse, and monitor, controller cards, etc. As explained in Chapter 2, *System Considerations* reputable server brands such as Compaq, IBM, and HP are recommended for Notes servers. Also, hardware level RAID technology is highly recommended to provide improved performance and data redundancy

It is important that the Notes server machine be placed in a secure location in a server room. From a Notes server machine, any person can gain access to Notes applications from the Notes user interface, bypassing Notes security. For this reason, the Notes server should be placed within a room where only authorized personnel have access.

Install the Operating System

Once all the hardware for the Notes server has been assembled and the Notes server is placed within a secure location, the operating system code is ready to be installed. The operating system is just a platform for Notes to run on top of. Hosting actual file and print activities are not necessary for this machine and are actually discouraged, as file sharing provides a potential security risk as well as a performance degradation for the Notes server code.

As mentioned earlier, Windows NT is currently the most popular operating system to house Notes servers, so we use Windows NT as an example of how to install a Notes server. Windows NT version

3.51 or 4.0 (if this is the preferred OS) should be installed with any necessary Service Packs that Microsoft has made available. As we write this book, Service pack 5 is out for version 3.51 of Windows NT and Service Pack 2 (plus patches) is available for version 4.0.

Once Windows NT is installed, the Notes administrator should configure any protocols or modem ports the Notes server may be using. For example, for TCP/IP installations, the static IP address of the machine should be set along with its proper subnet mask, DNS should be configured, and the default gateway should be added. If NWLINK will be used for SPX connections, the SAP agent and gateway services should be installed so that the Notes server may advertise itself within a Novell network.

The Windows NT machine may be added to a corporate Windows NT domain if so desired, but it is certainly not necessary. Again, Windows NT is only a platform that Notes will be running on. Windows NT domain authentication will not be taking place for Notes connections. It is highly recommended that the Notes server not be run on a Windows NT Primary Domain Controller or Backup Domain Controller. The Notes server is an intensive application and would burden the tasks of the Windows NT domain controllers. As mentioned, file and print sharing should not be granted to anyone except to Notes administrators, so that they may access Notes file remotely.

Traps

If file and print sharing is enabled on a Windows NT server running the Notes server, users with proper Windows NT access could access Notes applications as if they were on their local machines. This bypasses the Notes server security model, giving the user MANAGER access to Notes applications if Enforce a Consistent ACL *is not enabled on the database application. Users also run the risk of corrupting Notes database applications by not accessing them through a Notes server.*

Only a handful of Windows NT user accounts should be granted access to the machine. The Notes server(s) can be part of the corporate Windows NT domain, but should not be open for user access other than through Notes. Many organizations choose instead to create a separate Windows NT domain that only houses Notes servers. The Windows NT server should not have any users logged into the machine locally while the machine is unattended. This prevents unauthorized access.

For specific installation procedures of Windows NT server, you should consult the installation documentation provided with the Windows NT server package.

Install Notes Server Code

For a Windows NT installation of the Notes server, the install program extracts the server and administration files, creates the **NOTES.INI** file, and updates the Windows NT registry.

All files for the InterNotes and HTTP process are also copied to the Notes server. If you wish to use the InterNotes and/or HTTP process to integrate your Notes server with the Internet or other Intranet servers, you must perform additional configuration steps. These are described in Chapter 13, *Internet and Web Application Servers*.

You may install the Notes server directly from the Domino CD or from a shared directory on a network drive where the Notes installation files have been copied. To begin the installation for a Windows NT Intel machine, follow these steps:

1. Run the program **Install.exe** that is located in the **\W32INTEL\INSTALL** directory.

2. Click **I AGREE** once you have reviewed and agreed to the Domino Software License Agreement.

3. Type in your name and your company name within the proper fields. Do not check the **Install on File Server** box. The check box entry is not used by Notes server installs and is only for installing shared copies of Lotus Notes clients. Once completed, click **Next**. You will be prompted to verify the names. Click **Yes** if satisfied.

4. You will now see the Install Options screen as shown in Figure 7-1. Within the Notes Program Folder field, enter the directory where you wish to install the Notes server code and the Notes server data files. You may browse your local drives in order to choose a location by clicking the appropriate **Browse** button.

It is recommended that you install the Notes server code and Notes server data files in separate directories. This reduces the complexity of administration, as data files are easily located on the machine. The normal defaults are \NOTES for the Notes server files and \NOTES\DATA for the Notes server data files.

Figure 7-1

Notes Server
Install Options

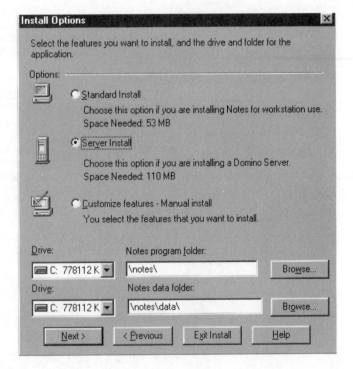

The three choices for installs are:

● **Standard Install:** This option is for Notes workstation installations only.

- **Server Install:** This is the standard Notes server install option. It consumes 110 MB of disk space plus any Notes applications you may have. For most organizations, this is the option to select.

- **Customize features:** This option lets you install only the features you select.

5. Click **Next** once you have selected your choices.

6. If you selected the **Customize features** install, the screen shown in Figure 7-2 appears to let you choose the features you wish. Click **Next** when finished.

Figure 7-2

Notes Server
Install Customizable
Options

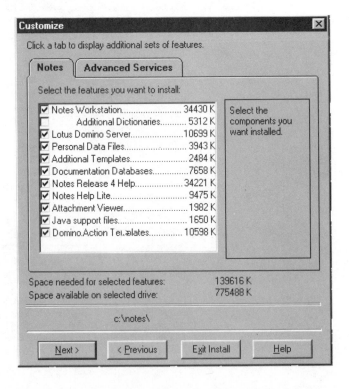

If you wish to install advanced services including Notes server clustering, partitioned servers, and billing services, you have to select the Customize features selection and then choose those options from the Advanced Services tab.

Tips

7. You are prompted for the program folder destination (Figure 7-3). Select the destination and click **Next**.

Figure 7-3

Notes Server
Install Program
Folder Selection

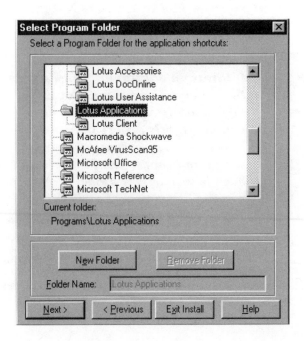

8. Next, you are prompted to begin copying the source files to your hard drive. All other programs should be closed. Click **Yes** to begin the copying.

9. When all files are copied, click **Done** to exit the install process.

Configure a New Notes Server (Create the First Server and Certifier ID Files)

Continuing from the above installation procedures, we are now set to configure the first Notes server within the company. All necessary Notes files should now reside on the Notes server's hard drive. Proceed as follows:

1. Start the Notes user interface. This is the Notes client workstation on the Notes server machine itself.

2. The Notes server setup screen appears (see Figure 7-4). Click on **The first Lotus Notes server in your organization** and then click **OK**.

Tips

If this is an additional Notes server within your organization, then click **An additional Lotus Notes server in your organization.** *For an additional Notes server, some of the following procedures will be slightly different. Also, the Notes server ID for an additional Notes server must be created before setting up the Notes server and should not be stored in the public Name and Address book for security reasons.*

Figure 7-4

Lotus Notes
Server Setup Screen

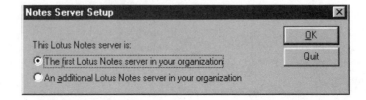

3. The First Server Setup screen appears, as shown in Figure 7-5.

Figure 7-5

Lotus Notes First
Server Setup Screen

First Server Setup	
Server name (e.g. Acme Server1):	OK
Chicago-Notes01	Quit
Organization name (e.g. Acme Corp):	
ACME	Advanced Options...
Administrator's last name: First name: MI:	
Thoams Scott	
Administration password (case sensitive):	
password	
Network type: Serial port:	
TCP/IP (None) Setup...	
Modem type:	
. Auto Configure (for unlisted modems, only) Script...	
☐ Server is also administrator's personal workstation	

Configure the following fields:

- **Server Name:** Enter the name of the Notes server. Guidelines for Notes server names are explained in detail in Chapter 4, *Naming Standards*.

- **Organization name:** Enter the name of the organization. This will be the name of the top-level hierarchy in a fully distinguished name. Guidelines for the Notes hierarchical naming standards are explained in detail in Chapter 4. The company's Organizational level certifier will be created from this name.

- **Administrator's last name:** Enter the last name of the Notes administrator. Guidelines for the Notes user names are explained in detail in Chapter 4.

- **First name:** Enter the first name of the Notes administrator.

- **MI:** If middle initials are going to be used, enter the middle initial of the Notes administrator. As explained in Chapter 4, most companies should not use middle initials unless necessary.

- **Administration password:** Enter the password for the Notes administrator's user ID file and certifier ID file. The Notes administrator's ID file will be created from the entries in the last name, first name, and MI fields.

Is this the password for the server-id or administrator's user-id?

Tips

We recommend you not assign a password to the Notes server ID file. One may be assigned after the Notes server is configured. However, most organizations choose not to assign a Notes ID password to the Notes server ID file as the Notes server will not automatically start without the password being entered. Also, any Notes API programs will prompted for the Notes server password if one is applied to the server ID file. Once a password to a server ID is assigned it cannot be removed! A new server ID would have to be created without a password, which would cause problems to existing users and servers when encryption is used.

IMPORTANT

- **Network type:** Enter the network protocol that will be used on this Notes server. Additional protocols may be added once the server is installed.

- **Serial port:** Enter the serial port, if any, that this Notes server will be using. Additional serial ports may be installed once the server is installed.

- **Modem type:** Enter the modem type attached to the serial port.

4. Once the above fields are set, click the **Advanced Options**-button. The screen shown in Figure 7-6 appears:

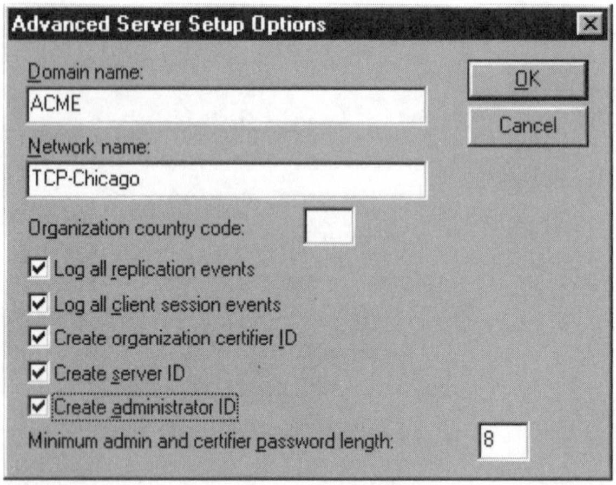

Figure 7-6

Lotus Notes
Advanced Server
Setup Options

Configure the following fields:

- **Domain Name:** Enter the domain of the Notes server. This is usually the company's name and normally matches the name of the organization certifier. For discussion on domain naming standards, consult Chapter 4, *Naming Standards*.

- **Network Name:** This is the name of the Notes named network the Notes server will belong to. Again for naming standards for Notes named networks, consult Chapter 4.

- **Organization country code:** This is an optional field that represents the country code for a hierarchically named server. Most companies do not use this field. For a more detail explanation of country codes, consult Chapter 4.

- **Log all replication events:** This check box will enable all replication events to be logged to the Notes log on the Notes server. This option may be turned on or off later, if desired, once the server has been configured. We recommend that you enable this option to assist in any troubleshooting you may need to perform.

- **Log all client session events:** This check box will enable all Notes client sessions to be logged to the Notes log on the Notes server. This option may be turned on or off later, if desired, once the server has been configured. We recommend that you enable this option to assist in any troubleshooting you may need to perform.

- **Create organization certifier ID:** Click this box so that the company's organizational certifier ID file is created. This box should be checked.

- **Create server ID:** Click this box so that the Notes server's ID file is created. This box should be checked.

- **Create administrator ID:** Click this box so that the Notes administrator's ID file is created. This box should be checked.

- **Minimum admin and certifier password length:** Enter the minimum number of characters for the password of the Notes administrator's ID file and certifier ID file.

But which password applies to which file?

5. Once all the above fields are configured, click **OK**. The Notes server (SERVER.ID), certifier (CERT.ID), and Notes administrator's (USER.ID) ID files are created and registered in the public Name and Address Book.

6. Next, you are prompted with the time zone screen (Figure 7-7). Select the proper time zone and Daylight Savings time option and click **OK**.

Figure 7-7

Lotus Notes Server
Time Zone Setup

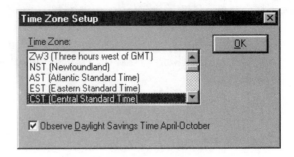

7. The first Notes server is now configured and ready to be run. For installation on Windows NT, the server should be started as a service. For other platforms, the Notes server icon may be used to start the Notes server.

Configure Windows NT Settings

Once the Lotus Notes server code is installed (assuming a Windows NT machine), Notes should be configured as a service so that it starts automatically upon Windows NT boot-up. Enabling Notes as a service allows the administrator to logout from the Windows NT machine, thus locking the NT desktop. Also, Windows NT Registry settings should be configured. To configure Notes as a service on Windows NT as well as proper registry settings, see Chapter 9, *Windows NT Integration*.

Set Security and Server Configurations

Before the Notes server is brought into production, not all Notes and Web users should be allowed access to the Notes server. Initially, security should be set on the newly registered server in the server document of the public Name and Address book to prevent people from gaining access once the newly created server comes on-line. It is a good idea to grant access just to the Notes administrators while testing and configuring the server. The fields to be set can be found in Chapter 6, *Public Name and Address Book Forms and Views* within the server document section. Once the Notes server is approved for production, the temporary restrictions can be lifted.

Depending on the class of Notes server, certain users will not need to access all servers. For example, Notes users should never have to access a hub or gateway server, and restrictions should be set to prevent this. Notes agent and *http* restrictions (if installed) need to be set as well. Proper groups should also be set to the proper fields; for example e.g. the Server Administration field should be filled with the company's Notes Administration group. Again, complete descriptions of the Notes server document can be found in Chapter 6.

All administration databases should be configured and proper ACL settings set. This includes the public Name and Address book, Notes log, administrations request database, statistics and reporting database(s), certification log, and mail router box.

Set Protocols, Modems, and other Server Settings

Once the server code is installed, configurations such as additional protocols, other modem(s), domain configurations, and other settings can be set. Most of the settings are either per the naming standards already defined, or dependent upon the administrator's desires (such as logging replication and client activity to the Notes log).

Configure the Necessary Connection Records

Once the Notes server is running, you can configure connection records to other Notes servers from the Notes administrator's workstation if the need exists. Necessary connection records include replication and mail routing (mail routing connections only if outside of local Notes named network) which have to be created in the public Name and Address book. Discussion on replication can be found in Chapter 10, *Replication.* Electronic mail can be found in Chapter 11, *Electronic Mail.*

Test Connectivity

Once the Notes server is on-line and configured properly, connectivity via the different network protocols and COM ports (if direct remote access is needed) should be tested. Testing should be done from several Notes workstations and/or Web browsers on different physical networks if applicable. Security concerns should be tested as well as any connection records to other Notes servers, if applicable.

Bring the Server into Production

Once the above issues have been addressed, the server is ready to enter production. Temporary security restrictions can now be lifted and the proper users can be allowed access to the Notes servers. Mail and Application servers are normally set for access by all users. Hub, Backup, and Gateway servers are normally set for access only by other Notes servers and administrators.

Fine-tuning may also be necessary, depending on the type of access and server loads the Notes server encounters. Notes administrators should monitor Notes logs and statistics databases to guarantee optimal performance. For example, if the server is a mail server, it may need to be configured for optimal performance for mail routing. Such a configuration item would include multiple mail threads if deemed necessary, based on the mail traffic encountered from viewing Notes logs. The public Name and Address book in version 4 of Lotus Notes now enables administrators to edit these settings without having to do them at each server console. See Chapter 8, *Administration Issues* for discussion on how to fine-tune Notes servers.

Client Installation Guidelines

The two main obstacles that surface when deploying and installing Notes clients' enterprise-wide deal with logistics and end-user education. The process of installing Notes on a workstation is not difficult. The problem lies in the amount of time required rolling out Notes for the first time to hundreds and sometimes thousands of PCs; this can be overwhelming. Also, most end users will not be familiar with how to use Lotus Notes. If, for example, the user is used to using another mail package such as cc:Mail, the problem of converting the user to the new platform will require even more effort, both from the administrator's and end user's standpoint.

The task of deploying the Notes workstation code to the individuals' workstations can be accomplished in a number of ways. Some methods are quicker than others but ignore many of the training issues that normally come back to haunt administrators. In many rollouts it actually ends up taking more time rolling out Notes to the users with no accompanied education than if a proper training procedure was put into place from the start. Without end user training, help desk calls surface and eat up much of the Notes administrators' time.

New Notes Client Installs

One method of deploying Notes surrounds the situation on a new install on a new, clean PC. Many organizations include Lotus Notes as part of the Windows or Windows NT image that is downloaded to each PC. In that way, the administrator only needs to visit each PC to configure Notes and copy the person's user ID file to the local machine.

Pull Notes Client Installs

Another type of method(s) is a push or pull installation from a network directory executed from the system file and login script. These types of installations involve a programmer to code a program using utilities such as WinInstall or WinBatch. This automates much of the procedure for the end-user. Although aimed at reducing administration overhead, many times these types of installations are not worth the time to program and deploy, especially in environments where there is not a corporate desktop standard. The issue of user IDs still requires intervention, as passwords can not be automated.

Software Distribution Notes Client Installs

With Notes version 4.5, other software distribution utilities may be used, such as Intel LANDesk, Microsoft SMS, and Tivoli. Information can be obtained from the respective companies as to what level they support for Notes. Most organizations are in the process of getting to a software distribution platform and are not ready to deploy

Notes in this manner. Also, company mail migration from cc:Mail to Notes mail may further inhibit this method.

Automated Notes Client Installs

If you install Notes clients from a shared directory on a network file server, the Notes response file can be edited to automate most of the installation procedures as well. This file is found in the installation directory of Lotus Notes. In the Windows environment, this is the **AUTONOT.RSP** file. For Windows 95 and Windows NT, this file is called **INSTNOT.RSP** file. Other platforms are not supported with this option. The response file can be edited to select which options you want installed. The **/A** switch should be used to automate the install. The **INSTNOT.RSP** file should follow the switch to specify the location of the response file. The format should look like the following:

```
\NOTES\INSTALL.EXE /A INSTNOT.RSP
```

The file is documented so that installable options can easily be set.

Scheduled Notes Client Installs

Another method of installing Notes to the corporate desktop involves a scheduled install or upgrade, where administrators visit each workstation and install Notes for the end user. This is usually the method of choice, as it reduces the number of potential help desk calls due to unforeseen problems.

Scheduled Notes Client Installs with End User Education

The final and preferred approach of Notes client deployment uses the above procedure of visiting each desktop, combined with a short end-user training session. Individuals sign up to have Notes installed on their desktop. While the installation is taking place, the end user attends a short (1 to 2 hour) training session on how to use Lotus Notes, specifically tailored to the organization's environment. The session can be taught by someone internal to the organization who is familiar with Lotus Notes, or someone from an outside educational firm—with the assumption that the firm takes some time to understand the Notes environment at the organization and customizes the materials accordingly. It is very important that users know how to use Notes mail if a conversion will be performed from another e-mail package. A few Notes applications within the organization's Notes infrastructure should be addressed in this session as well. Simple 1-page "cheat sheets" handed out with the high level issues also prove beneficial in these types of sessions

Notes Client Installation Steps

To perform a non-automated Notes client install on a Windows machine (assuming a 32-bit version), take the following steps. You may install the Notes client directly from the Domino CD or from a shared directory on a network drive where the Notes installation files have been copied. To begin the installation for a Windows Intel machine:

Notes

An automated install using the INSTNOT.RSP file may be used to automate these installation steps.

1. Run the program **Install.exe** which is located in the **\W32INTEL\INSTALL** directory.

2. Click **I AGREE** once you have reviewed and agreed to the Domino Software License Agreement.

3. Type in your name and your company name within the proper fields. Do not check the **Install on File Server** box. The check box entry is only used initially by a Notes administrator if you wish to install the Notes program files for use by Notes workstations to share the program files. Once completed, click **Next**. You will be prompted to verify the names. Click **Yes** if satisfied.

   Maybe we want this? Bandwidth?

4. You will now see the Install Options screen as shown in Figure 7-1, earlier in this chapter. Within the Notes Program Folder field, enter the directory where you wish to install the Notes client code and the Notes client data files. You may browse your local drives in order to choose a location by clicking the appropriate **Browse** button.

We recommend that you install the Notes workstation code and Notes workstation data files in separate directories. This reduces the complexity of administration, as data files are easily located on the machine. The normal defaults are **\NOTES** *for the Notes workstation files and* **\NOTES\DATA** *for the Notes workstation data files.*

The Notes program files can be run from a shared directory if desired, but if disk space on the local Notes client machine is not an issue, then we recommend you install the Notes program files on the local machine.

The three choices for installs are:

- **Standard Install:** This option is for Notes workstation installs only and should be selected.

- **Server Install:** This is the standard Notes server install option (should not be selected for a workstation install).

- **Customize features:** This option lets you install only the features you select.

5. Click **Next** once you have selected your choice.

6. If you selected the **Customize features** install, select the features you wish. Click **Next** when finished.

7. Next, you are prompted for the program folder destination. Select the destination and click **Next**.

8. You are prompted to begin copying the source files to your hard drive. All other programs should be closed. Click **Yes** to begin the copying.

9. When all files are copied, click **Done** to exit the install process.

Notes Server Advanced Services

The release of Domino (Notes) 4.5, contains two new services to help ease server loads and numbers. They are *Notes clustering* and *partitioning*.

Notes clustering provides load balancing and failover for up to six Notes servers. Real-time replication ensures that applications hosted on servers in a cluster remain synchronized. Load balancing enables administrators to define a particular threshold which, when exceeded, automatically passes new sessions on to another server in the cluster with more resources at its disposal. Notes clustering also provides failover, which ensures that in the event that a Domino server fails (whether due to a hardware or software problem), users accessing that server are seamlessly switched to the same application on another server in the cluster.

Partitioned servers let administrators run several logical Notes servers on one physical machine. This is especially advantageous when using a Domino server for HTTP applications. It stems from the technology used at public Notes networks, such as AT&T Network Notes, CompuServe, and Telstra. Partitioned servers for most organizations probably will not be very useful, as partitioning is aimed at companies (primarily ISPs) interested in hosting several Notes servers for other companies.

Also included in advanced services is Notes billing. Notes billing enables a Notes server to track different types of billing classes. Reports are then generated to a Notes billing application. This functionality is useful for implementing chargebacks within an organization.

Partitioning Notes Servers

Partitioned Notes servers can be installed on the Windows NT or UNIX platforms. It requires a Notes advanced server license and enables you to run several Notes servers on a single machine, providing scalability in the event that multiple physical machines are not available or desired. Partitioned servers are used extensively on the

Internet to provide shared slices of a machine for ISP customers. Notes security is employed on each virtual Notes server so that each can be its own separate domain if necessary.

If one partitioned Notes server fails or is shut down, it will not affect the other Notes servers running on that physical machine.

To install partitioned Notes servers on a single physical machine, the Notes administrator simply installs subsequent Notes installs in separate data directories. Each Notes server will then access these unique data directories and separate **NOTES.INI** files.

There are some important items that must be addressed when configuring partitioned Notes servers. The first is restricting the number of active users per server. The **Server_MaxUsers** setting within the **NOTES.INI** file must be set to limit the number of active users. This number is hardware dependent and also is associated with the total number of partitioned servers running on the machine. Notes logs as well as Notes server performance should be monitored to effectively set this number.

For partitioned Notes servers, the maximum number of concurrent transactions must be set so that the sum of all transactions on all Notes servers running on the physical machine not exceed 20. For example, if your organization is running 4 Notes servers on a single machine, each server should set the **NOTES.INI** variable **Server_Max_Concurrent_Trans** to **5**.

If the TCP/IP protocol is used, each server must use a unique IP address or port number. Unique IP addresses can be assigned to separate network cards in the machine, or to a single network card. If unique IP addresses will be used, then the **NOTES.INI** file of each partitioned server must have the **TCPIP_TcpIpAddress** entry added. An example would be:

```
TCPIP_TcpIpAddress=0,192.23.23.17:1352
```

where TCPIP is the port name, 192.23.23.17 is the IP address of the Notes server, and 1352 is the port number.

Traps

If the same IP address is used for all partitioned Notes servers with separate port numbers, you must assign one Notes server to be the port listening server. If this Notes server goes down, the other partitioned Notes servers will be inaccessible.

Each Notes server's **NOTES.INI** files must be configured to use the same TCP/IP address with multiple port numbers.

The listening port Notes server's **NOTES.INI** file must contain the following entries if there are a total of 3 partitioned Notes servers:

```
TCPIP_TcpIpAddress=0,192.23.23.17:1352
TCPIP_PortMapping00=CN=Server2/O=Org2,192.23.23.17:13520
TCPIP_PortMapping00=CN=Server3/O=Org3,192.23.23.17:13521
```

The second Notes server's **NOTES.INI** file will have the following entry:

```
TCPIP_TcpIpAddress=0,192.23.23.17:13520
```

The third Notes server's **NOTES.INI** file will have the following entry:

```
TCPIP_TcpIpAddress=0,192.23.23.17:13521
```

Notes Clustering

Notes clustering enables a Notes administrator to cluster up to 6 Notes servers in the same Notes domain to provide load balancing and redundancy. If a Notes server were to crash, the clustering capabilities would continue to work without interruption. Also, if a single Notes server becomes overburdened, clustering automatically re-routes users to a less taxed Notes server.

Notes clustering is quite different from Microsoft's, Novell's, or Digital Alpha's NOS clustering. A mix of hardware types can be supported in a Notes cluster.

The key to clustering is to create replicas of key Notes applications on each cluster server to provide real-time replication between the applications. The Notes clustering process then monitors and provides real-time replication.

Considerations that must be reviewed before setting up a Notes cluster include the following:

- All Notes servers must have a Lotus Notes version 4.5 Advanced Server license and all workstations must be at least version 4. All other types of clients cannot take advantage of the failover process.

- All Notes servers within a Notes cluster must be running a network protocol in common and the network link between them must be of high bandwidth. They also must all be in the same Notes domain.

- A Notes server may only be a member of a single Notes cluster.

Notes servers within a cluster are created and edited from within the public Name and Address book. Notes clustering also depends on the administration process of each Notes server.

To add a Notes server to the cluster, perform the following steps:

1. Open the public Name and Address book.

2. Enter the **Server\Servers** view.

3. Select the Notes servers you wish to add to the Notes cluster.

4. Click the **Add to Cluster** button.

5. You will then be prompted to add the Notes server(s) to an existing cluster or create a new Notes cluster.

Once the above steps are completed, the following items occur:

- The cluster database directory manager task (CLDBDIR) is started and added to the **ServerTasks** setting within the **NOTES.INI** file on the Notes server(s).

- The cluster replicator task (CLREPL) is started and added to the **ServerTasks** setting within the **NOTES.INI** file on the Notes server(s).

- The cluster database directory (CLDBDIR.NSF) is created and any databases residing on the Notes server(s) are added.

- The **Show Cluster** server console command is enabled.

All load balancing is based upon **NOTES.INI** settings of the Notes servers. These settings include:

- **Server_Availability_Threshold:** Use this setting to specify the level of workload before redirecting to another Notes server. This threshold is calculated every minute. If a redirection occurs, it is recorded to the Notes log.

- **Server_MaxUsers:** Use this setting to determine the maximum number of users for the Notes server before directing to another Notes server. In the event of redirection, it is recorded to the Notes log.

- **Server_Restricted:** Use this setting to prevent users from accessing Notes applications on a specific server. In the event of redirection, it is recorded to the Notes log.

If failover ever occurs in the event of a downed Notes server, it is recorded in the Notes log.

The cluster database directory application (CLDBDIR.NSF) shows all databases that will be replicated in real-time between Notes servers within a Notes cluster. The database also enables a Notes administrator to enable access to Note applications on each Notes server in the cluster. Once Notes clustering is enabled, it is from this database that clustering is controlled. A replica copy of this application, along with any other applications that will be replicated within the cluster, must exist on every Notes server in the cluster.

Tips

Attention should be paid as to what Notes applications will be replicated in real-time between Notes servers within a Notes cluster. Notes applications such as Notes logs that are not considered business critical should not be set, as this will only cause additional overhead to the cluster.

Notes Billing Services

Notes billing may be enabled on a Notes server by loading the **billing** task from the Notes server console. This task may also be added to the **NOTES.INI** file setting **ServerTasks** to enable this program to load automatically upon server startup. The following classes are available which will be reported to the billing Notes application (BILLING.NSF):

- **Session.** This tracks when a user or server reads or writes to a Notes application, and the start and end time of the transactions.

- **Database.** This class tracks when Notes applications are opened and closed and how long they were open.

- **Document.** This class tracks all read and write activity for specified Notes documents.

- **Replication.** This class tracks replication events that are initiated by the billing server to other Notes servers and clients.

- **Mail.** This class tracks all Notes mail messages that the billing server transfers to other Notes servers.

- **Agent.** This class tracks the time elapsed when a user or server runs an agent on the billing server.

Notes Server Placement

This section discusses different methods of placing Notes servers within your environment. These approaches assume that a corporate wide area network (WAN) is in place and is accessible to both Notes servers and clients. For smaller Notes installations, this section will not be applicable. Two approaches will be considered, mostly based on the availability and the comfort level of an organization's WAN environment.

Lotus claims a version 4.5 Notes (Domino) server will now support up to 2000 concurrent users per server. Keep in mind that this machine must be running Windows NT or UNIX, have multiple processors, and plenty of RAM. It probably would not be wise for organizations to try to expect to house 2000 mail users per server. Half that number might be feasible, assuming the machine has the necessary horsepower.

Centralized Notes Server Approach

Centralizing the Notes servers takes a glass house approach where all the Notes users within the company access the Notes servers from a central location across the WAN. For this to happen, a comfort level of the availability and reliability of the company's WAN must be reached. If the WAN were to fail, users would not be able to access their mail or Notes applications. TCP/IP would have to be deployed to all workstations and DNS would need to be established. It is not recommended to use the SPX protocol across the WAN for Notes access.

Proper bandwidth must exist to remote locations for users to efficiently access Notes. Requirements do not have to be very extensive, as users would only be accessing data periodically. Considerations should be weighed in terms of the number of users per location verses the pipe speed (bandwidth) to that location. For example, a 56KB pipe would be more than enough to support a handful of Notes users, but what must be weighed is that amount of other traffic already being used by that pipe. The average Notes user will probably check mail 3 times a day, so spikes can be expected in the morning, after lunch, and at the end of the day. What also must be considered is if the Notes users are accessing mail as well as Notes applications, the bandwidth demands will grow. All in all, Notes is not a very WAN-intensive application; data is only passed as needed. Pages are gathered, giving the user a full screen of data to read and edit. Only when the Notes user requests another page does another network request proceed.

Notes traffic on the WAN will generally not put a significant burden on most remote sites. However, locations with larger numbers of Notes users will probably want to consider a WAN bandwidth increase. The number and size of Notes applications are also factors in the pipe speeds to remote locations. The bandwidth requirements are dynamic as the Notes infrastructure grows, and should be monitored daily and reacted to as needs change.

The centralized approach has these advantages:

- Less administration, as administrators have all servers in one location.

- Remote Notes servers would not exist and remote administrators would not be necessary.

- If there is a problem, Notes servers are easily accessible.

- Very few Notes connection documents are needed (very little replication—data is more up to date)

- No analog connections to remote servers.

Some disadvantages of this approach:

- If Notes server maintenance or problems arise, the number of affected Notes users is high.

- If the WAN fails, users will be unable to access the Notes network.

- Bandwidth requirements may need to be increased to remote locations.

- A large number of centrally located dial-in lines must be administered for remote Notes access.

Distributed Notes Server Approach

The distributed approach places Notes servers in each or your company's locations replicating back to a central Notes hub server. This is the approach most organizations take and exploits the greatest strength of Notes, which is its replication engine.

Some advantages to the distributed approach are:

- Local Notes server access is not affected by WAN outages.

- Bandwidth to remote sites does not need to be increased.

- Remote dial-in is at local servers.

- There is no WAN overhead for end user access.

- It provides greater room for growth in all locations. As more Notes applications and mail users are added, the Notes servers are able to accommodate them very easily, as opposed to a centralized approach where server loads are much greater.

Some disadvantages to the distributed approach are:

- Greater administration of Notes servers, including database distribution and server maintenance.

- More Notes servers to monitor.

- Slower to identify problems.

As mentioned before, most organizations architect Lotus Notes in a distributed approach or a hybrid of a distributed approach. Lotus Notes was designed from its core centering on replication. This collaborative data distribution is Notes' greatest strength. Although this distributive Notes server approach requires more administration, it is the preferred method of most Notes shops, especially when considering a WAN environment and its accompanying bandwidth issues.

Chapter 8

Administration Issues

Within this chapter we focus on the issues that face Notes administrators on a daily basis. This includes the monitoring of your Notes infrastructure using the different administration tools, upgrading Notes components, as well as creating and maintaining Notes ID files.

Notes ID Files

Notes ID files are one of the most important items within a Notes infrastructure. Without these files, a Notes user or server cannot operate. There are three types of Notes ID files: server, user, and certifier ID files. A certifier ID file is used to create new Notes user and server ID files. A certifier ID file is also used to cross-certify existing server, user, or certifier files of other organizations to allow authentication to your Notes environment. The following sections explain how to create new ID files.

Creating User ID Files

A Notes user ID file consists of six components:

- **User Name.** This is the name of the Notes user.

- **Notes License Number.** This license number assures that the ID is a legitimate North American or International ID file. It cannot be changed once created.

- **Public and Private Keys.** These keys are used for various security measures, such as authenticating with a Notes server. During authentication, a challenge-response sequence is initiated between the Notes client and Notes server. Every Notes user's public key within a single domain is also stored within the public Name and Address book. With this public key, a challenge is composed that only the User ID file with the appropriate private key may unlock. If not completed properly, authentication with the Notes server fails. This public-private key authentication is based upon public key cryptography licensed from RSA.

- **Encryption Keys.** If any Notes administrator or Notes developer creates a key to encrypt certain fields within a Notes application, that encryption key is stored within the user's ID file.

- **Certificate(s).** An ID file must contain at least one certificate. For hierarchical user ID files, an ID file may only contain one hierarchical certificate. Cross-certification is needed to access other hierarchical organizations. However, an ID file may contain several flat certificates.

- **Password.** The password for a user ID is stored within the ID file as well. It is not stored on the Notes server.

The user ID file for the Notes administrator is automatically created when the first Notes server within your company is created. In order to set up additional users on Notes, you must first register those new Notes users. The person registering new users must have at least AUTHOR access with the UserCreator role assigned. If you and the new Notes users are defined in a Windows NT domain, you can replicate the new Notes users from the Windows NT User Manager program. You may also choose to create new Windows NT users from Lotus Notes. For details on integrating and synchronizing users between Lotus Notes and Windows NT, refer to Chapter 9, *Windows NT Integration*.

Registering a new person will create a person document within the public Name and Address book, the user's ID file, and create the user's mail file (if so desired). To register new Notes client users, follow the steps detailed below. We will discuss how to register non-Notes client users (browser users) in Chapter 13, *Internet and Web Application Servers*.

1. From the Notes administrator's Notes user workstation, click **File**, **Tools**, **Server Administration**.

2. Click the **People** icon, and choose **Register Person**. Click **Yes** to indicate you have purchased the required Notes ID license for the person.

3. Type in the password for the Notes certifier ID.

4. The Register Person dialog box, shown in Figure 8-1, will appear:

Figure 8-1
Register Person
Dialog Box

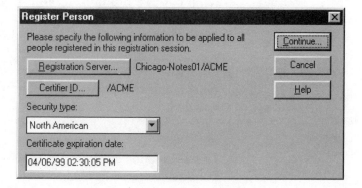

The following options need to be configured:

- **Registration Server:** Select the Notes server in which to register the Notes user(s).

Traps

If the registration server is different from the home (mail) server of the user, then the user(s) will not be able to be set up until the registration server replicates with the user(s) home Notes server.

- **Certifier ID:** Select the certifier ID file to register the person. If a hierarchical certificate is used, this is the level in the tree where the user will be registered.

- **Security Type:** Select either the North American or International ID file type.

- **Certificate expiration date:** Select the expiration date of the certificate for the user ID file(s). The default is two years.

- **Add NT User Account(s)** (Optional): If your machine is running Windows NT and the users are also authenticating with a Windows NT domain, enable this option to create the user within the Windows NT domain as well. See Chapter 9, *Windows NT Integration* for more detail.

5. When you're finished with configuration, click **Continue** when finished.

6. The user name specifics for registering a person will appear in the Basics dialog box (Figure 8-2):

Figure 8-2

User Name Basics
Dialog Box

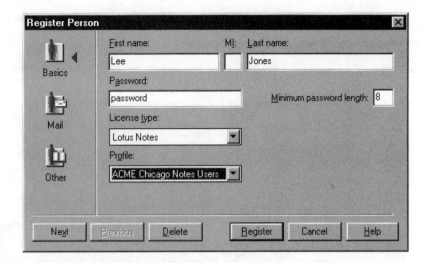

Configure the following fields:

● **First, MI, and Last Name:** Enter the user's first and last name. Only use the middle initial if necessary (See Chapter 4, *Naming Conventions,* for more details on the use of middle initials).

● **Password:** Enter the password for the user. It may be changed by the user once his or her Notes desktop is configured. The password is case sensitive.

● **License Type:** Select the Notes license type for the user. This can be Lotus Notes, Lotus Notes Desktop, or Lotus Notes Mail.

● **Profile:** Enter the profile, if any, for the user. The profile can be configured by the Notes administrator so that when a Notes user is first created, some of the user's information is automatically set. This could include database icons for the user's desktop, Notes server phone numbers, and Internet browser settings. For a greater description of profiles, see Chapter 6, *Public Name and Address Book Forms and Views.*

● **Minimum password length:** Enter the minimum character length for the Notes user's password. We recommend that you use a minimum password length of 8. A Notes password cannot be cleared if a length is set. For a more detailed discussion of pass-word lengths, see Chapter 12, *Notes Application and Security Issues.*

7. Click the **Mail** icon. The Mail dialog box will appear, as shown in Figure 8-3:

Figure 8-3
User Name Basics
Dialog Box

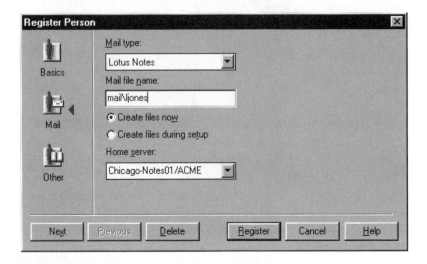

Configure the following fields:

- **Mail type:** Select the user's appropriate e-mail program, or none for no mail or mail not dependent on a Notes server.

- **Mail file name:** Enter the path relative to the Notes data directory and filename of the user's mail file.

- **Create files ...** Select whether or not to create the user's mail file now or when the user is set up.

Tips

If the "Create files during setup option" is selected, it speeds the user registration process.

- **Home Server:** Enter the name of the server that will store the user's mail file.

Traps

Many Notes administrators forget to change this selection to the appropriate server. If this setting is left as LOCAL, the newly registered user will not be able to receive any e-mail.

8. Click the **Other** icon. The Other dialog box, shown in Figure 8-4, appears:

Figure 8-4
User Name Other
Dialog Box

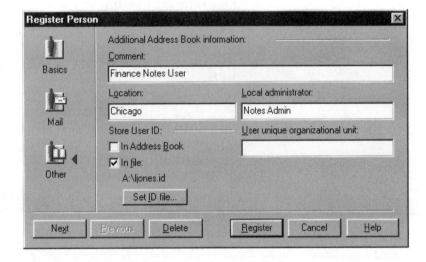

Configure the following fields:

● **Comment** (Optional): Enter a comment about the Notes user.

● **Location** (Optional): Enter a location for the user.

● **Store User ID:** Select whether or not to store the User's ID file in the public Name and Address book and/or on a floppy or network drive.

If the ID file is stored within the public Name and Address book and the user has AUTHOR access to the public Name and Address book (default), then the ID file will be removed from his or her person record and copied to the desktop of the machine where Notes is installed.

If you choose to create the ID file to a floppy or network drive, click the **Set ID File** button to change the target location of the file, if necessary.

Traps

It is highly recommended that you not store the ID file within the public Name and Address book for security reasons. If another user opens the public Name and Address book, they can detach the newly created user's ID file. They can then gain access to Notes information under the new person's identity if the password for the newly created ID file is known.

- **Local administrator** (Optional): Enter the local administrator's name.

- **User unique organizational unit** (Optional): Enter a unique organizational unit for user's within the same Notes hierarchy with the same user name. This field is rarely used—using a middle initial to distinguish users with the same name in the same hierarchy is preferred. See Chapter 4, *Naming Standards* for more details.

9. (Optional) Click **Next** to continue to register other Notes users: repeat the above steps for these users.

10. Click **Register** when you are ready to register the user(s).

You may also register persons from a text file. To do so, you must first create a text file with the following format:

```
Lastname;Firstname;MiddleInitial;organizationalunit;
password;Idfiledirectory;IDfilename;homeservername;
mailfiledirecotry;mailfilename;location;commenct;
forwarding address;profile name; local administrator
```

The file should contain one user per line.

Once the file is created:

1. Click **File, Tools, Server Administration.**

2. Click the **People** icon and select **Register From File.**

3. Follow the instructions on screen.

Creating Server ID Files

Like a Notes user ID, a Notes server ID file consists of up to six components including:

- **Server Name.** The name of the Notes server.

- **Notes License Number.** The license number assuring the ID is a legitimate North American or International ID file. It cannot be changed once created.

- **Public and Private Keys.** These keys are used for various security measures, such as authenticating with a Notes server. During authentication, a challenge-response sequence is initiated between the Notes client and Notes server or between two Notes servers. Every Notes user's and server's public key within a single domain is also stored within the public Name and Address book. With this public key a challenge is composed that only the user or server ID file with the appropriate private key may unlock. If not completed properly, authentication with the target Notes server or user fails. This public-private key authentication is based upon and licensed from RSA.

- **Encryption Keys.** If any Notes administrator or Notes developer creates a key to encrypt certain fields within a Notes application, those keys are stored within the user's ID file.

- **Certificate(s).** An ID file must contain at least one certificate. For hierarchical server ID files, an ID file may only contain one hierarchical certificate. Cross-certification is needed to access other hierarchical organizations. An ID file may contain several flat certificates.

- **Password.** The password for a server ID is stored within the ID file as well. It is not stored within the public Name and Address book on the Notes server.

The Notes server ID file for the first Notes server is automatically created when the first Notes server within your company is created. In order to set up additional Notes servers within your company, you must first register them. When you register a new Notes server, a server record in the public Name and Address book is created, a Notes server ID file is created, and the new Notes server is added to the group **LocalDomainServers**. The person creating a new Notes server must have at least AUTHOR access to the public Name and Address book with the ServerCreater role assigned.

To register a new Notes server, follow these procedures:

1. Click **File**, **Tools**, **Server Administration.**

2. Click the **Servers** icon and select **Register Server.**

3. Click **Yes** once you have agreed you have purchased the necessary license for the new Notes server.

4. Type in the password for the certifier ID file and click **OK**.

5. The registration server dialog box will appear (see Figure 8-5):

Figure 8-5
Register Notes
Server Dialog Box

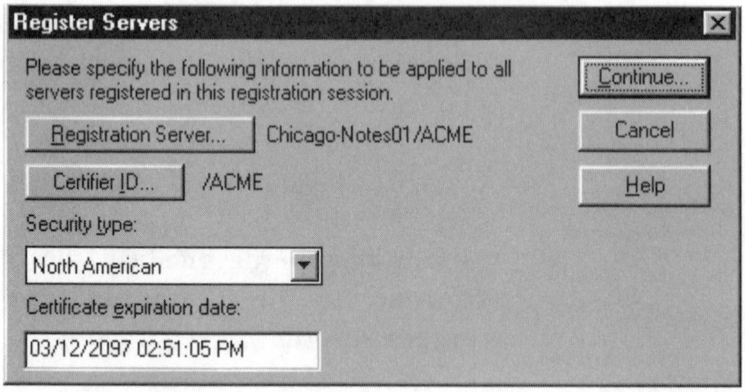

Configure the following fields:

● **Registration Server:** Select the Notes server in which to register the new Notes server.

- **Certifier ID:** Select the certifier ID file to register the server. If a hierarchical certifier is used, this is the level in the tree where the server will be registered.

- **Security Type:** Select either the North American or International ID file type.

- **Certificate expiration date:** Select the expiration date of the certificate for the server ID file. The default is 100 years.

6. Click **Continue** when finished.

7. The Register Server Basics dialog box shown in Figure 8-6, will appear:

Figure 8-6
Register Server
Name Basics
Dialog Box

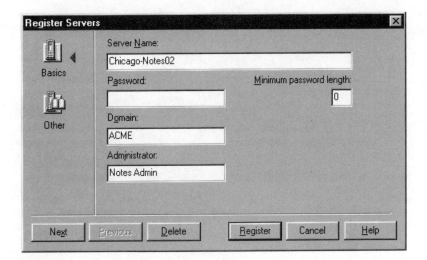

Configure the following fields:

- **Server Name:** Enter the name of the new Notes server.

- **Password:** Enter the password for the Notes server. The password is case sensitive.

Tips

It is recommended that you not use passwords on Notes server ID files. If you do assign a password to a Notes server ID file, you will be prompted to enter the Notes server password each time you restart the server or run a Notes API program.

- **Domain:** Enter the Notes domain where the new Notes server will exist.

- **Administrator:** Enter the Notes name or group that will administer the Notes server.

- **Minimum password length:** Enter the minimum character length of the password for the new Notes server ID file. We recommend that you use a minimum password length of 8. For a more detailed discussion of password lengths, see Chapter 12, *Notes Application and Security Issues*.

8. Click the **Other** icon. The Register Server Other dialog box will appear (See Figure 8-7):

Figure 8-7

Register Server
Name Other
Dialog Box

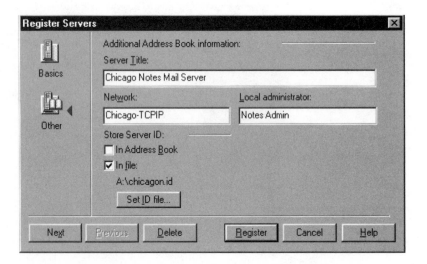

Configure the following fields:

- **Server Title:** Enter the title of the new Notes server. This descriptive title will appear in the server record of the domain's Name and Address book.

- **Network:** Enter the Notes named network to which this new Notes server belongs. See Chapter 6, *Public Name and Address Book Domain Structures,* for more details.

- **Local administrator:** Enter the Notes name or group that will administer this Notes server.

- **Store Server ID:** Select whether or not to store the new server's ID file in the public Name and Address book and/or on a floppy or network drive.

  If the server ID file is stored within the public Name and Address book, the ID file will be removed from server record and copied to the machine when the new Notes server is configured.

  If you choose to create the ID file to a floppy or network drive, then click the **Set ID File** button to change the target location of the file, if necessary.

Traps

We highly recommend against storing the ID file within the public Name and Address book for security reasons. If another user opens the public Name and Address book and detaches the newly created server ID file, that person can gain access to Notes information under the server identity if the password for the newly created ID file is known or one has not been assigned.

9. (Optional) Click **Next** to continue to register other Notes servers; complete steps 5–8 for these servers.

10. Once you are finished, click **Register** to register the new Notes server(s).

Creating Certifier ID Files

A certifier ID file is used to create new servers and users. For hierarchical ID files, a certifier ID file can also be used to create organizational unit certifiers as well as to certify other company's ID files (cross-certification).

From this definition, you can see the importance of the certifier ID file. Only administrators should have access to this file.

Organization Certifiers

The top level certifier (Organization certifier [O]) for a company is automatically created when the first Notes server is created. Normally, you never need to create another top level organization (O) certifier for your company unless you create one to set up an external Notes firewall domain. To create an organization certifier, follow these procedures:

1. Click **File**, **Tools**, **Server Administration**.

2. Click the **Certifiers** icon and choose **Register Organization.**

3. The Register Organization Certifier screen, shown in Figure 8-8, appears:

Figure 8-8

Register Organization
Certifier Dialog Box

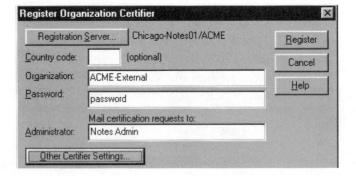

Configure the following fields:

● **Registration Server...** Click the button to change the Notes server in which to register the organization certifier.

● **Country Code** (Optional): Enter the Country Code, if desired, for the organization certifier. Most companies do not use country codes.

● **Organization:** Enter the name of the organization certifier.

● **Password:** Enter the password for the organization certifier. This is case sensitive.

- **Administrator:** Enter the name of the administrator who will handle recertification requests. All requests handled through e-mail will be mailed to this user or group.

Tips

It is useful to set up a group to handle recertification requests, so that one individual does not become bottlenecked by this process.

4. Click the **Other Certifier Settings** Button. The Other Certifier Settings dialog box, shown in Figure 8-9, appears:

Figure 8-9
Other Organization
Certifier Settings
Dialog Box

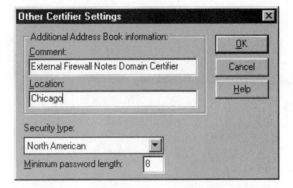

Configure the following fields:

- **Comment** (Optional): Enter a comment about the organization certifier.

- **Location** (Optional): Enter a location for the organization certifier.

- **Security Type:** Choose either the North American or International license type for the certifier.

- **Minimum password length:** Enter the minimum number of characters the password for the certifier. We recommend that you use a minimum password length of 8. For a more detailed discussion of password lengths, see Chapter 12, *Notes Application and Security Issues.*

5. When finished, click **OK** to return to the first screen and then click **Register.** You will be prompted on where to store the new organization certifier ID file.

Organizational Unit Certifiers

For larger companies, you may wish to create organizational unit certifiers to further break down your naming structure hierarchy. Normally, companies do this by department or geographic location. For example:

```
Scott Thomas/Chicago/ACME

Lee Jones/NY/ACME

or

Brad Hoyt/Finance/ACME

Joe User/HR/ACME

or

Scott Thomas/Finance/Chicago/ACME

Brad Hoyt/HR/Chicago/ACME
```

Organization unit certifiers may be created from organization certifiers or from other organizational unit certifiers, creating a hierarchy up to four levels deep. Complete discussions regarding hierarchical naming can be found in Chapter 4, *Naming Standards*.

To create an organization unit (ou) certifier, follow these procedures:

1. Click **File, Tools, Server Administration**.

2. Click the **Certifiers** icon and choose **Register Organization Unit**. Enter the password for the previous certifier if prompted (or click **Cancel**).

3. The Register Organizational Unit Certifier screen will appear
   (Figure 8-10):

Configure the following fields:

● **Registration Server...** Click the button to change the Notes
  server in which to register the organizational unit certifier.

● **Certifier ID:** Click the **Certifier ID** button to change the
  certifier ID file to register the new organizational unit certifier. The certifier ID file will be the parent of the new organizational unit and the level in the tree at which the new organizational unit certifier will appear.

● **Org Unit:** Enter the name of the organizational unit certifier.

● **Password:** Enter the password for the organizational unit
  certifier. This is case sensitive.

● **Administrator:** Enter the name of the administrator or
  group who will handle recertification requests. All requests
  handled through e-mail will be mailed to this user or group.

4. Click the **Other Certifier Settings** button and the Other
   Certifier Settings dialog box, shown in Figure 8-11, appears:

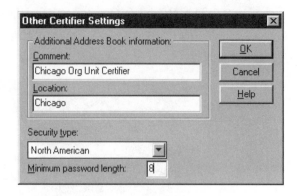

Configure the following fields:

- **Comment** (Optional): Enter a comment about the organization unit certifier.

- **Location** (Optional): Enter a location for the organization unit certifier.

- **Security Type:** Choose either the North American or International license type for the certifier.

- **Minimum password length:** Enter the minimum number of characters the password for the certifier.

5. Click **OK** to return to the previous screen. Click **Register** to register the new organizational unit certifier ID file. You will be prompted as to where to save the new file. Enter the filename and path for the new organizational unit certifier ID file.

Flat Certifiers

Flat names existed exclusively from the earliest version of Notes up through version 2. With the release of version 3.0 of Notes, hierarchical naming was introduced. Flat certifiers and naming conventions are still available with release 4.0 of Notes for backwards compatibility. However, if your company is on a flat Notes naming structure, it is recommended that you convert to a hierarchical naming structure to take advantage of many of the enhancements unavailable in a flat named environment.

A flat certifier may be applied to any hierarchical ID file to enable authentication between a hierarchical and a flat ID file. Obviously, a flat certifier applied to two flat ID files will enable authentication between to the two ID files. It should be noted that a flat certifier applied to two different hierarchical IDs will *not* enable authentication. Only cross-certification will enable authentication in this situation.

To create a flat certifier, follow these procedures:

1. Click **File, Tools, Server Administration.**

2. Click the **Certifiers** icon and choose **Register Non-Hierarchical.**

3. The Create Non-Hierarchical Certifier ID dialog box will appear (see Figure 8-12):

Figure 8-12

Non-Hierarchical Certifier Settings Dialog Box

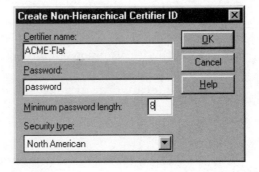

Configure the following fields:

● **Certifier name:** Enter the name of the flat certifier.

● **Password:** Enter the password for the certifier. This is case sensitive.

● **Minimum password length:** Enter the minimum number of characters for the password.

● **Security type:** Select either the North American or International license type.

4. Click **OK** when finished. You will then be prompted to enter the name and location of the ID file.

Converting Flat ID Files to Hierarchical ID Files

With version 4 of Lotus Notes, Notes administrators are now able to convert a user or server ID from a flat naming structure to a hierarchical naming structure. The administration process on a Notes version 4 server handles this conversion.

Before you can actually begin the conversion process to convert a flat ID file to a hierarchical ID file, some preliminary steps must be completed:

- All Notes servers within the infrastructure must be running at least version 4 of Lotus Notes and should be running the administration process.

- A certification log should be created.

- A hierarchical naming standard should be set (see Chapter 4, *Naming Standards*, for details).

Notes

If you have a mixed environment of different versions of Notes servers, any databases on version 3 Notes servers will not have their ACL entries changed, nor any author or reader name fields by the administration process. If you have any Notes version 4 servers that are not yet version 4.5, author and reader name fields will not be renamed by the administration process.

Once these items are in place, you can begin to convert flat ID files to hierarchical ID files.

Tips

You should convert all Notes servers to a hierarchical naming structure before converting any flat users to a hierarchical naming structure.

Flat Server Name to Hierarchical

This procedure assumes that there are both hierarchical and flat Notes servers within the infrastructure. If all Notes servers are of a flat naming structure, then the first Notes server will have to be manually converted to a hierarchical naming structure. Subsequent servers then may follow these steps:

1. Click **File, Tools, Server Administration.**

2. Click the **Servers** icon and select **Servers View.**

3. Select the server document to convert and click **Actions, Upgrade Server** to **Hierarchical.**

4. Select the hierarchical certifier to use and enter the password.

5. Click **Upgrade.**

6. After Notes processes the request, click **OK**. Repeat the above steps for additional flat Notes servers.

Flat User Name to Hierarchical

In order to convert flat user names from flat to hierarchical, the administrator performing the conversion must have at least AUTHOR access to the public Name and Address book with the UserModifier role assigned. The person also must have at least AUTHOR access to the certification log.

1. Make sure all Notes servers have been converted to hierarchical named servers.

2. Open the public Name and Address book within the People view.

3. Select the user(s) that you wish to convert.

4. Click **Actions, Rename Person.**

5.   Click **Upgrade to Hierarchical.**

6.   Select the hierarchical certifier to use and enter the password.

7.   Enter the expiration date for the certificate and click **Upgrade**.

8.   Once Notes processes the request, click **OK.**

Renaming User Names

Renaming user names follows the same procedures as converting a flat user name to a hierarchical user name. To change a user's common name, perform the following steps:

1.   Make sure all Notes servers have been converted to hierarchical named servers.

2.   Open the public Name and Address book within the People view.

3.   Select the user(s) that you wish to convert.

4.   Click **Actions, Rename Person.**

5.   Click **Change Common Name.** Instead, you may also click **Request Move to New Certifier** if you wish to move the user to a different level or position within your hierarchical tree.

6.   Select the hierarchical certifier that was originally used to create the person and enter the password.

7.   For a name change, enter the new user name and click **Rename**. For a move to a new certifier, enter the new certifier name and click **Submit Request.**

8.   Once Notes processes the request, click **OK.**

For moving of users to a different certifier, these additional steps must be followed:

9. Open the Administrations Request database and enter the Name Move Requests View.

10. Click **Actions, Complete Move** for the selected entries.

11. Select the new certifier ID file for the user(s) and enter the password.

12. Click **Certify**.

Notes users may also request a name change manually from their own Notes workstation by performing the following steps (this assumes that Notes mail is being used):

Tips

In order to use the referenced mail functionality, it is necessary to use the Notes mail.

1. Click **File, Tools, User ID.** Enter the password and click **OK.**

2. Click the **More Options** icon.

3. Click the **Request New Name** button.

4. Enter the new common name and click **OK.**

5. Enter the Notes administrator's name within the TO field and click **Send.**

Once the Notes administrator receives the name request change, he or she should perform the following steps:

1. Open the e-mail message containing the name request change.

2. Click **Actions, Certify Attached ID File.**

3. Select the certifier ID file that was used *originally* to create the user and enter its password.

4. Change any of the desired settings (expiration date, password length, registration server) and then click **Certify.**

5. Confirm the name change and click **OK.**

6. An e-mail message will appear sending the ID file back to the person. Click **Send.**

7. The Notes administrator must now manually change any ACL settings of any database to reflect these changes, including the person's mail file.

The Notes user now must perform these final actions:

8. Open the new e-mail message with the name change request.

9. Click **Actions, Accept Certificate.**

The user's name is now changed.

Deleting Notes Users

To remove a Notes user from the Lotus Notes infrastructure, you must delete all Notes ID files, remove the person record from the public Name and Address book, remove their Notes mail file, and remove all entries of the person from group records and ACL entries of Notes applications. This can be done through a manual process, making sure that all steps listed above are accomplished.

Also, with release 4.0 and higher of Lotus Notes servers, the administration process can be used to automate user deletions (the administration process is explained later in this chapter). To delete a Notes user using the administration process, follow these procedures:

1. Open the public Name and Address book on the Lotus Notes server.

2. Choose the **People** view and select the user(s) to delete.

3. Click the **Delete** button and select **Yes** to continue. The dialog box shown in Figure 8-13 appears:

Figure 8-13
Delete User
Dialog Box

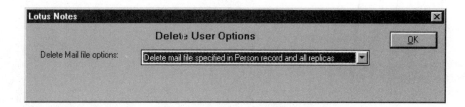

4. Select one the following three options and click **OK**.

● **Delete just the mail file specified in Person record.** This will delete only the mail file(s) for the person(s) specified in the public Name and Address book. Any other replica copies of the user(s) mail file(s) will not be removed.

● **Delete mail file specified in Person record and all replicas.** This will delete all replica copies of the user(s) mail files on all Notes server(s).

● **Don't delete the mail file.** This option will not delete a user(s) mail file.

5. Now select one of these two options:

● **Yes,** to immediately delete all references in the public Name and Address book of the user(s) and database ACL entries.

● **No,** to post a request in the administration database and have the references removed according to the "Interval setting" for the administration process within the server record of the public Name and Address book.

Tips

After a person is deleted, it is recommended that you place the person within a "deny access group" that appears within a Notes server document.

Recertifying ID Files

With release 4 of Lotus Notes, users and servers can be automatically recertified through the administration process. To recertify a Notes ID file, follow these procedures:

1. Click **File, Tools, Server Administration.**

2. Click the **People** icon and choose the People view.

3. Highlight the user(s) you wish to recertify.

4. Click **Actions, Recertify Person.**

5. Select the certifier ID file that was used to originally create the person(s) and enter its password.

6. Click **Certify** once all settings are accepted (expiration date).

A Notes user may request recertification manually through Notes mail by performing the following steps:

1. From his or her workstation, the Notes user clicks **File, Tools, User ID.**

2. Click the **Certificates** icon.

3. Enter the name of the Notes administrator in the **To** field of the e-mail message.

4. Click **Send** and then **Done.**

Once the Notes administrator receives the recertification request, he or she performs the following steps:

1. Open the e-mail message and click **Actions**, **Certify Attached ID File**. Select the certifier ID file to use and enter its password.

2. Click **Certify** and then **Send** once all settings are accepted (expiration date, password length, registration server).

The user then performs the following steps:

1. Open the e-mail message and choose **Actions**, **Accept Certificate**.

2. Enter the password and click **OK.**

The user is now recertified.

Assigning Multiple Passwords to ID Files

In version 4 of Lotus Notes, you are able to assign multiple passwords to ID files. This is especially helpful for certifier ID files, where it can be implemented so that two or more people must enter a separate password for the ID file in order to create a new user, server, or organizational unit certifier. Subsets may also be devised so that only a specific number of the total passwords assigned are needed to access the ID file. For example, the ACME certifier might have three separate passwords for the ID file, but only two of the three passwords are needed to access the ID file. In this manner, no one person is assigned complete authority of an ID file, especially in the case of certifier ID files.

To assign multiple passwords to a user, server, or certifier ID file, follow these procedures:

1. Click **File**, **Tools**, **Server Administration**.

2. Click the **Certifiers** icon and click **Edit Multiple Passwords.**

3. Select the ID file to assign the passwords to. The screen shown in Figure 8-14 appears:

Figure 8-14

Multiple Passwords
Dialog Box

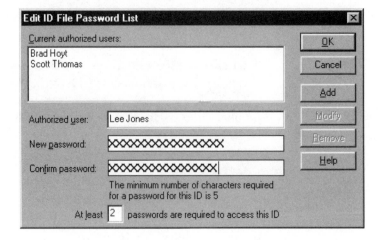

4. Within the Authorized User field, enter one of the user names.

5. Enter that user's password in the New Password field.

6. Retype the password in the Confirm Password field.

7. Click **Add**.

8. Other users need to repeat steps 4–7.

9. Enter the number of passwords required to access this ID file.

Forcing Password Changes on User ID Files

A Notes administrator may force password changes on user ID files with version 4.5 and higher Notes workstations and servers. In order to use this feature, the server document of the Notes server and the person document of the user must be enabled. For details on which fields within the records to enable, refer to Chapter 6, *Public Name and Address Book Forms and Views*.

Tips

In order to force password changes for Notes users, the Notes server must be configured to check passwords of user ID files. This is done by enabling the "check passwords" field in the security section of the server document within the public Name and Address book.

Once the server document of the Notes server has been set to check for Notes ID passwords, the following steps must be performed on the person document of the Notes user:

1. From the public Name and Address book, select the user(s) for whom you wish to enable password checking.

2. Click **Actions**, **Set Password Fields** and then click **Yes** to continue. The following diagram will appear (Figure 8-15):

Figure 8-15
Password Checking
Dialog Box

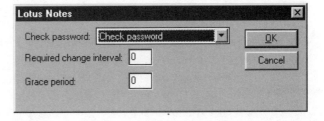

3. Select **Check Password**. (The other setting of **Lockout ID** will not let the user ID logon to the Notes server.)

4. Within the **Required Change Interval** field, enter the number of days after which users are required to change their password. An entry of 0 does not require password changes.

5. Within the **Grace Period** field, enter the number of days a user has to change their password before being locked out of the server.

6) Click **OK**.

Maintaining ID Files

Unlike most other operating systems and mail packages, Lotus Notes uses private/public key encryption. The way Notes handles this process is by storing the individual's private key in the user ID file. Within this file exists the user's name, copies of the user's public and private keys, and password. It is very important that users understand this concept and are familiar with the location of this file. If a user ID file is copied by another user and that second user knows the first person's password, this second person can gain entry to all applications accessible to that user ID even if the first person changes his password on the original ID file. With Notes 4.5, an administrator can force a password change in the user's local user ID file as explained in the previous section.

This same concept holds true for server IDs as well. The ID files contain the server name, password (if required), and public/private keys.

From this discussion, the significance of the user and server ID files can be seen. Keeping a backup of the ID file is a must, especially when encryption is used for mail. If a user loses his or her ID file and it has to be recreated in Notes, the new user ID file obtains a new private and public key. This means any encrypted mail will be unreadable by the new user ID, even if the mail file is accessed at the Notes server. If a user forgets his or her password, the ID file also must be recreated, unless a backup exists containing the original password.

To avoid the above situation, a backup of the user ID file should be made. Organizations handle this in different manners, depending on the security structures in place. The issue that is debated is that if someone else has a copy of another person's user ID file, that second person may gain access to all resources granted to the first user, even if the password has been changed and the documents are encrypted.

Some organizations handle this issue by putting the responsibility on the end user to keep backups of their user ID file. In this manner, administrators or anyone else cannot be blamed for accessing other peoples' data. Many times, though, users do not make backups and administrators are forced to recreate users. Often, the user is unable to read their mail due to encryption.

Other organizations keep user ID files in public directories or worse yet, in the public Name and Address book. These methods should be avoided for obvious reasons. If a person acquires another person's password, or another user simply makes a copy of the file from the public directory or public Name and Address book, he can assume that person's identity.

The preferred method, assuming it follows the security model of the organization, is that after an administrator creates a user, the ID file is copied to a secured directory or Notes database application only accessible to a few administrators. The passwords are reset to the same password for all ID files and only the administrators can access the files in case of emergency or loss by the end user. Another copy is then given to the end user with instructions on changing its password. Administrators can create multiple ID files at the same time from the administration server administration console on the administrator's workstation. The ID files can be created directly into the secure network directory where administrators can copy the files for local client Notes installations.

Most organizations accept the above method, as it eases the burden of administration in the event of loss of the ID file. Most organizations inform end users the mail system and Notes environment is owned by the company and the end-user has no privacy rights and administrators can access their personal information when deemed necessary by management.

How Lotus Notes user ID files are distributed to end users deals directly with how an organization decides to roll out Notes to the client desktops. If administrators install Notes at each desktop directly, which is usually the preferred method, the administrator copies the file from a secured network directory or from a floppy. The administrator should also instruct the end user to change his or her password.

Some organizations have automated scripted installs of Notes. This often causes configuration problems, especially when dealing with the user ID files and passwords, as it is difficult to automate passing the password to the ID file. Also, in environments where machine configurations differ from department to department, automated installations become increasingly difficult to manage.

A certifier ID is one of the most important pieces in the Lotus Notes design model. With the certifier ID, an administrator creates new users and servers. It can be thought of as a "stamper." Each ID must be "stamped" with a certifier ID and each server and user must have a "stamp" in common.

If someone were to get a hold of the certifier ID, this person could create an ID of any name he or she wishes. The intruder then would have all security privileges of the user he or she creates.

The certifier IDs should be kept under lock and key with unique passwords known only by a handful of people. As discussed earlier in the chapter, it is also possible to apply multiple passwords to the certifier ID so that more than one person must be present to create a new user or server. The ID files should not be kept in the Notes server directory; they should be kept on a floppy or secured network directory.

The sharing of user ID files should be discouraged at all times. User IDs and their appropriate access rights are easily defeated by sharing IDs. Sharing IDs as a method of delegating access to personal mail files or other databases should be discouraged as well.

Another key element of security for user ID files is passwords. All user and certifier ID files should be assigned a unique password. It is recommended that passwords be a minimum of 8 characters in length. Password protecting a user ID will not ensure its security, but it will certainly make it more difficult to breach the overall system security.

Since ID files can be freely copied using the operating system copy command, they are susceptible to misappropriation.

Maintenance and Upgrades of Notes Servers and Clients

Notes Server

In order to upgrade a Notes server, it must first be shut down. Many organizations implement scheduled downtime each month for maintenance to Notes servers: it is during this downtime that an upgrade should be performed. A set monthly time should be established; end users should be informed and aware that during this time, Notes will be unavailable.

Tips

It is advisable to restart a Notes server on a scheduled cycle such as a monthly schedule. Some Notes applications —for example, the public Name and Address book, the Notes log, and the Statistics and Reporting database—are always open and will build up deletion stubs. These deletion stubs will not be purged until the Notes server is restarted. As the number of stubs increase, the Notes server gets increasingly slower.

Notes Client

With version 4.0 and higher of Lotus Notes, Notes administrators may now upgrade Notes clients to newer versions through Notes mail. The Notes mail message includes two buttons. The first button shuts down the user's Notes client and performs an upgrade from a shared directory on a file server on the network. The second button then performs an upgrade to the Notes user's mail file.

Before an upgrade message is sent out, the Notes administrator must perform the following steps:

1. Copy the Notes source install directory from the Lotus Notes CD to a shared directory on a file server where all Notes users have access. For Windows 95 and Windows NT client machines, the directory on the Notes CD to copy is

\W32INTEL\INSTALL. Copy all other Notes client platforms that are necessary for each operating system supported in your organization. For example, if your company has Windows and Macintosh machines running the Notes client, you would create separate directories for each platform. On a Windows NT file server, the following directories should be created:

```
\\ACME01\APPS\Notes\WIN32
```

```
\\ACME01\APPS\Notes\Mac
```

2. Grant users the correct access rights in the Windows NT directory so that they may read and execute the files within the above directories.

Once these tasks are completed, a Notes administrator can send a Notes mail message to Notes users in order to perform a Notes client upgrade to their machines. To perform a Notes client upgrade in this manner, the Notes administrator performs the following tasks:

1. Open the public Name and Address book **Mail Users** using the Notes view.

2. Within this view, select the Notes user(s) you wish to upgrade.

3. Once all Notes users are selected, click the **Send Upgrade Notifications** button. The following screen, shown in Figure 8-16, appears:

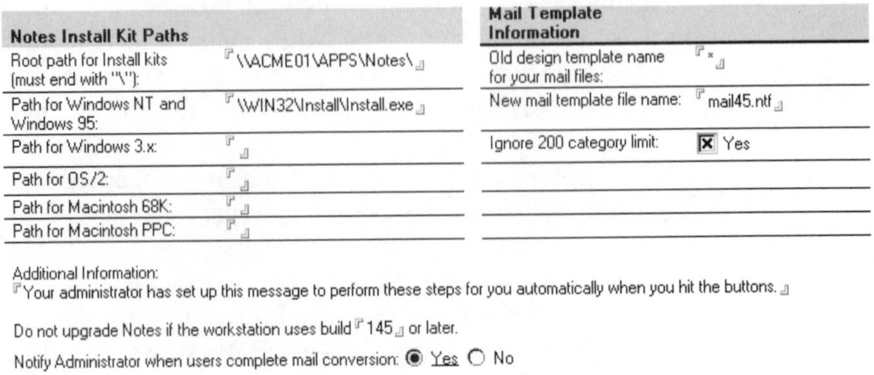

Figure 8-16

Notes Mail Upgrade Notification

Notes Install Kit Paths		Mail Template Information	
Root path for Install kits (must end with "\"):	\\ACME01\APPS\Notes\	Old design template name for your mail files:	x
Path for Windows NT and Windows 95:	\WIN32\Install\Install.exe	New mail template file name:	mail45.ntf
Path for Windows 3.x:		Ignore 200 category limit:	☒ Yes
Path for OS/2:			
Path for Macintosh 68K:			
Path for Macintosh PPC:			

Additional Information:
Your administrator has set up this message to perform these steps for you automatically when you hit the buttons.

Do not upgrade Notes if the workstation uses build 145 or later.

Notify Administrator when users complete mail conversion: ◉ Yes ○ No

4. Within the **TO**: field, enter the recipients of the Notes client upgrade notification.

5. Fill the **Root path for Install kits** field with the path, including server name, of the root of the install kit. Using our above example this would be \\ACME01\APPS\Notes\. It is recommended that you use UNC names for the server and resource; if drive letters are used, some users may not have the same drive mappings. Also, the end of the path statement must end with a "\".

6. Paths and program names for Notes client installs: in each of these fields, enter the path for the client(s) that will be used within your organization. Using our example for Windows 95 and NT users, this would be \WIN32\Install\Install.exe.

7. The **Old design template name for your mail files** field should contain the name of the template that was used for the user's current mail file. An * within this field defaults to **any**.

8. The **New mail template file** name field should include the name of the new mail template. If the default is going to be used within your organization for version 4.5 of Lotus Notes, this field will contain the entry mail45.ntf.

9. The **Ignore 200 category limit** checkbox should be checked if you wish to ignore the 200 category limit within the user's mail file.

10. The **Additional Information** field should contain any additional information you wish the user to see when the message is opened.

11. The **Do not upgrade Notes if the workstation uses build XXX or later** field determines whether or not the specified Notes user's client should be upgraded. If a Notes user's build number of his or her client is less than the specified number, the Notes client will receive the first button that will enable the Notes user to perform an upgrade. A Notes user's build number can be determined by performing the *@Version* function on a Notes user's desktop.

12. The **Notify Administrator when users complete mail conversion** field will notify the Notes administrator when a Notes user's mail file is upgraded.

Once all fields are configured, the Notes administrator e-mails the message to the intended recipients. They open the Notes mail message, and if the Notes user's build number is less than the specified number set by the Notes administrator, the user sees the two buttons.

The Notes user clicks the first button, and the user's Notes client closes. The user's machine then runs the Notes installation program. The user should follow the steps to install the Notes client on his or her machine as defined in Chapter 7, *Installation Guidelines,* making sure to install Notes in the same directory as the older version. The installation program fills the target fields with the current location of Lotus Notes on the user's machine based on settings in the user's NOTES.INI file. Once the upgrade is complete, the Notes user restarts the Notes client.

Once the upgraded Notes client is running, the Notes user enters his or her Notes mail file and opens the original Notes mail message. The Notes user now clicks the second button, which will upgrade the user's Notes mail file based upon the template set by the Notes administrator. When this button is pressed, a background program initiates and the user is prompted for his or her Notes password. Once the password is entered, the user's Notes mail file is upgraded. If the Notes administrator has specified an e-mail alert, a mail message will be sent informing the administrator of the completed upgrade.

This automated procedure can certainly help organizations save time and resources, as it is now possible to upgrade Notes clients without visiting every workstation. However, it should be noted that some sort of warning and possibly training should be offered to users before the Notes mail upgrade notification is sent out.

Traps

The Notes administrator should forewarn Notes users of a Notes upgrade before actually sending out a Notes e-mail upgrade notification. The upgrade notification e-mail requires the users to perform a Notes client installation. For some users, this may prove intimidating. Some training may be necessary.

Changing Lotus Notes License Types

The need may arise to change a Notes user's license type. The three different types available include: Notes Mail, Notes Desktop, and Lotus Notes (refer to Chapter 1, *Lotus Notes in Your Organization* for explanations of each license type). To change a user's Notes license type, perform the following steps:

1. Open the Notes user's person record in the public Name and Address book.

2. Move to the Administration section of the document.

3. Within the Notes client license field, enter the new license type. Figure 8-17 shows this entry:

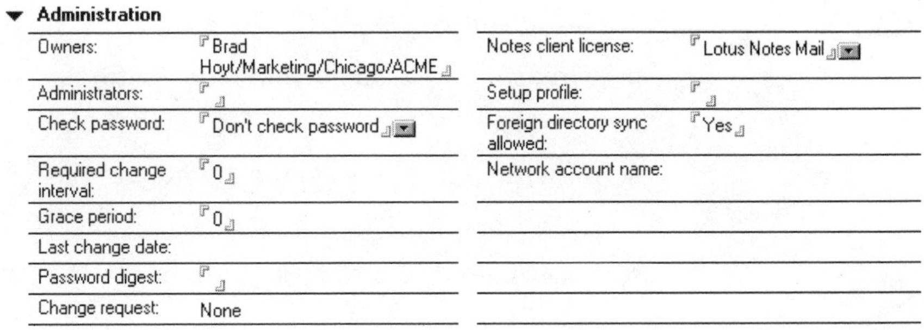

Figure 8-17

Changing a Notes Client License Type

Administration			
Owners:	Brad Hoyt/Marketing/Chicago/ACME	Notes client license:	Lotus Notes Mail
Administrators:		Setup profile:	
Check password:	Don't check password	Foreign directory sync allowed:	Yes
Required change interval:	0	Network account name:	
Grace period:	0		
Last change date:			
Password digest:			
Change request:	None		

4. Save the document.

The next time the user logs into the Notes server, the license change automatically takes effect.

Notes Administration Tools

There are several administration tools and databases available within Lotus Notes version 4 that the Notes administrator should monitor at least on a daily basis. The following sections discuss these databases and tools.

Notes Administration Process

New with version 4 of Lotus Notes is the Notes administration process. It is a significant addition designed to save the administrator time by automating much of the Notes administration tasks. These tasks include:

- Deleting user, servers and group documents from the public Name and Address book.

- Recertifying Notes ID files.

- Renaming users and servers.

- Creating and deleting users' mail files.

- Creating replicas of Notes applications.

- Moving databases from a cluster server.

- Adding and removing servers from a Notes cluster.

- Enabling password checking during authentication.

- Removing user names from ACL, reader, and author name fields of Notes applications.

- Converting users and servers from a flat to a hierarchical naming standard.

Tips

The Notes administration process will only perform most of these tasks if you use a hierarchical ID naming structure for your Notes infrastructure.

The administration process automatically initiates when a Notes server is started. However, before a Notes administrator can take full advantage of the tool, proper configurations of the process must be set and ACL access must be assigned on each Notes application. The administration process task (named *adminp* on a Notes server) must interact with the public Name and Address book, all Notes applications that have an administration server set, the administration requests Notes application, and the certification log Notes application. Notes administrators must also have the proper ACL access to these Notes applications.

Setting the Administration Server for the Public Name and Address Book

The first step you need to perform is to assign an administration server for your public Name and Address book. This is performed as follows:

1. Shut down the Notes server process on the Notes server that will be the administration server for the public Name and Address book.

2. Start the Notes user interface (Notes client program) on the Notes server.

3. Check to see if a wildcard replica of the Administration Requests (ADMIN4.NSF) database already exists on the server. If so, delete the database. The Administration Requests database is a wildcard replica if it does not appear in the list of databases when you choose **File, Database, Open.**

4. Open the public Name and Address book locally on the Notes server (**File, Database, Open.** Select **Local** for the server, and **NAMES.NSF** for the filename).

5. Click, **File, Database, Access Control.**

6. Click the **Advanced** icon.

7. The following page will appear (see Figure 8-18):

Figure 8-18

Administration
Server Setting for
Public Name and
Address Book

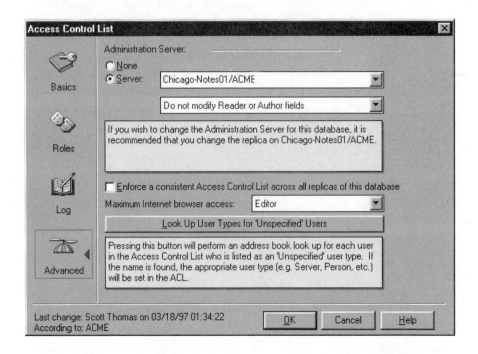

8. Within the Administration Server fields, enter the Notes server name to administer the public Name and Address book. Keep the other field set to **Do Not Modify Reader or Author fields**. Enabling this setting will slow the process, and you should never need to edit any author or reader name fields within the public Name and Address book.

9. Make sure that a Notes certification log exists. If it doesn't, you will need to create a Notes certification log on the Notes server (see the "Certification Log" section within this chapter for details).

10. Shut down the Notes user interface and restart the Notes server.

Traps

It is important to note that the administration process for the public Name and Address book is intensive. For smaller Notes installations, the administration Notes server for the public Name and Address book can be the same Notes server that houses the Notes applications for that company. However, for larger installations, the process may become too much of a burden on the server. A dedicated server may be needed whose only job is to perform administration requests.

By default, the administration process uses three threads to process administration requests. If you have multiple processors installed on your machine and would like to improve performance of the administration process, you may add threads. This setting is configured within the server document of the Notes server. See Chapter 6, *Public Name and Address Book Forms and Views* for the exact configuration. Once this field is modified, the administration process on the Notes server must be shut down and restarted to take effect.

Once this task is complete, the Notes server creates the administration requests database (ADMIN4.NSF). It is within this database that all administration requests post. Actual requests are not entered into this database; requests are initiated from buttons within the public Name and Address book. This Notes application only houses requests where the adminp server task then carriers out the request. Every Notes server within your domain will have a replica of this Notes application. The administration Notes server creates these replicas.

Tips

The Notes administrator should monitor the administration requests database daily for any errors that may occur, and to track all requests being performed by the administration process.

Configuring Proper ACL Access to Perform Administration Procedures

Once the above tasks are completed, you now must configure ACL settings on the public Name and Address book, the administration requests database, and the Notes certification log. Most administration tasks that are performed within the public Name and Address book require at least AUTHOR access (with Create documents enabled) to the administration requests database. Unless changed by the Notes administrator, this is the default access of the database. Some tasks, such as renaming users in a different hierarchy and deleting users' mail files, require at least EDITOR access (with Delete documents enabled) to the administration requests database. Servers within your domain will need access rights to the administration requests database as well. As with most Notes applications, the LocalDomainServers group should have MANAGER level access.

The Notes certification log requires that users performing administration tasks have at least AUTHOR access (with Create documents enabled).

Setting the Administration Server for Notes Database Applications

In order for the administration process to modify ACL settings for a Notes application within your domain, you must set an administration server per Notes application. To perform this action on one or more Notes applications, perform the following tasks:

1. Click **File**, **Tools**, **Server Administration...**

2. Click the **Database Tools** icon. The following dialog box, shown in Figure 8-19 appears:

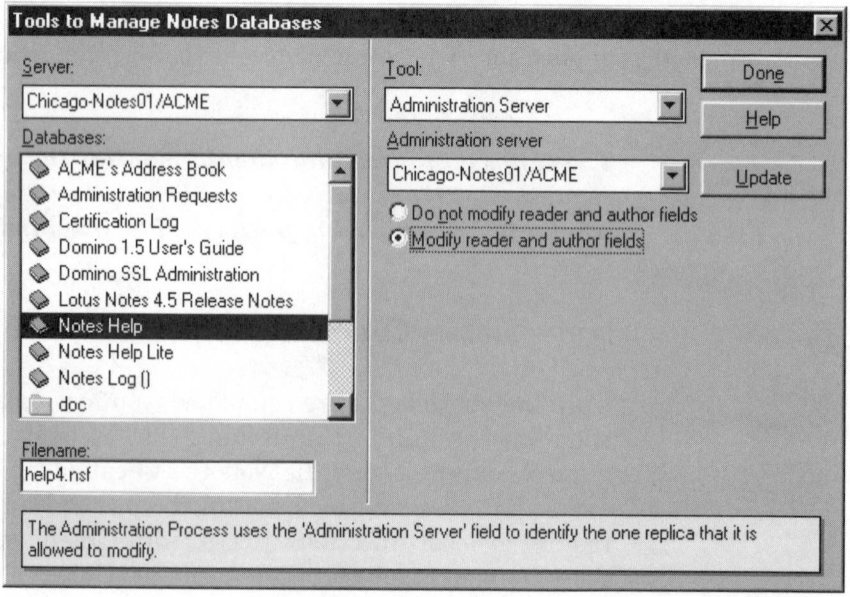

Figure 8-19
Administration
Server Settings for
Notes Applications

3. Within the Server box, select the Notes server you wish to use to access the Notes applications.

4. Within the **Tool** box, select **Administration Server.**

5. Within the **Databases** box, select the database(s) for which you wish to set the administration server.

6. Within the **Administration Server** box, select the Notes server that will be the administration server for the Notes application(s).

7. If you wish to have the administration process update READER and AUTHOR name fields for the Notes application(s), select **Modify Reader and Author fields.**

8. When finished, click **Update.**

The administration server for a single database may be viewed or set by clicking the **Advanced** icon within the database's ACL settings, as well as through the **Server Administration** console. If a "key" icon appears next to any server entry within the ACL of any database application, this specifies the ACL entry as the administration server.

Tips

You only need to set the administration server once per database replica. In other words, if a Notes application exists on multiple Notes servers and is a replicating application, once you set the administration server on the Notes application, the setting is passed through replication to all replica copies on all Notes servers.

Scheduling the Administration Process

As explained in Chapter 6, *Public Name and Address Book Forms and Views* within the "Server document" section, scheduling of the administration process can be set. The timing of requests depends on the type of administration that is set. Table 8.1 lists the available requests and at what point they are executed:

Request	Timing
Create Mail File	Immediate
Initiate Rename in Address Book	Per "interval" field set in the the server record
Rename Person in Address Book	Per "interval" field set in the server record
Rename in Access Control List	Per "interval" field set in the server record
Rename in Person Documents	Per the "execute once a day..." field set in the server record
Rename in Reader/Author Fields	Per the "Start Executing..." fields set in the the server record
Move Person's Name in Hierarchy	Performed by Notes administrator
Delete Obsolete Change Requests	Per the "execute once a day..." field set in the server record
Initiate Rename in Address Book	Per "interval" field set in the server record
Rename Server in Address Book	Per "interval" field set in the server record
Rename in ACL	Per "interval" field set in the server record
Rename in Person Documents	Per the "execute once a day..." field set in the server record
Rename in Reader/Author Fields	Per the "Start Executing..." fields set in the the server record
Delete Obsolete Change Requests	Per the "execute once a day..." field set in the server record
Re-certify Person in Address Book	Per "interval" field set in the server record
Re-certify Server in Address Book	Per "interval" field set in the server record
Delete in Address Book	Per "interval" field set in the server record
Delete in Person Documents	Per the "execute once a day..." field set in the server record
Delete in ACL	Per "interval" field set in the server record
Delete in Reader/Author Fields	Per the "Start Executing..." fields set in the the server record
Get Information for Deletion	Immediate
Approve File for Deletion	Done by Notes administrator
Request File Deletion	Immediate
Delete Mail File	Per "interval" field set in the server record
Delete Unlinked Mail File	Per "interval between purging mail..." field set in the server record
Resource Add	Immediate
Resource Delete	Immediate
Approve Resource Delete	Done by Notes administrator
Set Master Address Book	Per "interval" field set in the server record
Set Password Information	Per "interval" field set in the server record
Change User Password in Address Book	Immediate
Check Access for New Replica Creation	Immediate
Create Replica	Immediate
Add Server to Cluster	Immediate
Remove Server from Cluster	Immediate
Check Access for Move Replica Creation	Immediate
Move Replica	Immediate
Monitor Replica Stub	Per "interval" field set in server record
Delete Original Replica After Move	Per "interval" field set in server record
Copy Servers' Certified Public Key	Per "interval" field set in server record
Place Server's Notes Build Number in Server Record	Per "interval" field set in server record

The Notes administrator can tell which databases on a Notes server have the administration server set per database, as well as which have the Reader and Author Names fields set. To do so, type the following at the Notes server console:

```
tell adminp show databases
```

You may also override any scheduled settings for the administration process and force an immediate execution by typing the following at the Notes server console:

```
tell adminp process request
```

where *request* is one of the following settings:

- **Interval.** This setting initiates all immediate and interval-based requests.

- **Daily.** This setting processes all new and modified administration requests to update person documents within the public Name and Address book.

- **Delayed.** This setting processes all requests that are scheduled per the "start executing..." setting.

- **Time.** This setting processes all requests that are based on the "delete unlinked mail..." setting.

- **All.** This processes all requests of all types except those based on the "delete unlinked mail..." setting.

Server Directory and Database Links

A Notes database application may exist within the Notes data directory or in any subdirectory relative to the data directory. Notes applications may also exist outside the data directory by using directory links. Directory links can also provide another layer of security by limiting Notes access to the directory itself. To create a directory link, follow these procedures:

1. Click **File, Tools, Server Administration.**

2. Make sure the proper Notes server is highlighted, then click the **Server** Icon.

3. Select **Directories** and **Links.**

4. The Manage Directories and Links screen, shown in Figure 8-20 then appears.

Figure 8-20

Manage Directories and Links Dialog Box

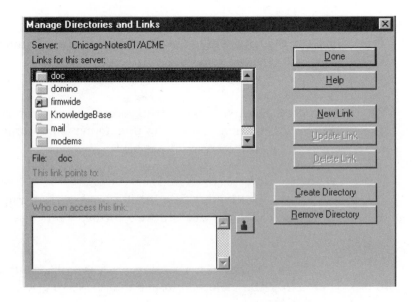

5. To create a new directory link, click **New Link**. The Create a New Link dialog box appears (see Figure 8-21):

Figure 8-21

Create a New
Link Dialog Box

Create a New Link

Server: Chicago-Notes01/ACME
File:
firmwide.dir

OK

Cancel

Help

Link
⦿ Directory Link   ⦾ Database Link

This link points to:
F:\firmwide

Who can access this link:
Jim Carlson
Brad Hoyt/Marketing/Chicago/ACME

Configure the following fields:

- **File:** Within this field, enter the name of the directory link as
  it will appear to users relative to the Notes data directory on
  the Notes server. In other words, the physical location of the
  directory on the operating system the Notes server is running
  on may exist on a different drive and/or directory relative to
  the Notes data directory. Because this is a directory link, it
  will appear as another directory relative to the Notes data
  directory when a user performs a **File**, **Database**, **Open**.

Traps

*It is recommended that you not create a directory link that
points to another file server that will house a Notes application.
This causes additional overhead for the network, as a user enters
the network card to access the Notes server, then the Notes server
will traverse again to the network to access the Notes applica-
tion(s). In the event of a file server or partial network failure,
the Notes application(s) may not be accessible in this scenario.*

- **Link.** Click the **Directory Link** radio button. Notes will
  automatically add the .DIR extension to the name of the link
  within the **File** field above.

- **This link points to:** Enter the path to where this link points to the operating system of the Notes server. This directory can be created from the operating system of the Notes server or by using the Manage Directories and Links screen (see the next section for details).

- **Who can access this link** (Optional): Enter the users, groups, and/or servers that may access this directory. If an entry is input into this box, only those users will be able to browse the directory.

6. Click **OK,** then **Done.**

You may also use the Manage Directories and Links screen shown in Figure 8-17 to create a new operating system level directory on the Notes server. To do so, perform the following procedures:

1. From the Manage Directories and Links screen click the **Create Directory** button. The screen shown in Figure 8-22 appears:

Figure 8-22

Create a
New Directory
Dialog Box

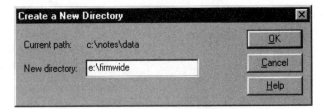

2. Within the New Directory field, enter the new directory name including the drive and full path.

3. Click **OK,** then **Done.**

Also from the Manage Directories and Links screen shown in Figure 8-20, you may create a Notes database link. A database link is used to point to a single Notes database outside the data directory of the Notes server. To create a Notes database link, follow these steps:

1. Click **File, Tools, Server Administration.**

2. Highlight the Notes server on which to create the Notes database link and click the **Servers** icon.

3. Click **Directories** and **Links**. The Manage Directories and Links screen appears as shown in Figure 8-20.

4. Click **New Link**. The screen shown in Figure 8-23 appears:

Figure 8-23

Create a New Notes Database Link Dialog Box

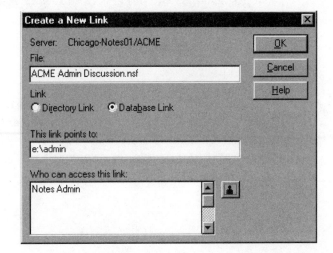

Configure the following fields:

● **File:** Within this field, enter the name of the database link— the physical location of the Notes application on the operating system where the Notes server is running.

Traps

We recommend that you not create a Notes database link that points to another file server that will house a Notes application. This will cause additional overhead for the network, as a user will enter the network card to access the Notes server, then the Notes server will traverse again to the network to access the Notes application. In the event of a file server or partial network failure, the Notes application may not be accessible in this scenario.

- **Link.** Click the **Database Link** radio button. Notes will automatically add the .NSF extension to the name of the link within the **File** field above.

- **This link points to:** Enter the complete path to where this link points on the Notes server's operating system.

- **Who can access this link**(Optional): Enter the users, groups, and/or servers that may access this linked database.

5. Click **OK,** then **Done.**

Tips

If any modifications and/or deletions are needed to a database link, directory link, or operating system directory, the Manage Directories and Links screen shown in **Figure 8-20** *can be accessed to perform these operations.*

Notes Logs

The Lotus Notes logs represent the complete audit trail for the actions of each server. The Notes log is created automatically the first time a Notes server is run. Replication, mail routing, database size and usage, phone calls, and all events and errors are recorded within this database. Every morning and periodically throughout the day, the Notes administrator(s) should scan the Notes logs on each Notes server for any errors or inconsistencies.

The Notes log may be opened by simply performing a **File, Database, Open** on the specified Notes server, and then highlighting the Notes log and clicking **Open**.

You may also open the log on a Notes server by following these steps:

1. Click **File, Tools, Server Administration**

2. Select the desired Notes server.

3. Click the **System Databases** icon.

4. Click **Open Log.**

Tips

The Notes Log on every Notes server is one of the most important tools for a Notes administrator. The administrator should make it a point to monitor the logs throughout the day to ensure proper overall health of each Notes server.

The Notes log file can become quite large. To speed searches for specific events, you may perform a log analysis from the Notes server administration panel to search for a string of words within a Notes log file. To do so, follow these steps:

1. Click **File, Tools, Server Administration**.

2. Select the Notes server to administer.

3. Click the **Servers** icon.

4. Choose **Log Analysis**. The screen shown in Figure 8-24 appears:

Figure 8-24
Log Analysis
Dialog Box

Server Log Analysis	☒

For Server: Chicago-Notes01/ACME

[Results Database...]

Log Analysis on Local

Report on the activity in the last: [2]   days

Enter comma separated keywords to search for:

Chicago-Notes02/ACME

| Start | Start and Open | Cancel | Help |

5. Click the **Results Database** button. The following screen (Figure 8-25) appears:

Figure 8-25

Results Database
Dialog Box

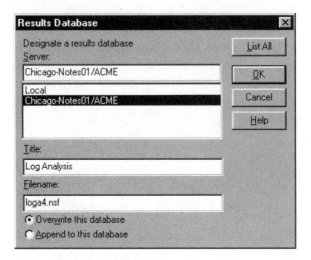

6. Specify the location to store the results of the search and click **OK**.

7. In the Server Log Analysis dialog box, enter the number of days and the search criteria and click the **Start** button to start the search. Click the **Start and Open** button to start the search and then view the results database.

Database Catalog

The database catalog (CATALOG.NSF) lists all databases existing on the server excluding any databases designated not to be listed (such as mail databases). The catalog server task which is scheduled to run at 1:00 AM every morning on the Notes server is responsible for populating this database with all Notes applications, as well as removing any old selections. All Notes servers and administrators should be granted MANAGER access to this application. All other users will only need READER access.

Tips

It is recommended that you create a REPLICA copy of the Notes database catalog on every Notes server within your organization. This enables users and administrators to see all databases within the entire infrastructure and on which server they exist. From an administration standpoint, the catalog quickly shows the person where databases exist and if replication IDs for the application are correct.

The Notes database catalog may be opened by simply performing a **File**, **Database**, **Open** on the specified Notes server, then highlighting the catalog application and clicking **Open**.

You may also open the Notes database catalog on a Notes server in the following way:

1. Click **File**, **Tools**, **Server Administration.**

2. Select the desired Notes server.

3. Click the **System Databases** icon.

4. Click **Open Catalog.**

Certification Log

The Notes certification log (CERTLOG.NSF) keeps track of all Notes users and servers registered within your organization. By default, the certification log is *not* created. We recommend that you create a certification log before you begin registering any new users or servers.

The certification log tracks all servers and users displaying the following:

● Name, license type, and ID number.

● Date of certification and expiration.

● Name, license type, and ID number of the certifier ID used to create or recertify the ID file.

To create a new certification log, follow these procedures:

1. Click **File**, **Database**, **New**. The dialog box shown in Figure 8-26 appears:

Figure 8-26
New Dialog
Box

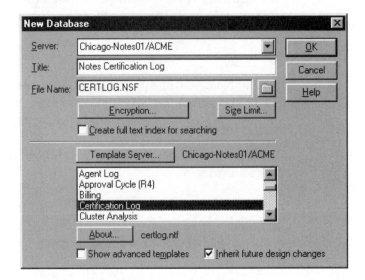

2. Click the **Template Server** button and select the server housing the Notes templates. Highlight the **Certification Log** template.

3. Within the **Server** field, select the server where the Notes administrators will be registering new users and servers.

4. Within the **Title** field, enter the database title.

5. In the **Filename** field, type **CERTLOG.NSF.**

6. Click **OK**.

7. Repeat these steps to create a certification log on other Notes servers where you want to register new Notes users and servers.

To open the certification log once it has been created, select **File, Database, Open** on the specified Notes server. Highlight the desired selection and click **Open**.

You may also open the Notes certification log on a Notes server as follows:

1. Click **File**, **Tools**, **Server Administration.**

2. Select the appropriate Notes server.

3. Click the **System Databases** icon.

4. Click **Open Certification Log.**

Statistics and Event Monitoring

The Notes statistic reporting and event monitoring procedures can be used to monitor such items as communications, mail, replication, resources, Notes database security changes, and server statistics. The information can be reported to a central database repository for all Notes servers within the infrastructure. Alerts can also be e-mailed to a particular person.

These mechanisms make it easy for a Notes administrator to get a quick snapshot of the "health" of all Notes servers within the environment. Also, replication and security problems can quickly be observed.

In order to configure the process, the server task **report** must be loaded on each server. The report server task collects the statistics of the Notes server and reports them within the statistics reporting database (STATREP.NSF).

This can be done from the console or remote console by typing the following line:

```
load report
```

The task should also be added to each Notes server's **Server-Tasks** setting within the NOTES.INI file on the Notes server(s).

This task automatically creates the following when loaded:

- Statistics and Events database (**EVENTS4.NSF**) in the server's data directory. This database is used to configure the Statistics and Reporting.

- Statistics collection database (**STATREP.NSF**).

The Statistics and Events database (**EVENTS4.NSF**) is where you specify the Notes server(s) to monitor for statistics and where to log the data. This is shown in Figure 8-27 below:

Figure 8-27
Notes Server
Statistics
Configuration

| 🖳 Save Server To Monitor | 🖳 Delete | ☞ Exit |

Server to Monitor

Chicago-Notes01/ACME

Basics:

Server name:	Chicago-Notes01/ACME	Server administrators:	Notes Admin
Server title:	Chicago Notes Mail Server	Report method:	Log to Database
Domain name:	ACME	Enter server name: Database to receive reports:	Chicago-Notes01/ACME statrep.nsf
Collection interval in (minutes):	120	Analysis interval:	○ Daily ○ Monthly ● Weekly ○ Never
Server description:			

Description:
Report statistics for server Chicago-Notes01/ACME, to database 'statrep.nsf' on server Chicago-Notes01/ACME.
Sample statistics every 120 minutes.
Analize statistics weekly.

The Statistics database then collects the statistics from the Notes server(s) within your domain. You may specify a statistics collection database (**STATREP.NSF**) for each server in the Notes domain, or a single master collection database for all Notes servers.

Tips

For larger Notes installations, it may be beneficial not to use a master collection database—it will grow quite large, and the mail router on each Notes server may have to be used to deliver the statistics to the single collection database.

The **event** server task can be used along with the **report** server task to collect more information about a Notes server as well as alert

Notes administrators of specific events. The **event** server task is responsible for monitoring statistics and events that appear within the Notes server console. These include communication, mail, replication, resources, security, server statistics, and database update console events.

To run the **event** server task, type the following at the Notes server prompt:

```
load event
```

For each type of event you wish to report, you must create an Event Monitor document within the Statistics and Events database (**EVENTS4.NSF**). These events then can be configured within this document to notify via e-mail, log to a database, relay to another server, through SNMP, or logged to the Windows NT event viewer.

The following screen shows a security event that may be configured when using the **event** server task:

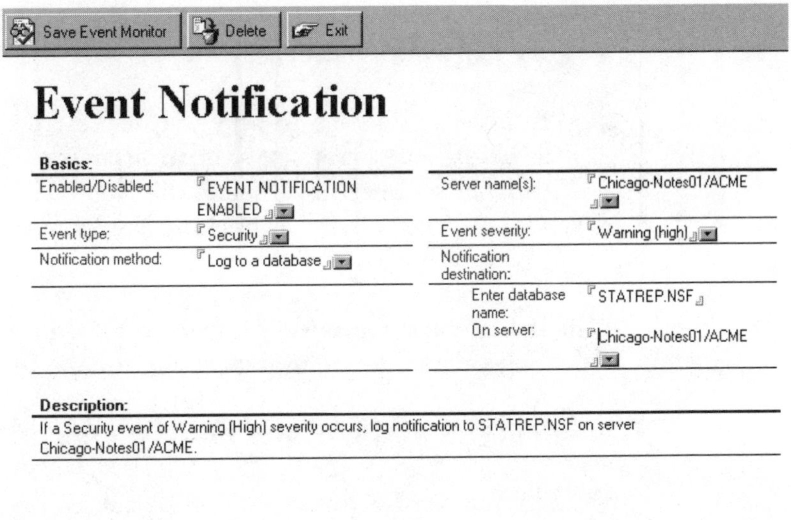

Figure 8-28
Notes Server Event Configuration

The **collect** task can be used to collect statistics from multiple servers and only needs to be run on a single Notes server. It will not give as detailed report as if the **report** task is used; however, unlike **report**, it only needs to be run on a single server.

To use the **collect** task instead of **report**, type the following command at the Notes server console:

```
load collect
```

If any of these programs are to be used, they should be appended to the **ServerTasks** entry in the **NOTES.INI** file(s) on the Notes server(s).

Tips

Within the Statistics and Events database (EVENTS4.NSF) it is possible to edit the alerts to suppress the number of error occurrences. This prevents the Notes servers from reporting errors continuously, possibly mailing or logging thousands of documents every time an error occurs at a console. It would be beneficial to set error alerting to once every 10 minutes.

Remote Notes Server Console

With release 4.5 of Lotus Notes, the console of a Notes server can be monitored in real time from a Notes workstation. In order to use the remote console feature for a Notes server, you must be listed in the Administrators field of the Notes server document in the public Name and Address book.

To access the remote server console from a Notes workstation, click **File**, **Tools**, **Server Administration**. Click the **Console** icon. Within the **Server** field, select the Notes server to monitor. You may view real-time activity by clicking the **Live Console** box.

To send a command to the Notes server, simply enter the command in the **Server Console Command** field. The **Commands** button lists the available commands you may send to the Notes server.

Windows NT Event Log and Performance Monitor

The Windows NT event log and performance monitor can be used to monitor the performance of the system components of the machine. Items such as network, processor, disk I/O, and memory should be monitored. In the event of continued strain on any of these processes, additional hardware may be needed. Consult Chapter 9, *Windows NT Integration* for details on these two products.

NotesView

SNMP

NotesView is an add-on program that runs on HP's Openview as well as IBM's Netview products. It is SNMP-compliant and can be used to monitor Notes servers within an organization's environment. It does give the administrator a little more control over the Notes environment, but is more of a graphical monitoring tool that can be used in the event a threshold is surpassed.

Third-Party Products

There are a number of third-party products available to help administer a Notes network infrastructure. One of the most popular products available for Windows 95 and Windows NT machines is *PC Anywhere. PC Anywhere* is a popular tool that enables administers to remotely control Windows NT and Windows 95 machines over a LAN and/or a WAN environment. Another remote access tool that has proven beneficial in NT environments is *Remotely Possible*. Both applications can be invaluable in the event a Notes server program has crashed while Windows NT or Windows 95 is still running, as the Notes server is otherwise inaccessible.

Data Backup

If there is an enterprise backup solution in place at your company, the Notes servers should be included within the corporate backup strategy. If not, the Notes administrators will be responsible for backing up the data. It may be beneficial to have a separate Notes server in charge of replicating all mission-critical Notes applications from each Notes server within the company. Then a complete backup could be made of that single Notes server.

Backing up Notes presents some unique issues in comparison to backing up other data. Notes replicates among servers, so databases that have replica copies on other servers actually have backups on other machines. For this reason, many organizations only back up hub servers where replicating databases exist. Other application servers are only backed up for databases that do not replicate to any other server.

Tips

If you include your Notes servers in a nightly backup, do not down the Notes server during the backup. There are several scheduled processes that run every night on a Notes server, and if the Notes server is not running during the late hours, the processes will never run. The result will be poor and erratic Notes server performance over time. Instead, implement a backup solution allowing backup of open files.

Important

Notes administrators often do not back up mail. In light of recent court rulings concerning electronic mail, many organizations do not back up any e-mail whatsoever. In fact, many companies automatically purge users' mail after seven days.

Restoration of data presents another problem within Lotus Notes. If data from a replicating database is corrupted or deleted and the database replicates with other servers, the data cannot be simply restored from backup. If the database is restored from backup and placed on the Notes server, the next time the server replicates, the data will be deleted the next time replication occurs. Notes tracks the time and dates of all documents within a database, including all deletions. For this reason, deletions will be replicated back into database applications.

Not (easily) possible with Aresere

The procedure used to restore individual documents is as follows: the database is restored to a temporary location and the desired documents are copied and pasted back into the original database (using the clipboard). Notes now will treat these pasted documents as new documents within the old database and will replicate them back into the environment.

If the Notes administrator is going to be responsible for backing up Notes data using tape backups, he or she should have a proper tape rotation scheme in place. This includes the proper number of tapes (DLT or DAT, depending on the format) for the rotation. Normally, most companies have a tape for each weekday that is rotated. The Friday and end of the month tape is pulled from the rotation each week and each month and stored at a secure, off-site location.

Chapter 9

Windows NT Integration

This chapter provides you with insights into how version 4.5 of Lotus Notes integrates with the Microsoft Windows NT Server and workstation. In environments where Windows NT Servers provide file and print services, seamless integration of Notes and NT are invaluable to system administrators. Lotus has provided some valuable integration points between the operating system and Notes that enhance the user experience and minimize the cost of administration.

With release 4.5 of Lotus Notes comes direct integration with Windows NT. This includes both Windows NT versions 3.51 and 4.0.

The integration features include:

- **Single password logon.** This enables Notes workstations running on Windows NT machines to accept Windows NT passwords. This way, password entries for Lotus Notes are not necessary. Single sign-on is only available to Notes users running the Windows NT operating system.

- **Lotus Domino directory synchronization with the Windows NT domain**. This allows administrators to create and delete users within Notes; the user will then automatically be created or deleted within the Windows NT domain. This works in the opposite direction as well.

● **Windows NT event logging and performance monitoring.** Lotus Notes server events can be logged and managed through the Windows NT event viewer. Performance statistics for the Notes server can also be viewed through the Windows NT performance monitor.

Single Logon

In order for users running Lotus Notes on the Windows NT platform to use the single logon feature, the option must be installed when the Notes workstation is created. Single password logon can be found within the Customized features selection. For details on how to install a Notes workstation, see Chapter 7, *Installation Guidelines.*

Tips

You must be a Windows NT user with administrator privileges in order to install the single logon feature. The feature will install a Windows NT service as well as configure the Windows NT registry of the machine.

Once the Lotus Notes single logon is installed on a Windows NT machine, it will run as a native Windows NT service. This may be viewed within the services list found in the Windows NT control panel. This selection is shown in Figure 9-1 below:

Figure 9-1
Single Logon
Service Entry

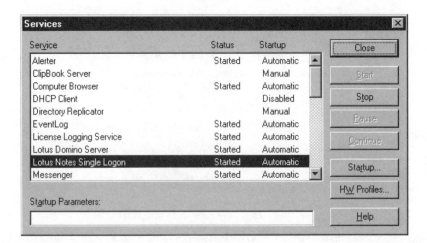

This service can be started or stopped from within the Windows NT Service control panel. It can also be disabled upon startup of the Windows NT machine.

The single logon service is transparent to the user. The user logs onto the Windows NT system as usual by pressing **Ctrl+Alt+Del** and enters his or her Windows NT user name, domain and password. Once a valid Windows NT logon is established and the user launches Lotus Notes, the user is not prompted for his or her Lotus Notes password. What happens instead is the single logon service sends a request to unlock the Lotus Notes ID file which then unlocks the user ID.

In order for the single logon service to work, the passwords for Windows NT and Lotus Notes must be identical. If they are not, the single logon service will present the user with the dialog box as shown in Figure 9-2 below:

Figure 9-2
Synchronize
Lotus Notes
Password Dialog Box

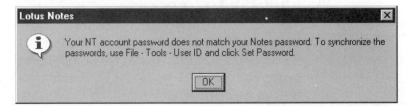

Lotus Notes will then prompt the user for the Notes password. To take advantage of the single logon service, the Notes password and Windows NT password *must* be the same. To change the password for a Lotus Notes ID, click **File, Tools, User ID**, and press the **Set Password button**.

Traps

It should be noted that if a user logs off Notes (presses F5) or has an automatic timeout set, the single logon service will log the Notes users back into Lotus Notes once the workstation becomes active. This could provide unauthorized access to otherwise secure Notes applications.

As explained in Chapter 8, *Administration Issues* and Chapter 12, *Notes Application and Security Issues*, Lotus Notes uses public/private key authentication. For this reason, a Notes ID is necessary as every user's private key and password is stored within the ID file. Windows NT, on the other hand, stores user information (including a user's password) within domain security databases stored on Windows NT domain controller machines. With the single logon service, the Lotus Notes logon procedure is less of a hassle for the user. However, neither the Lotus Notes nor Windows NT security model is compromised as only the password is passed between the systems. Because of this fact, any user ID file containing the same password will work on the same machine.

The single logon service is only available for Windows NT workstations or servers. It will not work on any other platform, such as Windows 95.

Notes Directory Synchronization with Windows NT Domain

With release 4.5 of Lotus Notes, administrators may now register or delete users within Lotus Notes and the person will be automatically be registered or deleted within a Windows NT domain. The converse is true as well. If a Windows NT administrator adds, deletes, or changes the name of a user within the Windows NT domain, the change can automatically be propagated to the public Name and Address book within Lotus Notes. Lotus Domino directory synchronization is handled by the Notes User Manager Extension. Existing Windows NT accounts may also be added to the Notes public Name and Address book.

In order for an administrator to take advantage of the synchronization features, the user synchronization selection must be installed on the administrator's Notes workstation. For details on how to install a Notes workstation, see Chapter 7, *Installation Guidelines*.

To maintain user accounts, a Notes administrator running Lotus Notes version 4.5 or higher on a Windows NT machine within a Windows NT network environment may now choose to either use the Windows NT User Manager or the public Name and Address book of Lotus Notes. Following are the different options available to control user accounts within Lotus Notes and Windows NT.

Tips

> ***To use these registration features within Lotus Notes and Windows NT, the administrator must have the appropriate rights to the public Name and Address book. Also, the administrator must be a member of the local Administrator Group or local Account Operator Group in Windows NT to add user accounts using the Windows NT User Manager.***

Register New Users from Lotus Notes

To create a user within Notes and Windows NT using the Lotus Notes registration utility, follow these steps:

1. Click **File, Tools, Server Administration**.

2. Click the **People** icon and choose **Register Person**.

3. Click **Yes** that you have purchased the required license for Lotus Notes. The dialog box shown in Figure 9-3 appears:

Figure 9-3
Registering New Windows NT and Notes Users from Lotus Notes

Register Person	✕
Please specify the following information to be applied to all people registered in this registration session.	Continue...
Registration Server... Chicago-Notes01/ACME	Cancel
Certifier ID... /ACME	Help
Security type: North American	☑ Add NT User Account(s)
Certificate expiration date: 04/18/99 03:05:52 PM	NT Group Name: Domain Users

4. Click the **Registration Server** button to select the proper Notes registration server.

5. Click the **Certifier ID** button to select the proper certifier ID file to register Notes users.

6. Select either the North American or International ID type.

7. Change the expiration date for the Notes user if desired.

8. Select the **ADD NT User Account(s)** check box to create the Notes user within Windows NT as well.

9. In the NT **Group Name** field, enter the name of the Windows NT group in which you wish to place all user account(s). Click the down arrow to see a list of all available NT groups. If this field is left blank, all accounts will be placed within the Windows NT group USERS.

10. Click **Continue**. The user name specifics for registering a person will appear in the Basics dialog box, as shown in Figure 9-4:

Figure 9-4

User Name
Basics Dialog Box

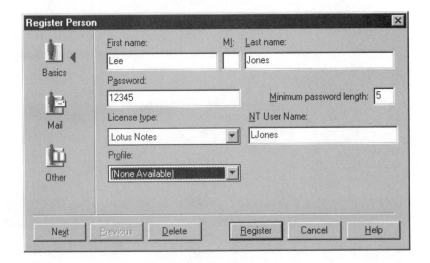

Configure the following field:

- **First name, MI, and Last name:** Enter the user's first and last name. The middle initial is not recommended unless necessary.

- **Password:** Enter the password for the user. The user may change it once his or her Notes desktop is configured. The password is case sensitive.

- **License Type:** Enter the Notes license type for the user: Lotus Notes, Lotus Notes Desktop, or Lotus Notes Mail.

- **Profile:** Enter the profile, if any, for the user. The Notes administrator can configure the profile so that when a Notes user is first created, some of the user's information is automatically set. This could include database icons for the user's desktop, Notes server phone numbers, and Internet browser settings. For a more detailed description of profiles, see Chapter 6, *Public Name and Address Book Forms and Views.*

- **Minimum password length:** Enter the minimum character length for the Notes user's password. If the length is set to any number but zero, a user will never be able to clear the password, only change it.

- **NT User Name:** This field contains the user name as it will appear within the Windows NT domain.

11. Click the **Mail** icon. The Mail dialog, shown in Figure 9-5, appears:

Figure 9-5
User Name
Mail Dialog Box

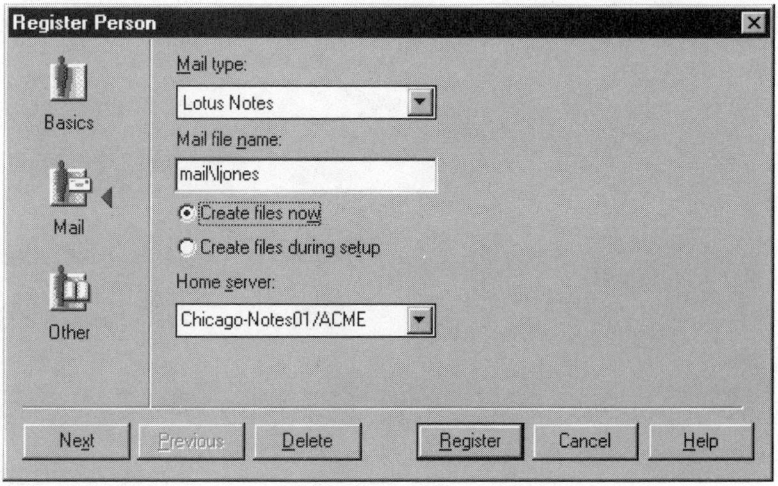

Configure the following fields:

- **Mail type:** Select the user's appropriate e-mail program, or **none** for no mail.

- **Mail file name:** Enter the path relative to the Notes data directory and filename of the user's mail file.

- **Create files... :** Select whether or not to create the user's mail file now or when the user is set up.

- **Home server:** Enter the name of the server that stores the user's mail file.

Traps

Many Notes administrators forget to change this selection to the appropriate server. If this setting is left as LOCAL, the user will not be able to receive any e-mail.

12. Click the **Other** icon. The Other dialog box will appear (see Figure 9-6):

Figure 9-6
User Name
Other Dialog Box

| Register Person | ☒ |

Basics

Mail

Other ◄

Additional Address Book information:

Comment:

Location: Chicago   Local administrator:

Store User ID: User unique organizational unit:
☐ In Address Book
☑ In file:
    A:\ljones.id
    Set ID file...

Next   Previous   Delete   Register   Cancel   Help

Configure the following fields:

- **Comment** (Optional): Enter a comment about the Notes user.

- **Location** (Optional): Enter a location for the user.

- **Store User ID**: Select whether or not to store the user's ID file in the public Name and Address book and/or on a floppy or network drive.

If the ID file is stored within the public Name and Address book and the user has AUTHOR access to the public Name and Address book (default), then the ID file will be removed from his or her person record and copied to the desktop of the machine where Notes is installed.

If you choose to create the ID file to a floppy or network drive, then click the **Set ID File** button to change the target location of the file, if necessary.

Traps

We highly recommend against storing the ID file within the public Name and Address book for security reasons. If another user opens the public Name and Address book and double clicks on the newly created user's ID file, that other person can gain access to Notes information under the new person's identity if the password for the newly created ID file is known.

- **Local administrator** (Optional): Enter the local administrator's name.

- **User unique organizational unit** (Optional): Enter a unique organizational unit for users within the same Notes hierarchy with the same user name. This field is rarely used, a middle initial is more commonly used to distinguish users with the same name in the same hierarchy. See Chapter 4, *Naming Standards,* for more details.

13. (Optional) Click **Next** to continue to register other Notes users. Complete steps 10–12 for these users.

14. Click **Register** when you are ready to register the user(s).

Once you have completed these steps, Lotus Notes will create a Windows NT account using the following fields:

- **NT User Name.** This name is filled in with the Notes user's first name and last name.

- **Password.** This is created from the user's Lotus Notes password.

- **NT Group Name.** The user is added to the Windows NT group specified by the administrator.

Tips

Windows NT accounts will only be created if you register new Lotus Notes users. If you add a person document within the public Name and Address book (by pressing the **Add Person** *button), a Windows NT account will not be created.*

Delete Users from Lotus Notes

You may delete users within Lotus Notes and Windows NT from Lotus Notes if you are running Lotus Notes on a Windows NT machine. You must also have the proper security rights within Lotus Notes and Windows NT to perform this operation. Follow these procedures to delete a user within both systems using Lotus Notes:

1. Open the public Name and Address book on the Lotus Notes server.

2. Choose the **People** view and select the user(s) to delete.

3. Click the **Delete** button and **Yes** to continue. The diagram box shown in Figure 9-7 appears:

Figure 9-7
Delete User
Dialog Box

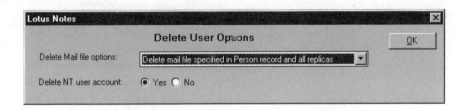

4. Select one the following three options and click **OK**.

    ● **Delete just the mail file specified in Person record.**
      This deletes only the mail files for the persons specified in
      the public Name and Address book. Any other replica
      copies of the users' mail files will not be removed.

    ● **Delete mail file specified in Person record and all repli-
      cas.** This deletes all replica copies of the users' mail files
      on all Notes servers.

    ● **Don't delete the mail file.** This option will not delete a
      user's mail file.

5. Select the **Yes** radio button to delete the user from the Win-
    dows NT domain as well as Lotus Notes. Lotus Notes immedi-
    ately searches the Windows NT domain and deletes the user
    from Windows NT.

6. Once you select your desired option above, you will be prompted
    with one of these two options:

    ● **Yes** to immediately delete all references in the public Name
      and Address book of the user(s) and database ACL entries.

    ● **No** to post a request in the administration database and
      have the references removed according to the "Interval set-
      ting" for the administration process within the server
      record of the public Name and Address book.

Tips

*The Administration Process enables you to perform this opera-
tion on both systems (Lotus Notes and Windows NT). Simply
deleting a person record in the public Name and Address book
will not remove the Lotus Notes user from Windows NT.*

Register New Users from Windows NT

You may register a new user within Lotus Notes and Windows NT from the User Manager program within Windows NT. You must have proper rights within Lotus Notes and Windows NT to perform these operations. When you register a new Lotus Notes user from Windows NT a new person record, Notes ID file, and mail file is created within Lotus Notes. To register a new user within Lotus Notes and Windows NT, from Windows NT, follow these steps:

1. Start the User Manager program from Windows NT.

2. From the User Manager, click Notes, **Enable Notes User Registration** so that a check mark appears next to the entry. Figure 9-8 shows this setting:

Figure 9-8

Windows NT
User Manager

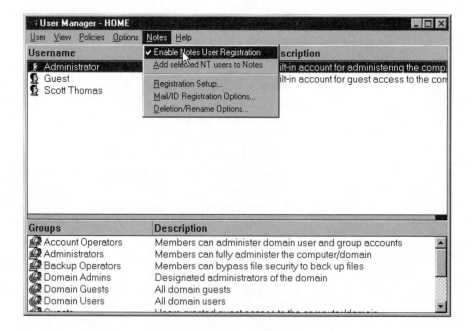

3. Click **Notes, Registration Setup**. The dialog box shown in Figure 9-9 appears:

Figure 9-9
User Manager
Registration Setup
Dialog Box

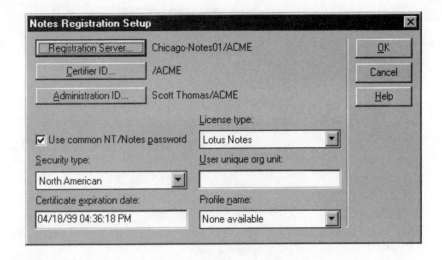

Configure the following fields:

- **Registration Server:** Select the Notes server in which the new user(s) will be registered.

- **Certifier ID:** Select the certifier ID file to register the new user(s).

- **Administration ID:** Select the user ID to use to connect to the Notes server. This is normally the Notes administrator's ID file.

- **Use Common NT/Notes Password:** Select whether or not the user(s) will have the same Windows NT and Notes password.

- **Security Type:** Select the type of encryption to use, (either North American or International).

- **Expiration Date:** Change the expiration date of the user(s) ID files, if desired.

- **License Type:** Specify the license type of the user(s) ID files. The default is Lotus Notes.

- **User Unique Organizational Unit** (Optional): Enter a unique organizational unit for users within the same Notes hierarchy with the same user name. This field is rarely used; a middle initial is more commonly used to distinguish users with the same name in the same hierarchy. See Chapter 4, *Naming Standards* for more details.

- **Profile Name:** Enter the profile, if any, for the user. The Notes administrator can configure the profile so that when a Notes user is first created, some of the user's information is automatically set. This could include database icons for the user's desktop, Notes server phone numbers, and Internet browser settings. For a more detailed description of profiles, see Chapter 6, *Public Name and Address Book Forms and Views.*

4. Click **OK.**

5. Click **Notes, Mail/ID Registration Options**. The following dialog box appears (see Figure 9-10):

Figure 9-10

User Manager Mail and ID Setup Dialog Box

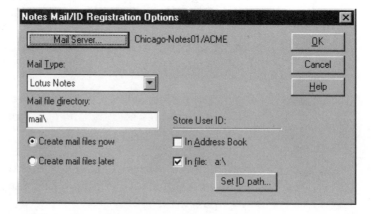

Configure the following fields:

- **Mail Server Button:** Select the mail server for the user(s).

- **Mail Type:** Select the mail type for the user(s).

- **Mail Directory:** Select the location on the mail server for the user(s) mail files.

- **Create Files:** Select when to create user mail files.

- **Store User ID File:** Select whether or not to store the user's ID file in the public Name and Address book and/or on a floppy or network drive.

If the ID file is stored within the public Name and Address book, and the user has AUTHOR access to the public Name and Address book (default), then the ID file will be removed from his or her person record and copied to the desktop of the machine where Notes is installed.

If you choose to create the ID file to a floppy or network drive, then click the **Set ID Path** button to change the target location of the file if necessary.

Traps

We highly recommend against storing the ID file within the public Name and Address book for security reasons. If another user opens the public Name and Address book and double clicks on the newly created user's ID file, that other person can gain access to Notes information under the new person's identity if the password for the newly created ID file is known.

6. Click **OK.**

7. Now you are able to create new users in Lotus Notes and Windows NT. Click **User, New User.** The following dialog box, shown in Figure 9-11, appears:

Figure 9-11
User Manager
New User
Dialog Box

New User		×
Username:	Lee Jones	Add
Full Name:	Lee Jones	Cancel
Description:		Help
Password:	********	
Confirm Password:	********	

☑ User Must Change Password at Next Logon
☐ User Cannot Change Password
☐ Password Never Expires
☐ Account Disabled

Groups	Profile	Hours	Logon To	Account	Dialin

8. Fill in the necessary fields. The required fields for Lotus Notes include **Username**, **Full Name,** and **Password.**

9. Click **Add.**

10. The Notes user information screen appears, as shown in Figure 9-12:

Figure 9-12
Notes User
Information
Dialog Box

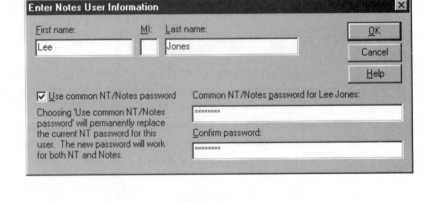

Configure the following fields:

- **First Name:** Enter the user's first name.

- **Last Name:** Enter the user's last name.

- **Use Common NT/Notes password:** Select this if you want the user to have the same password for Lotus Notes and Windows NT.

- **Common Password:** Enter the common password for the user.

- **Confirm Password:** Confirm the password entry.

11. Click **OK**. To add additional users, repeat steps 7-10.

12. Click **Close** when finished. The new user(s) are now added to the Windows NT domain.

13. You are prompted to add the new users to Lotus Notes. Click **Begin Registration** to add the new user(s) to Lotus Notes.

14. The user(s) are now created within Lotus Notes.

Register Existing Windows NT Users in Lotus Notes from Windows NT

Within Windows NT, you may register existing Windows NT users who currently do not have Lotus Notes accounts in Notes. You must have appropriate rights within Windows NT and Lotus Notes to perform this operation. Follow these steps:

1. Start the User Manager program from within Windows NT.

2. From the User Manager, click **Notes**, **Enable Notes User Registration** so that a check mark appears next to the entry (See Figure 9-8).

3. Click **Notes**, **Registration Setup**. See Figure 9-9.

Configure the following fields:

- **Registration Server:** Select the Notes server in which the new user(s) will be registered.

- **Certifier ID:** Select the certifier ID file to register the new user(s).

- **Administration ID:** Select the user ID to use to connect to the Notes server. This is normally the Notes administrator's ID file.

- **Use Common NT/Notes Password:** Select whether or not the user(s) will have the same Windows NT and Notes password.

- **Security Type:** Select the type of encryption to use, (either North American or International).

- **Expiration Date:** Change the expiration date of the user(s) ID files if desired.

- **License Type:** Specify the license type of the user(s) ID files. The default is Lotus Notes.

- **User Unique Organizational Unit** (Optional): Enter a unique organizational unit for users within the same Notes hierarchy with the same user name. This field is rarely used; a middle initial is more commonly used to distinguish users with the same name in the same hierarchy. See Chapter 4, *Naming Standards*, for more details.

- **Profile Name:** Enter the profile, if any, for the user. The Notes administrator can configure the profile so that when a Notes user is first created, some of the user's information is automatically set. This could include database icons for the user's desktop, Notes server phone numbers, and Internet browser settings. For a more detailed description of profiles, see Chapter 6, *Public Name and Address Book Forms and Views*.

4. Click **OK.**

5. Click **Notes, Mail/ID Registration Options**. The dialog box shown in Figure 9-10 appears.

Configure the following fields:

- **Mail Server:** Select the mail server for the user(s).

- **Mail Type:** Select the mail type for the user(s).

- **Mail Directory:** Select the location on the mail server for the user(s) mail files.

- **Create Files:** Select when to create user mail files.

- **Store ID File:** Select whether or not to store the User's ID file in the public Name and Address book and/or on a floppy or network drive.

If the ID file is stored within the public Name and Address book, and the user has AUTHOR access to the public Name and Address book (default), then the ID file will be removed from his or her person record and copied to the desktop of the machine where Notes is installed.

If you choose to create the ID file to a floppy or network drive, then click the **Set ID Path** button to change the target location of the file, if necessary.

Traps

We highly recommend against storing the ID file within the public Name and Address book for security reasons. If another user opens the public Name and Address book and double clicks on the newly created user's ID file, that other person can gain access to Notes information under the new person's identity if the password for the newly created ID file is known.

6. Click **OK.**

7. You are now ready to add existing Windows NT users to Lotus Notes. Within the User Name window of the User Manager program, select the Windows NT account(s) you wish to register within Lotus Notes.

8. Click **Notes, Add Selected Users To Notes.**

9. If you are adding more than one Windows NT user to Lotus Notes, you will be prompted for the following registration options:

   ● **Prompt for the name and password of each selected user.** If you select this option, you will be prompted to enter Notes information within the Notes Information Dialog box for each user as shown in Figure 9-12.

   ● **Register selected users at once without additional prompts.** If you select this option, random passwords for Notes users will be generated. The passwords will be copied to the New User Passwords Notes application (**NTSYNC45.NSF**). This is a local Notes application on your Notes workstation that must be created manually using the template NTSYNC45.NTF. The database holds

the passwords for each user; however, the passwords are
encrypted and can only be viewed using that person's ID
file. Also, the passwords are only for Notes. Windows NT
passwords are not created in this manner.

10. Click **OK** to begin to register Windows NT users within Lotus
Notes.

Delete Users in Windows NT

From within Windows NT, you may delete a Notes and Windows NT
user simultaneously, assuming you have proper security rights to
both systems. To delete a Notes and Windows NT user from Windows
NT, follow these steps

1. Start the User Manager program from Windows NT.

2. Click **Notes, Deletion/Rename Options.** The dialog box
shown in Figure 9-13 appears:

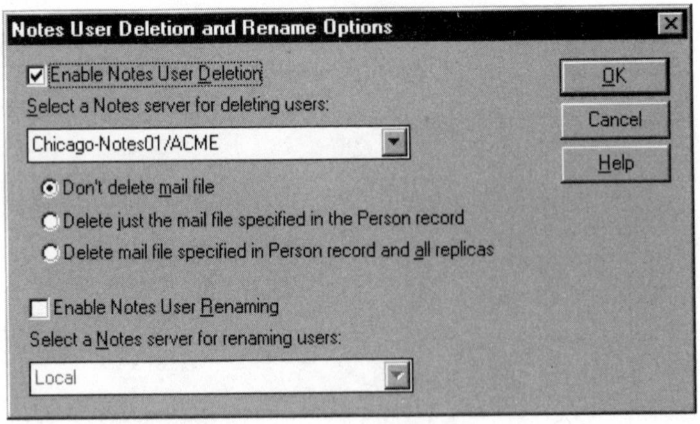

Figure 9-13
User Deletion Settings
Dialog Box

3. Click **Enable Notes User Deletions.**

4. Click the name of the Notes server where the public Name and
Address book exists to perform the deletions.

5. Select one the following three options:

- **Delete just the mail file specified in Person record.** This will delete only the mail files for the persons specified in the public Name and Address book. Any other replica copies of the users' mail files will not be removed.

- **Delete mail file specified in Person record and all replicas.** This will delete all replica copies of the users mail files on all Notes servers.

- **Don't delete mail file.** This option will not delete a users mail file.

6. Click **OK.**

7. Now highlight the users) to delete within User Manager and click **User, Delete**.

8. Click **OK** to delete users from both systems.

The administration process on a Notes server handles all deletions for Lotus Notes. It should also be noted that the Notes full name or short name must match the Windows NT full name or user name, respectively.

Rename Users in Windows NT

From within Windows NT, you may rename a Notes and Windows NT user simultaneously, assuming you have proper security rights to both systems. To rename a Notes and Windows NT user from Windows NT, follow these steps:

1. Start the User Manager program from Windows NT.

2. Click **Notes, Deletion/Rename Options**. The dialog box shown in Figure 9-14 appears:

Figure 9-14
User Rename
Settings
Dialog Box

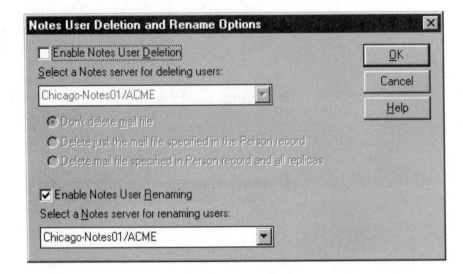

3. Click **Enable Notes User Renaming**.

4. Click the name of the Notes server where the public Name and Address book exists to perform the renaming.

5. Click **OK**.

6. Highlight the user to rename within the User Manager program and click **User, Rename**.

7. Enter the user's new user name.

8. Click **OK**.

Tips

You may use the Windows NT user manager program on both a Windows NT Workstation and Windows NT Server. However, in order to create or delete Windows NT accounts from within Notes, you have to be logged on to a Windows NT domain rather than a workgroup.

Notes Server Monitoring with Windows NT Event Log and Performance Monitor

Within Lotus Notes version 4.5 and higher, a Notes administrator may add the Notes server process to the Windows NT Event log and performance monitor. This allows administrators to record and view all Notes/Domino and operating system events in a single location.

Windows NT Event Log

To enable Notes events to be logged to the Windows NT event log, the new option **Log to NT Event Viewer** has been added to the Notification Method field of the Event Notification form in the Notes application **EVENTS4.NSF**. This option only appears if the Domino server is running on Windows NT.

Lotus Notes server events will appear in the Application view of the Windows NT Event Viewer, as shown in Figure 9-15:

Figure 9-15
Windows NT
Event Log

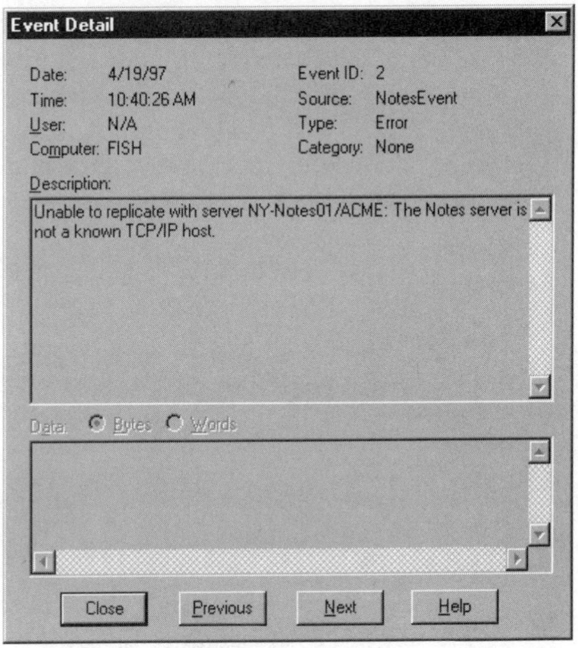

Table 9.1 shows the severity levels for Lotus Notes server events within the Windows NT Event Log.

Table 9.1

Lotus Notes
Server—Windows
NT Event Log
Entries

Lotus Notes Server Severity Level	NT severity level
Fatal and Failure	Error
Warning (high and low)	Warning
Normal	Informational

Windows NT Performance Monitor

The Windows NT performance monitor can be used to monitor the performance of the system components of the machine. Items such as network, processor, disk I/O, and memory should be monitored. In the event of continued strain on any of these processes, additional hardware may be needed.

With version 4.5 of Notes, the Notes server is now an item within the performance monitor of Windows NT. To add the Notes server as an item within the Windows NT performance monitor, follow these steps:

1. You may need to install **lodctr.exe**, **unlodctr.exe**, and **regini.exe** on your Windows NT system. These executables can be installed from the Windows NT Resource Kit, Windows NT Device Development Kit, or the Lotus Notes custom installation setting of Notes performance monitor. Refer to Chapter 7, *Installation Guidelines* for more details.

2. Open a command prompt on the Windows NT machine.

3. From the Notes program directory on the Notes server, type **notesreg.bat *directory*** where *directory* is the full path to the Notes program directory.

4. Lotus Notes will be a selection within the Window NT performance monitor.

Figure 9-16 shows an example of the Lotus Notes entry within the Windows NT performance monitor.

Figure 9-16

Windows NT
Performance
Monitor

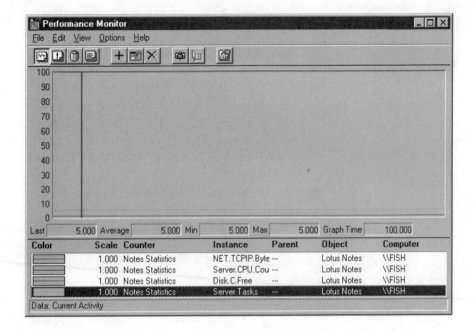

Configuring Windows NT Servers to Run Lotus Notes Servers

For optimal performance on the Windows NT environment, the following two registry settings should be configured. This includes both versions 3.51 and 4.0 of Windows NT. The first is listed below:

```
HKEY_LOCAL_MACHINE\System\CurrentControlSet\Control\Session
Manager\Memory Management\LargeSystemCache
```

By default, Windows NT has this setting set to 1. Lotus recommends that the setting be changed to 0.

The following values are accepted:

● **3—Minimize Memory Used.** This option is used so that the Windows NT server minimizes its memory usage and accepts a low number of network connections (up to 10 concurrent connections). This would be unusable for a Lotus Notes server due to the number of connections supported.

- **2—Balance.** This option initially allocates memory for up to 64 network connections. Again, this would be an unacceptable number of concurrent connections for a Lotus Notes server.

- **1—Maximize Throughput for File Sharing.** This option enables the Windows NT server to initially allocate memory for an unlimited number of connections (up to 71,000 network connections). This is the default setting and should be used if the Windows NT server is used for file and print activity.

- **0—Maximize Throughput for Network Applications.** This option initially allocates memory for the Windows NT server for an unlimited number of connections, but does not set aside much memory for cache. This is the recommended setting for a Notes server.

The second registry setting that should be changed on a Notes server is the following:

```
HKEY_LOCAL_MACHINE\System\CurrentControlSet\Control\
PriorityControl\Win32PrioritySeparation
```

By default, this is set to 2. Lotus recommends that this setting be changed to a value of 0. By lowering this value, foreground applications will not get as much processor time. For Notes servers, this is the ideal setting, as no other foreground applications should be running on the Windows NT machine.

Tips

These two registry setting changes can be made by using the Registry Editor (REGEDT32.EXE found in the WINNT35\SYSTEM32 or WINNT\SYSTEM32 directory of the Windows NT machine). Using this program, you should have knowledge of how the registry operates.

Traps

If an incorrect setting is made, disastrous effects could befall the Windows NT machine.

The preferred method to make the necessary registry settings is to use the Control Panel within Windows NT.

To change the **LargeSystemCache** registry setting with the Windows NT Control Panel, perform the following steps (Windows NT version 4.0 is shown):

1. From within Windows NT version 4.0, open the **Control Panel** icon.

2. Open the **Network** icon.

3. Click the **Services** tab and highlight the **Server** entry.

4. Click **Properties**.

5. The Server Optimization settings dialog box, shown in Figure 9-17, appears:

Figure 9-17
Windows NT
Server Optimization
Dialog Box

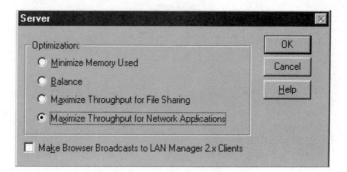

6. Select **Maximize Throughput for Network Applications**.

7. Click **OK** and **Close**. You must restart the Windows NT machine for the change to take place.

To change the **Win32PrioritySeparation** registry setting from the Windows NT Control Panel, perform the following steps (version 4.0 of Windows NT is shown):

1. From within Windows NT version 4.0, open the **Control Panel** icon.

2. Open the **System** icon.

3. Click the **Performance** tab. The dialog box shown in Figure 9-18 appears:

Figure 9-18

Windows NT
Server Tasking
Dialog Box

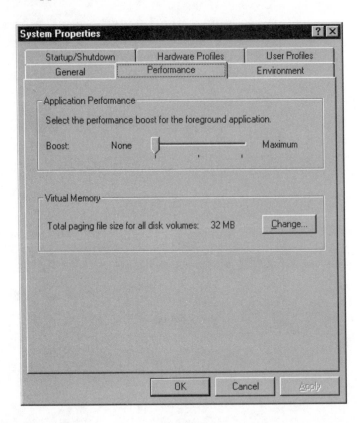

4. Move the application performance selector to the far left setting (**None** setting). This changes the Windows NT registry setting to zero from the default of two.

5. Click **OK**.

Configuring Lotus Notes Server to Run as a Windows NT Service

To configure a Windows NT machine to run a Lotus Notes server as a service, you will need to select the Notes service install selection when installing the Notes server. Refer to Chapter 7, *Installation Guidelines*, for details on how to make this selection.

To add an entry within the registry of the Windows NT machine for the Lotus Notes server, follow these steps:

1. Open a command prompt on the Windows NT machine.

2. Change to the directory where the Lotus Notes program is installed (e.g. C:\NOTES).

3. Type the following line from the command prompt:

```
NTSVINST -c
```

Tips

The NTSVINST –d command will remove the Lotus Notes server from the service registry entry.

4. Close the command prompt.

5. Open the **Control Panel** of the Windows NT machine.

6. Open the **Services** icon.

7. Highlight the **Lotus Domino Server** as shown in Figure 9-19:

Figure 9-19
Lotus Notes Server
Service Entry

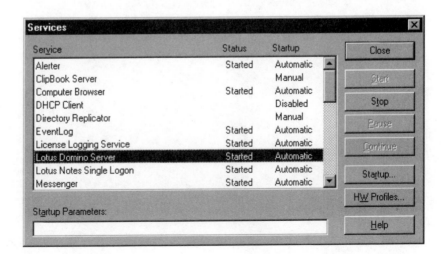

8. Click the **Startup** button.

9. Click **Automatic** to have the server startup automatically when the Windows NT machine begins. Leave the entry so that the Notes server is able to use the system account.

10. Click **OK**.

11. Click the **Start** button to start the Notes server as a service.

12. Click **Close**.

Traps

You should always start and stop a Notes server from the SERVICES panel of the Windows NT machine. If you start a Notes server by running it from the icon, the Notes server program will be closed when you log off of the machine.

What about minimum password length / password value

of server.id.

Should it be ∅ ie password can be cleared ?

10

Replication

Replication is the heart of Lotus Notes and is responsible for much of what the product is today. Many different products have tried to accomplish what Lotus has achieved with its replication engine, with minimal success. Replication has made it possible for all users, both in the office and remotely connected, to effectively and efficiently share information regardless of location or time zones. Replication also makes it possible for people to share information without accessing a central database.

In this chapter we discuss Notes replication in detail, present several model replication structures, address access control issues, provide administration tips, and discuss fine-tuning replication.

Definition

Replication is simply the exchange of data between two Notes servers or a Notes server and a client. This action occurs between common databases in either a bi-directional or one-way mode. The Lotus replication engine automatically synchronizes data between like Notes database applications so that the end result after a replication event is two identical Lotus Notes applications containing the same information. On a Notes server, the replication engine is a program that runs on the server. For Notes replication to occur between two machines, the machines must share a protocol in common that is enabled within Notes.

Notes servers and clients replicate databases by what is termed a *replica ID*, not by database title or file name. Each database has its own unique replica ID number. It can be compared to the concept that every person in America is identified by his or her social security number, not his or her name. In fact, to Notes at both the file system and application name levels, duplicate names can exist. It is the replica ID number that matters to Notes and is looked up by a Notes server or client when replication commences. Notes will replicate all like databases based on like replica IDs between servers and/or clients. This includes all databases that exist in the data directory of Notes as defined in the NOTES.INI file, as well as in any directory/database links. If any database does not exist within the data directory or one of its subdirectories or links, the Notes server or client will not replicate the database.

Figure 10-1 shows where the replica ID can be found on a Notes database application:

1. Click **File**, **Database**, **Properties**.

2. Click the **Information** tab.

Figure 10-1
Notes Database
Replica ID Information

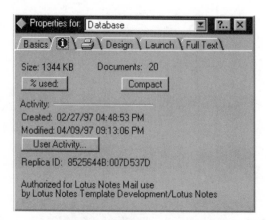

When a replication process begins between two servers, the initiating server first builds a list of replica IDs of its databases. The receiving server then also builds a list of replica IDs independent of database titles and filenames. If any like matches exist, the servers then determine if documents have been changed or added. Any documents that have been changed are identified and the date and time of creation ascertained. The initiating server then begins to push its data to the receiving server (assuming default replication settings and proper security access are in place). The initiating server then pulls any data from the second Notes server. For this reason, only the initiating server will have entries in its Notes log for replication events (again, assuming defaults for replication are in place).

With release 4 of Lotus Notes, replication now occurs at the field level of Notes database applications rather than at the document level. This feature is automatically used for version 4 Notes servers and clients. Prior to release 4, within a Notes application every new document and every edited document was replicated in full to all replica databases throughout the Notes infrastructure. This produces a lot of unneeded overhead. For example, take a large existing document within a Notes application containing a large number of fields. If a person were to edit just one field of the document, without field level replication enabled, the entire document (all fields including the ones that were not edited) would be replicated to all other Notes replica databases. However, if the machines were both running Notes version 4, only the edited field would be replicated between the replica databases; the other fields within the document would be skipped.

Tips

In order to take advantage of field-level replication, the two replicating machines must both be running at least version 4.0 of Lotus Notes. If one of the servers or clients is running an earlier version, field-level replication will not be used.

If a new document is ever added to a Notes application, it is added to all replica copies within the Notes infrastructure at the next scheduled replication event, assuming proper security rights. Replication of documents and fields for existing documents to other replicas are based upon sequence numbers and dates. For example, if a document exists in location A and location B, and a user edits a field in the application in location B, location B's change will replicate to location A and reflect the edit. This is because the sequence number of the field that was edited was incremented by one. The sequence number for the document containing the edited field will also increment by 1. To view the sequence number of a document, click **File**, **Document Properties** while within the document. The sequence number appears within the document ID number following the letters *SN* (Sequence Number). The sequence number for a document can be found as shown in Figure 10-2:

Figure 10-2
Document Sequence Number

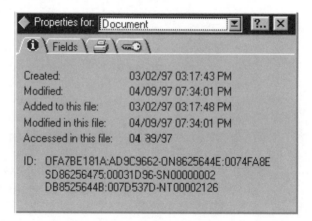

To view the sequence number of a field, click **File**, **Document Properties** while within the document, then click the **Fields** tab and highlight the field you would like to view. The sequence number appears in the data box following the **Seq Num** entry. The sequence number for a field can be seen in Figure 10-3:

Figure 10-3
Field Sequence
Number

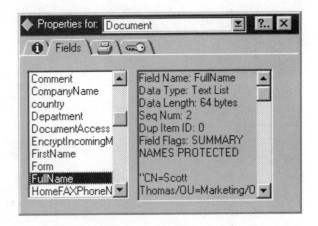

Tips

In order for replication to occur between two Notes machines within the same Notes domain and organization certification hierarchy, the Notes servers must be allowed access to each other based on the Access server field within each Notes machine's server documents. Also, all Notes database applications to be replicated must allow each server proper access in the ACL of the database.

Replication Structures

When you have more than one Notes server within your organization, you must set up a replication structure between Notes servers, even if you do not have any Notes applications created. This is because the public Name and Address book for your organization must replicate in order to contain all administration updates. Administration is only done to one public Name and Address book within your Notes infrastructure. Replication then carries those changes to other Notes servers.

There are three major models of replication between Notes servers including a hub and spoke architecture, hierarchical architecture, and the peer-to-peer architecture. The sections that follow define and explain each architecture.

Peer-to-Peer Model

A peer-to-peer replication architecture is used for smaller Notes environments. In this type of architecture, all Notes servers replicate with one another. Figure 10-4 depicts such a replication architecture:

Figure 10-4
Peer-to-Peer
Replication Model

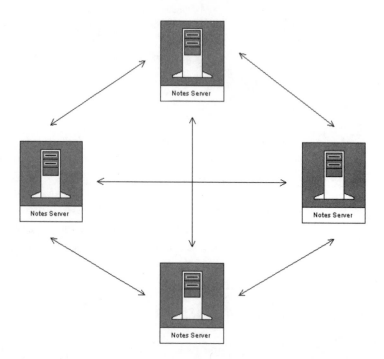

Companies should consider using a peer-to-peer replication architecture only if the total number of servers within the Notes domain is less than 6. If the environment contains more than this number of Notes servers, or if the environment is anticipated to grow past this number of Notes servers, another replication architecture is recommended. For example, under this peer-to-peer architecture, six Notes servers would require 15 replication connection records within the public Name and Address book to connect all Notes servers. The equation used to figure the number of connection documents is $n*(n-1)/2$ where n is the total number of servers.

Peer-to-peer replication is a somewhat inefficient means of distributing data, especially as the total number of Notes servers grows.

Peer-to-peer replication architecture does offer more reliable replication as all servers replicate with one another. However, the administrative overhead and complexity outweighs such an approach in larger Notes environments.

Hierarchical or Binary Tree Model

This type of replication architecture is arranged in a pyramid where a top level Notes server replicates with servers below itself. Those children Notes servers then are responsible for replicating with their children, and so on. Such an architecture is depicted in Figure 10-5:

Figure 10-5
Binary Tree
Replication
Model

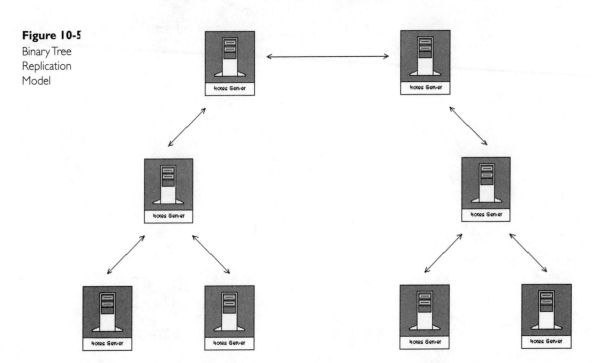

This type of replication architecture is a more efficient means of distributing data than the peer-to-peer model; however, it is not as efficient as a hub-and-spoke architecture. The main fault with this type of architecture is that if one server fails in replication, all others fall behind. Organizations that are spread internationally may want to consider such an architecture where distances and prices concerning those connections are an issue.

Hub-and-Spoke

The hub-and-spoke replication architecture is the most popular replication architecture—especially for larger Notes installations—as it offers the most efficient means of distributing data. With this type of design, there is a central Notes server or a combination of servers (hubs), responsible for replicating to outer Notes servers (spokes). The hub(s) are responsible then for calling all spoke servers and distributing data to the Notes servers. Such an architecture is shown in Figure 10-6:

Figure 10-6

Hub-and-Spoke
Replication
Model

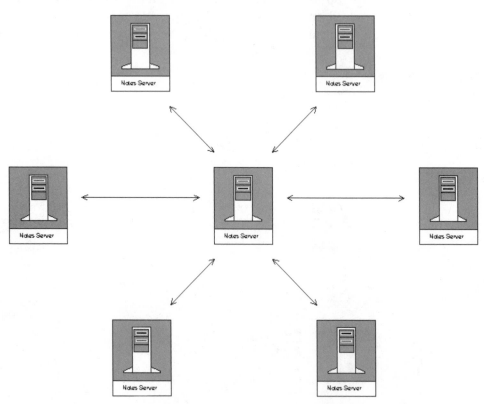

This type of replication model centralizes Notes administration, as all connection records are from the hub(s) to spokes and all replication events appear within the hub Notes logs, as the hub(s) Notes server initiates the replication event. If your environment is running multiple protocols, the hub Notes servers can be configured so that it also runs multiple protocols; it replicates with Notes servers running those protocols acting like a bridge between the two environments.

Tips

*A **hybrid hub-and-spoke and hierarchical model** can be used in organizations with regional servers. These regional servers then act as top-level servers replicating to child servers. This method can be effectively used to maintain consistent and timely replication between hub and spokes, while providing local efficiencies.*

Connection Records

Replication is set through connection records in the public Name and Address book. Settings such as times to replicate, frequency of replication, and priorities of databases are set in the records (high, medium, low). Creating a connection record within the public Name and Address book is detailed in Chapter 6, *Public Name and Address Book Forms and Views.*

Tips

Unlike mail connection records, replication connection records are only needed on one Notes server. The initiating Notes server will pull and push all documents, as replication is a two way process (assuming default replication configurations). Once a replication connection record is created for a Notes server, you do not have to create another connection record for the target Notes server.

Connection Types

Within this section, we further examine the connection document a Notes server needs to establish replication.

There are several types of connection records that may be created to establish connectivity to another Notes server for replication. We will look at the local area network connection, dialup modem, passthru server, and remote LAN service.

If you have multiple connection documents set to a target Notes server, Notes tries to connect to the target Notes server in this order:

1. Local area network

2. Remote LAN service

3. Dialup modem

4. Passthru server

If a connection fails, Notes tries the next type of connection record in the order listed above.

Local Area Network Connection Record

The local area network connection should be used to connect two Notes servers with a common protocol through a LAN or WAN environment. Figure 10-7 shows this type of connection record:

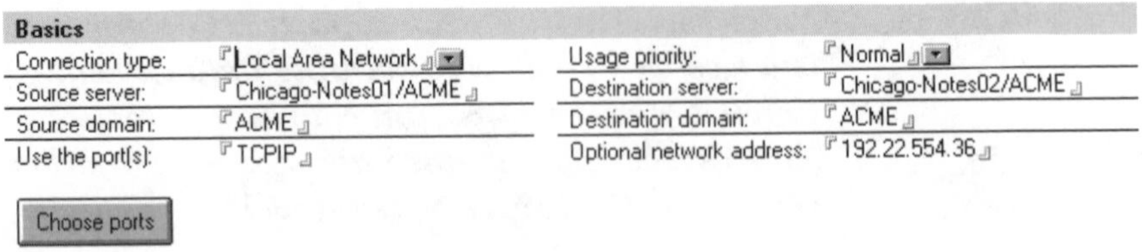

Figure 10-7
LAN Connection
Record

Once this type of connection record is set, you can configure the following fields related to this type of connection:

● **Connection type:** As stated before, this should be Local Area Network.

● **Source server:** Enter the source Notes server. This is the Notes server initiating the replication. All information concerning the replication is recorded within this Notes server's log. No information appears in the target Notes server's Notes log.

- **Source domain:** Enter the source Notes server's domain.

- **Use the port(s):** You may press the **Choose Ports** button to select which network port(s) to use to connect with the target Notes server. It tries each port in the order listed within this field. For information on how to set up a port within Notes, see Chapter 3, *Network Protocols*. If you leave this field blank, Notes will use all available ports on the source Notes server to try to connect to the target Notes server, based on the order in which the ports are configured in the Notes server setup.

- **Usage Priority:** If you leave this field as **Normal**, Notes will use this connection record first to try to connect to the target Notes server. If you set this field to **Low**, Notes uses other methods first to tries to connect to the target Notes server and try this connection record last.

- **Destination server:** Enter the destination Notes server to replicate with.

- **Destination domain:** Enter the destination domain of the target Notes server.

- **Optional network address:** Enter the network address of the Notes server. For TCP/IP networks, enter the IP address of the target Notes server in the event there is a DNS failure (if DNS is used).

Dialup Modem Connection Record

Dialup connection records are used to connect two Notes servers that are not directly connected through a LAN or WAN environment. This type of connection record should be used if you have analog or digital modems, such as ISDN, that are directly connected to the Notes server *and* you wish the Notes server to perform the dial-up procedure. The Notes servers communicate using the Notes X.PC protocol. For connections that will use remote LAN services, such as Windows NT RAS, you need to use a remote LAN service connection record (explained later in this section).

Once you create a dialup modem replication connection record within the public Name and Address book, the screen shown in Figure 10-8 appears:

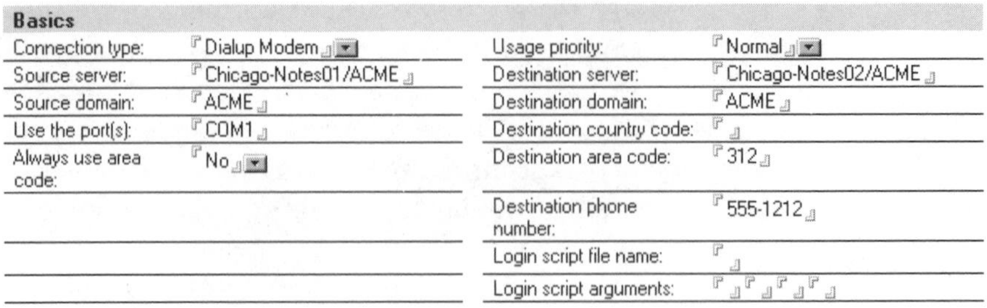

Figure 10-8
Dialup Modem
Connection
Record

Basics			
Connection type:	Dialup Modem	Usage priority:	Normal
Source server:	Chicago-Notes01/ACME	Destination server:	Chicago-Notes02/ACME
Source domain:	ACME	Destination domain:	ACME
Use the port(s):	COM1	Destination country code:	
Always use area code:	No	Destination area code:	312
		Destination phone number:	555-1212
		Login script file name:	
		Login script arguments:	

Once this type of connection record is set, you can configure the following fields related to this type of connection:

- **Connection type:** This should be Dialup Modem.

- **Source server:** Enter the source Notes server. This is the Notes server that initiates the replication. All information concerning the replication is recorded within this Notes server's log. No information appears in the target Notes server's Notes log.

- **Source domain:** Enter the source Notes server's domain.

- **Use the port(s):** Enter the port(s) to use to connect with the target Notes server. Each port is tried in the order listed within this field. Each COM port's number enabled in Notes relates to the actual physical port to which the modem is connected. For information on how to set up a port within Notes, see Chapter 3, *Network Protocols*.

- **Always use area code:** Enter whether or not to force this connection to use the area code for the phone number of the target Notes server.

- **Usage priority:** If you leave this field as **Normal**, Notes uses this connection record first to try to connect to the target Notes server. If you set this field to **Low**, Notes uses other methods first to try to connect to the target Notes server. It tries this connection record last.

- **Destination server:** Enter the destination Notes server with which to replicate.

- **Destination domain:** Enter the destination domain of the target Notes server.

- **Destination country code** (Optional): Enter the target Notes server's country code.

- **Destination area code:** Enter the target Notes server's area code.

- **Destination phone number:** Enter the 7-digit phone number of the target Notes server.

- **Login script file name:** If you dial in to a PAD to connect to an X.25 network such as CompuServe, enter the file name of the script you will use.

- **Login script arguments:** If you dial in to a PAD to connect to an X.25 network, enter the script arguments to use.

Passthru Connection Record

This type of connection will allow a source Notes server to specify an intermediary Notes server to act as a bridge. This bridge ultimately connects to a destination Notes server. In this manner, the source and destination Notes servers need not be running the same protocol. With this type of scenario, the intermediary (passthru) Notes server can be configured with multiple protocols to support such connections.

Once you create a passthru replication connection record within the public Name and Address book, the screen shown in Figure 10-9 appears:

Figure 10-9
Passthru
Connection
Record

Basics			
Connection type:	⸢Passthru Server ⸥▼	Usage priority:	⸢Normal ⸥▼
Source server:	⸢Chicago-Notes01/ACME ⸥	Destination server:	⸢NY-Notes01/ACME ⸥
Source domain:	⸢ACME ⸥	Destination domain:	⸢ACME ⸥
Use passthru server:	⸢Chicago-Notes02/ACME ⸥		

Once this type of connection record is set, you can configure the following fields related to this type of connection:

- **Connection type:** This should be Passthru Server.

- **Source server:** Enter the source Notes server. This is the Notes server that initiates the replication. All information concerning the replication is recorded within this Notes server's log. No information appears in the target Notes server's Notes log.

- **Source domain:** Enter the source Notes server's domain.

- **Use passthru server:** Enter the passthru (intermediary) Notes server to route through in order to reach the destination Notes server.

- **Usage priority:** If you leave this field as **Normal**, Notes uses this connection record first to try to connect to the target Notes server. If you set this field to **Low**, Notes uses other methods first to try to connect to the target Notes server. This connection record is tried last.

- **Destination server:** Enter the destination Notes server with which to replicate.

- **Destination domain:** Enter the destination domain of the target Notes server.

Tips

In order to use passthru, the Notes server requesting passthru service must be allowed passthru access and calling access in the passthru Notes server's server record in the public Name and Address book. These fields include the **Route through** *and* **Cause calling** *fields. In addition, the destination server via passthru must allow the calling Notes server access in the* **Access this server** *field in the passthru section of the server document. By default, all three fields allow* **no** *access.*

Remote LAN Service Connection Record

With version 4 of Lotus Notes, you can now use the operating system's remote LAN services to make a connection to a target Notes server. These type of systems include Microsoft's RAS (Remote Access Server) and SHIVA's remote node products, to name two. Basically, when using either of these types of products, the machine running remote LAN services becomes another node on the network. It is as if the machine were directly connected within the office. The difference is that all network activity is rerouted through the modem of the calling machine.

Lotus Notes version 4.5 currently supports the use of either Microsoft's LAN service (RAS) or AppleTalk Remote Access (ARA) on the machine doing the calling. The Microsoft RAS server and client provide connectivity through a PPP (Point to Point Protocol) connection. Within a PPP connection, the protocols the Notes servers are running (TCP/IP, SPX, etc.) are encapsulated within the PPP protocol. The RAS service can use either a standard analog modem or an ISDN device. These devices are configured within the Windows NT or Windows 95 RAS service. As far as the Notes servers are concerned, they are communicating via the network protocol, such as TCP/IP, as if the two machines were on the same LAN or WAN.

Once you create a Remote LAN Service replication connection record within the public Name and Address book, the screen shown in Figure 10-10 appears:

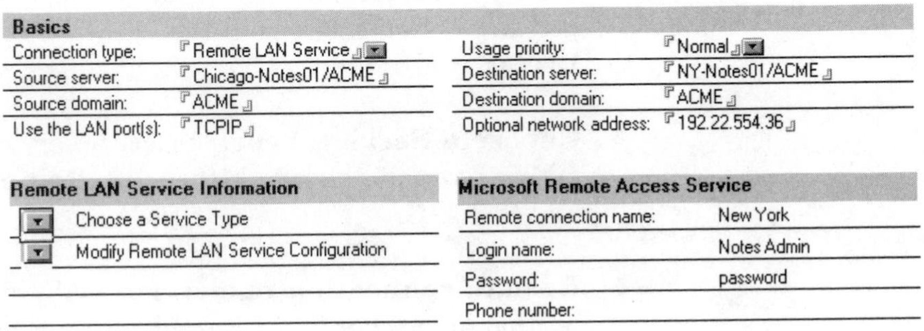

Figure 10-10

Remote LAN
Service
Connection
Record

Basics			
Connection type:	Remote LAN Service	Usage priority:	Normal
Source server:	Chicago-Notes01/ACME	Destination server:	NY-Notes01/ACME
Source domain:	ACME	Destination domain:	ACME
Use the LAN port(s):	TCPIP	Optional network address:	192.22.554.36

Remote LAN Service Information	Microsoft Remote Access Service	
▼ Choose a Service Type	Remote connection name:	New York
▼ Modify Remote LAN Service Configuration	Login name:	Notes Admin
	Password:	password
	Phone number:	

Once this type of connection record is set, you can configure the following fields related to this type of connection:

- **Connection type:** This should be Remote LAN Service.

- **Source server:** Enter the source Notes server. This is the Notes server that initiates the replication. All information concerning the replication is recorded within this Notes server's log. No information appears in the target Notes server's Notes log.

- **Source domain:** Enter the source Notes server's domain.

- **Use the LAN port(s):** Specify the port(s) that have been enabled on the remote LAN services of the operating system (RAS in Windows NT). It will try each port in the order listed within this field. For information on how to set up a port within Notes, see Chapter 3, *Network Protocols*.

- **Usage priority:** If you leave this field as **Normal**, Notes uses this connection record first to try to connect to the target Notes server. If you set this field to **Low**, Notes uses other methods first to try to connect to the target Notes server. It tries this connection record last.

- **Destination server:** Enter the destination Notes server with which to replicate.

- **Destination domain:** Enter the destination domain of the target Notes server.

- **Optional network address:** Enter the network address of the Notes server. For TCP/IP networks, enter the IP address of the target Notes server in the event there is a DNS failure (if DNS is used).

- **Choose a Service Type:** Select a service. For Windows NT or Windows 95, choose **Microsoft Remote Access Service** and click **OK**.

- **Remote connection name:** For RAS, enter the remote connection name that is configured within RAS.

- **Login name:** Enter the login name used to connect to the RAS server. This field may not be necessary if it has already been configured from the RAS connection.

- **Password:** Enter the password used to log into the RAS server. This field may not be necessary if it has already been configured from the RAS connection.

- **Phone number:** Enter the phone number used to log into the RAS server. This field may not be necessary if it has already been configured from the RAS connection.

- **Modify Remote LAN Service Configuration:** Use this field to modify any of the above remote LAN services parameters.

Replication Priority

A Notes administrator or Notes database manager may specify three possible priority settings for a Notes database application: **High**, **Medium**, and **Low**. Connection records for replication can be set to replicate all types or a subset of each type of application. In other words, a connection record that replicates every hour could be created to only replicate **High** priority databases with a target Notes server. Still another connection record with the same target Notes server could be created to only replicate **Medium** and **Low** databases once or twice a day.

Within a Notes connection record, this setting is established with the **Replicate databases of...** field of the connection document, as shown in Figure 10-11:

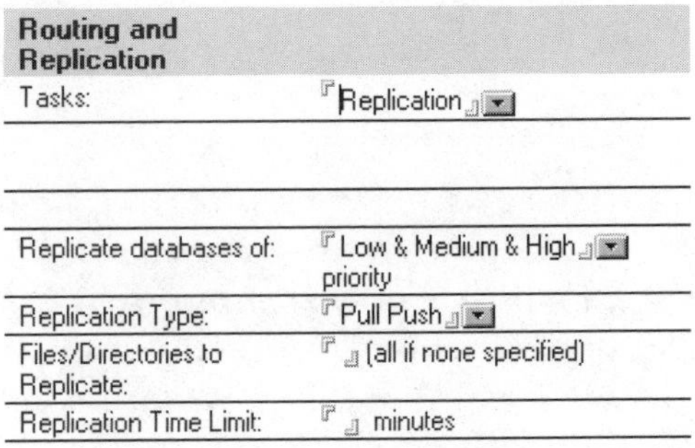

Figure 10-11

Replication Fields within a Connection Record

Routing and Replication	
Tasks:	Replication
Replicate databases of:	Low & Medium & High priority
Replication Type:	Pull Push
Files/Directories to Replicate:	(all if none specified)
Replication Time Limit:	minutes

On a Notes database application, the priority of the database can be set by entering the replication settings of the Notes application, as shown in Figure 10-12:

Figure 10-12
Notes Database
Priority Setting

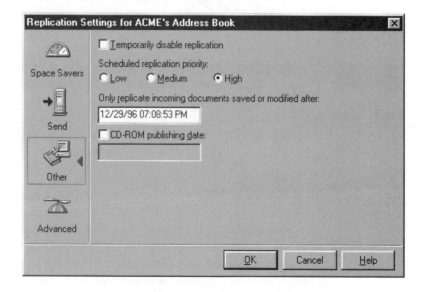

This is done as follows:

1. Highlight the Notes database icon and click **File**, **Database**, **Properties**.

2. Click the **Replication Settings** button.

3. Click the **Other** icon.

4. The replication priority for the Notes application can be set.

Tips

Before using the replication priority, you should consider the administrative requirements necessary to take complete advantage of this capability. It has been our experience that organizations taking advantage of replication priority settings often do so without a strategy for effectively using and managing this feature.

Scheduling

Lotus Notes enables you to schedule replication at a specific time each day or to specify a range of times with a repeat interval. Scheduling times is handled within the **Scheduled Connection** section of the Notes connection record within the public Name and Address book. This section is shown in Figure 10-13:

Figure 10-13
Notes Connection
Record Replication
Schedule

Scheduled Connection	
Schedule:	⌜ENABLED ⌟▼
Call at times:	⌜08:00 AM - 10:00 PM⌟ each day
Repeat interval of:	⌜60⌟ minutes
Days of week:	⌜Sun, Mon, Tue, Wed, Thu, Fri, Sat⌟▼

There are four different types of schedules that may be established: one specific time, a list of times, time range with a repeat interval, and time range without a repeat interval.

- **One specific time.** To replicate with a target server at one specific time each day, enter that time within the **Call at Times** field. Populate the **Repeat interval of** field with a value of zero. The initiating Notes server will then call once each day at this time. If there is a failure, the initiating Notes server will retry for an hour. If a connection still is not established after this hour, replication will not be retried until the next day.

This type of connection is usually used to replicate Notes applications of **Low** priority.

- **A list of times.** This type of connection will replicate with the target Notes server at the times entered within the **Call at times** field of the Notes connection document. To replicate at 8:00 am, 12:00 pm, and 4:00 pm each day, you would enter those three times within the **Call at times** field. A value of zero should be entered within the **Repeat interval of** field. If the connection fails, the target Notes server will continue to try to connect for up to an hour. If after an hour the connection still has not been established, replication will not commence until the next scheduled time within the **Call at times** field.

This type of schedule is usually used to replicate Notes applications of **Medium** and/or **Low** priority.

- **Time range with a repeat interval.** With this type of schedule, the initiating Notes server will replicate with the target Notes server for a specified time range, repeating every certain number of minutes. You may wish to have your Notes server replicate with a target Notes server from 8:00 am to 10:00 pm every two hours. For this type of configuration, you should enter the times **8:00 am–10:00 pm** in the **Call at times** field, and **120 minutes** within the **Repeat interval of** field.

If the first replication attempt is unsuccessful, the initiating Notes server will continue attempting until the end of the specified time range or at the next time of repetition.

This type of connection record is usually used to replicate databases of **High** priority.

- **Time range without a repeat interval.** With this type of schedule, the initiating Notes server will replicate with the target Notes server once commencing at the beginning of the specified time range. If the scheduled replication is successful, replication will not occur until the next day. However, if the attempt is unsuccessful, the initiating Notes server will retry continuously throughout the time range. For this type of configuration, you should enter the schedule within the **Call at times** field and enter a value of zero in the **Repeat interval of** field.

If the first replication attempt is unsuccessful, the initiating Notes server will continue attempting until the end of the specified time range; however, the time between each call attempt will increase. This type of connection record is usually used to replicate databases of **Low** or **Medium** priority.

Tips

If mail routing is going to be enabled within the connection record as well as replication, issues surrounding routing mail should be considered. See **Chapter 11,** *Electronic Mail, to understand how e-mail is routed based on con-nection records. It may be necessary to create one connection record for e-mail and another connection record for replication to the target Notes server, depending on your organization. It should also be noted that e-mail that is destined for the target server is also delivered during the replication cycle regardless of the mail settings within the connection record.*

The **Days of the week** field can also be set to schedule replication only on certain days of the week. It may be valuable to create two connection records for replication to a target Notes server where one record is only for Monday–Friday and the other connection record is for Saturday and Sunday.

When establishing connection records within a hub-and-spoke replication architecture, you may wish to stagger connection records from the hub to spoke servers with a call range of times without a repeat interval. This makes it so a hub Notes server does not try to replicate with multiple spoke servers at the same time (assuming only one replicator is enabled on the hub server). Also, using this staggered approach reduces the likelihood a Notes server will be skipped as the call range is increased. For example, the hub Notes server may be set to replicate with Notes spoke server A at 8:00 am–10:00 am, spoke B at 9:00 am–11:00 am, and spoke C at 10:00 am–12:00 pm. With this type of scheduling, each Notes server is guaranteed at least an hour of replication time. In the event of failure, there will also be a retry period of two hours to each spoke Notes server.

Tips

If your company is spread throughout different time zones, you should replicate with spoke Notes servers within a later time zone first. This ensures that these people see more timely data before people residing in earlier time zones. In the United States, you would replicate with servers in the Eastern time zone before those in the Pacific time zone.

It is recommended that an organization with a hub-and-spoke replication structure set replication schedules so that **High** priority databases must be scheduled to replicate from the most distant point within any hub Notes server within four hours. **Medium** and **Low** priority databases should then replicate with a hub Notes server within 24 hours. Close attention must be paid so that developers understand the impact of classifying a database application as high priority. If large applications classified as **High** priority begin appearing within the infrastructure, replication may not be accomplished within this time window. Twenty-four hours is usually the standard that organizations try to target for all Notes applications to be replicated throughout the Notes network.

Notes logs need to be monitored daily to ensure that timely replication is indeed happening. Notes statistics and monitoring may need to be configured as well to alert Notes administrators of a replication failure, especially for business-critical Notes applications. Additional bandwidth and/or replication tasks may need to be added on hub servers in order to keep this time window open. Remote locations using analog connections should be watched closely as the number of Notes applications increase.

Traps

Unless you have multiple replicators (server processes) configured on the initiating Notes server, do not schedule replication to occur at the same time on different ports or to multiple Notes server destinations. For example, do not schedule replication with two different connection records from server A to server B at 1:00 pm on both ports SPX and TCP/IP.

You may also limit the amount of time the initiating Notes server may replicate with the target Notes server. This setting is especially useful for remote locations using analog connections where cost is an issue. It is also useful for large Notes infrastructures where the replication time window for each server is a set, small window. To specify a time limit, populate the **Replication Time Limit** field with the desired number of minutes. If the field is left blank, Notes will take as much time as necessary to complete replication. Most of the time, you should leave this field blank. Figure 10-11 shows the location of this field within a Notes connection record.

Replication Direction

Within a replication connection document, you specify which server sends and/or receives documents. This is defined in the **Replication Type** field as shown in Figure 10-11. The choices are **Pull-Push, Pull-Pull**, **Push-Only**, and **Pull-Only**. Specifying a different replication type does not affect the replication process in terms of how the program works. It only affects in which direction replication occurs and which server does the work.

- **Pull-Push.** This is the default setting within Notes. With this type of replication, changes are distributed to both Notes servers. The initiating server first pulls the changes from the target server, then the initiating server pushes any changes to the target Notes server. The replicator program on the initiating Notes server does all the work of replication; all data concerning the replication event is recorded only in the initiating Notes server's log file. The replicator program on the target Notes server is not run in this type of replication.

- **Pull-Pull.** This type of replication is also a two-way distribution of data to both Notes servers. This model distributes the workload of replication where each Notes server's replicator program is run. Each Notes server pulls data from one another; both replication programs on each server are running.

- **Push-Only.** This type of replication is a one-way process where the initiating Notes server pushes changes to the target Notes server only. No updates are added to the initiating Notes server in any Notes application. Only the target Notes server receives updates to Notes applications.

- **Pull-Only.** This type of replication is a one-way process where the initiating Notes server only pulls changes to itself from the target Notes server. No updates are added to the target Notes server in any Notes application. Only the initiating Notes server receives updates to Notes applications.

Tips

The Pull-Only and Push-Only replication types can be used in combination to pull during one time interval and then push during another. This would be used in combination with **pull** *and* **push** *connection records in the Name and Address book. This type of replication scheme could be used in the hub-and-spoke scenario to allow all hub servers to gather new and/or modified documents and then push all changes out to servers, thus guaranteeing that all replica copies of databases were updated within a given replication cycle.*

Specifying Specific Databases to Replicate

Within the **Files/Directories to Replicate** field, as shown in Figure 10-11, you may specify which databases to replicate. By default, and assuming all database priorities are selected, all databases in common between two Notes server that are located within each Notes server's data directory, subdirectories relative to the data directory, and any database/directory links are replicated. To enable replication of specific Notes application(s), enter the directory and/or database application, separated by semicolons. For example, to replicate Notes applications in the \ADMIN subdirectory relative to the Notes data directory, you would enter:

```
\ADMIN
```

in the **Files/Directories to Replicate** field within the Notes connection document.

Tips

Wildcard entries (*) are not allowed within this field. If you have a Pull-Pull replication connection, this field will only affect replication of the initiating server. The target server will pull all databases from the initiating Notes server.

Disabling Replication to a Notes Server

There may be times where a Notes administrator or Notes database manager wishes to disable replication of a specific Notes database application or even an entire Notes replication connection record.

Any connection record to a target Notes server within the public Name and Address book can be temporarily disabled by editing the document and changing the **Schedule** field to **Disabled**.

Traps

If you disable a connection record for replication, and the connection record is also used for mail routing, mail routing will also be disabled to this server, assuming the target Notes server is not on the same Notes named network.

A single Notes database can be disabled as well. The Notes administrator or database manager can do this as follows:

1. Highlight the Notes database application and click **File**, **Database**, **Properties**.

2. Click the **Replication Settings** button.

3. Click the **Other** icon.

4. Click the **Temporarily Disable Replication** checkbox.

An alternate method follows:

1. Click **File**, **Tools**, **Server Administration**.

2. Highlight the desired Notes server and click the **Database Tools** icon.

3. Select the proper Notes server and database(s).

4. Select **Replication** from the **Tool** field.

5. Click the **Disable** radio button (see Figure 10-14).

Figure 10-14

Disable Replication
for Notes Applications

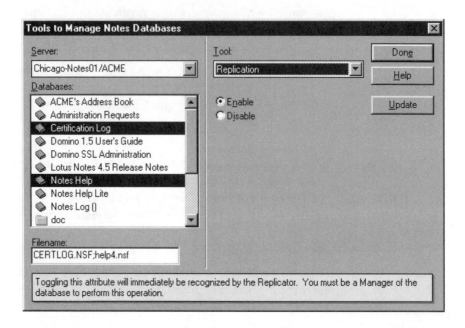

Tips

***You must have MANAGER access to the Notes database
application(s) in order to temporarily disable replication.***

ACL Database Settings and Effect on Replication

Just like Notes users, Notes servers have limited access to Notes
applications based upon the access control list (ACL) security
settings of Notes applications. If two Notes servers have replica
database application(s) in common but do not have proper access,
replication will not occur between the applications. Following
are the different ACL settings for a Notes application, and the
effect upon replication between two Notes machines. Table 10.1
shows a Notes database residing on Server B. Server A has been
assigned the following ACL rights to the Notes application on Server
B. The second column shows the replication results to the application on Server B.

Table 10.1
Database ACL
Effects upon
Replication

Replica Notes Application Residing on Server B	
ACL Assigned to Server A	**Result to Notes Application on Server B**
No Access	No changes or updates sent or received from Server A.
Depositor	This ACL setting only applies to users, not servers.
Reader	Changes and updates are sent to Server A. No new documents or updates to current documents are received from Server A
Author	Changes and updates are sent to Server A. New documents are received from Server A; updates to existing documents are not received from Server A.
Editor	Changes and updates are sent to Server A; new documents and updates to existing documents are received from Server A.
Designer	Changes and updates are sent to Server A. New documents are received from Server A; updates to existing documents are received from Server A. Design changes to the Notes application are received from Server A.
Manager	Changes and updates are sent to Server A. New documents are received from Server A; updates to existing documents are received from Server A. Design changes to the Notes application are received from Server A. All ACL settings to the Notes application are received from Server A.

Tips

We recommend that for all of your Notes applications within your Notes domain, you assign the LocalDomainServers group with MANAGER access. This allows all documents to be replicated and keeps the ACL of the application current. For databases that will be replicated outside of your Notes domain, the highest level of access ever recommended is EDITOR. Many times READER access is sufficient if no updates are going to be received from the external Notes server.

Traps

If the setting **Enforce a consistent ACL across all replicas of this database** *is enabled on a Notes application, replication will not occur for the application unless both replicating Notes servers have MANAGER access to the database. This setting is found within a Notes application in the* **Advanced ACL settings** *of a Notes application. See Figure 10-15.*

Figure 10-15
Enforce Consistent
ACL Setting
for Notes Applications

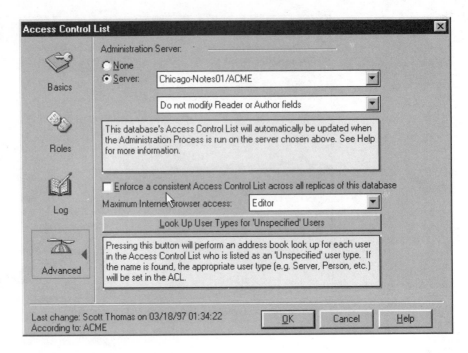

If an ACL change is made on two different replica copies of a Notes database application where the replicating Notes servers both have MANAGER access, the most recent change will prevail on both replica copies at the next scheduled replication.

Tips

Deploying Replica Copies of Applications

Deploying new replica databases within a Notes infrastructure should always be performed from the Notes administrator's desktop machine. By default, a new replica of a Notes application may not be created by any Notes user from a Notes workstation. The field **Create new replica databases** within the Notes server document controls who may create new replica Notes database applications on the Notes server. We recommend you populate this field with a group within your company that will be responsible for creating and maintaining replica Notes applications.

In order to create a new replica, follow these steps:

1. Click **File**, **Tools**, **Server Administration**.

2. Click the **Database Tools** icon.

3. Select **Create A Replica** from the Tool field.

4. Select the source Notes server from the **Server** field.

5. Select the destination Notes server from the **Destination Servers** field.

6. Select the Notes application(s) to create new replica copies.

7. (Optional) Click the **More Info** button to change the file name(s) of the new replica application(s).

8. Click the **Create** button to create the new replica Notes application(s). The Notes administration process carries out the request.

The following figure shows the new replica creation dialog box:

Figure 10-16
Create a New Replica
Notes Application(s)
Dialog Box

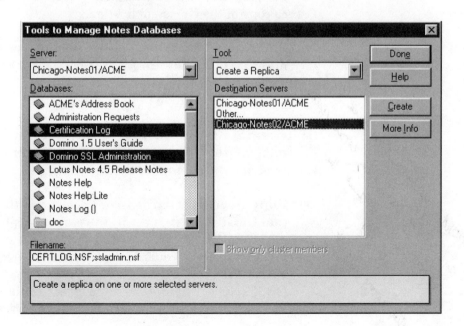

You can also create a new replica copy of a Notes database copy without using the administration process on a Notes server. To do so, follow the procedures below:

1. Highlight the database and click **File**, **Replica**, **New Replica**.

2. The New Replica dialog box appears as shown in Figure 10-17:

Figure 10-17
Create a New
Replica Database

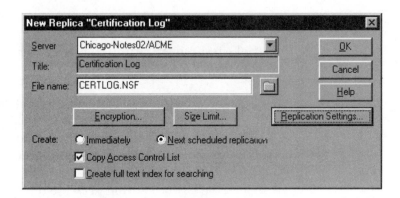

Configure the following fields:

- **Server:** Enter the destination Notes server for the new replica copy of the Notes application.

- **File Name:** Enter the destination file name and directory (if necessary) on the target Notes server. The database will appear in the data directory of the target Notes server or in a subdirectory relative to the data directory.

- **Create:** Select whether or not to create the replica copy immediately or during the next scheduled replication by selecting the appropriate radio button.

- **Copy Access Control List:** Select whether or not to replicate the ACL as it is set in the current replica copy. If you do not select to replicate the ACL, LocalDomainServers, OtherDomainServers, the administration server, and you will appear with MANAGER access. The Default access will be set to DESIGNER. The database designer could set other default access control attributes that would then take effect.

Several public address book by creating workstation local replica previously without this selected.

* replication history lost *

- **Create full text index for searching:** This checkbox will create a full-text index of the database on the target Notes server. You may create a full text index later if you decide not to create one at the time of creating the new replica copy.

- **Encryption:** Press the **Encryption** button if you wish to encrypt the database.

- **Size Limit:** Press the **Size Limit** button if you wish to set the absolute size the database application may reach. Once the database is created, the setting may not be changed.

- **Replication Settings:** Press the **Replication Settings** button to change any of the replication settings of the database, such as configuring a selective replication formula.

The remote administrators may obtain information on available applications from the Notes catalog, which lists all Notes and applications in the Notes infrastructure. It also lists what servers they are located on and the directory in which they reside. Many times users are alerted to new database applications available, and the Notes users should contact the local Notes administrator where available to create a stub on their local Notes server. The database catalog (unless modified) allows users to add a database application to their workspace by clicking a button.

Clearing Replication History

The replication history of a database determines to what extent replication has occurred between two Notes machines. Before replication begins between two machines, the replication history of each database is checked to determine where the previous replication left off.

If you experience problems replicating documents between two applications, the history may be viewed and cleared by performing the following steps:

1. Highlight the Notes database in question and click **File**, **Replication**, HISTORY. The following screen will appear (Figure 10-18):

Figure 10-18
Replication History
Dialog Box

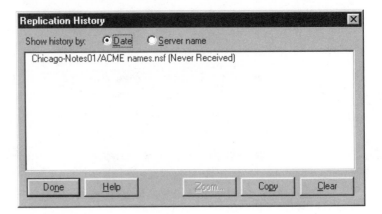

2. You may view the replication history of the database. If you want to clear the history, press the **Clear** button. You must have MANAGER access to the application in order to clear the history.

Tips

If you clear the replication history of the Notes application, replication will begin from the cutoff date of the application. If no cutoff date is specified, the entire database will replicate again. Care should be taken when clearing the history, especially for larger applications and where replication occurs over slow links.

Selective Replication

A Notes administrator or database manager may configure a Notes application so that only a subset of the database replicates to a target Notes server or client workstation. For example, a Notes application could replicate documents to or from a target machine based upon date, user name, specific fields, or document type. This can be done by selecting the views or fields desired, or even by creating a formula to select the desired documents.

To configure a selective replication formula, follow these steps:

1. Highlight the desired Notes database application and click **File**, **Database**, **Properties**.

2. Click the **Replication Settings** button, and then click the **Advanced** icon. The screen shown in Figure 10-19 appears:

Figure 10-19
Creating Selective
Replication Settings

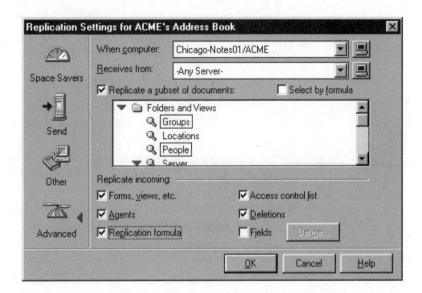

3. You can now select only the documents listed in the views by clicking the desired view(s), or you may create a formula to select the desired documents by clicking the **Select by formula** check box.

4. Fill in the source and target Notes machines in their respective fields.

5. Select the incoming items to replicate by checking any desired check boxes listed in the **Replicate incoming** section. This includes any fields desired by using the **Fields** check box.

Traps

Care should be exercised when creating selective replication formulas, as creating multiple types can lead to confusion when troubleshooting replication.

Replication and Save Conflicts

Replication conflicts occur in Notes applications when two or more users edit and save changes to the same document in the same Notes application on different Notes servers. When the next scheduled replication occurs, Notes flags the document as a replication conflict.

A save conflict is the same as a replication conflict except the action happens on the same server. Two or more users edit the same document in the same Notes database on the same server.

Replication and save conflicts can be handled in a number of ways. Further discussion on replication and save conflicts can be found in Chapter 12, *Notes Applications and Security Issues*.

Forcing an Unscheduled Replication

A Notes administrator may force an unscheduled replication by typing in the following command from the Notes server console or from a Notes remote server console:

```
Replicate Chicago-Notes01/ACME

Push Chicago-Notes01/ACME

Pull Chicago-Notes01/ACME
```

The fully distinguished Notes server name should be used following the command. The replicate command initiates replication in a two-way direction between Notes servers. The push command is a one-way command that only pushes changes to the target Notes server. The pull command is a one-way command that only pulls changes from the target Notes server.

A connection document must exist from the initiating Notes server to the target Notes server for these console commands to work. They should be used in the event a replication is necessary that cannot wait for the next scheduled replication. If the command with server name is followed by a database name, only that database will be replicated. The complete path relative to the initiating Notes server's directory must be entered. For example:

```
Replicate Chicago-Notes01/ACME admin\discuss.nsf
```

Fine-Tuning Replication

Depending on your Notes infrastructure, you may need to change some parameters of your Notes server to offer better performance. The rest of this chapter describes some of the settings that are available to accomplish this within Notes.

Enabling Multiple Replicators

With the release of Notes 4.0, a Notes server is now able to support multiple replication tasks to service multiple spoke Notes servers simultaneously. This gives the administrator the ability to replicate with more Notes servers and to broaden the infrastructure's daily replication window.

To enable multiple replicators on a Notes server, add the following setting to the Notes server's **NOTES.INI** file:

```
REPLICATORS = number
```

where *number* is the number of replicators to run on the Notes server.

This setting can also be configured from a configuration document within the public Name and Address book. For details on how to perform this action, see Chapter 6, *Public Name and Address Book Forms and Views.*

If the setting is added in either manner to the **NOTES.INI** file as explained above, the Notes server must be restarted for the change to take place.

If you wish to have an additional replicator running immediately without having to restart the Notes server, you may run it from the console or remote console of the Notes server by entering the following command:

```
load replica
```

NOTES.INI Settings

Table 10.2 shows the **NOTES.INI** settings that affect replication of a Notes server. Any values may be added or changed by editing the **NOTES.INI** file on the Notes server, or by adding a configuration document within the public Name and Address book. For details on how to perform this action, see Chapter 6, *Public Name and Address Book Forms and Views*.

Table 10.2
Replication
NOTES.INI
Settings

NOTES.INI Setting	Description
Log_Replication	Specifies whether or not replication sessions are logged to both the Notes server console and Notes application log.
Repl_Error_Tolerance	Specifies the number of replication failures of the same type the Notes server will allow before terminating replication between the two Notes machines.
ReplicationTimeLimit	Specifies the time in minutes to allow replication between two Notes servers.
Replicators	Specifies the number of replicator server tasks to run on a Notes server. The server must be restarted to take effect.
Repl_Push_Retries	Specifies the number of times a Notes server will attempt to replicate with a target Notes server.
ServerNoReplRequsts	Causes the Notes server to refuse all replication requests from other Notes servers.
ServerPullReplication	Forces the Notes server to pull changes from a target Notes server, but will not allow target Notes servers to pull changes.
ServerPushReplication	Will not allow the Notes server to pull changes, but will allow target Notes servers to pull changes.

11

Electronic Mail

With the release of Notes version 4.5, a variety of mail protocols and platforms are now supported, including Notes mail along with MAPI, POP3, SMTP, cc:Mail, and X.400. A Notes mail server can be accessed by a Notes mail client, a MAPI client (such as Microsoft's Exchange), a Web Browser, or a POP3 mail client. Gateway products (or MTAs) enable mail users to exchange mail with any SMTP, cc:Mail, or X.400 mail system.

If the Notes mail client is used, you get one of the industry-leading products in terms security, incorporating digital signatures and encryption using RSA's encryption algorithm. Notes mail also now incorporates built-in group scheduling and calendaring to support Notes users both in and outside the office. The scheduling and calendaring system may also be tied to other systems, including OfficeVision and Lotus Organizer.

Notes Mail Client Specifics

Unlike many other e-mail systems, each user has a separate file for his or her mail repository. A mail database for a user is simply just another Notes database application. This means that all the security and functionality measures incorporated into a Notes database are also part of a user's mail file. This includes forms, views, ACL, encryption, full-text indexes, rich-text fields including file attachments, and replication to name a few items that can be exploited for Notes user mail files.

Figure 11-1 shows a sample Notes e-mail message:

Notes mail databases are created by the administrator upon creation of the Notes user ID file. Once the Notes user is configured, that user may create new documents within his or her mail file. These new mail database documents are actually new Notes mail documents. From within a new e-mail message, Notes mail users may address e-mail messages to others within the Notes domain by clicking the **Address** button, which does a lookup on all users and groups who are available Notes recipients. Recipients can be populated within the **To**, **cc** and **bcc** fields of the message via Notes' type ahead feature. The body of the message is a rich text field that supports all types of rich text, including file attachments.

Within the delivery options of a Notes mail message, is the ability for the user to assign a priority to the e-mail. These are shown in Figure 11-2:

Figure 11-2

Notes Mail
Delivery Options

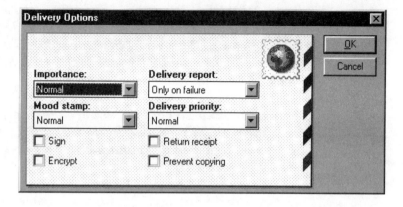

The following options are available:

- **Importance** and **Mood Stamps:** Importance and mood stamps are only for the appearance and tone of the message and have no functional importance.

- **Delivery report:** A delivery report enables a user to specify the level of reporting from the Notes mail router. The default is to only have only the router return an error when the message is not delivered. The other options include the ability to receive a report even for successful deliveries, or to receive no reports at all.

- **Delivery priority:** A Notes mail message may be addressed with the priorities **low**, **normal**, and **high**. These priorities are explained later in this chapter.

- **Sign:** A Notes mail message may be signed to guarantee the sender is authentic.

- **Encrypt:** A Notes mail message may be encrypted with the recipient's public key so that only the recipient may read the message. Only the body of the message is encrypted. A Notes mail message can only be encrypted when the recipient's public key is available to the sender. Public keys are stored within the public Name and Address book.

Tips

Notes Mail encryption is not available for remote users, non-Notes mail users, nor for Notes users outside of the sender's Notes domain. However, if the sender has a copy of the Notes mail recipient's public key stored in his or her personal address book, the message can be encrypted.

Tips

Many companies forbid the use of Notes mail encryption, as only the recipient's Notes ID file may unlock the e-mail message. The encrypted message cannot be read by any administrator ID file or server ID file.

- **Return Receipt:** This option enables the sender to receive a Notes mail message back once the recipient opens the original message.

- **Prevent copying:** This option prevents the recipient from copying, printing, or forwarding the message once opened.

Connection Records

Like replication connection records between Notes servers, it is necessary create mail connection records between Notes servers in order to route Notes mail. The structure should follow the same replication structure that is defined for replication of Notes databases. This includes either a peer-to-peer, binary tree, or hub-and-spoke architecture. Refer to Chapter 10, *Replication*, for details on replication architectures.

Mail connection records may be a part of a replication record where both mail routing and replication are enabled within a single connection record. However, unlike replication records where only the calling Notes server needs a replication connection record, mail connection records are necessary for each Notes server to provide mail routing in both directions.

Tips

For Notes servers on different Notes named networks, mail connection records within the public Name and Address book are necessary for both Notes servers to provide two-way mail routing between them. A Notes mail connection record is necessary to route mail from A to B, and another separate mail connection record is necessary to route mail from Notes server B to A.

Notes servers on the same Notes named network do not require connection records between them. Notes named networks are explained in detail in Chapter 5, *Public Name and Address Book Domain Structures*. Servers simply pass mail to each other without the need of mail connection records.

Tips

Although replication connection records are necessary between Notes servers in the same Notes named network, mail connection records are not *needed. Notes mail is automatically transferred to Notes servers on the same Notes named network; mail connection records only cause increased complexity in the design of the architecture, as they represent unneeded overhead to the public Name and Address book.*

There are several types of connection records available for routing Notes mail. The four main types are Local Area Network, Dialup Modem, Passthru Server, and Remote LAN Service. For example on how to configure these four types of connection records, refer to Chapter 10, *Replication*. Connection records can be created for X.25 and SNA networks as well. Options also exist to create connection records to route cc:Mail, X.400, and SMTP mail, if those add-on products are installed on the Notes server. Figure 11-3 shows a sample Mail connection record:

Figure 11-3
Notes Mail
Connection
Record

Basics			
Connection type:	⌜Local Area Network⌟ ▾	Usage priority:	⌜Normal⌟ ▾
Source server:	⌜Chicago-Notes01/ACME⌟	Destination server:	⌜NY-Notes01/ACME⌟
Source domain:	⌜ACME⌟	Destination domain:	⌜ACME⌟
Use the port(s):	⌜TCPIP⌟	Optional network address:	⌜192.22.554.36⌟

[Choose ports]

Scheduled Connection		Routing and Replication	
Schedule:	⌜ENABLED⌟ ▾	Tasks:	⌜Mail Routing⌟ ▾
Call at times:	⌜08:00 AM - 10:00 PM⌟ each day	Route at once if:	⌜1⌟ messages pending
Repeat interval of:	⌜60⌟ minutes	Routing cost:	⌜1⌟
Days of week:	⌜Sun, Mon, Tue, Wed, Thu, Fri, Sat⌟ ▾		

For configuring a mail connection record, the following fields should be considered:

- **Schedule:** Specify whether or not this connection should be enabled or disabled.

Traps

If you disable a mail connection record where replication is also enabled, both replication and mail routing will be disabled. If you wish to have different mail routing and replication schedules, you may wish to create two separate connection records with the target server: one that schedules and controls mail routing, and the other that schedules and controls replication.

- **Call at times:** Enter the times or a range of times to route normal priority Notes mail messages to the target Notes server. This field assumes that the **Route at once if** field is greater than 1. Let us take an example setting a range of 8:00 am to 10:00 pm with a repeat interval of 120 minutes where the **Route at once if** field is set to 5. Normal Notes mail messages will be delivered between this time period every 2 hours, or until either the threshold of 5 pending messages is reached or a high priority Notes mail message is sent. If just specific times are entered, such as 10:00 am and 2:00 pm, normal priority Notes mail will only be routed at those two times unless a high priority message or the **Route at once if** field threshold has been reached.

Tips

Low priority mail messages are only delivered between 12:00 am and 6 am for Notes servers on the same Notes network or on different Notes named networks even if normal or high mail messages are being routed during a Notes server to server connection. Normal mail messages are routed only during a scheduled connection, when the Route at once if *field threshold has been reached, or along with a high priority mail message. High priority mail messages are always routed to the target server immediately.*

Tips

If your servers are connected via dedicated lines, you should consider having the Route at once if *field set to 1. This will automatically route all mail of normal or high priority. If you are using slow or dial-up connections, it is advisable to set the* Route at once if *field to 5 or higher.*

- **Repeat interval of:** This field should only be used if a range of times is specified within the **Call at times** field above. This field represents how often to repeat mail routing (and replication, if replication is enabled within this connection record as well) within the call at times range.

- **Days of week:** Specify the days of the week this connection record should route mail to the target Notes server.

- **Tasks:** Specify if this connection record will be used for Notes mail routing, replication, cc:Mail routing, X.400 mail routing, and/or SMTP mail routing, if these products are all installed.

- **Route at once if:** Specify the number of normal priority mail messages to hold until the Notes server calls or connects to the target Notes server to deliver the mail. If the threshold is matched, the Notes server will call regardless of the set time schedule. Also, if any high priority messages are sent, the Notes server will call regardless of the contents of this field and deliver that message along with any normal priority messages pending.

- **Routing cost:** This number is used by Notes mail routers to determine the least costly path in order to deliver Notes mail messages where there are multiple paths for delivery. For Notes servers on the same Notes network, there is no need to configure this value as no mail connections are necessary. This number is set by default to 1 for LAN connections and 5 for dialup connections; the value can range from 1 to 10. Caution should be taken when changing these values. Normally, there will be no need to change this value unless you want to force Notes to always use a particular route where multiple routes exist.

Notes Mail Routing

The Notes mail router on every Notes server is responsible for routing mail from the sender to the receiver's mail database. This may include multiple Notes server hops until the message is finally delivered.

Tips

A Notes mail server message may take a maximum of 25 hops. This prevents an undeliverable mail message within a routing loop from creating a Notes mail flood.

The Notes mail router on each server uses the public Name and Address book (**NAMES.NSF**) and the router mail box (**MAIL.BOX**) to determine the destination of the Notes mail message. When a sender addresses a Notes mail message to a recipient, the following happens:

- If the recipient exists on the same Notes server as the sender, the router automatically moves the Notes mail message from the router mailbox and places the message into the receiver's Notes mail application database (see Figure 11-4).

Figure 11-4
Notes Mail
Routing—Same
Notes Server

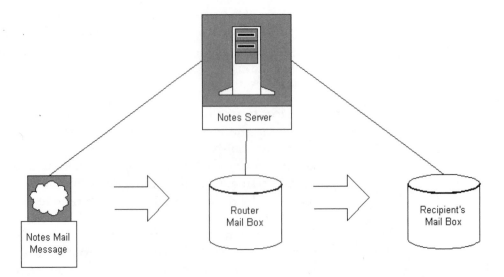

- If the recipient exists on another Notes server and the target Notes server is within the same Notes named network, the message is automatically transferred from the sender's Notes server's router mailbox to the target Notes server's router mailbox. The router server task on that Notes server then moves the message from the MAIL.BOX database (router mailbox) to the recipient's Notes mail database. Note that no mail connection records between the Notes servers are necessary for this routing to occur. Figure 11-5 shows this routing path.

Figure 11-5

Notes Mail Routing—Different Notes Server, Same Notes Named Network

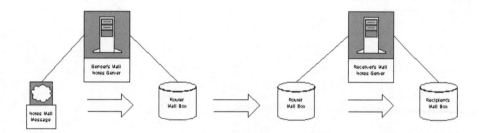

- If the recipient exists on another Notes server and the target Notes server is on a different Notes named network, the sender's mail server looks for a mail connection record to the target Notes server. If one exists, the message is automatically transferred to the target Notes server's router mail box from the sender's Notes server's mailbox. The router server task on that Notes server then moves the message from the mailbox database to the recipient's Notes mail database (Figure 11-6).

Figure 11-6

Notes Mail Routing—Different Notes Server, Different Notes Named Network

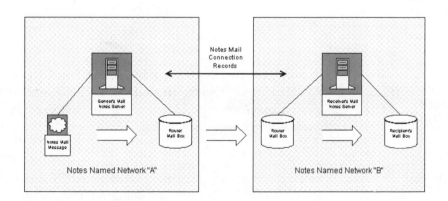

● If the recipient exists on another Notes server that does not have a direct mail connection record to the target Notes server, the message is transferred to each Notes server's router mail box along the path until the message reaches the recipient's Notes server's mailbox. The router server task on that Notes server then moves the message from the mailbox application database to the recipient's Notes mail application database (See Figure 11-7).

Figure 11-7

Notes Mail
Routing—Multiple
Notes Server Hops

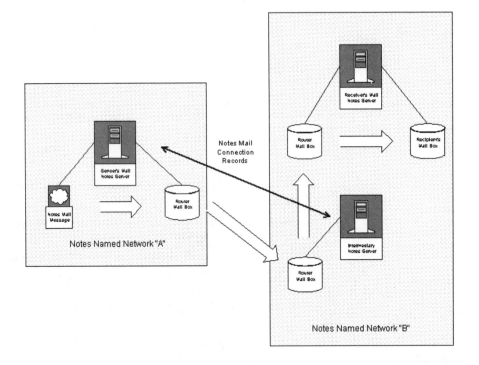

Tips

If multiple mail routing paths exist to a target Notes server, the mail router routes a mail message based on the least cost per connection record, as set in the routing cost field of each mail connection document.

Notes mail routers may also route Notes mail to other Notes servers within other Notes domains, assuming there is a connection record path the Notes routers can successfully follow to deliver the message. In order for a user to send a Notes mail message to a user within another Notes domain, each domain must be appended to the recipient's name from left to right. Let us take for example Notes mail user Scott Thomas within the ACME domain who wants to send a Notes mail message to Brad Hoyt in the ABCompany Notes domain. If a Notes mail connection record existed between a Notes server within the ACME domain to a Notes server within the ABCompany domain, the message could be delivered successfully. Notes user Scott Thomas within the ACME Notes domain would need to address his message as follows:

```
Brad Hoyt @ ABCompany
```

Scott's Notes mail server would look within its public Name and Address book to determine which Notes server in the ACME domain had a mail connection record to a Notes server within the ABCompany Notes domain. Once determined, Scott's Notes mail server would deliver the message to the router mailbox of the Notes server within the ACME domain where the mail connection existed. This ACME Notes server would then deliver the message to the ABCompany Notes server.

From there, the ABCompany Notes server would look within its public Name and Address book to determine the location of Brad's Notes mail database. The Notes server's mail router would then deliver the Notes mail message to Brad's mail Notes server's router mailbox. The router on Brad's server would then deliver the message to his mail database.

Notes mail may also be addressed across multiple Notes domain paths. Intermediary Notes domain(s) may exist between the sender and receiver, assuming proper connection records along the path. To take our example again, let us consider a third Notes domain called *Middledomain*. Let us assume that an ACME Notes server has a mail connection record to a Notes server in the Middledomain. Also let us assume that a Notes server in the Middledomain has a mail connection record to a Notes server in the ABCompany domain. For Scott to address a Note mail message to Brad, the following format would be used:

```
Brad Hoyt @ ABCompany @ Middledomain
```

Within our example, no Notes server within the ACME domain knows how to route Notes mail to the ABCompany Notes domain. Because of the way Scott has addressed his e-mail message, Scott's Notes mail server would look only at the last domain appended to the recipient. Scott's Notes mail server will look within its public Name and Address book to determine which Notes server in the ACME domain had a mail connection record to a Notes server within the Middledomain Notes domain. Once determined, Scott's Notes mail server would deliver the message to the router mailbox of the Notes server within the ACME domain where the mail connection existed. This ACME Notes server would then deliver the message to the Middledomain Notes server.

At this point, the ACME Notes server has stripped the last portion of the appended domain from the Notes mail message. From here, the Middledomain Notes server looks within its public Name and Address book to determine which Notes server in its domain has a connection record to a Notes server in the ABCompany domain. This Middledomain Notes server delivers the message to the router mailbox that has a mail connection record to the ABCompany domain. This Notes server then delivers the message to the ABCompany's mail router mailbox.

From here, the ABCompany Notes server would look within its public Name and Address book to determine the location of Brad's Notes mail application database. The Notes server's mail router would then deliver the Notes mail message to Brad's mail Notes server's router mailbox. The router on Brad's server would then deliver the message to his mail application database.

The diagram in Figure 11-8 depicts this multiple domain path:

Figure 11-8

Notes Mail
Routing —
Multiple Notes
Domain Hops

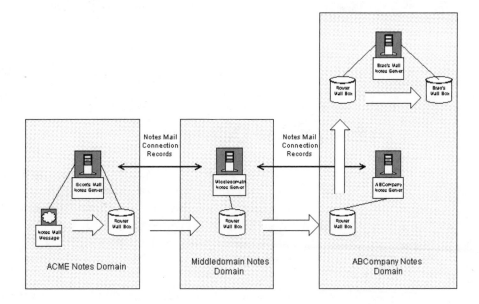

To avoid confusion for Notes mail users where there will be Notes mail routing to external domains where the target domain is not adjacent to the users' Notes domain, as depicted in the example above, a Notes administrator may create a non-adjacent domain connection record in the public Name and Address book. This would make it so that Notes mail users only need to type the user name and append only the recipient's Notes domain to the message. To illustrate, in our example instead of Scott addressing his memo as:

```
Brad Hoyt @ ABCompany @ Middledomain
```

he would only have to address the memo as:

```
Brad Hoyt @ ABCompany
```

The non-adjacent domain record in ACME's public Name and Address book would handle the translation. Figure 11-9 shows an example of such a record in ACME's public Name and Address book:

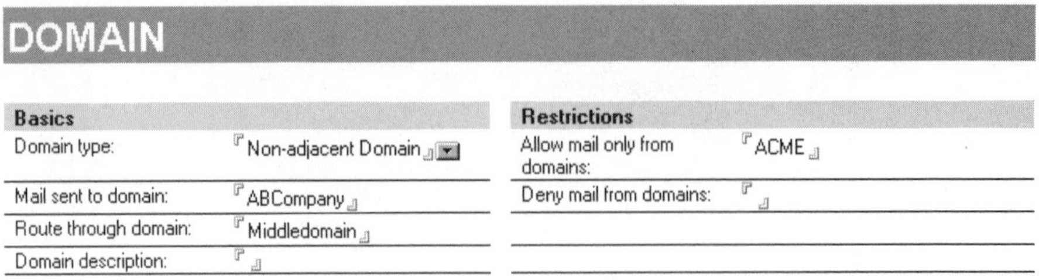

Figure 11-9

Non-Adjacent
Connection
Record

DOMAIN

Basics		Restrictions	
Domain type:	Non-adjacent Domain ▾	Allow mail only from domains:	ACME
Mail sent to domain:	ABCompany	Deny mail from domains:	
Route through domain:	Middledomain		
Domain description:			

Forcing Mail Delivery

Like replication, a Notes administrator may force a Notes server to deliver any pending Notes mail immediately—including low priority mail—by typing the following command from the Notes server console or remote Notes server console:

```
route servername
```

where *servername* is the name of the destination Notes server. You should enter the fully distinguished name of the Notes server. If there are any spaces within the server name, the fully distinguished server name should be encompassed within quotes, ("Chicago Notes01/ACME").

If you wish to shut down the mail router on a Notes server, you may do so by typing the following command from the Notes server console or remote Notes server console:

```
tell router quit
```

If you wish to start it again, type the following command:

```
load router
```

POP3 Support

With the release of Lotus Notes version 4.5, any POP3 (Post Office Protocol version 3) mail client may access a Notes mail server and its Notes mail database. Popular POP3 mail clients include Eudora,

Netscape Mail, and Microsoft Internet Explorer Internet Mail. POP3 requires the TCP/IP protocol and listens over port 110 on the TCP/IP protocol stack. In order for you to utilize a Notes server as a POP3 mail post office, you need to install the POP3 server task on the Notes server and install the SMTP MTA on at least one Notes server within your organization.

For POP3 client users, you need to do the following:

- Create a person record within the public Name and Address Book.

- Manually create a Notes mail database for each POP3 client.

Within the person record for the POP3 mail client, the **HTTP password** field is used for the POP3 mail user's password. This password will be encrypted once the document is saved. Also the **first**, **last**, **shortname**, and **full name** fields should be filled.

To load the POP3 mail server task on a Notes server, type the following line from the Notes server console:

```
load POP3
```

This task should be added to the **NOTES.INI** file within the **ServerTasks** setting to ensure the task automatically loads upon Notes server startup.

To stop the POP3 task, type the following from the server console:

```
tell POP3 quit
```

You must purchase a Domino Mail Access License for every POP3 mail client in your organization accessing the Notes server.

Browser Access

You may also access a Notes mail application from any Web browser such as Netscape Navigator, Internet Explorer or Mosaic. In order to perform this type of operation, the HTTP process must be loaded on the Notes mail server and TCP/IP must be enabled on both the Notes server and client running the Web browser. Also, you will need to purchase a Domino Mail Access License for every mail client in your organization who will be accessing the Notes server with a Web browser.

Mail Router Database (MAIL.BOX)

Every Notes server running the router server task in order to route Notes mail will have the Notes database, MAIL.BOX, which is located within the Notes server data directory. This application will not appear to users when they perform a **File**, **Database**, **Open**. Administrators need to add this application to their desktops by specifying MAIL.BOX within the filename field when performing a **File**, **Database**, **Open**. By default, the access is set to DEPOSITOR. This lets all users and servers place Notes mail messages into the application in order to route Notes mail.

Tips

We recommend that you add the Notes administration group with MANAGER access to the MAIL.BOX Notes application in order to monitor electronic mail on the Notes server and to delete dead messages from the mailbox database.

It is within this application that Notes administrators should monitor mail routing. At times, dead or undeliverable mail will appear. Notes administrators should delete any dead mail or release it by clicking the **Deliver Mail** button within the application. Releasing any messages should only be performed by Notes administrators when they know the actual recipient exists and there was not any addressing error by the sender. Once the button is pressed, the mail router will attempt to deliver the message again. Otherwise, the message(s) should be deleted from the application.

The mail router mailbox may also be opened from a Notes administrator's desktop by following these steps:

1.   Click **File**, **Tools**, **Server Administration.**

2. Highlight the desired Notes server and then click the **System Databases** or the **Mail** icon.

3. Click **Open Outgoing Mailbox.**

Tracing Mail

If the Notes administrator is experiencing problems sending mail from one Notes server to another, a Mail Trace may be run to troubleshoot any potential routing problems. When using this utility, a trace report will be returned by every Notes version 4 or higher server between the sending and receiving Notes servers. This utility can be compared to the TCP/IP trace route (tracert) utility. To run a mail trace between two Notes servers, perform the following steps:

1. Click **File**, **Tools**, **Server Administration.**

2. Click the **Mail** icon and click **Send Mail Trace**. The screen shown in Figure 11-10 appears:

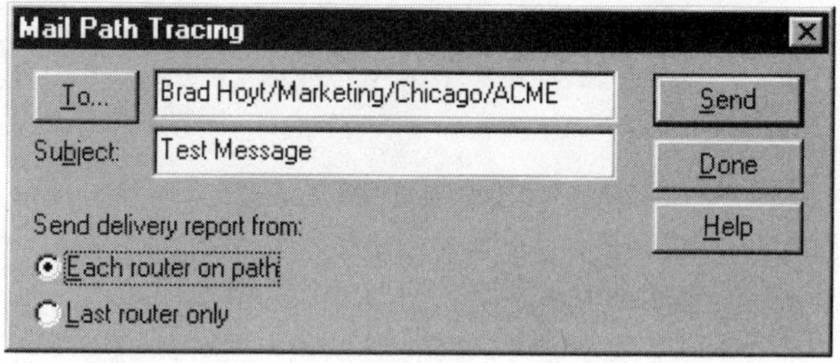

Figure 11-10

Mail Trace
Dialog Box

3. Within the **To** field, enter the recipient on the target Notes server. You may press the **To** button to search the public Name and Address book.

4. Select the delivery report option from the radio buttons. Select **Each router on path** to receive a mail trace report back from every Notes server between the sender and receiver Notes mail server. Select **Last router only** to only receive a mail trace report from the receiving Notes mail server.

5. Click **Send**.

Multi-Threaded Mail Configuration

On a Notes version 4 or higher mail server, you may run multiple mail threads in order to simultaneously route mail to multiple Notes servers. Each connection to a Notes server to route mail consumes one thread on a Notes server. The **NOTES.INI** setting **MailMaxThreads** determines the number of threads to allow on a Notes server. The default setting is one thread per port. This setting may be changed within the **NOTES.INI** file or by configuring a configuration document within the public Name and Address book. Refer to Chapter 6, *Public Name and Address Book Forms and Views*, for details on how to create a configuration document.

Shared Mail

With the release of version 4 of Lotus Notes, Notes administrators may configure Notes servers to utilize a shared Notes application to store users' mail. Simply speaking, Notes can be configured to store electronic mail messages in a single Notes database for messages intended for multiple recipients.

The shared Notes mail application database is also called the *single copy object store* and is the repository Notes application where all users access a multiple-recipient mail message. Users may still perform the same functionality as if the Notes mail message existed within their own Notes mail application; the Notes mail server running shared mail transparently to all shared mail users performs these actions. The shared mail server keeps tracks of all shared mail messages and automatically deletes unneeded shared mail messages once all users have marked a message for deletion.

A Notes mail message can be divided into two parts; the summary and non-summary data. The summary data includes all header information including the **To**, **cc**, **bcc**, **Subject**, and **From** fields of an e-mail message. The non-summary data is the body of the text, including all file attachments.

If shared mail is enabled on a Notes server, the mail router splits the message, only delivering the summary data to recipients. All non-summary data is delivered to the shared Notes mail application. When a Notes user opens a Notes mail message when connected to the network, the message is displayed from the shared application database transparently to the user. If the user decides to delete a message that is being shared, only the summary information is deleted from the user's personal Notes mail database. For remote users who are replicating their mail databases, all data (including summary and non-summary information) is replicated to his or her remote machine.

In terms of security, the shared Notes mail application is encrypted so that only the server ID file that created the shared application may access it. The ACL of the database is set so that only the server ID can access the application as a server, meaning that only the server process may access the file, and the user interface on the server machine will not be allowed access. The shared application does not contain any views and none may be added. The shared mail application cannot be added to any user's desktop.

Tips

If you allow users to encrypt incoming and outgoing mail bound for a shared Notes application database, the message will not be stored within the shared application. Instead, it is stored in each user's personal mail files. Only unencrypted mail messages can be stored within a shared mail application.

When shared mail is installed on a Notes mail server, two Notes database applications are created. The first is called **MailOBJ.NSF**; it is a database link that points to the actual shared Notes mail application. This is the default name used by the shared mail process and will exist within the data directory of the shared mail Notes server. It is created automatically once shared mail is enabled. The second Notes application that is created is the actual shared Notes mail database. The Notes mail server will also create this once the Notes administrator enables shared mail.

To install shared mail on a Notes mail server, type the following command from the Notes server console:

```
tell router use "shared mail database"
```

where *shared mail database* is the name of the Notes database that will store users' mail messages. A descriptive name such as **USERMAIL.NSF** is recommended. Notes will automatically create the database link **MAILOBJ.NSF** and the shared Notes mail application **USERMAIL.NSF**—as named by the administrator.

There are two different ways to configure shared mail on a Notes server. The first method of shared mail uses the **NOTES.INI** setting of **Shared_Mail=1.** This type of shared mail only routes mail to the shared Notes mail application if the message is destined for two or more recipients. Initially, the Notes mail router places the message within the receiver's personal mail file. If the message is intended for two or more people, then the message is written to the shared Notes mail database (**USERMAIL.NSF**) and the message for the first recipient is removed from his or her mail file in favor of the shared Notes mail store. If a Notes mail message is only sent to one person, the shared message store is not used. Figures 11-11 and 11-12 depict these scenarios:

Figure 11-11
Share_Mail=1,
One Receiver

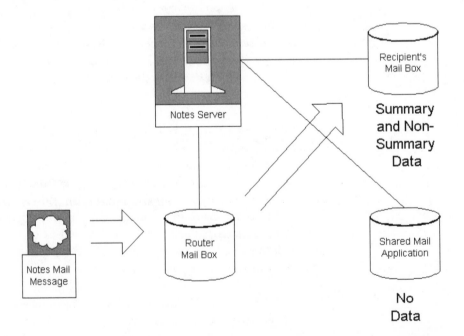

Figure 11-12

Share_Mail=1,
Multiple Recipients

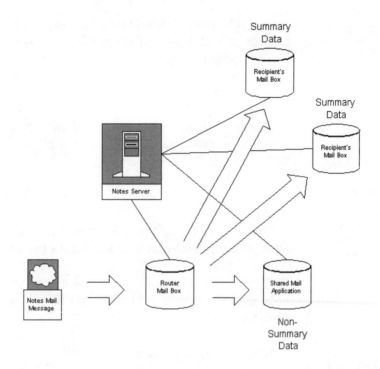

The second method to configure shared mail uses the **NOTES.INI** setting of **Shared_Mail=2.** This is the default setting when shared mail is first installed on a Notes mail server. This type of configuration will use the shared mail message store regardless of the number of intended recipients. Even if the recipient is not on the mail server, the message is written to the message store. The message is then removed once the mail router determines a recipient is not on the mail server. Figure 11-12 is the method the Notes mail router will use to deliver all mail to users, even if there is only one recipient.

Tips

For Notes servers that will be housing shared Notes mail as well as being involved in multiple mail transfers to other Notes mail servers, this is not the ideal setting. The setting Shared_Mail=1 would be more efficient.

After all users delete the summary information for a mail message in their personal mail applications, the Notes server process **Object Collect** will remove the message from the shared Notes mail database application. This task will run every morning at 2 A.M. The process can also be run manually from the Notes server console by typing the following line:

```
load Object Collect USERMAIL.NSF
```

If you wish to link a mail file that has messages that are not included in the shared mail Notes application database, type the following line:

```
load object link STHOMAS.NSF USERMAIL.NSF
```

This will link Scott Thomas' mail file to the shared mail message store and move all non-summary data to this application.

If you wish to remove a user's mail from the shared message store back into the user's personal mail file, type the following command from the Notes server console:

```
load object unlink STHOMAS.NSF
```

This will unlink the user's mail file and move all non-summary data back into the user's mail file.

Traps

If you specify the shared Notes mail application file name instead of the user's name, all user mail files will unlink.

Statistics concerning shared mail can be gathered by typing the following line from the Notes server console:

```
show stat Object
```

Tips

Very few organizations use the shared mail function of Lotus Notes for a few main reasons. The low price of additional mail disk space, administration of the central mail repository, and the risk of corruption to a central database outweigh the advantages of shared mail on Lotus Notes mail servers. For these reasons, we recommend you not use this feature within your environment.

Controlling Mail File Sizes

Most organizations either set very liberal or no size limits at all for mail files, given that the price of disk drive space is far cheaper than the administrative costs of restricting and monitoring the limits of user mail files.

The default maximum size of any Notes application (a mail file is just another Notes application) is 1 gigabyte. The maximum absolute size (which can be changed at the time the database is created) is 4 gigabytes. Needless to say, end users should not be permitted to have mail file sizes of 1 gigabyte. For this reason, quotas can be established on mail files. Once a database quota has been reached on a mail file, a user can continue to receive mail (above the quota limit), but will not be able to save or send mail until the mail file is cleaned or archived. Quotas are explained within Chapter 12, *Notes Applications and Security Issues*.

Archives can be set by users to automatically archive electronic mail. This is found in the archives view of a person's Notes mail file. Archives may be established on a Notes server or on a user's local desktop. Figure 11-13 shows the possible settings:

Figure 11-13

Notes Mail
Archive Agent

In light of current laws, regulations, and legal precedent, many organizations now enforce very strict mail retention policies. If your organization does not have e-mail retention policies, we recommend that minimum policies be established and enforced, if only to better manage your disk usage requirements.

Investigate + document policy

Converting Notes Mail

The CONVERT server utility can be used to upgrade Notes mail databases from version 3 to version 4 format. The utility will run on every document in the user's Notes mail database application. Read and unread marks will be unaffected and the file format of the database will not be changed. To run the utility, type the following command on the Notes server command prompt:

```
load convert database name
```

where *database name* is the filename of the user's Notes mail database application. You may use wildcards to convert more then one user's mail file, such as:

```
load convert mail\*.nsf
```

Moving User Mail Files

A Notes administrator may move a user's mail file to another server by simply making a new replica of the Notes mail application on the target server. The Notes administrator may also perform this task from the operating system by copying between servers assuming the two machines have file sharing enabled. Once the user's Notes mail database application has been copied, the user's person record must be edited to reflect the move. The Notes server field and/or mail file location should be edited. Please refer to Chapter 6, *Public Name and Address Book Forms and Views*, for exact details of the fields involved.

Traps

For multi-mail Notes server environments, administrators should take caution before moving user mail files. Once the person record is edited, the change must replicate to all Notes servers to have effective mail routing. If done in the middle of the day, a mail loop could incur as some Notes servers will point the person to the original Notes mail server, and servers where the change has been received will point to the new location. A Notes administrator should make Notes mail file moves at the end of the day and edit the person record on the user's original Notes server. If a move must take place during business hours, the person record change should be done on the server where the user's mail file originally resided.

Delegation

If users wish other users to access their Notes mail, this can be done simply by adding the other user's name to the ACL of the Notes mail application. If READER access is granted, then the other user will only be able to read e-mail messages. No new messages or replies will be allowed. If the original user would like the other user to respond to messages, EDITOR access will be needed; however, the **From** field will contain the second user's name.

Delegation may also be performed from the Mail tools menu.

Message Transfer Agents (MTAs)

Lotus offers three different MTAs that can be installed on Notes servers. The SMTP and cc:Mail MTAs are free of charge and may be downloaded from the Lotus Web site. The Lotus X.400 MTA is available at a cost to the customer. Also at a cost, Lotus offers a pager gateway as well as a fax gateway.

If you have a cc:Mail environment, Lotus now offers a cc:Mail-to-Notes-mail conversion program free of charge. This product, along with the cc:Mail MTA, will provide a seamless transition from cc:Mail to Notes mail. The cc:Mail MTA will provide electronic mail transport to and from the cc:Mail network to the Notes mail net work. It will also provide cc:Mail post office directory replication to the Notes mail public Name and Address book. It is especially important to have the MTA running during the migration when both cc:Mail users and Notes mail users exist.

The SMTP (Simple Mail Transport Protocol) MTA should be installed to provide mail transport to and from the Internet as well, as to any other SMTP mail machine with Notes mail. If you are planning on supporting POP3 clients on the Notes mail server as well, the SMTP MTA is necessary.

The pager gateway should be installed so that Notes mail users are able send pages to paging services via Notes mail. Installation is very straightforward and one gateway should suffice for the use of all users within a Notes infrastructure. With the cc:Mail MTA installed, cc:Mail users would also be able to use the Notes pager gateway if desired.

The Notes fax gateway provides both inbound and outbound fax capabilities. The inbound side does come with OCR software and fax workstation ID capabilities to route faxes to Notes mail users' mailboxes. Ease of use and installation are certainly its strong points, especially on the outbound side. The Notes mail user simply composes an electronic mail message with the fax number and recipient name and appends an **@FAX** to send the electronic message to a fax recipient. The gateway handles the rest.

However, the Notes fax gateway probably is not the proper business solution for larger organizations. It is not meant for large volumes of faxes, especially on the inbound side. It is meant for the small occasional fax sent by Notes users. For an enterprise solution, organizations would be better off looking for a product designed to handle larger volumes of inbound and outbound faxes.

Calendaring and Group Scheduling

With the release of version 4.5, built-in calendaring and group scheduling is incorporated into user Notes mail files. Within the calendars, users can create the following:

- Appointments

- Personal Meetings

- Business Meetings where schedules can be set and other people may be invited.

- Events

- Anniversaries which serve as reminders such as birthdays, wedding dates, etc.

Once a user fills his or her schedule, the free time database on the Notes server (**BUSYTIME.NSF**) is filled with the updates. Only the schedule manager program on the Notes server has access to the free time database. The free times system can also be integrated with Lotus Organizer or IBM OfficeVision. Remote Notes users may also replicate the free time database to perform free time searches.

The free time system on the Notes server consists of two Notes server programs, the schedule manager (**SCHED.EXE**) and the calendar connector (**CALCONN.EXE**). When the Notes 4.5 server is installed, these tasks are automatically installed within the **ServerTasks** entry in the server's **NOTES.INI** file so that they run automatically.

Virus Scanning

Normally, virus scanning is handled at the desktop level on each PC. A memory-resident program should be in place that scans for a virus anytime a file is accessed.

To avoid a virus outbreak through electronic mail transport, it may be worthwhile to investigate electronic mail scanning products for Lotus Notes mail. There are a few products on the market that will scan each incoming and outgoing mail message on the server, including attachments, for a virus. However, this does put additional burden on the Notes servers, and may require more hardware in order to support such products, especially as mail volume increases.

Although this would help reduce the number of affected PCs, a better solution would be to institute a policy of installing virus scanners locally on each PC. Not only would this reduce overhead on the Notes mail routers, it would help prevent the spread of a virus through the sharing of floppy disks as well.

Notes Mail Server Parameters

There are several **NOTES.INI** settings that may be applied to a Notes mail server to determine how mail is controlled and routed upon a server. The next two sections explain these settings.

Router Logging

All mail events by default are not logged to the miscellaneous events section of the Notes log. Instead, they are logged to the mail routing events section of the Notes application. To control the type of logging that will occur on a Notes mail server, the **NOTES.INI** variable **Log_Mailrouting=** should be modified. Values include:

- **10—Minimal:** This setting will only report fatal and error messages related to mail routing.

- **20—Normal:** This setting will only report fatal, error, warning, and infoterse (major and minor component events) messages related to mail routing.

- **30—Informational:** This setting will only report fatal, error, warning, infoterse (major and minor component events), and info-verbose (greater detail of infoterse events) messages related to mail routing.

- **40—Verbose:** This setting will report all events related to mail routing.

NOTES.INI Settings

The following table shows all **NOTES.INI** settings that effect mail routing.

Table 11.1

NOTES.INI
Settings for Notes
Mail Servers

NOTES.INI Variable	Description
Log_MailRouting	Specifies the level of detail for mail routing reported to the Notes log.
MailCompactDisabled	Enables or disables the compaction of the mail router mailbox every evening.
MailDisablePriority	Causes the mail router to ignore the delivery priority of Notes mail messages.
MailDynamicCostReset	Allows the mail router program to use the original least-cost mail routing once the server boots.
MailEncryptIncoming	Forces all incoming mail to be encrypted for users.
MailLowPriorityTime	Specifies the time for the mail server to route low priority mail messages.
MailMaxThreads	Determines the number of threads for the server to allocate in order to route Notes mail messages.
MailServer	Specifies the Notes server to use for mail (used mostly by Notes client machines).
MailSystem	Specifies the type of mail system the machine should use (used mostly by Notes client machines.)
MailTimeout	Specifies the number of days a Notes server waits until returning undeliverable mail back to the sender.
MailTimeoutMinutes	Specifies the number of minutes a Notes server waits until returning undeliverable mail back to the sender
POP3Domain	Specifies the Internet domain for a Notes POP3 server.
POP3Port	Specifies a port other than the default of 110 for the POP3 mail server task.
POP3_Enable_SSI	Enables the uses of Secure Sockets Layer (SSL) on a Notes POP3 server task.
ReportUseMail	Allows the reporter server task to use Notes mail in order to deliver statistics.
SecureMail	Forces the Notes server to encrypt and sign all outbound Notes mail messages of Notes mail users.
Share_Mail	Specifies what type of shared mail to use on the Notes mail server.

Remote Access to Lotus Notes

Similar to the discussion concerning Notes server installations and locations within Chapter 7, *Installation Guidelines*, is the issue of remote Notes dial-in access. Remote dial-in gives the capabilities to remote Notes clients to replicate and/or view on-line Notes applications, including their Notes mail applications. The same two approaches can be considered when handling remote dial-in procedures. One is a centralized, one location dial-in approach with access to remote locations provided by an organization's WAN infrastructure. The other approach is a distributed approach with dial-in access provided at each location.

The centralized approach has the advantage in that administration would be handled in one location. All resources could be managed and tracked fairly easily. Long distance charges would be assessed, unless a toll free number was established. Replication time to remote users would also be impacted as data would have to be passed through the WAN from remote locations to the dial-in facility. Stability and pipe-speed of the WAN is a major factor in determining whether this would be a viable solution.

A large number of dial-in modems need to be established in order to use this approach. There is a heavy amount of administration with this type of dial-in infrastructure, as all remote access for the entire organization's community occurs in this one location. Notes users incur a long distance charge, unless a toll-free number is established.

Figure 11-14 depicts this type of approach:

Figure 11-14
Centralized Dial-In
Approach

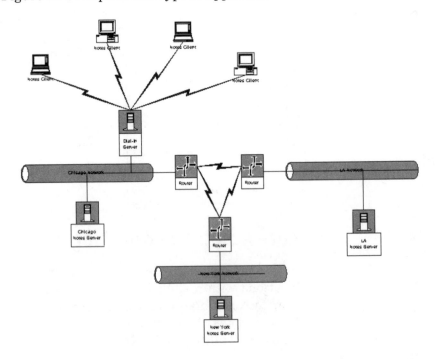

A distributed approach provides dial-in capabilities at each site. A bank of modems is established at each location and the WAN is not a factor in replication. This solution provides faster throughput to Notes users; however, Notes administrators have the responsibility of monitoring modem connections in several locations. Notes users have the luxury, though, of having a local call (in most cases) when accessing their mail files and Notes applications.

Figure 11-15 depicts the distributed approach:

Figure 11-15
Distributed
Dial-In Approach

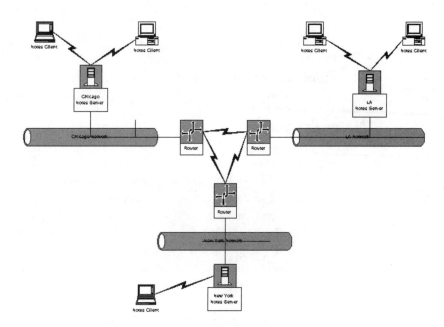

Whichever dial-in approach is used, a PBX huntgroup is recommended so that dial-in users only need one phone number to remember.

Tips

Microsoft's Remote Access Server (RAS)

Microsoft's Remote Access Server provides remote node connectivity for users through standard analog lines, ISDN, x.25, and SNA connections. Shiva products also provide this type connectivity. When a RAS client dials in and establishes a PPP connection, the remote operating system (Windows NT or Windows 95) becomes a node on that network segment as if it were connected on the LAN in the office. Throughput obviously will be limited to the speed of the modem; however, all resources including file and print (Novell and NT file servers) as well as Notes Servers are accessible. Lotus Notes version 4.0 and higher supports RAS connections directly so that Notes can automatically launch a RAS connection from Windows 95 or Windows NT.

Nothing needs to be done on the Notes server to support this functionality. However, on the network where the Notes server exists, a Windows NT RAS server or Shiva remote dial-in product must be installed. The RAS server handles all connectivity issues with the remote client and enables the remote PC to become another node on the network, in order to connect to the target Notes server with the proper network protocol.

Notes Passthru

New with version 4.0 of Lotus Notes is a feature called *Notes passthru*. This feature enables Notes users to dial into a Notes server and not only access that Notes server, but also traverse other network and modem ports to access other Notes servers. This provides a central dial-in point to the entire Notes infrastructure (assuming proper security rights are granted). Only Notes resources are accessible using this procedure; other NT and Novell file and print services are not accessible.

Passthru may also be used to provide connectivity between two Notes machines where no protocol in common is available. The passthru server then acts as a protocol gateway between the source and destination server. If Server A is running SPX, Server B is running SPX and TCP/IP, and Server C is running TCP/IP, Server A and C may communicate via Server B.

In order for passthru to work, the Notes administrator must install analog or digital modems on a Notes server. Also, the administrator must configure the proper fields on the passthru Notes server's (and any destination Notes server's) server document within the public Name and Address book to allow client passthru access. These fields include:

- **Access this server through Passthru:** This field allows users, groups, and servers to access this server as a passthru destination. If this field is left blank, then **no** users or servers can access this Notes server as a passthru destination.

- **Passthru route through:** This field should be populated with users, servers, or groups you wish to access the Notes server for passthru to another Notes server destination. If this field is left blank, then no user or server will be able to use this Notes server as a passthru server.

- **Passthru cause calling:** This field designates which servers, groups, or users may force the Notes server to call or contact another server and act as an intermediary (passthru) contact to another Notes server. If this field is left blank, no destinations are allowed to be called.

- **Passthru destinations allowed:** This field lists all destination Notes servers that are allowed. If this field is left blank, then all Notes servers are possible destinations via passthru.

Traps

By default, NO ACCESS is allowed to passthru Notes servers and to connect to destination servers via passthru Notes servers. The restrictions must be configured within the server documents of the respective Notes servers.

On the client machine, connection record(s) needs to be configured in order to access a Notes server through a passthru Notes server.

The following are advantages for using Notes passthru:

- A passthru Notes server allows a client the ability to only have to dial into a single Notes server and then access other Notes servers via the passthru Notes server.

- A passthru Notes server enables other Notes servers and clients to connect to it and access other Notes servers where a protocol in common is not present between the source and destination Notes machines. The passthru Notes server acts as a "stepping stone."

- A passthru Notes server can ease the load on a network modem pool, as modems may be added to a dedicated passthru Notes server.

There are also limitations to passthru:

- The hard-coded limit is 10 hop counts for passthru. The practical limit is four; typically, only 1 or 2 hops are ever used.

- A version 3 Notes server cannot act as a passthru Notes server, but can be the ultimate destination Notes server.

Chapter 2

Notes Application and Security Issues

Although this book is not written with the Notes database designer in mind, Notes administrators must consider issues regarding the proper administration and security of both the Notes infrastructure and Notes applications. This chapter addresses those and other security issues.

Security Measures

When people think of data, one of the main issues and concerns that arises is security. Lotus Notes incorporates the industry's best security measures including access control, private/public key encryption, and digital signatures.

Lotus Notes has several mechanisms that interact with each other to form the basis of a secure environment. These security mechanisms are Physical Security, Certificates (Certification), Authentication, Access Control, and Encryption. The certification and authentication mechanisms are sometimes included in the general category of authentication. In order to provide a more practical approach to Notes security, they will be addressed as separate and distinct items.

The following sections discuss the different layers of security within Lotus Notes. There are several layers; each layer is hit the first time a Notes client or server connects with another Notes server.

Physical Security

Physical security is the cornerstone of the Notes security model. Without it, a Notes network cannot be considered secure. *Physical security* is defined as having all relevant system components in appropriate locations with tightly controlled and/or limited access. Physical security is the most common point of overall security failure.

The Notes security model will only be reliable if physical security of key components is maintained. These key components are server machines, certifier ID files, server ID files, and user ID files.

Access to the Notes Server Machine

All Notes servers within an organization must be located in areas with limited access (a locked room). The Notes server should be kept in a secure room away from the average user. Only proper administrators should ever be allowed access to the machine itself. While it is recommend that the room be environmentally controlled, this is not a necessity.

Tips

It has been our experience that microcomputer server class machines are less prone to component failures when consistent temperature and humidity levels are maintained.

Notes server consoles should be password protected using keyboard and/or screensaver locks and by using the set secure *password* command on the Notes server console. By using the "set secure" Notes server command, most server console functionality is disabled. These passwords should be known by as few administrators/technicians as possible. Random passwords should be used and be changed periodically (at least every 90 days). For Windows NT machines hosting Notes servers, Windows NT should have all users logged off from the machine.

Run as service? ✗

Traps

We do not recommend applying passwords to any Notes server ID file. If you apply a password to the Notes server ID file, the Notes server will not automatically restart in the event of server downing either through planned or unplanned outages. For this reason it is better to use the "set secure password" capability.

We also do not recommend the use of a "power on" password. This creates problems in "lights-out" data centers, where a server would not come back online in the event of unplanned or planned power outages.

One of several weaknesses in the Lotus Notes security model is the inability to secure information in databases that are located on a server (or workstation) using only the Access Control Lists. Any local database—a database located on a machine's hard disk (or other local media)—is accessible via the Notes user interface without regard to the actual ACL restrictions. What this means is that anyone who has physical access to a server (or workstation) can access any database, make changes, and view information in applications located on that machine. The only exceptions to this are to encrypt fields within documents or to encrypt the entire database itself. Also, a Notes administrator or manager may enable the *Enforce consistent ACL across all replicas of this application* field within the ADVANCED section of a database's ACL. In the case of encrypted fields, the encrypted information will not be accessible unless the ID has the associated encryption key. If the entire database is encrypted, only the ID file that encrypted the database will be able to access the data. If the ADVANCED ACL setting to enforce local ACL access is enabled, all servers and/or users must be listed with MANAGER access in order to replicate the application. Encryption is explained later in this chapter.

Access to Certifier ID Files

All certifiers should be physically secured and accessible by as few individuals as possible. Since certification is a key mechanism of Notes security, it is important that strict control of certificates be maintained. It is recommended that there be only one administrator certifying users, a backup at the organization level, and one main and one backup person at the organizational unit level. If an unauthorized (or formerly authorized) user gains access to an organization's certificates, they could conceivably apply certificates to their ID file or create "dummy" users to gain access to proprietary and confidential information. Chapter 8, *Administration Issues*, gives more detail on how to keep certifier ID files secure, including applying multiple passwords to the file.

Access to User ID Files

The Notes security model uses a User ID file for authentication, access control and encryption. The User ID file contains the following:

- **User Name:** This is the name of the Notes user.

- **Notes License Number:** This is the license number assuring the ID is a legitimate North American or International ID file. It cannot be changed once created.

- **Public and Private Keys:** These keys are used for various security measures such as authenticating with a Notes server. During authentication, a challenge-response sequence is initiated between the Notes client and server. Every Notes user's public key within a single domain is also stored within the public Name and Address book. With this public key, a challenge is composed that only the User ID file with the appropriate private key may unlock. If not completed properly, authentication with the Notes server is not granted. This public-private key authentication is based upon and licensed from RSA.

- **Encryption Keys:** If any Notes administrator or Notes developer creates a key to encrypt certain fields within a Notes application, the encryption keys are stored within the user's ID file.

- **Certificate(s):** An ID file must contain at least one certificate. For hierarchical user ID files, an ID file may only contain one hierarchical certificate. Cross-certification is needed to access other hierarchical organizations. However, an ID file may contain several flat certificates.

- **Password:** The password for a user ID is stored within the ID file as well. It is not stored on the Notes server.

User ID files can be freely copied using the operating system **copy** command, making them susceptible to misappropriation. If the password of an ID is compromised (or none exists), any user can access the Notes server. An administrator with release 4.5 of Lotus Notes can force a password change and render other copies of the ID file useless with the old password. For details on this procedure, consult Chapter 8, *Administration Issues*. There is also no way to change a password if a user forgets their IDs password. There is no foolproof method for securing a user ID. It is recommended that IDs be password-protected during creation. A comprehensive user awareness program should also be undertaken to give users an appreciation for the significance of the Notes user ID file.

Passwords

Another key element of physical security is passwords. All users IDs should be assigned a unique password. Organizational guidelines should reflect the necessity of periodic password changes. With the release of version 4.5 of Lotus Notes, administrators can force users to change passwords on user ID files. For details on this procedure, see Chapter 8, *Administration Issues*. Passwords should be a minimum of 8 characters in length.

Users should also be instructed to log off of their Notes workstations by pressing **F5**. Also, a user may set his or her preferences to have Notes automatically log them from Notes at a preset time interval within user preferences.

Certification and Authentication

Certification is the mechanism by which user ID files are certified. Certification is an integral part of the authentication process.

Every Notes ID—whether it be a server or user ID—contains a certificate. If one Notes ID is to authenticate with another (user-to-server or server-to-server), then the two IDs must share a common certificate. This is the first level of security. If the two IDs share a common certificate, the authentication process proceeds. If the authentication "handshake" between the two IDs is successful, then the security process is passed up to the next security layer.

Authentication is the process used to validate that a user ID can access a given Notes server. This process occurs as a challenge and response between a workstation and a server, or between two servers. When a client attempts to establish a connection with a server, validation occurs. This validation process establishes trust of the client's public key. The second step is authentication, the actual challenge and response interaction that uses the public/private keys of the client and server (or server-to-server). This is done by the Notes server in a client/server challenge (the target Notes server performs this if two Notes servers are attempting a connection). The target Notes server sends a random number to the initiating ID file (server or client). The initiating ID file then encrypts the random number with the ID's private key and sends it back to the target ID file (server or client). The target ID file then decrypts the challenge message with the initiator's public key. If successful, this process is then repeated in the opposite direction. If this reverse scenario is then successful, authentication between the two ID files is granted.

Server Access

After successful authentication takes place, the server checks its server record in the public Name and Address book, as well as any **NOTES.INI** variables that secure the server.

There are some variables within the NOTES.INI file that have equivalent settings within the public Name and Address book. The Server documents access list within the public Name and Address book will override any NOTES.INI variables.

Tips

Server access lists add an additional layer of security to Notes servers. By using access lists, access can be granted or denied to a server, or particular ports on the server even if the user is certified to access the server. Server access lists are controlled through the Server Record in the public Name and Address book and/or in the **NOTES.INI** file of the server. Port level access is achieved through a **NOTES.INI** variable on each server.

Table 12.1 lists the different settings available to secure a Notes server. It is recommended that you use Notes groups, rather than individual server and/or user names, within the fields for easier administration. More details on fields within a Notes server document within the public Name and Address book can be found in Chapter 6, *Public Name and Address Book Forms and Views.*

For Web Browser access to a Notes server via the HTTP process, the Restrictions section of the server document with related fields do not apply. The fields within the Restrictions section only apply to Notes users.

Tips

Access List	Description
Only allow server access to users listed in this	This field is found in the server document in the Address Book public Name and Address book. If set to **yes**, only people within the same domain of the server will be allowed access to the server. If set to **yes** you must add other servers that need access to this server into the Access Server field.
Access Server	Place any users and/or servers that need access to this Notes server within this field. If you set the field above this field to **yes** you must enter other users not within your domain and any serv er within or outside your domain in this field; otherwise, access will not be granted. Servers within the domain should be OK. If this field is left blank, all certified users and/or servers will be allowed access, assuming the field above is set to **no**.
Not access server (N&A Book)	Denies access to users, servers, and groups to this Notes server.
Create new databases (N&A Book)	Enter a Notes group that will be allowed to create new database applications on this Notes server. If the field is left blank, *all* users will be allowed to create new databases.
Create replica databases (N&A Book)	Enter the Notes group that will be allowed to create new replica databases on this server. If the field is left blank, *no one* will be able to create new replica applications.
Access this server through passthru (N&A Book)	Enter the users, servers, or groups that are allowed access to this server via a passthru server. If this field is left blank, *no one* will be allowed access via passthru.
Use this server as a passthru server. (N&A Book)	Enter the users, server, or groups that may use this server as a passthru server to reach another server. If this field is left blank, *no one* will be allowed to use this server as passthru server.
Allow Anonymous Notes Connections	If you set this field to **yes** within a Notes server document, all Notes users will be allowed access to the Notes server, regardless of certificates held. In other words, authentication will not take place between the two ID files. Access will be granted with these types of connection using the user name "Anonymous," which can be placed within ACLs of databases and other server access fields.
Compare public keys against those stored in the public Name and Address book.	Set this field to **yes** to check users' public keys within their user ID files against those public keys stored within your domain's public Name and Address book. This is useful in the event a "dummy" or "fake" ID has been created to access the Notes server.
Allow_Access (NOTES.INI)	Same function as Allow Access field within the public Name and Address book; only is used if that field is left blank.
Allow_Access_portname (NOTES.INI)	Specifies the servers, users, and groups that may access this server at the specified port. There is no an equivalent setting within a server record.
Allow_Passthru_Access (NOTES.INI)	Same function as the server record equivalent. Only used if the server record field is left blank.
Allow_Passthru_Callers (NOTES.INI)	Same function as the server record equivalent. Only used if the server record field is left blank.
Allow_Passthru_Clients (NOTES.INI)	Same function as the server record equivalent. Only used if the server record field is left blank.
Allow_Passthru_Targets (NOTES.INI)	Same function as the server record equivalent. Only used if the server record field is left blank.
Create_File_Access (NOTES.INI)	Same function as the server record equivalent. Only used if the server record field is left blank.
Create_Replica_Access (NOTES.INI)	Same function as the server record equivalent. Only used if the server record field is left blank.
Deny_Access (NOTES.INI)	Same function as the server record equivalent. Only used if the server record field is left blank.
Deny_Access_portname (NOTES.INI)	Specifies the servers, users, and groups that are denied access to this server at the specified port. There is no equivalent setting within a server record.
Server_Restricted	Specifies whether or not the Notes server will accept requests to Open Database requests. There is no equivalent setting with the public Name and Address book.

Traps

Use caution when enabling anonymous Notes connections to a Notes server, as defined in the server document within a Notes server. If enabled, authentication will not take place between the two Notes ID files and access will be determined using the "Anonymous" name within server access fields and database ACL settings. If the name "Anonymous" does not appear, the DEFAULT settings for the unauthenticated user will be used.

Directory links on a Notes server may also be used to limit access to directories on a Notes server. *Directory links* are text files that allow you to create a database directory unrelated to the server's Notes data directory. Directory links can be used to locate application databases to a new drive without user confusion and, more importantly, to control access to a directory tree. By using directory links, you are adding an additional layer of security to database access. For details on how to create directory links, consult Chapter 8, *Administration Issues*.

Execution Control Lists (ECL)

Execution Control Lists (ECL) control what types of actions may occur on a user's workstation. These include the following:

- **Access to the file system:** Controls whether or not user(s) may attach or detach files to and from Notes.

- **Access to the current database:** Allows user(s) the ability to read and modify the current Notes application.

- **Access to environment variables:** Allows user(s) access to environment variables within the **NOTES.INI** file on the machine.

- **Access to non-Notes databases:** Allows user(s) access to external Note applications through non-Notes database drivers (e.g. ODBC).

- **Access to external code:** Allow user(s) the ability to run programs associated within DLLs unknown to Lotus Notes.

- **Access to external programs:** Allow user(s) the ability to run other external programs.

- **Ability to send mail:** Allow user(s) the ability to send mail.

- **Ability to read other Notes applications other than the current one:** Allow user(s) the ability to read data from Notes applications other than the current application.

- **Ability to modify databases other than the current one:** Allow user(s) the ability to modify data in Notes applications other than the current Notes application.

- **Ability to export data:** Allow user(s) the ability to print, copy to the clipboard, and import and export data from the Notes workstation.

- **Access to the Notes workstation security ECL list:** Allow user(s) to edit the current ECL of the Notes workstation.

In order to set the ECL for a new Notes workstation, follow these steps:

1. Open the public Name and Address book.

2. Click **Actions, Edit Administration ECL**. The Execution Control List dialog box appears as shown in Figure 12-1.

3. Select **Default** or click **Add** and add specific users and/or groups.

4. Select the different levels of access for each group and/or user.

5. Click **OK**.

You may also edit the ECL on a workstation after initial setup by following these steps:

1. Click **File**, **Tools**, **User Preferences**.

2. Click the **Security Options** button. The Execution Control List dialog box appears, as shown in Figure 12-1.

3. Highlight the user's name and change the preferences.

4. Click **OK**.

Figure 12-1

Execution Control
List Settings

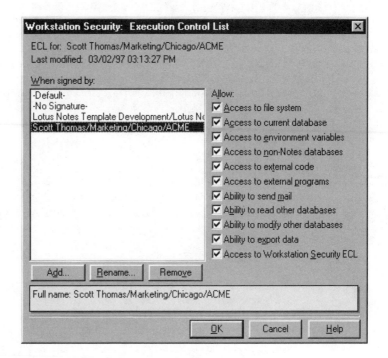

If you wish to edit the ECL of a workstation after the initial workstation setup, you must visit that workstation or send a Notes mail message with a button containing the following formula:

```
@RefreshEcl ("","")
```

The ECL is evaluated for the workstation based on the signature of the current Notes object.

Notes Database Access

In order for a user or server to gain access to a Lotus Notes application, the user or server must be listed in the access control list (ACL) of the database or be a member of a group in the ACL of the database. If a user is listed in the ACL of a database they will be granted access to the database at the level specified. The levels of access control in Notes version 4 are Manager, Designer, Editor, Author, Reader, Depositor, and No Access (in descending order). For entries of READER access and higher, each level attains those privileges of the level below it (e.g. AUTHOR access has all privileges of READER access plus those of AUTHOR access). Database ACLs are used to limit access to Notes applications, as well as controlling how replication occurs between two servers and between servers and clients.

Most companies assign responsibility to the Notes application owner to define who receives access to his or her database application. This is certainly the best approach to take in regards to managing Notes application ACLs. The Notes administration overhead associated with maintaining the ACLs of all databases would be too great.

Tips

We highly recommend that you use group names from the public Name and Address book to assign access rights to a Notes application. Using specific user names will become very tedious to manage once the number of Notes applications within a company grows. Also, when using hierarchical naming, wildcards may be used within a database ACL to grant access to an application. For example, an ACL entry of `*/Chicago/ACME` *could be used within a database ACL to grant access to only those users and servers created with the /Chicago/ACME certifier.*

Tips

We recommend that the Notes admin group is added with MANAGER access to all applications within the Notes infrastructure in the event an administrator must make changes.

The different levels of Access Control that may be assigned to a Notes application are listed below (assuming no Roles or Reader or Author Fields):

- **No Access:** The Notes ID or browser user is not granted access to the database.

- **Depositor:** The Notes ID or browser user is able to create documents, but may not view any documents within the database.

- **Reader:** The Notes ID or browser user is able to read documents but not create any documents within the database. A Reader may also create personal agents within the Notes application that may run against any document to which they have proper access.

- **Author:** The Notes ID or browser user is able to read all documents as well as create new documents. However, the server or user is only able to edit those documents the user or server created itself. This setting should be used rather than EDITOR access to avoid replication and save conflicts.

- **Editor:** The Notes ID or browser user is able to read, create, and edit all documents.

- **Designer:** The Notes ID or browser user is able to read, create, and edit all documents. In addition, the user is able to edit and create Forms, Views, and create a Full-Text Index.

- **Manager:** The Notes ID or browser user is able to read, create, and edit all documents. In addition, if using the Notes client, the user is able to edit and create Forms, Views, and Full-Text Indices. Manager access also allows the editing of the ACL of the database itself. Each Notes application requires at least one entry with MANAGER access.

The manager of a Notes application can also select from seven different levels of access to grant to users and/or groups. Each level contains options, which can be selected or deselected based on the level. These options include:

- Create documents

- Delete documents

- Create personal agents

- Create personal folders/views

- Create shared folder/views

- Create LotusScript agents

To configure the access control list for a Notes database application, follow these procedures:

1. Highlight the Notes database application and click **File**, **Database**, **Access Control**. The dialog box shown in Figure 12-2 appears:

Figure 12-2

Notes Database
Access Control
List Settings

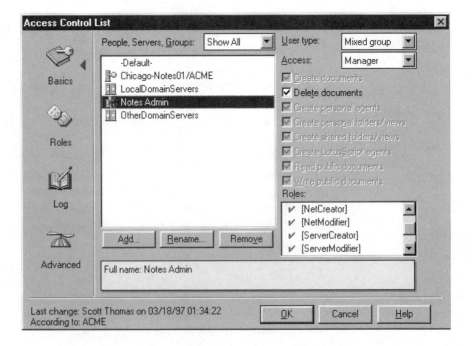

2. Highlight each entry to configure the access for each server, user, or group. The access field assigns the rights per entry.

3. For each entry in the ACL, assign its type. Choices include: Person, Server, Mixed Group, Person Group, and Server Group.

4. Click the **Add**, **Rename**, or **Remove** buttons to add, rename, or remove an ACL entry for the database. Entries allowed are groups, servers, users, or hierarchical wildcards (e.g. `*/ACME` would allow all ID files with the /ACME certifier). The entry **Default** is applied to any user or server not specifically listed or a member of any group.

5. Assign any additional settings that you desire, such as the ability to create or delete documents within the dialog box. Also assign any roles if available.

6. Click **OK**.

Tips

As another security measure, it is recommended that you set Default access to NO ACCESS for each Notes database application. You then should assign groups that need access specifically to the Notes application.

Tips

If a user appears specifically within the ACL of a Notes database ACL and also is a member of a group that appears in the ACL of the database, the user's name will prevail. If a user belongs to two or more groups that all appear within the ACL of the database, the group with Higher ACL access will prevail.

There are also additional ACL settings available within a Notes application. To access these settings, click the **Advanced** icon within the access control list dialog box, as shown in Figure 12-2. The dialog box shown in Figure 12-3 then appears:

Figure 12-3

Notes Database
Advanced Access
Control List Settings

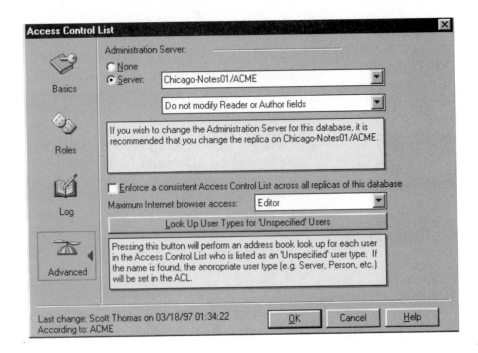

The following fields are available:

- **Administration Server:** This field specifies which Notes server will act as this application's administration server.

- **Enforce a consistent ACL across all replicas of this database:** When enabling this dialog box, ACL settings on all replica copies of this Notes application will remain the same. However, every server replicating the application must have MANAGER access or the database will not replicate with this box checked. Also, with the box checked, the ACL will be enforced even on local machines. It is not intended to be a security feature, as a Notes add-on product may bypass this feature.

- **Maximum Internet browser access:** This setting will limit the maximum access that is allowed for Web browsers accessing this Notes application. Even if the Web browser user is listed with higher access in the database's ACL, this setting will limit the access.

- **Look up User Types for "Unspecified" Users** button: Use this button if there are any entries within the database's ACL with an unspecified entry. This button will look up these entries within the public Name and Address book and assign the type of entry. ACL types will then appear as icons next to each ACL entry of the database.

Tips

It is highly recommended that you assign a type for each entry within the database's ACL. If an entry is left unspecified—for example, a person is left unspecified—another person could create a group with the same name as that person and be allowed access to the database with that person's rights. By specifying that a person listed is of type "person," a group with the same name as the person would not be allowed.

Using Roles

Roles allow the application designers and managers to group together users who should have access to certain design elements within the database. Roles are specified at the database level in the Access Control List. These roles can then be used in place of individual names in design elements such as form and view access lists, authors and readers fields, and sections. This eases the burden of maintaining lists of individual names. Other advantages to using roles in an application include the following:

- Roles allow application designers to centralize security. Access to a design element can be changed by including or excluding an individual from the role at the ACL level, rather than modifying the list of users in every field and access list. This also avoids the need to update all of the documents every time a security change is made.

- Roles provide group control to managers who might not have access to create a group in the public Name and Address book.

- Since roles are listed in the ACL dialog box, a manager is more likely to remember to include a user in the correct roles when modifying the ACL. If the manager was required to review all design elements, this would be much more difficult to maintain.

- Roles are easily included in formulas. They are represented as text strings in brackets (`"[Product_Managers]"`).

Notes Database Access to Forms, Views, Folders, and Documents

Control can be set to limit access to views, forms, folders, and documents of Notes applications. Similar to database ACLs, individuals and Notes groups can be added to a form, view, or folder of a Notes application. For a form, follow these procedures:

1. Enter the Notes application and then enter the design of the form.

2. Click **Design**, **Form Properties.**

3. Click the **key** tab. The dialog box shown in Figure 12-4 appears:

Figure 12-4

Notes Database
Advanced Access
Control List Settings

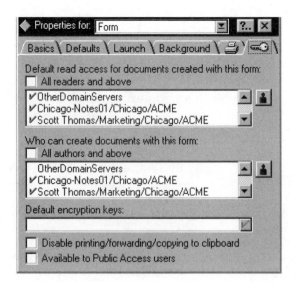

4. From within this box, select which users, servers, and/or groups that may either read or create using this form.

This same procedure may be followed in order to assign access rights to views and folders within a Notes application.

To limit access to certain documents, AUTHOR and READER fields may be used within a Notes application. If a READER name field is used within a Notes application, only users or members of groups listed within this field may read the document

If an AUTHOR name field is used within a Notes application, only users listed within this field may create or edit the document, assuming users only have AUTHOR ACL access. Those users or servers with EDITOR access or higher will be able to edit the document, regardless of the contents of an AUTHOR field within a document.

Encryption and Digital Signatures

Lotus Notes is one of the most secure packages on the market today in regards to electronic mail, information sharing, and document collaboration. Lotus Notes uses the dual key RSA Cryptosystem to encrypt data. For bulk data, the RC2 and RC4 algorithms are used. For key management, the RSA algorithm is used. RSA encryption is recognized as the only encryption system without an exposed point of compromise. As with earlier version of Lotus Notes, North American version 4 uses a 128-bit encryption key to encrypt data. The International version is limited by government export laws to a key length of 48 bits. For this reason, a North American Notes mail user sending an encrypted e-mail message to an International Notes mail user will only have the message encrypted with the 48-bit length key. By law, only users within North America are allowed to use the North American version of Lotus Notes or use a North American user ID file.

Encryption can be used to secure electronic mail and can be used to create encryption keys. These keys can be given to users and server IDs, and can then be used to encrypt fields within a Notes database form. Only those Notes IDs possessing the proper encryption key are able to access the field or document. Encryption of mail can be forced at the Notes server (refer to Chapter 11 for settings) or voluntarily by the user. Encryption keys can be created to secure database fields as follows:

1. Click **File**, **Tools**, **User ID** and then click the **Encryption** icon. The dialog box shown in Figure 12-5 appears:

Figure 12-5

Notes Encryption
Key Dialog Box

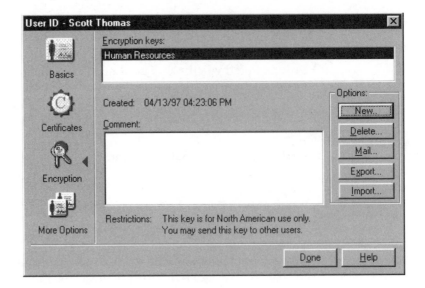

2. Click the **New** button to create a new encryption key. Once completed, you may apply it to fields within a Notes application's form.

3. Click the **Mail** button to e-mail the encryption key to others. This lets them access databases encrypted with this key.

4. Click the **Export** button to place the key on a floppy disk to distribute to others. Other people would then click the **Import** button to add the encryption key to their user ID file.

Digital signatures are used to verify that the document or field is from or edited by the user ID it states it is from. The private key of the user ID generates the signature when the document is opened; the key is then compared against the public key in the Public Name and Address book.

Version 4.0 and higher of Lotus Notes now supports encryption of local databases with a user ID or server ID. Once encrypted, only the ID that encrypted the database is able to access the data. This is especially useful for remote users where a local copy of Notes databases do not follow the Notes security model, as they do not exist on Notes servers. To encrypt a Notes application, follow these steps:

1. Highlight the Notes application and click **File**, **Database**, **Properties**.

2. Click the **Encryption** button. The dialog box shown in Figure 12-6 appears:

Figure 12-6

Notes Database
Encryption
Dialog Box

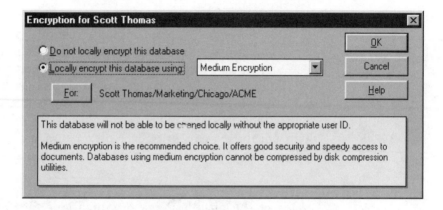

3. Select the level of encryption and change the user if necessary by pressing the **For** button.

4. Click **OK**.

Lotus Notes enables the client and/or server to encrypt data over the network. If either the client or the server is set to encrypt data, then both ends encrypt over the wire. Although the process slows performance, data can not be "sniffed" while in transit. To encrypt data over the network for a server or workstation:

1. Click **File**, **Tools**, **User Preferences**.

2. Click the **Ports** icon.

3. Click the **Encrypt Network Data** radio box.

Lotus Notes Applications

As stated at the beginning of this chapter, it is not our intention to focus on Notes application issues—rather, the administration, configuration, and security of a Notes infrastructure. However, there are some high level issues concerning Notes applications that should be addressed in order to maintain a healthy Notes network.

One of the key ingredients for successful Notes deployment and adoption is the design of a simple but useful Notes database application. Most users will be unfamiliar with Notes, and a simple database application that is accessed by a majority of users every day will familiarize them with the interface. Simple discussion databases and bulletin board-announcement databases are popular starting applications. Human resource databases are other good candidates. Such databases can provide Notes users with information easily while getting the user used to navigating their desktop.

One of the pitfalls many organizations face because of the ease and popularity of Lotus Notes is trying to use Notes as the all-in-one solution for every business need. The envelope is pushed on what Notes is designed to do, and applications fall short in expectations for performing operations that would be better suited to a relational database or other type of system. Although performance has been greatly increased with version 4.0 of Notes, applications requiring that functionality should still remain on relational database systems.

Lotus Notes should be used for:

- Company-wide information flow

- Forms-driven workflows

- When multiple users need access to a group information base

- Large amount of tasks/orders to coordinate

- Team-oriented applications

- High demand for application flexibility

- Mail enabled application support

- Discussion threaded applications

- Rapid prototyping to develop specs for full scale relational system

- Unstructured data

Lotus Notes should be avoided for:

- Relational type data models (Notes is not a relational database)

- Central–real-time data access

- High volume and transaction type applications

- Extremely large database applications

Notes Application Policies

Before a Notes application is rolled out into production, the application should go through a review process to make sure it adheres to standards set by the organization's Notes development team. Notes users should be encouraged to present ideas for application development, or to develop applications themselves on their local machines (or in a development Notes environment set by the Notes administration team).

Notes Application Roll-Out Requirements

- First, a Notes development team should be assembled. Their job is to define and develop standards that will apply to all Notes development—both ongoing and future development projects. It is this review team that will decide when applications adhere to the standards set to allow a Notes application to be replicated and accessed on the production Notes network.

- Understand the business need for the application. Before an application is approved for development, the application should satisfy a business need. A preliminary project plan should be established and approved by the necessary management teams in terms of what the application is to accomplish. All business units should agree on the plan.

- Interviews and workshops should be held to provide feedback from management as well as end users. Obtain information as to what the end user would like to see and get from the database application.

- Requirements for the application should be set. What problems and tasks the database will solve should be agreed upon and documented by the development team. Priorities then should be assigned to each requirement. Details include the number of documents, forms, and views expected. How many users will need to access this database and at what locations? Will the database need to be full-text indexed? Will Web browsers access the application through Domino?

- Once the necessary information is gathered, it should be reviewed and resources needed to complete the project should be estimated. The project plan should be amended and reviewed to include any estimates along with any additions from the interviewing process.

- With the project plan in place, a prototype of the application can now be built. The prototype should include all of the requirements of the application, while following the basic guidelines for Notes application development set by the Notes application development team.

- Once the prototype is built, a pilot team should be assembled of a few Notes users to test the application. A time period should be set and feedback should be gathered and reviewed from the pilot team. Suggestions should be reviewed and applied to the application during this testing phase. Once user acceptance has been reached, the application is ready for the production review phase.

- The application now should go through the quality assurance phase before it is released into production. The application should meet all criteria set by the Notes development standards committee. Once the application is reviewed and has passed all requirements, it is ready to be passed to the Notes administration team for deployment in the production Notes network.

Notes Application Design Requirements

It is very important that database standards be set and adhered to for all production Notes applications. Notes users within your company should feel comfortable that all Notes applications have the same basic look and feel. A few requirement examples are listed below:

- Notes buttons should be in a similar location in all applications.

- A standard set of views should be used across all applications.

- Colors for different types of forms should be uniform on all Notes applications (for instance, all response documents are yellow).

- Input validation and translation fields should be required on each form where applicable.

- Every database should include the standard About and Using Document.

- The use of Notes application templates should be defined and used when appropriate for Notes applications.

- Notes Administrators should be added to all application ACLs with MANAGER access. Group names, rather than individual names, should be used to grant access. **Default** access should be set to **none**.

Tips

You can create default ACL attributes in database templates by including the user name or group in brackets. For example, to have the group Notes Admin *always be created when a template is used to create a new database, include* [Notes Admin] *in the ACL list with the appropriate access level.*

Legacy Application Tie-Ins with Notes Applications

There are a number of third party programs that work in conjunction with Notes that pull and push (some even replicate) data to and from other data sources. Such sources include DB2, Oracle, and Sybase, to name a few. Products include ReplicAction by Casahl Technologies and NotesPump by Lotus Development Corporation. These products are designed to pull and push data to larger relational-type database applications. With these add-ons, Notes provides more of a reporting mechanism to end-users. This is especially popular for applications with remote users; Notes is powerful and efficient in delivering information easily to such users. Many organizations take advantage of this by incorporating one of these products to pull information from large relational databases, and distribute the information on a daily basis to the necessary people via Lotus Notes.

Further information on these products can be found on their respective Web sites; all companies offer trials of the product. The products are fairly easy to use and can run on production Notes machines, but it is advisable to place the engines on their own machine if possible.

It is important not to try to replace these types of relational databases with Notes. Notes is not designed to perform many of these types of transactions. Notes can be used as a reporter in most cases, but should not be expected to do more.

Controlling Notes Application Sizes

With version 4.0 and higher of Lotus Notes, the absolute size a database may grow to is 4 gigabytes (up from 1 gigabyte). The default size upon creation of an application is still set to 1 GB. The maximum size of a database may not be changed once it is created. A new copy or a new replica must be made in order to change the maximum size.

It should be noted that once a database's size gets to 1 GB, performance problems might begin to be encountered by Notes users. Additional hardware may be added to the Notes application server such as RAM and processors, but this may prove to be an expensive solution. Databases that get to this size may be candidates to be split into multiple applications by the Notes development team. Figure 12-7 shows the absolute size settings dialog box for a Notes application:

Figure 12-7

Notes Database
Absolute Size
Settings

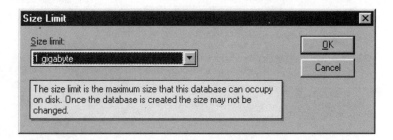

Quotas may also now be set with version 4.0 and higher of Lotus Notes. Warnings are sent to the log, console, and administrators when the size of the application reaches the quota size. This is beneficial when using Notes mail to prevent people from letting their mail files get too large. Quotas enable mail files to continue to receive e-mail once the quota is reached, but prevents users from adding anymore documents. Alerts may be set to alert administrators when a database reaches a specified size. To create or adjust the quota for a Notes application, follow these procedures:

1. Click **File**, **Tools**, **Server Administration.**

2. Click the **Database Tools** icon.

3. Within the **Tool** field, select **Quotas.**

4. Within the **Server** field, select the Notes server to administer.

5. Within the **Databases** area, highlight the Notes application(s) to set Quota information.

6. Within the **Quota** field, enter the quota for the application.

7. Within the **Warning Threshold** field, enter the threshold-warning amount for the application.

8. Click **Done**.

Figure 12-8
Notes Database
Quota Settings

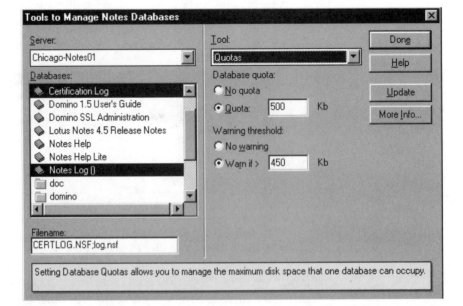

Notes Application Full Text Indexing

Lotus Notes supports full-text indexing on a database level. Full-text indices may be created so that users may find information in a database in seconds. When a full text index is created for a Notes application, a subdirectory is created with the filename of the database with a **.FT** extension. It is within this subdirectory that the index for the application is stored.

Any Notes administrator or manager with ACL access of DESIGNER or higher may create an index on one or more Notes applications. For an index to be created upon multiple Notes applications, each database must have the design property of **Include in multi database indexing** enabled.

It should be noted that full-text indexing takes server resources as well as disk space. The average size of the index can be calculated to be roughly one half the size of the database itself. For example, a 500 MB database would have roughly a 250 MB index.

To create a full-text index for a Notes application, follow these steps:

1. Click **File**, **Tools**, **Server Administration.**

2. Click the **Database Tools** icon.

3. Within the **Tools** field, select **Full Text Index.**

4. Within the **Server** field, select the Notes server to administer.

5. Highlight the database(s) to create a full-text index.

6. Specify whether or not the index should include case sensitivity, file attachments, and/or encrypted fields.

7. If you wish to exclude words, click the **exclude words in stop word file** and specify that file name in the box.

8. Click **Create.**

You may also create a full-text index for a database by highlighting the database icon and selecting **File**, **Database**, **Properties** then clicking the **Full Text** tab.

You may prevent users from full text indexing databases upon a Notes server by using the line Update_No_Fulltext=1 *within the* NOTES.INI *file of the Notes server.*

Corrupted Notes Applications

At times a Notes application may contain corrupted documents, views, and/or folders. Corruption of a Notes application is usually caused by the improper shutdown of a Notes server (server crash, power failure, not shutting down the Notes server before shutting down the machine), improper database access through a Notes API program, or accessing a Notes application directly through the file system by two or more users or servers by-passing a Notes server.

The Notes server program FIXUP can be used to attempt to fix damaged databases. It can be run from the Notes server console on any unopened Notes applications. Type the following command from the server console:

```
load fixup mail\sthomas arguments
```

For applications that are opened, the Notes server should be shut down and the fixup program run on a Notes application from the command prompt against the database. Take note, though; depending on the platform, the proper prefix for the program must be used. For example, to run Fixup on the public Name and Address book on a Windows NT server, shut down the Notes server, open a command prompt, and type the following from the Notes directory:

```
nfixup data\names.nsf arguments
```

Arguments include:

- **-L** Reports all events to the Notes log. Without this option, only databases with problems will be reported.

- **-V** This option will prevent Fixup from running on Notes application views.

- **-N** This option prevents Fixup from purging corrupted documents from the Notes application.

Updating Notes Application Views and Full Text Indexes

The **updall** Notes server program is responsible for updating all database views that have been accessed at least once and all full text indexes for all Notes applications on the Notes server. By default it runs automatically at 2:00 AM, as specified within the Notes server's **NOTES.INI** file. It may also be run manually from the Notes server console by typing the following:

```
load updall arguments
```

Optional arguments include:

- **-V** updates views that have been accessed at least once and skips full text indexes

- **-C** builds all unused views and full text indexes

- **-R** rebuilds all database views that have been accessed at least once as well as all full text indexes. This option should only be used on corrupt databases.

- **-F** updates all full text indexes and skips database views

- **-X** rebuilds all full text indexes

- **-S** updates all full text indexes that have designations of scheduled frequencies Scheduled, Hourly, and Immediate

Notes Database Compaction

The compact server utility program regains any disk space lost within a database due to document deletions. A document, once deleted, is only flagged for deletion. The actual content of the document remains in the database until the database is compacted, or when a new document fills this void. However, the document has been deleted may not be undeleted. Once the database contains 10% of what is called white space, the database should be compacted. The amount of this white space may be gathered from either the Notes log or by highlighting the database in question and performing a **File, Database, Properties**, and clicking the **information** tab, then **% used**. Anything less than 90% is a candidate for compaction.

When you compact a Notes application and it is in Notes version 3 format, the application will be converted to the version 4 file format. To prevent this from happening, the application should be renamed with a **.NS3** file extension.

The compact program can be run in several manners. Compact can be run at the server or remote console by typing the following from the Notes server console:

```
load compact argument
```

Optional arguments include:

- **-D** discards any built view indexed in addition to compacting

- **-L** allows users to continue to access a database during compaction (slows process)

- **-S** *value* compacts all databases with a percentage of white space of *value* or more

- **-R** compacts Release 3.x databases without changing to Release 4.x format

This will run compact on all Notes databases on the Notes server. If you specify a database afterwards, such as `load compact MAIL\STHOMAS.NSF`, it will only run on that database.

You may also run the compact utility as follows:

1. Click **File**, **Tools**, **Server Administration.**

2. Click the **Database Tools** icon. The dialog box shown in Figure 12-9 appears.

Figure 12-9

Notes Database
Compact Settings

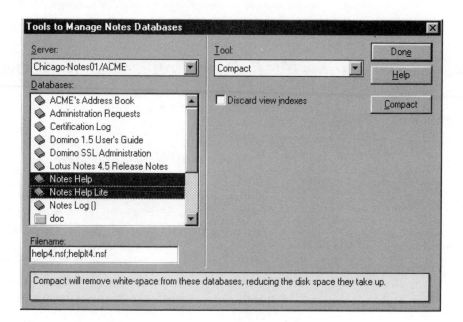

3. From the **Tool** field, select **Compact**.

4. Within the **Server** field, select the Notes server for administration.

5. Within the **Databases** field, select the application(s) to compact.

6. Click **Compact.**

Finally, the compact server program can be run within a program document in the public name and address book. Consult Chapter 6, *Public Name and Address Book Forms and Views* for discussion on program documents.

Tips

The compact server utility is resource intensive and should only be run at off-hours. Also, if a database is being compacted, all users will be unable to access the database until the task is completed. When a database is compacted, an actual copy of the database is temporarily made; enough disk space is needed on the server is needed to make this temporary copy.

Notes Application Replication and Save Conflicts

Replication conflicts occur in Notes applications when two or more users edit and save changes to the same document in the same Notes application on different Notes servers. When the next scheduled replication occurs, Notes flags the document as a replication conflict.

A save conflict is the same as a replication conflict, except the action happens on the same server. Two or more users edit the same document in the same Notes database on the same server.

There are a number of ways to handle save and replication conflict. First, when designing the application, this problem should be kept in mind. For large, intensive applications where people need to modify the same document in the same database, Notes is probably not a good solution. Granting only *author* access to a Notes application will eliminate this problem, as users will only be able to edit their own documents.

Lotus has helped resolve these problems in Notes version 4.0 and higher with a process called *merging conflicts*. The merging conflicts process must be enabled by the designer of the database. The setting can be found by entering the design of a form of a database and then selecting **Form Properties** (see Figure 12-10). At the bottom right-hand corner of the **Basic** tab is a check box where this option can be selected.

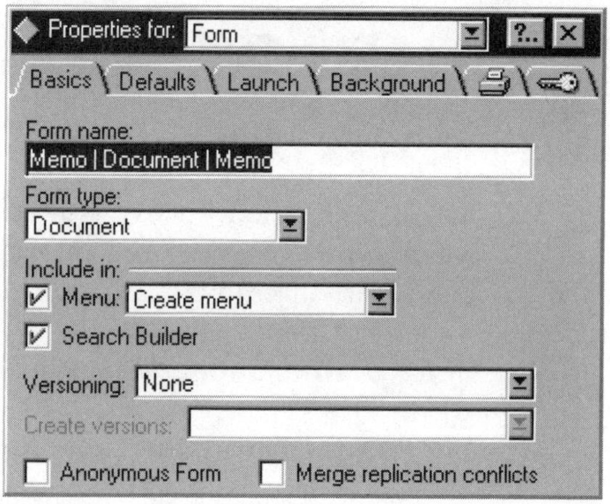

Figure 12-10

Database Merge
Conflicts Setting

When a person edits the same document as someone else either on the same server or on a different server without merging conflicts, a replication or save conflict is flagged. With merging conflicts enabled on the form(s) within the database, a replication or save conflict may not necessarily occur in the above scenario. If two people edit the same document either on the same or on a different server, and the fields edited are different, Notes will merge the two documents together as one document without flagging a replication or save conflict. However, if the document edited and saved has a change done to the *same* field, then a replication or save conflict will still occur.

It must be noted that if this feature is turned on, it may actually make some documents incorrect in what type of data is expected. Take, for example, a Notes application where merge conflicts is enabled, and the application has two fields: user and location. One user edits a document and changes the user's name. Another person edits the same document at the same time and changes the location. With merge conflicts on, the document now has a new user's name with another new location, making the document incorrect. Great care and planning must be considered before enabling this feature.

Most organizations give responsibility to the Notes database manager to scan for replication and save conflicts. If there is an occurrence, the database manager decides which document should be the "winner." Many times, this involves the manager to cut and past information from one document and to another. The manager then deletes the old document.

Analyzing a Notes Database

A Notes administrator or manager may analyze a particular database by running a database analysis. This tool gathers information from the replication history, user activity dialog box, and the Notes log, and stores the gathered information within a results database. To run a database analysis:

1. Click **File**, **Tools**, **Server Administration.**

2. Click the **Database Tools** icon.

3. Within the **Tool** field, select **Analyze A Database** (see Figure 12-11).

Figure 12-11

Database Analysis Settings

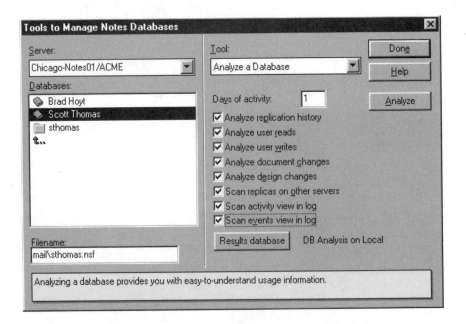

4. Within the **Server** field, select the Notes server to administer.

5. Within the **Databases** field, select the application to analyze.

6. Within the **Days Of Activity** field, select the number of days to evaluate.

7. Select any other settings you wish reports on from the radio boxes.

8. Click the **Results Database** button to change the location of the results database.

9. Click **Analyze.**

Updating a Notes Application's Design

A Notes developer may create a design template for a Notes application to control the design elements for the database. A notes database can be set to accept design changes from this template. Every evening at 1:00 AM, the server program **design** will run and update the design of all Notes applications that have their design based upon templates. To run the program manually, type the following command from the Notes server console:

```
load design
```

The automatic update is controlled via **NOTES.INI**. It can be disabled or rescheduled.

Viewing NotesIDs of Notes Documents

At times, a Notes document will become corrupted. Running the compact server program will more than likely fix any corrupted documents within a Notes application. However, before running compact, you may be able to view the contents of the damaged Notes document by the following procedure:

1. Open the Notes log where the damaged Notes application resides and copy its hexadecimal NoteID number.

2. Click **File, Tools, Server Administration** and click the **Database Tools** icon.

3. Within the **Tool** field, select **NoteID** (see Figure 12-12).

Figure 12-12

Viewing the
Contents of a
Notes Document
with a NoteID

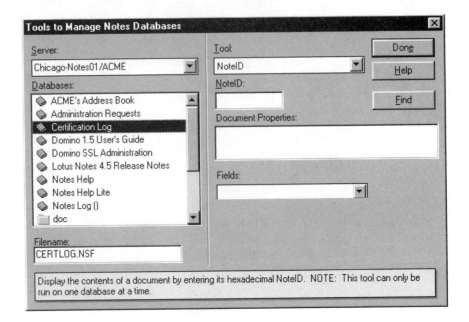

4. Within the **Server** field, select the Notes server to administer.

5. Within the **Database** field, select the Notes application to view.

6. Within the **NoteID** field, enter the document's hexadecimal value.

7. Click **Find** to view the contents of the document.

13

Internet and Web Application Servers

With the release of version 4.5 of Lotus Notes comes one of the most exciting products available for Internet/Intranet servers today. You may now configure your Notes server to run the HTTP process to serve Notes applications and/or HTML pages to any Web browser, thus creating a world-class Web server that contains all of the Notes administration, replication and security features. You may also configure your Notes server as an InterNotes server so that any Notes client, regardless of protocol, may access HTML web pages from your company's Intranet Web servers or even from Internet Web servers. There are many more components so tightly coupled to Notes that we do not consider them as independent components for the sake of this book. Many of these additional components have been discussed in previous chapters, including the SMTP e-mail gateway, and POP3 client e-mail support.

InterNotes Web Navigator

You may configure a Notes server to act as an InterNotes server responsible for connecting to Web servers, pulling those HTML pages into a central repository Notes application so that any Notes client may view them. Because the Web pages are stored within a Notes application on the InterNotes server, a Notes client does not have to run TCP/IP and does not have to connect to the target Web server directly. Figure 13-1 shows this type of connectivity:

Figure 13-1
InterNotes Server
Connectivity

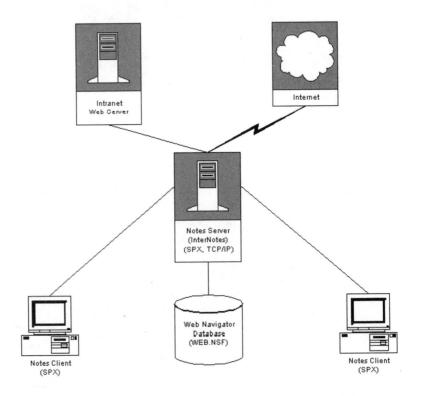

Requirements for the Internet server include the following:

- TCP/IP must be enabled (as well as any other protocol) for Notes client connectivity.

- The Notes server must run the Web Navigator server program.

- The Web Navigator must be configured within the Web Navigator database (**WEB.NSF** is the default filename).

- For Internet Web connectivity, the InterNotes server must have a direct connection to the target Web servers (an Internet connection).

Traps

Connecting your internal network to the Internet raises potential security risks. Consult **Chapter 5** *and refer to the external connectivity section for issues surrounding opening your Notes server to external contact.*

Installation and Configuration

To start the InterNotes Web server task on a Notes server, type the following command from the Notes server console:

```
load web
```

If you wish this task to begin every time the Notes server is started, the task must be added to the **ServerTasks** line within the server's **NOTES.INI** file. Once the server task begins, the Web Navigator database (**WEB.NSF**) is created. Within this database, the administration document is also created. It is within this document that you should configure the settings for the InterNotes server. To open the document, follow these steps:

1. Open the Web Navigator database (**WEB.NSF**) on the Notes server running the WEB server task.

2. Click the **Database Views** icon from within the home navigator page.

3. Click on the **All Documents** button.

4. Click **Actions, Administration.** The screen shown in Figure 13-2 appears:

Figure 13-2

InterNotes Server
Configuration
Settings

✎ Enable Purge agent	✪ Enable Refresh agent	🌐 Go to Notes resource site

Web Navigator Administration
Chicago-Notes01/ACME

Server Basics		Purge Agent Settings	
InterNotes server name:	CN=Chicago-Notes01/O=ACME	Purge agent action:	Delete page ▾
Maximum database size:	500 MB	Purge to what % of maximum database size:	60 % ▾
Save author Information:	☐	Purge documents older than:	30 ▾ Days
Save HTML in Note?	☐	Purge documents larger than:	512KB ▾
		Purge Private documents:	☐ _ Warning!

HTML Preferences			
Anchors:	Underline/Blue ▾	Fixed:	Courier ▾
Body Text:	Times 11 ▾	Listing:	Courier ▾
Plain:	Courier ▾	Address:	Times ▾

Only fonts Helvetica, Times and Courier are supported.

Tips

You must have MANAGER access with the WebMaster role assigned in order to view this configuration document. Also, the document can only be viewed from within the ALL DOCUMENTS view of the application.

The following fields can be configured:

- **InterNotes server name:** This field is configured by default once the WEB server task is loaded on the Notes server. To change the name, enter the new Notes server name with its fully distinguished name.

- **Maximum database size:** Enter the maximum available size in megabytes for the Web Navigator Notes application.

- **Save author information:** If you wish to save the Notes user name of the individual who retrieved the Web page into the Web Navigator application, click this box.

- **Save HTML in Note:** If you wish to have the HTML code stored for the retrieved Web page within the Notes document, check this box.

- **Purge agent action:** When the purge agent is run upon this database, you may have the agent either delete the eligible document or reduce the eligible document. Deleting the document will remove all contents of the Notes document from the Web Navigator database. Reducing the document will remove all portions of the document and will leave only a URL pointing to the original Web page.

- **Purge to what % of maximum database size:** Enter the percentage amount you wish to have the purge agent reach.

- **Purge documents older than:** Specify the number of days old the documents within the Notes application should be that the purge agent should delete.

- **Purge documents larger than:** Specify the maximum size a document may be before the purge agent will delete the document.

- **Purge Private documents:** Specify whether or not the purge agent should be allowed to delete documents stored in Notes users' private folders.

- **HTML Preferences:** Specify the appearance of Web page documents within the Notes application.

5. Documents within the Web Navigator database may be refreshed automatically on an InterNotes server by running the Refresh agent. Click the **Refresh Agent** button to run this agent.

Tips

You must have proper security rights within the server document of the InterNotes server in the public Name and Address book to run restricted LotusScript agents.

6. Exit the document and save your changes.

To further configure the settings for the InterNotes server, follow these procedures:

1. Open the server document housing the WEB server task within the public Name and Address book.

2. Move to the Web Retriever Administration section of the document. Figure 13-3 shows this section:

Figure 13-3

InterNotes Server Administration Settings

▼ Web Retriever Administration

Web Retriever Management		Internet Site Access Control	
Web Navigator database:	web.nsf	Allow access to these Internet sites:	×
Services:	HTTP, FTP, GOPHER	Deny access to these Internet sites:	×.playboy.com ×.mtv.com
Concurrent retrievers:	25		
Retriever log level:	Terse		
Update cache:	Once per session		
SMTP Domain:	acme.com		

Configure the following fields:

● **Web Navigator database:** This field represents the Notes database application that will host all remote Web site pages.

● **Services:** This field controls what services can be accessed using the InterNotes server. These include FTP, GOPHER, HTTP, HTTPS, and FINGER.

● **Concurrent retrievers:** This field represents the maximum number of processes or threads that are permitted to access remote Web sites. The web program only creates a new retriever as required.

- **Retriever log level:** This field represents the level of logging that will be recorded to the Notes log database on the Notes server. The levels include None, Terse, and Verbose.

- **Update cache:** This entry controls how often the document within the Web Notes application is updated.

- **SMTP Domain:** This field represents the domain used to route SMTP mail.

- **Allow access to these Internet sites:** This field controls what sites users are able to connect to. Wildcards (*) may be used if desired. For example, *.com allows users to connect to any site ending with **.com**.

- **Deny access to these Internet sites:** This field controls what sites users are not allowed to connect to. Like the allow access field, wildcards may be used. ***.acme.com** would prevent users from connecting to any server within ***.acme.com**. You may also directly enter the IP address of a target site. This field overrides any sites that may be available within the **allow access field** listed above.

3. Exit and save your changes.

You may unload the WEB retriever task by typing the following line from the server console:

```
tell web quit
```

On each Notes client, you also must specify the InterNotes server for the client to use. This setting can be found within the location document within each user's personal Name and Address book. Before the creation of a Notes user, the Notes administrator may specify an InterNotes server within a Profile Record within the public Name and Address book. When the new user is created, the profile can be assigned to the user, thus populating this field on the user's Notes workstation.

Personal Web Navigator

Domino 4.5 now includes a personal Web Navigator. This allows
Notes client users to access Web pages directly without using an
InterNotes Server. The database also allows users to store browsed
Web pages for later use. The personal Web Navigator is configurable
from the user's Notes clients. If your organization already has a
standard Web browser, Notes clients can be configured to use the
browser of their choice. This is done in the location document of the
personal Name and Address book for each Notes client.

Web Publisher

The InterNotes Web publisher task enables Notes administrators to
convert Notes applications to HTML files. These converted files can
then be moved or copied onto a Web server for Web browser access.
This program is being phased out by Lotus in favor of the Domino
server (HTTP program described within the next section). The Web
Publisher add-on program can still be used, but the HTTP program
is now a better solution for serving Notes applications to Web
browsers. The Web Publisher program must be installed on the target Notes server. Once installed, the following server task must be
started from the Notes server console:

```
load webpub
```

This line can also be added to the **ServerTasks** entry within the
NOTES.INI file of the server so that the task will begin automatically upon server startup.

Once the task is loaded, the Web Configuration database
(**WEBCFG.NSF**) is created. It is from within this Notes application
that you configure the settings for the Web Publisher. This includes
target directory locations for the converted Notes application(s)
(HTML files), Notes applications in which to convert, and schedules
as to when and how often to publish the Notes applications.

Domino (HTTP Server Program)

The Lotus Domino Server 4.5, powered by Notes, is an integrated Internet standards-based Web server. The Domino server is the tried and true Notes server, with integrated support for standards-based Internet protocols such as TCP/IP, HTTP, SMTP/MIME, X.400, Java, Netscape Plug-Ins, ActiveX, POP3, HTML, MAPI, SNMP, CGI support, and animated GIFs.

What Domino now does is make a Notes server's architecture much more open, specifically to Web browsers and other Web servers. With Domino installed on a server, any Web browser is capable of accessing a Notes application, which includes Notes mail. This openness actually makes it so that a Lotus Notes client is not needed to access Notes applications. Obviously, functionality would be lost, but it shows the commitment Lotus (IBM) has to opening up Notes to Intranet/Internet standards.

Because the back end is still Notes, administrators can control what Web browsers access with the built-in security features of Lotus Notes. This includes server access, database access, view access, and form access. You may even develop Notes applications that dynamically generate information for Web browsers depending on the user name accessing the information. Also, because the back end is still Lotus Notes, you are very easily able to replicate Notes applications to other Notes servers running the HTTP process. Replication is the bidirectional information moving process that so many other Web servers still are unable to accomplish. Also, documents can be edited and saved by a Web browser directly within the Notes application (another feature that is unavailable to Web servers).

The Domino server can also be used to serve standard HTML files as well. This gives the flexibility to a company to host both Notes applications and Web pages on a single server.

Once the HTTP program is loaded, a Domino server will convert a Notes application on the fly and transparently, including navigators, views, documents, and links into HTML for access by any requesting Web browser. The server task actually speaks in native HTTP. A Web browser may also access HTML pages on the Notes server if such pages exist on the Notes server. Figure 13-4 depicts this interaction between the Domino server and Web browser:

Figure 13-4
Domino Server
and Web Browser
Interaction

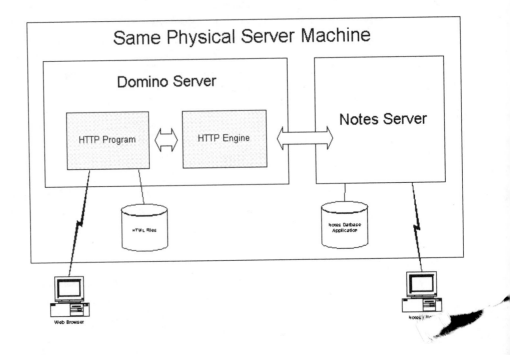

Installation

As with all Web servers and Web browsers, TCP/IP is required in order to connect to a Notes server running the HTTP server process. TCP/IP must be installed and running on the Notes server machine and on the Notes server itself. Also, any client machine running a Web browser must also have a valid TCP/IP address configured. For details on the TCP/IP protocol, consult Chapter 3, *Network Protocols*.

To start the HTTP server process upon a Notes server, type the following command from the Notes server command line:

```
load http
```

Once loaded, any Web browser with TCP/IP connectivity to the machine will be able to access any Notes applications and/or HTML

Web pages on the Notes server, assuming proper security restrictions. If you want this task to begin every time the Notes server is started, the task must be added to the **ServerTasks** line within the **NOTES.INI** file on the Notes server.

Tips

We recommend that the Notes server running the HTTP server task have at least 1 gigabyte of disk space and a minimum of 64 megabytes of RAM.

Configuration

Configuration for the HTTP process is handled in the server record for the Notes server within the public Name and Address book. To configure the HTTP process, follow these steps:

1. Open the server record of the Notes server running the HTTP process and move to the HTTP Server section.

2. The following screen appears, as shown in part in Figure 13-5.

Figure 13-5
HTTP Server
Configuration
(Section 1)

▼ **HTTP Server**

Basics		Operational Information	
TCP/IP port number:	80	Cache directory (for GIFs and file attachments):	domino\cache
TCP/IP port status:	Enabled	Garbage collection:	Enabled
SSL port number:	443	Garbage collection interval:	60 minutes
SSL port status:	Enabled	Maximum cache size:	50 (MB)
Host name:		Delete cache on shutdown:	Disabled
DNS lookup:	Disabled	Image conversion format:	GIF
Default home page:	default.htm	Interlaced rendering:	Enabled
Maximum active threads:	40		
Minimum active threads:	20	Default lines per view:	30
		Default character set group:	Western

Configure the following fields:

- **TCP/IP port number:** This field represents the port number of the HTTP process to listen for HTTP requests. Port 80 is the default used by all HTTP Web servers and clients. Other than port 80, no port below 1024 should ever be used. If another port is going to be used for the HTTP process, clients must specify the port used. For instance, another popular port to use to listen for HTTP requests is port 8008. For a Web browser to access a Domino server running the HTTP process, the user would have to specify the server name and port number, for examplek `http://www.acme.com:8008/`.

If the port number is changed, the Domino server must be restarted.

- **TCP/IP port status:** This field specifies the status of the TCP/IP port. Either this port and/or the SSL port must be enabled to use the HTTP process.

- **SSL port number:** Similar to the TCP/IP port number, the SSL port number is the number that is set for the HTTP process to listen for HTTPS requests (secure sockets). The default in the industry for the port number is 443 and should not be changed.

- **SSL port status:** This field must be enabled for the HTTP process to accept SSL requests. It may be enabled along with the TCP/IP port if desired. If this port is enabled while the Domino server is operating, the server must be restarted.

- **Host name:** This field contains the fully qualified host name for the Notes server. This should be the address as defined in DNS. If the Notes server is not registered within DNS, the IP address should be used here. If the field is left blank, then the Notes server will use the address defined in the operating system's TCP/IP configuration.

- **DNS lookup:** This field determines whether or not the HTTP process will look up the qualified host name of Web browsers contacting the server. If it is enabled, the Notes server will lose some performance in order to process each lookup. Also, if the field is enabled and logging is enabled, then the actual machine (host) names of clients will be logged rather than the IP addresses of the requesting machines.

- **Default home page:** This field represents the name of the HTML page you wish to use for the server's home page. If you decide to use an HTML home page, the file must be placed within the Domino HTML directory and the **Home URL** field must be blank.

If a Notes database application is going to be used for the home page, then this field should be left blank.

- **Maximum active threads:** This specifies the maximum number of threads that can be used for answer browser requests. The more hardware the Notes server contains (processors, RAM, etc.), the higher the number of threads the Notes server running the HTTP process will be able to handle.

- **Minimum active threads:** This is the minimum number of active threads the Notes server will keep open, even if the threads are idle. Like the **Maximum active threads** field, the more hardware that is available to the server, the higher this number may be set.

- **Cache directory:** This directory stores images and file attachments. When a Web browser requests an image or file attachment, it is stored within this directory. If the item is requested again, the image is displayed from this directory, which improves performance. This directory is located in the Notes data directory.

- **Garbage collection/interval:** These fields specify if garbage collection is enabled and if so, at what interval. Files that are no longer needed will be deleted, beginning with the least accessed files.

- **Maximum cache size:** This field specifies the maximum size the cache directory may reach. Once this size is reached, the Domino server will automatically delete unnecessary files. If more disk space is available, this size may be adjusted accordingly.

- **Delete cache on shutdown:** If this field is enabled, the Domino server will clear the contents of the cache directory when the server is shut down.

- **Image conversion format:** This field determines what format to convert images to. The choices are either JPEG or GIF formats.

- **Interlaced rendering:** If GIF format is enabled, GIF images will be rendered progressively to Web browsers, as if the image is being gradually "filled in."

- **Default lines per view:** This setting defines the number of lines the HTTP process will use to display a Notes database application view. This setting will affect all Notes applications on the Notes server.

- **Default character set group:** This field represents which character set to use when Web browsers access the Domino server.

Figure 13-6 shows the second section of the HTTP server configuration.

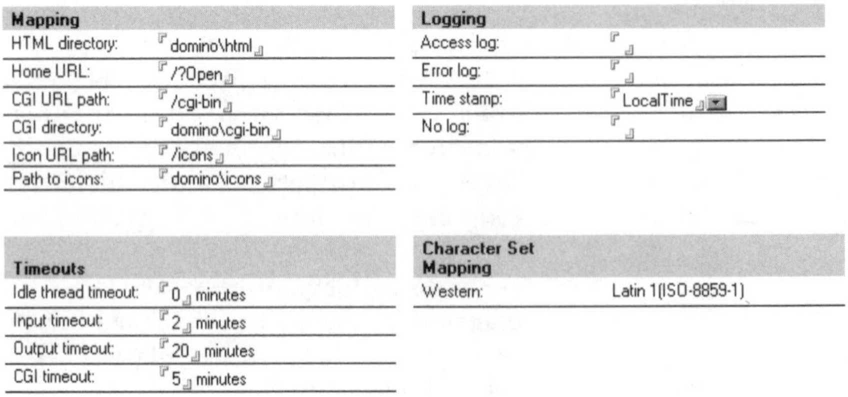

Figure 13-6
HTTP Server
Configuration
(Section 2)

Mapping	
HTML directory:	domino\html
Home URL:	/?Open
CGI URL path:	/cgi-bin
CGI directory:	domino\cgi-bin
Icon URL path:	/icons
Path to icons:	domino\icons

Logging	
Access log:	
Error log:	
Time stamp:	LocalTime
No log:	

Timeouts	
Idle thread timeout:	0 minutes
Input timeout:	2 minutes
Output timeout:	20 minutes
CGI timeout:	5 minutes

Character Set Mapping	
Western:	Latin 1(ISO-8859-1)

Configure the following fields:

- **HTML directory:** This field specifies the directory for HTML files that will be hosted by the Domino server. A Domino server can host Notes applications and/or HTML files to any standard Web browser.

- **Home URL:** Within this field enter the about document, navigator, or Notes database application for users to access when a Web browser first contacts the Notes server. If an HTML document is going to be used for the server for the home page instead, leave this field blank. The default setting of **/?Open** will list all Notes applications available on the Notes server assuming this security option is enabled. To designate a specific database for the Domino home page, an entry such as **/home.nsf** may be used.

- **CGI URL path:** This field contains the URL path for CGI programs. Note that this is not the path as related to the file system of the Notes server.

- **CGI directory:** This field specifies the directory location of the CGI program files. The path is relative to the data directory of the installed Notes server.

- **Icon URL path:** This field contains the URL path for icons. Note that this field does not represent the operating system path.

- **Path to icons:** This field represents the directory location of the icons. This field is also relative to the data directory of the Notes installation.

- **Access log:** This field represents the path and/or filename of the access log for HTTP access statistics. If you do not wish to have Web client requests logged, leave the field blank. The information can be logged to either a Notes database or the NCSA standard log file format. If you will be using a Notes application, create a Domino Web Server log using the included template (**DOMLOG.NTF**).

Tips

You can actually log to both a Notes database and NCSA standard log files. To do this, enter both the text file name and the domino database file name separated by a comma. Logging to both types of files is useful if you wish to analyze your logs using HTTP reporting tools like Microsoft Interse' or Webtrends.

- **Error log:** This field represents the path and/or filename of the error log for HTTP errors. If you do not want to log errors, leave the field blank. The log information can be logged to either a Notes database or the NCSA standard log file format. If you want errors to report to the Domino Web Server log (**DOMLOG.NTF**), specify this application.

- **Time stamp:** This field specifies if the logs are recorded using the local time of the Notes server or Greenwich Mean Time (GMT).

- **No log:** This field is used to not log certain clients within the access log. For example, you may not wish to log users internal to your company, but still wish to log all hits from external clients. Such an example within this field may look like: ***.acme.com.**

3. Once completed, **Save** and **Exit** the server record.

Figure 13-7 shows sample entries within a Domino Notes log using the Notes application to trace HTTP connections:

Figure 13-7

Domino Log

Date	User	Address	Request
04/16/97 02:19:50 PM	-	192.2.2.2	GET / HTTP/1.0
04/16/97 02:20:01 PM	Scott Thomas	192.2.2.2	GET / HTTP/1.0
04/16/97 02:20:01 PM	-	192.2.2.2	GET /icons/abook.gif HTTP/1.0
04/16/97 02:20:01 PM	-	192.2.2.2	GET /icons/afolder.gif HTTP/1.0
04/16/97 02:20:11 PM	Scott Thomas	192.2.2.2	GET /mail/sthomas.nsf?OpenDatabase HTTP/1.0
04/16/97 02:20:16 PM	Scott Thomas	192.2.2.2	GET / HTTP/1.0
04/16/97 02:20:21 PM	Scott Thomas	192.2.2.2	GET /mail/sthomas/archive.nsf?OpenDatabase HTTP/1.0
04/16/97 02:20:31 PM	Scott Thomas/Mar	192.2.2.2	GET /mail/sthomas/archive.nsf?OpenDatabase HTTP/1.0
04/16/97 02:20:41 PM	Scott Thomas/Mar	192.2.2.2	GET /CERTLOG.NSF?OpenDatabase HTTP/1.0
04/16/97 02:21:26 PM	-	192.2.2.2	GET /mail/sthomas/archive.nsf?OpenDatabase HTTP/1.0
04/16/97 02:21:31 PM	Scott Thomas	192.2.2.2	GET /mail/sthomas/archive.nsf?OpenDatabase HTTP/1.0
04/16/97 02:21:46 PM	Scott Thomas/Mar	192.2.2.2	GET /mail/sthomas/archive.nsf?OpenDatabase HTTP/1.0
04/16/97 02:21:46 PM	Scott Thomas/Mar	192.2.2.2	GET /mail/sthomas/archive.nsf/$icon?OpenIcon HTTP/1.0
04/16/97 02:24:22 PM	-	192.2.2.2	GET / HTTP/1.0
04/16/97 02:24:28 PM	sthomas	192.2.2.2	GET / HTTP/1.0
04/16/97 02:24:28 PM	-	192.2.2.2	GET /icons/abook.gif HTTP/1.0
04/16/97 02:24:28 PM	-	192.2.2.2	GET /icons/afolder.gif HTTP/1.0
04/16/97 02:24:58 PM	-	192.2.2.2	GET / HTTP/1.0
04/16/97 02:25:28 PM	Lee Jones	192.2.2.2	GET / HTTP/1.0
04/16/97 02:25:28 PM	-	192.2.2.2	GET /icons/abook.gif HTTP/1.0
04/16/97 02:25:28 PM	-	192.2.2.2	GET /icons/afolder.gif HTTP/1.0
04/16/97 02:25:38 PM	Lee Jones	192.2.2.2	GET /help4.nsf?OpenDatabase HTTP/1.0

To show the statistics for the HTTP server task, type the following command from the Notes server console:

```
show stat domino
```

You may stop the HTTP server task by typing the following line from the Notes server console:

```
tell http quit
```

Virtual Web Servers

You may host (run) multiple HTTP servers upon a single machine. This is especially useful for companies where hardware is not readily available or for ISPs that wish to host multiple Web servers for their customers. Each Domino Web server must be configured within its own TCP/IP address, home URL, default home page, CGI path, and icons directory. The Notes data directory for all servers, however, is the same for all virtual servers.

In order to set up multiple virtual servers on a single machine, you must first create a virtual server document within the Domino Web Server Configuration database (**DOMCFG.NSF**). If you have not yet created this database, do so using the Domino Web Server Configuration template (**DOMCFG.NTF**).

Create a virtual server document for each additional Web server you would like to run on the machine. The settings for each virtual server will override any setting within the server document in the public Name and Address book.

Within this database you may also create documents to map Domino URLs and directories to disguise the actual locations of directories, map collections of URLs to a new location, and redirect one URL to another URL.

Using the Domino Site Creator Notes Application

Shipped with the Notes Domino CD is the Notes application Domino.Action Site Creator, which will walk a Notes administrator through the tasks of setting up and configuring the HTTP process to host HTML Web pages and Notes applications to Web browsers. To use this application, create the site creator database using the Notes database template, **SITEACT.NTF**.

Once this Notes application is created, you may select and configure the key elements of your World Wide Web site. Once the configuration steps are complete within this Notes application, the application will create your Web site as a set of databases that can be displayed both in Notes and via a Web browser.

Once the site is running, this Notes application can be used to maintain configuration and security settings for the Web pages.

Security

There are several security issues to address when running the HTTP process on a Notes server. Because the back end is a Notes server, many of the security measures that are a part of the Notes server and its applications are applied to Web browser access. Within this section, we address some of the security concerns and configurations of the product.

HTTP User Names

In order to allow Web browser access for individuals, you must create person records within the public Name and Address book for each Web user. In addition, you may also allow anonymous HTTP connections to the server, which allows all Web browsers access to the server. Anonymous users will be known as the person "Anonymous" and the name "Anonymous" should be placed in database ACLs to control access to applications for anonymous Web browser users. Passthru server access is not allowed for Web browsers.

Users are granted access to the Domino server and any of its applications through a challenge/response mechanism. Users are only challenged for a user name and password when they attempt to access something that is restricted. After the correct user name and password are provided, access to the resource is granted. User names are gathered from the first entry listed in the user name field of a person record and the password is gathered from the HTTP password field within the person record. Password entries are encrypted within the HTTP password field. Web browser users may be members of groups within the public Name and Address book as well. Figure 13-8 shows these locations:

Figure 13-8
Web Browser
Person Record

PERSON: Lee Jones
Lee Jones

Name	
First name:	⌐ Lee ⌐
Middle initial:	⌐ ⌐
Last name:	⌐ Jones ⌐
User name:	⌐ Lee Jones ⌐
Short name and/or Internet address:	⌐ ⌐
HTTP password:	⌐ (355E98E7C7B59BD810ED845 AD0FD2FC4) ⌐

Tips

If you do not allow anonymous Web browser connections to the Domino server, the server level authentication uses either the short name field or any entries within the user name field. However, for Notes database access, only the first entry within the user name field of a person record is used for authentication. This means for Notes users accessing a Domino server through a Web browser as well as Notes, the person must use his or her fully distinguished Notes name for database access. Passwords are also case sensitive. For users accessing a Notes server via HTTP, you are not required to create hierarchical user names.

Figure 13-9 shows the dialog box presented to Web users in order to access a Notes resource:

Figure 13-9

Web Browser
Authentication
Dialog Box

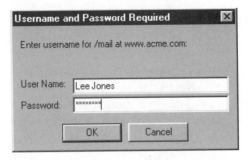

Within the HTTP section of the Notes server document of the public Name and Address book, the following fields should be configured as displayed in Figure 13-10:

Figure 13-10

HTTP Server
Security Settings

▼ **Security**

Security settings		SSL settings	
Compare public keys against those stored in Address Book:	○ Yes ◉ No	Accept SSL site certificates:	○ Yes ◉ No
Allow anonymous Notes connections:	○ Yes ◉ No	SSL key file:	⸢ keyfile.kyr ⸥
Allow anonymous HTTP connections:	◉ Yes ○ No		
Allow HTTP clients to browse databases:	◉ Yes ○ No		
Check passwords:	○ Enabled ◉ Disabled		

- **Allow anonymous HTTP connections:** If this entry is set to **No**, then the Notes server will not allow Web browser access unless a user name and password are provided. When set to **Yes**, anonymous access will be granted to the server and to any database that has the Default access in the ACL of Reader or above. The user will be treated as the user name "Anonymous," which may be placed within the ACL of the Notes application to restrict access.

- **Allow HTTP clients to browse databases:** If this field is set to **Yes** Web browsers will be able to see a list of Notes databases when issuing an OpenServer URL command. If set to **No** Web browsers will not see a list but will be able to open a

Notes application directly if the URL is known. An example URL to browse a server is `http://ACME`. If ACME is the Notes server running the HTTP process and listed within DNS, a listing of databases on that server will be listed in a manner similar to the **File**, **Database**, **Open** command within the Notes user interface.

Web Browser Database Access

Within each Notes application, you may specify individual access to the application through the ACL of the database. If the DEFAULT access is set to NO ACCESS, Web browser users will be prompted for a user name and password. If the name and password are correct, they will receive the security privileges set per their name or group within the ACL of the application. The exception is the setting within the ADVANCED section of the ACL of the Notes application. For Web browsers, the ACL access is limited by default to EDITOR access as the highest setting. So if a Web browser user is listed with DESIGNER access, but the maximum setting for Web browsers is only EDITOR, the user will only have EDITOR access. This setting is shown in Figure 13-11.

Tips

You can force a Web browser user to always be prompted for a password when accessing a database by appending &Login as an argument to a URL command. For example `http://www.acme.com/fun.nsf&Login` *would open the default view in* **fun.nsf***, but before doing so it would prompt the user for a user ID and password even if they had already provided this information during the current session.*

Figure 13-11
Maximum Database Access for Web Browsers

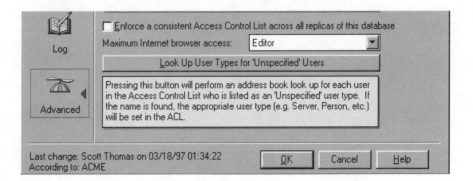

SSL Security

The Domino HTTP server supports the SSL security protocol for privacy and authentication. SSL encryption, like the standard Notes encryption, uses the RSA cryptosystems public/private key methodology. The SSL support augments the standard Notes authentication and encryption capabilities available to only Notes clients. When a Domino server is configured to use SSL, transactions between Web browsers and the server can be encrypted. SSL does not affect transactions between Notes clients and Notes servers.

In order for SSL to work, the server is required to have a unique pair of related public and private keys. These keys are used to initiate encrypted transactions between the server and browsers. Both Web servers and browsers store these keys in key ring files. There are two types of keys that can be used by Domino: self certified, and those supplied by commercial certificate authorities such as Verisign (http://www.verisign.com).

Tips

To find out more about SSL, check out RSA's FAQ at
http://www.rsa.com/rsalabs/newfaq/ql34.html.

To manage SSL key rings in the Domino environment, you should use the Domino SSL Administration database. This database allows you to create a self-certified key ring or create and send a request to a commercial certificate authority. The Domino SSL Administration database allows you to submit a certificate request directly to Verisign, or you can follow other certificate authorities procedures for submitting certificate requests.

In order to add SSL security to multiple Domino servers inside your organization the administration team can create an Intranet Certificate Authority. This too is done within the Domino SSL Administration database simply by creating a certification authority key ring. This would take place within the "Certificate Authority— Create Certificate Authority Key Ring" section of the SSL Administration database. If you decide to create your own Intranet CA, you will need to dedicate one or more administrators to process these requests (this is not a full-time job).

Once a signed certificate is received from either a commercial or internal CA, you must merge the certificate into the key ring. Copying the file to the Notes server and then using the SSL Administration database to merge the certificate into the key ring does this.

Traps

SSL certificates are host name and URL sensitive, meaning that if you change the server name and or URL, users may not be able to authenticate and encryption may not occur. Careful planning is necessary before implementing SSL security.

Administration

Most HTTP administration is a handled by standard Notes administration tasks. There are, however, a few administration tips and traps that relate only to HTTP.

Tips

You may not delete, fix up or run the compact database process against databases that have been accessed through the HTTP process. In order run these procedures against Notes databases that have been accessed through HTTP, you will need to unload the HTTP server process. You may stop the HTTP server task by typing the following line from the Notes server console:

```
tell http quit
```

Traps

If you have the compact process set to compact database every morning, any database accessed through the HTTP server process will not be compacted.

Tips

The Domino Advanced services provides the ability to build custom billing applications to gather information about mail traffic, or measure how specific applications are being used. This information is useful for ISPs charging for server access and or usage, as well as for internal chargeback in an Intranet. For more information on the Advanced Services, consult Chapter 7, Installation Procedures.

Traps

The Domino HTTP server process allows Web browsers to attach files to documents where the designer has enabled this capability. In order to attach files from a Web browser, the browser must support RFC 1867. At present only Netscape 2.x or above browsers support file attachments.

Traps

The Domino server will cache databases for faster access. This can sometimes cause problems when you are trying to do some types of database administration (see compacting, above). You could also experience anomalies when designing, testing and or redesigning applications. To clear the cache, type the following line from the Notes server console:

```
dbcache flush
```

Tips

If desired, administrators can set up cross database and cross server full-text searching, referred to as site searching. This provides functionality that users are accustomed to on most Web sites.

Tips

You should always read the Domino HTTP release notes and troubleshooting guide if you encounter problems with the HTTP process. Another excellent source of information is the Domino and Iris Web sites at `http://domino.lotus.com` *and* `http://www.notes.net,` *respectively.*

Web Browser Access

From a Web browser, a user may access Notes servers running the HTTP server process, open Notes applications (including Notes mail applications), and open HTML web pages. Within Notes applications, assuming proper security access, users may create, edit, and delete documents.

When Web browsers first access a Domino server, the user will see either an HTML page, Notes navigator, or an about document of a Notes application, as specified within the server document within the public Name and Address book. If one of these three items is not defined, a user will see a list of Notes applications available on the Notes server assuming the administrator has not disabled Web browsers from browsing Notes applications on the Notes server. Figure 13-12 shows this example:

Figure 13-12

Browsing Notes Databases through a Web Browser

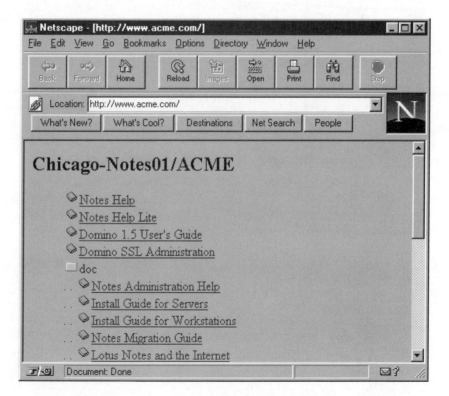

From this database list, a Web browser may enter the Notes application by clicking the link. A list of views within the application will appear. Figure 13-13 shows what a typical Notes application looks like through a Web browser:

Figure 13-13
Viewing a Notes
Application through
a Web Browser

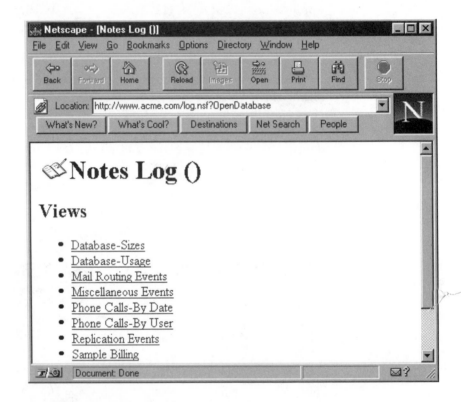

APPENDIX A

LOTUS NOTES 4.6

As of the writing of this book, Lotus Development Corporation and Iris Associates had released Notes 4.6 Pre-release 1. This pre-release product, to be delivered sometime in the summer of 1997, shows the evolution of Notes from a client dedicated specifically to interaction with a Notes/Domino server to that of a stand-alone application.

This chapter is intended to provide you an overview of the Notes 4.6 functionality and address any apparent impact it may have on new or existing Notes/Domino infrastructures.

As we discussed earlier in this book, Lotus Notes has become the stand-alone product used to not only access Domino servers but design Domino applications. The Notes moniker is attached to the client application while the Domino name is applied to the server running the core Notes engine.

What is Notes 4.6?

Lotus Notes 4.6 is an application that allows users to access Domino applications as well as non-Domino hosted applications. These applications are Internet mail, Internet/Web access and Personal Information Management (PIM)—calendaring, scheduling, and contact management.

The 4.6 release will combine major usability enhancements with Internet standards-based messaging systems. While the Domino server has supported SMTP and POP3 clients, the Notes client did not allow users access to those services. Release 4.6 changes that, and, in fact, provides a number of enhancements that will allow it to compete with similar applications from Microsoft (Outlook) and Netscape (Communicator components). The most significant of these enhancements is its ability to be used in stand-alone mode—it does not require a Domino server to function.

There are also enhancements that provide a more pleasing interface for desktop information management through updated templates and *Personal Portfolios*. The *Personal Portfolios* allow users to combine several of their most frequently used applications into one application. The applications are not physically combined into one Notes application database, but appear to the user as if they were. This functionality presents to the user a seamless view of their personal productivity tools—calendaring and scheduling, e-mail, etc.—as well as allowing them to perform seamless full-text searches.

Some of the functionalities users will be able to perform with Notes 4.6 include:

- Access POP3 Internet mail from the Notes client

- Use Microsoft's Internet Explorer in place of the Notes Web Browser (IE actually is used as an ActiveX component)

- Save Web pages browsed through Microsoft Internet Explorer directly into a Notes database as Notes documents

- Use Lotus WordPro or Microsoft Word as their e-mail editor

Impact on Existing Notes and Domino Infrastructure

The Notes 4.6 release will have little apparent impact on an existing Domino infrastructure. The 4.6 release is focused on end-user usability enhancements and not on server-side processes.

The impact on the Notes (client side) environment is difficult to gauge, but there will be some impact on administrative activities. This is due mostly to more extensive user configuration parameters, but there may also be some potential desktop resource issues because of things like Personal Portfolios. Administrators will also find that user training procedures and associated materials will need to be updated to reflect the PIM capabilities of Notes 4.6.

The configuration of most of the enhanced functionality is accomplished through modifications in the Location properties in each user personal Name and Address Book application. The administrative impact of these changes will vary based on your existing approach and policies and procedures.

Domino 4.6

While Lotus has not publicly release a pre-release version of the Domino 4.6 server, they have articulated plans to increase the price, add an Internet mail server, and provide additional server-side functionality. The enhanced functionality includes support for more Internet standards such as IMAP 4.0 (Internet Mail Access Protocol), Network News Transfer Protocol (NNTP), Lightweight Directory Access Protocol (LDAP), and Secure Sockets Layer version 3 (SSL3) certificate authorization and management. Lotus has also indicated that there will be better Java integration—allowing for Java applets to be stored in the Notes Object store—and the ability to administer a Domino server from a Web browser.

The 4.6 release of Notes and Domino will have significant positive impact on users with what we believe will be limited and manageable impact on administrators. It is encouraging to see Lotus extending the capabilities of the Notes client while at the same time supporting "open standards."

APPENDIX B

NOTES SERVER ERROR MESSAGES

Error Message	Type	Description
A duplicate recipient was specified and will be ignored	Mail	A user is listed twice within a Name and Address Book or appears within multiple cascaded Name and Address Books.
A NetWare DLL could not be found	Comm	If Novell's SPX protocol is being used for Notes, some DLL's cannot be found. *See Chapter 3.*
A NetWare library could not be loaded because a function is missing from the DLL	Comm	If Novell's SPX protocol is being used for Notes, some DLL's cannot be found. *See Chapter 3.*
A passthru message was received without the necessary context	Security	Passthru is not configured properly. *See Chapter 11.*
A path to the server could not be determined from the Connection records and Address Book	Security	Connectivity via Notes to a Notes server is not possible via the network in the Name or modem
A port with that name already exists	Comm	A port already exists in Notes with that name. *See Chapter 3.*
A transient network error or network adapter failure has truncated a message from a client. If it recurs, run the appropriate adapter diagnostics.	Server	This occurs when a network card is malfunctioning or is improperly configured.

Access control is set in <Destination Server database> to not replicate forms or views from <Source Server database>	Replica	This is a normal message when the ACL of the target database is set to DESIGNER. *See Chapter 10.*
Access control is set in <Destination Server database> to not replicate forms views or edits from <Source Server database>	Replica	This is a normal message when the ACL of the target database is set to AUTHOR. *See Chapter 10.*
>Access control is set in <Destination Server Pathname> to not allow replication from <Source Server Pathname>	Replica	This is a normal message when the ACL of the target database is set to NO ACCESS. *See Chapter 10.*
Access to data denied	Resource	This is a normal message received when access is not permitted to a resource such as a directory link. *See Chapter 8.*
Activity logging enabled for <Database Name>	Misc	This is a normal message when activity logging is enabled for a database under database Properties.
Added connection to server <Server Name> to catalog	Misc	When a connection record is added within the public Name and Address Book, it is also added to the database catalog.
Added database <Database Name> to catalog	Misc	This is a normal message stating a database is added to the catalog when the server task "catalog" is run. *See Chapter 12.*
Added database <Database Name> to Cluster Database Directory	Server	This is a normal message when Notes clustering is enabled. *See Chapter 7.*
Additional ports may not be enabled while the server is running	Comm	A port (modem or network) may not be added while the Notes server is running

AMgr: Agent <Agent Name>, cannot convert next run time to text	Server	The server cannot interpret the text data as type time.
AMgr: Another Agent Manager detected on the system, only one allowed	Server	Within the Agent Restrictions section of the Name and Address Book, the setting is only set to one allowable agent. *See Chapter 6.*
An OS/2 error has occurred. The code is <Decimal Error Code> (<Hex Error Code>) Consult your OS/2 documentation or ask for assistance.	Resource	This is a error received when running Notes on an OS/2 platform.
An unexpected authentication message was received	Security	An error has occurred during authentication. *See Chapter 12.*
Another system is using the same server name as this system	Comm	You have brought up a Notes server that is already using that server name.
AppleTalk is currently enabled on this port	Resource	AppleTalk protocol is installed. *See Chapter 3.*
AppleTalk is not installed on this system	Comm	The Notes AppleTalk driver is trying to be loaded but the machine's OS/2 does not have AppleTalk enabled.
At least one network port requires the Notes Server to be restricted to a single process, and that process has exceeded the maximum number of threads.	Server	The maximum number of allowable threads have been exceeded on a network port.
Attachment has been modified or corrupted since signed!	Misc	A digital signature has been corrupted or compromised. *See Chapter 12.*
Attempted encryption operation is not allowed outside of North America	Security	An International version of Notes is trying to perform an encryption option only allowed by North American versions. *See Chapter 12.*

Beginning consistency check of databases:	Server	This is a normal message once a Notes server starts.
Building list of databases to replicate with <Server Name>	Replica	This is a normal message once a Notes server begins a replication event. See *Chapter 10.*
Call has finished	Comm	This is a normal message once an analog Notes connection is finished.
Call in progress...	Comm	This is a normal message while an analog Notes connection is running.
Call timer expired	Comm	This message is displayed once the call timer setting within the port setup of Notes has been reached. See *Chapter 3.*
Can't perform this operation on running task	Server	An attempt to run a process or program is not able to run on the target Notes server.
Can not find the user or public key information in the Name and Address Book	Misc	The public key of the Notes server or user cannot be found within the server or person record of the public Name and Address book. See *Chapter 6.*
Cannot access or create the ID file	Security	Access to a Notes ID file has failed.
Cannot add the encryption key to your ID file. A key with that name already exists.	Security	An encryption key must have a unique name. See *Chapter 12.*
Cannot allocate database object - database would exceed its disk quota	Misc	If a database quota has been set, the threshold will not be allowed.
Cannot create database - the specified filename is a directory	Misc	A database name cannot be the same as a directory name.

Cannot create thread	Resource	Usually signifies server overload. Additional hardware may be necessary.
Cannot do that to an NSF that may be in use	Misc	An operation is trying to be performed on a database that is in use by another process on a Notes server.
Cannot find event types database . <DB Name>	Misc	The EVENTS4.NSF database cannot be located. It may need to be created.
Cannot locate required login information	Comm	A login problem was encountered such as in Microsoft's RAS.
Cannot read file	Resource	A file cannot be read as it may not exist.
Cannot store document; database has too many unique field names. Please ask your administrator to compact the database.	Misc	This may happen to the mail router database (MAIL.BOX). The server task,compact, will clear the deletion stubs. See Chapter 12.
Cannot support multiple processes using Notes in this environment	Resource	Some environments will not support multiple processes such as Windows 3.1.
Cannot write or create file (file or disk is read-only)	Resource	The floppy disk is write protected.
Cannot write to file (possibly it is READ-ONLY or the disk is out of space or not ready)	Resource	The disk drive may be full. Files may need to be deleted, the compact server task run, or additional drive space may need to be added.
Cataloger was unable to open database <Database Name>:	Misc	The cataloger server task was unable to open the target data base. See Chapter 12.

Cleared replication history in <Destination Database>	Replica	A user with manager access to a Notes database has cleared the replication history of the database. *See Chapter 10.*
Clearing modem's DTR	Comm	This is a normal message when an analog Notes connection terminates.
Command or option is not recognized	Server	A server console command was issued that is not supported or recognized by Notes.
Communications port hardware is not configured or enabled	Resource	A Notes COM port driver is enabled but it is not enabled on the operating system of the machine.
Communications port hardware not present or in use by another device	Comm	A COM port on the machine is not available or is in use by another program.
Compacting database <Database Name> (<Database Title>)	Server	The server task, compact, is running on a Notes database. *See Chapter 12.*
Compaction of the database was stopped prematurely because another user modified it while it was being compacted.	Misc	If a user is within a Notes application while the server task compact is being run, the task will terminate. Make sure no users are within an application before the task is run. *See Chapters 8 and 12.*
Copied access control list into <Destination Database> from <Source Database>	Replica	When two servers replicate a database with manager access, the ACL will also pass. *See Chapters 10 and 12.*
Could not detect carrier or dialtone; or phone was busy or did not answer	Comm	A normal message for Notes analog users and servers where a dialtone is not present.

Could not establish dialog with remote system	Comm	A common error where the two analog Notes machines cannot handshake correctly. The most likely cause is an incorrect modem MDM file on one of the machines. *See Chapter 3.*
Could not locate server document for <'Server Name'> in Stats & Events Types . Config DB	Server	Within the EVENTS4.NSF database, a server is not configured. *See Chapter 8.*
Could not open the ID file	Security	The target ID file could not be opened.
Created database catalog: <Catalog Pathname>	Misc	This message is shown when a database catalog is created, usually by the catalog server task.
Created database Cluster Database Directory:<Cluster Directory Name>	Server	Message displayed when a Notes cluster is created. *See Chapter 7.*
Data Directory cannot be accessed. Check the path given in the DIRECTORY= line in your NOTES.INI file.	Server	The Notes data directory cannot be located on the machine.
Database already contains a document with this ID (UNID)	Misc	Every document within a Notes application is associated with a Notes ID number. A document is trying to be created or replicated to a database with that number.
Database has been corrupted and can't be repaired; cannot open	Misc	A database is corrupted. Fixup or Updall may be able to repair it. *See Chapter 12.*
Database is corrupt — Cannot allocate space	Misc	A database is corrupted. Fixup or Updall may be able to repair it. *See Chapter 12.*
Database is currently being indexed by another process	Server	A second index task is trying to run against a database.

Database is not full-text indexed	Server	A full text search was trying to be performed against a database. Create a full text index. *See Chapters 8 and 12.*
Database object has been deleted	Misc	A document is trying to be accessed that was already deleted.
Database (.nsf) has grown too large; use File New Replica to recreate your file as a Notes Version 3 database capable of 1GB.	Server	A version 3 error for Notes databases. Actually database sizes can grow up to 4gigabytes.
Device or unit number already in use	Comm	A device number for a protocol is already in use. Common for NetBIOS.
Directory does not exist	Misc	A non-existent directory was trying to be accessed.
Disconnected from Server	Comm	A user or server was disconnected from the target Notes server.
Disk or network error (reading swap file) - cannot continue	Resource	For OS/2 users, the swapper file could not be read.
Document attachment is invalid	Misc	A file attachment type that is not supported by Notes.
Document has been modified or corrupted since signed! (data)	Misc	The document has been modified or compromised since it was sent by the original sender.
Document has been modified or corrupted since signed! (signature)	Misc	The document has been modified or compromised since it was sent by the original sender.
Document is not signed	Misc	The document does not contain a digital signature. *See Chapter 12.*
Drive is not ready	Resource	The floppy disk is not being read properly.
Driver already in use	Comm	A Notes driver is already being used.

Driver could not allocate memory for communications buffers	Comm	The driver, usually a COM driver, does not have enough communi cation buffers allocated for use.
Entry not found in index or view's index not built	Misc	The view should be built or rebuilt. This can be done using the updall server task. *See Chapter 12.*
Error attempting to load or run <Program Name> : <Additional Error Information>	Server	An error occurred while trying to invoke a Notes server program.
Error Compacting database <Database Name>	Server	An error was encoun tered while trying to compact a database. *See Chapters 8 and 12.*
Error fixing view <View ID> in <Database Name>	Server	The server task, updall, encoun tered an error while trying to update a view. *See Chapters 8 and 12.*
Error fixing views in <Database Name>	Server	The server task, updall, encoun tered an error while trying to update a view. *See Chapters 8 and 12.*
Error full text indexing document NT <Note ID> in database <Database Name>	Server	An error occurred while trying to full text a database. *See Chapters 8 and 12.*
Error full text indexing <Database Name>	Server	An error occurred while trying to full text a database. *See Chapters 8 and 12.*
Error getting list of AppleTalk Zones	Comm	An error when AppleTalk cannot correctly communicate on an AppleTalk network. *See Chapter 3.*
Error handling possible update conflict in <Destination Database>	Replica	A possible replication problem was encountered. *See Chapter 10.*

Error in Acquire or Connect Script; check the log file, Miscellaneous Events view, for further information.	Comm	An acquire or connect script error has occurred. *See Chapter 3.*
Error looking up name in Name & Address Book (names.nsf)	Misc	An error has occurred looking up a user's name within the Name and Address Book. *See Chapters 5 and 6.*
Error opening modem command file	Comm	A modem MD file could not be opened. *See Chapter 3.*
Exceeded maximum folder count in database.	Misc	The maximum count of 256 folders for a database has been exceeded.
Exceeded maximum limit of 300MB of shared memory	Resource	The maximum limit for shared memory has been exceeded.
Exchanging Read Marks between <Destination Database> and <Source Database>	Replica	The Notes server and client are exchanging read marks between database(s).
Field is too large (15K) or View's column & selection formulas are too large	Misc	A field or view's contents contain too much data.
Field names must be 250 characters or less	Misc	A field name within a Notes form may only be 250 characters or less in length.
File already exists	Resource	A database is trying to be created within a filename that already exists.
File does not exist	Resource	A database is trying to be accessed with a filename that does not exist.
File is in use by another program	Resource	A file is trying to be accessed that is already being used by another program.
File is not an object store. Rename it so that the router can create an object store with that name	Mail	The shared mail object store is not configured properly. *See Chapter 11.*

File name too long or invalid file name syntax	Resource	The filename being used is too long.
File not found or not a Notes database format.	Misc	A file is trying to be opened by Notes and is not in standard Notes database
File object is truncated - file may have been damaged	Misc	File is damaged. If it is a Notes application, the server task fixup can be run to try to repair it. *See Chapters 8 and 12.*
File truncated - file may have been damaged	Resource	File is damaged. If it is a Notes application, the server task fixup can be run to try to repair it. *See Chapters 8 and 12.*
Finished compacting <Database Name>, <KBytes> bytes recovered (<Percent Saved>)	Server	This message tells that the server task, compact, has finished running and tells the amount of space recovered. *See Chapters 8 and 12.*
Finished replication with server <Server Name>	Replica	This messages tells that replication has finished with the target Notes server. *See Chapter 10.*
Finished updating usage statistics	Misc	This message tells that the statistics server task has completed. *See Chapter 8.*
Finished updating views in <Database Name>	Server	This message tells that the index server task has completed up--dating database views.
Folder directory is corrupt. Please run Fixup to repair it	Misc	File is damaged. The server task fixup can be run to try to repair it. *See Chapters 8 and 12.*
Folder has no free space but should have	Misc	File may be damaged. The server task fixup can be run to try to repair it. *See Chapters 8 and 12.*

Folder is corrupt. Please run Fixup to repair it.	Misc	File is damaged. The server task fixup can be run to try to repair it. *See Chapters 8 and 12.*
Folder replication not supported by remote server	Misc	Target Notes server does not support older replication. Usually a v3 target Notes server.
Form has been deleted	Misc	The Notes database form has been deleted that the document is using.
Formula Error	Misc	The document, view, field, or agent formula contains an error.
Full text directory links must contain a valid directory name	Server	The full text index is configured improperly. *See Chapters 8 and 12.*
Full text error from Topic; see log for more information	Server	The full text index may contain an error(s). *See Chapters 8 and 12.*
Full text index not found for this database	Server	The database has been full text indexed, but the actual index cannot be located. *See Chapters 8 and 12.*
Full text indexing documents in <Database Name>	Server	The full text index is being built. *See Chapters 8 and 12.*
Groups cannot be nested more than 20 levels deep.	Mail	Groups nesting error encountered. *See Chapter 6.*
Groups cannot be nested more than 6 levels deep when mailing.	Mail	Groups nesting error encountered. *See Chapter 6.*
Help Section cannot be located	Misc	The help section of a Notes application cannot be located.
ID's certificate is invalid	Security	An ID file's certificate is invalid. *See Chapter 12.*

ID file cannot be created	Security	An ID file cannot be created. See *Chapter 8.*
ID file not found in Name & Address Book	Misc	A Notes workstation is being configured for setup with the option of obtaining the ID file from the public Name and Address book. The ID file, however, does not exist. See *Chapter 8.*
Idle	Replica	A server task is running but idle.
In the [386Enh] section, add: NetHeapSize =<Desired Heap Size>	Server	For Windows 3.1 users, the NetHeapSize needs to be increased.
Incorrect console security password	Server	A console password has been set on the Notes server, but has been incorrectly entered. See *Chapter 12.*
Index corrupted - will be rebuilt automatically when database is closed or server is restarted	Misc	A database index is corrupted. Can be manually rebuilt using the updall server task from the server console. See *Chapter 12.*
Initializing	Replica	Replication server task is initializing replication with a target Notes server.
Insufficient arguments. Enter 'HELP' for the correct syntax.	Server	A server console command was entered without the appropriate arguments.
Insufficient disk space	Resource	Not enough disk space is available on the Notes machine. Run com pact Notes server task, delete files, or add additional disk space.
Insufficient IPX sockets are available. Consult NetWare documentation to increase the maximum number of sockets.	Comm	See *Chapter 3.*

Insufficient IPX sockets, SPX sessions, or TLI endpoints are available. Consult NetWare documentation to increase these resources.	Comm	*See Chapter 3.*
Insufficient memory - a Notes memory pool is full	Misc	A Notes memory pool has been exhausted. Increase the pool. *See Chapter 6 - "Configuration Documents."*
Insufficient TCP sockets are available. Consult your vendor's TCP/IP documentation to increase the maximum number of sockets.	Comm	*See Chapter 3.*
Internal error in network operating system	Comm	An error occurred within the OS network driver.
Internal error in Notes NetWare port driver	Comm	The Notes SPX network driver reported an error.
Internal error in Notes TCP port driver	Comm	The Notes TCP network driver reported an error.
Mail Conversion Utility failed	Mail	The mail convert server program failed. *See Chapters 8 and 11.*
Mail held in outgoing mailbox for transfer. to 1 user	Mail	*See Chapter 11.*
Mail held in outgoing mailbox for transfer to <number of> users.	Maill	*See Chapter 11.*
Mail submitted for delivery. (1 Person/Group).	Mail	A Notes mail message was transferred for 1 user. *See Chapter 11.*
Mail submitted for delivery. (<Number of> People/Groups).	Mail	A Notes mail message was transferred for X users. *See Chapter 11.*
Mailconv: Categories to folder conversion failed on <Database Name>	Mail	The mail convert server program failed. *See Chapters 8 and 11.*

Mailconv: Design replacement failed on <Database Name>	Mail	The mail convert server program failed. *See Chapters 8 and 11.*
Mailconv: Failed to build a list of mail files in <Database Name>	Mail	The mail convert server program failed. *See Chapters 8 and 11.*
Mailconv: Failed to build a list of mail files in <View Name>:View	Mail	The mail convert server program failed. *See Chapters 8 and 11.*
Mailconv: Failed to open database <Database Name>	Mail	The mail convert server program failed. *See Chapters 8 and 11.*
Mailconv: Failed to open template file <File Name>	Mail	The mail convert server program failed. *See Chapters 8 and 11.*
Mailconv: Failed to open textfile <File Name>	Mail	The mail convert server program failed. *See Chapters 8 and 11.*
Mailconv: Invalid Option	Mail	The mail convert server program failed. *See Chapters 8 and 11.*
Mailconv: Missing file name	Mail	The mail convert server program failed. *See Chapters 8 and 11.*
Mailconv: No database found that matches <Database Name>	Mail	The mail convert server program failed. *See Chapters 8 and 11.*
Mailconv: Skipping database : <Database Name>Template does not match the specified old template name	Mail	The mail convert server program failed. *See Chapters 8 and 11.*
Mailconv: When using the -d option you must specify old and new templates	Mail	The mail convert server program failed. *See Chapters 8 and 11.*
Make call to server	Comm	For analog Notes users, asks to make call to target Notes server.

Maximum hop count exceeded. Message probably in a routing loop.	Mail	Mail message "ping ponging" between Notes servers. Maximum hop count is 25. *See Chapter 11.*
Message contains too many recipients (over 4 megabytes).	Mail	*See Chapter 11.*
Modem command file contains an illegal character sequence	Comm	Modem MDM file contains an illegal AT command. *See Chapter 3.*
Modem command file variable is not recognized	Comm	Modem MDM file contains an illegal AT variable. *See Chapter 3.*
Modem could not detect dial tone	Comm	Modem could not detect dial tone. *See Chapter 3.*
Modem lost carrier	Comm	The modem lost the connection to the target Notes server.
Name and Address database contains no Connection document for that server	Comm	The Notes server is trying to connect to a target Notes server but does not have a connection record within the public Name and Address book. *See Chapters 6, 10, and 11.*
Name & Address Book contains a Connection entry with no schedule information	Comm	The connection record does not have any scheduling information with the target Notes server. *See Chapters 6, 10, and 11.*
Name & Address Book database (names.nsf) does not exist	Misc	The Notes machine does not have a Name and Address Book. One must exist in order to operate. *See Chapter 5.*

Name & Address database does not contain a server entry for this server	Server	The Notes server cannot start unless an entry within the public Name and Address book exists for the Notes server. *See Chapters 6 and 7.*
NETBIOS not loaded or not running	Comm	The NetBIOS protocol is not configured. *See Chapter 3.*
NETBIOS unit number specified in NOTES.INI is too large	Comm	The NetBIOS unit number is not configured. *See Chapter 3.*
NetWare AppleTalk is not installed or could not be initialized	Comm	The AppleTalk protocol is not configured. *See Chapter 3.*
NetWare IPX is not installed or could not be initialized	Comm	The IPX protocol is not configured. *See Chapter 3.*
NetWare IPX/SPX could not be initialized: Insufficient conventional memory. Try loading fewer DOS device drivers or TSRs.	Comm	The IPX protocol is not configured properly .on the machine *See Chapter 3.*
NetWare IPX/SPX could not be initialized: No IPX/SPX control blocks (ECBs) available.	Comm	The IPX protocol is not configured properly on the machine. *See Chapter 3.*
NetWare IPX/SPX could not be initialized: Packet size is too large.	Comm	The IPX protocol is not configured properly on the machine. *See Chapter 3.*
NetWare IPX/SPX error: Lock failed, possibly due to insufficient memory	Comm	The IPX protocol is not configured properly on the machine. *See Chapter 3.*
NetWare is not started or the netware.drv Windows driver is not installed.	Comm	The IPX protocol is not configured properly on the machine. *See Chapter 3.*
NetWare service advertising (SAP) failed to start	Comm	On Windows NT, the SAP agent is required. *See Chapter 3.*

NetWare SPX is not installed or could not be initialized	Comm	The SPX protocol is not configured. *See Chapter 3.*
Network adapter not installed or not functioning	Comm	The network card is malfunctioning or is not installed.
Network adapter not working; check cable	Comm	The network card may not be functioning or the cable may be loose.
Network adapter too busy to handle request	Comm	The network card may be too busy.
Network authentication message is too short	Security	A possible network authentication occurred.
Network driver has not been initialized	Comm	The network driver on the OS has not initialized.
Network error due to transient network condition or hardware failure	Comm	A network error occurred.
Network error: message has been corrupted	Security	A Notes document or message has been corrupted due to a network error.
Network error: message has incorrect sequence number	Comm	A network packet was received out of sequence order. *See Chapter 3.*
Network not started	Comm	The networking software on the OS has not yet been started.
Network operation did not complete in a reasonable amount of time; please retry	Comm	The network is timing out. Due to an unreachable network/server or an overloaded network/server.
Network operation was canceled	Comm	The network operation was canceled usually due to a person pressing Control-Break on the keyboard.

Network traffic is being encrypted at the server's request...	Security	All data with the target Notes server is encrypted over the network with the Notes port settings. *See Chapters 3 and 12.*
New mail has been delivered to you!	Mail	A new mail message has been delivered to the user's mail database.
Newly disabled ports will remain active until the program is restarted	Comm	The network port will remain active until the Notes program is restarted.
No certificates in common	Security	Two user ID files do not have a certificate in common. *See Chapters 8 and 12.*
No databases to replicate on that server	Replica	The target Notes server does not have any replica databases in common to replicate.
No documents were deleted	Misc	A request to delete documents was made, but none were deleted.
No mail sent	Mail	A request to send mail was made, but no mail was sent.
No Name & Address Book database found.	Mail	A search was made for a Name and Address Book, but none was found.
No route found to domain. \<Domain Name> from server \<Server Name> via server \<Server Name>. Check Server, Connection and Domain documents in Name & Address Book	Mail	A Notes mail message was sent to a specified Notes domain, but the target Notes server did not have any connection records pertaining to that domain. *See Chapter 11.*

No route found to domain <Domain Name> from server <Server Name>. Check Server, Connection and Domain documents in Name & Address Book	Mail	A Notes mail message was sent to a .specified Notes domain, but the home mail server did not have any connection records pertaining to that domain. *See Chapter 11.*
No such port known	Comm	A request to access a Notes port driver was initiated, but no such port is configured within Notes. *See Chapter 3.*
None of the selected databases has a replica on the server	Replica	A request to replicate a specific database was initiated, but the target Notes server does not have a database with the same replica ID on the server. *See Chapter 10.*
Not authorized to open destination Replica database		A request to open a target Notes database was denied. The database ACL is set to not allow access. *See Chapter 12.*
Not authorized to open source database	Replica	A request to open a target Notes databasewas denied. The database ACL is set to not allow access. *See Chapter 12.*
Not replicating <Destination Server database> (not authorized to read <Source Server database>)	Replica	The ACL of the target Notes application is set not to allow replication to the initiating Notes server. *See Chapters 10 and 12.*
Notes requires a newer NetWare OS/2 Requester, v1.3f (NSD4) or later.	Comm	Notes requires the latest network drivers. *See Chapter 3.*
Notes requires a newer NetWare OS/2 Requester, v2.0b or later.	Comm	Notes requires the latest network drivers. *See Chapter 3.*

Notes requires newer NetWare SPX.SYS and SPDAEMON.EXE files, v3.0b or later	Comm	Notes requires the latest network drivers. *See Chapter 3.*
Notes requires newer NetWare SPX.SYS and SPDAEMON.EXE files, v3.0g (July 23, 1992) or later	Comm	Notes requires the latest network drivers. *See Chapter 3.*
Notes requires System 7.0 or later	Resource	Notes requires at least System 7.0. *See Chapter 2.*
One or more of the source document's attachment are missing. Run Fixup to delete the document in the source database.	Misc	Document may be corrupted. Run the server task fixup. *See Chapters 8 and 12.*
Partially replicated <Destination Server database> (due to previously reported error)	Replica	A replication error has occurred. *See Chapter 10.*
Passthru connect to remote server failed	Security	A passthru connection failed. *See Chapter 11.*
Passthru function codes is not recognized	Security	A passthru connection failed. *See Chapter 11.*
Periodic full text indexer - Error full text indexing <Database Name>	Server	An error occurred on the full text index of a database. *See Chapters 8 and 12.*
Periodic full text indexer error	Server	An error occurred on the full text index of a database. *See Chapters 8 and 12.*
Periodic full text indexer not started - need to specify HOURLY, DAILY, WEEKLY program argument	Server	Full text index settings not configured. *See Chapters 8 and 12.*
Periodic macro agent - Error opening macro <Macro Name> in <Database Name>	Server	An error occurred opening a Notes agent. *See Chapters 8 and 12.*

Periodic macro agent - Error opening running <Macro Name> in <Database Name>	Server	An error occurred opening a Notes agent. *See Chapters 8 and 12.*
Periodic macro agent - Error opening <Database Name>	Server	An error occurred opening a Notes agent. *See Chapters 8 and 12.*
Periodic macro agent - Error searching <Database Name> for macros	Server	An error occurred opening a Notes agent. See *See Chapters 8 and 12.*
Port specified in Connection document in Address Book (to reach that server) is not configured on this system	Comm	The Notes port is not configured within the server document. *See Chapter 6 - "Server Documents."*
Program shutdown in progress	Comm	Notes program is shutting down.
Recipient's Name & Address Book entry does not specify a mail file	Mail	The person record for the recipient must be configured to specify a mail file. *See Chapter 6 - "Person Documents."*
Remote user's identity is fraudulent	Security	Under the security section of the server document, check public keys is enabled and the ID file is assumed fraudulent. *See Chapters 6 and 12.*
Remote user failed authentication	Security	The user failed to authenticate with the Notes server. *See Chapter 6.*
Removed database <Database Name> from catalog	Misc	The catalog server task removed a database from the Notes catalog. *See Chapter 12.*
Removed database <Database Name> from Cluster Database Directory	Server	The adminp server task removed a database from a Notes cluster. *See Chapter 7.*

Replicating files with <Server Name>	Replica	The Notes machine is replicating with the target Notes server. *See Chapter 10.*
Replicating <Destination Database> from <Source Database>	Replica	The Notes machine is replicating with the target Notes server. *See Chapter 10.*
Replication cannot proceed because it cannot maintain uniform access control list on replicas	Replica	The Notes database has "Enforce Consistent ACL Across All Replicas" enabled. *See Chapters 10 and 12.*
Replication history in <Destination Server database>is corrupted and cannot be repaired. Please make a new replica copy of the database.	Replica	The replication history is corrupted in the Note database. *See Chapter 10.*
Replication history is corrupted. Use File Database Copy (Replica) to clear the history.	Replica	The replication history is corrupted in the Note database. *See Chapter 10.*
Replication is disabled for this database	Replica	Replication has been disabled for the database. *See Chapter 10.*
Replication is disabled for <Database Name>	Replica	Replication has been disabled for the database. *See Chapter 10.*
Replicator added <number of> document(s) to <Destination Database> from <Source Database>	Replica	Replication has finished and is reporting all document replicated. *See Chapter 10.*
Replicator deleted duplicate document in <Database Name>	Replica	The Notes replicator task found duplicate documents and deleted the duplicate. *See Chapter 10.*
Replicator deleted <number of> document(s) in <Destination Database> from <Source Database>	Replica	The replicator task is reporting the number of deleted documents for the recent replication event. *See Chapter 10.*

Replicator unable to build list of local databases - insufficient memory in pool.	Replica	The memory pool on the Notes server does not have enough resources to spawn a replication event.
Replicator updated <number of> document(s) in _<Destination Database> from <Source Database>_	Replica	The replicator task is reporting the number of updated documents for the recent replication event. See Chapter 10.
Reporter: Updating values from Configuration document	Server	See Chapter 8.
Requesting system's ID is the same as the server's ID. You cannot use the same ID on two systems.	Server	You have tried to access a Notes server with the same ID file that is running the Notes server.
Router task not running	Server	The Notes mail router task is not runningon the Notes server. See Chapter 11.
Router: Beginning mailbox file compaction	Mail	The Notes mail router mail box (MAIL.BOX) is being compacted. See Chapters 11 and 12.
Router: Completed mailbox file compaction	Mail	The Notes mail router mail box (MAIL.BOX) was compacted. See Chapters 11 and 12.
Router: Connection from server <Server Name> not used; Server not found in Address Book.	Mail	A connection document to a Notes server within the same domain was found to a non-existent Notes server. See Chapters 10 and 11.
Router: Error opening Name & Address Book <Database Name>	Mail	The public Name and Address book could not be opened.
Router: Error reading public key for <Server Name>from the Name & Address Book	Mail	The server key within the server document could not be read. See Chapter 6.

Router: Error searching mailbox file <Database Name>	Mail	The Notes server mail router database (MAIL.BOX) could not be opened. *See Chapter 11.*
Router: Mailbox file <Database Name> is corrupt	Mail	The Notes server mail router database (MAIL.BOX) is corrupted. Either delete it and the Notes server will recreate upon startup or try to run fixup. *See Chapters 11 and 12.*
Router: No messages transferred to <Server Name>	Mail	No mail messages were transferred to the target Notes server. *See Chapter 11.*
Router: Transferred <Message Count> messages to <Server Name>	Mail	The Notes mail router is specifying the number of mail messages transferred. *See Chapter 11.*
Router: Unable to compact mailbox file <Database Name>	Mail	The compact server task is unable to compact the mail router mail box while it is open. *See Chapters 11 and 12.*
Router: Unable to find view <View Name> in Address Book	Mail	The mail router is looking for a specific view within the Name and Address Book and cannot locate it. *See Chapters 6 and 11.*
Router: Unable to open mailbox file <Database Name>	Mail	The Notes mail router is trying to deliver mail to a target Notes server, however, the server is not responding or accepting deliveries. *See Chapter 11.*
Server is not a cluster member	Replica	The Notes server is not a member of a Notes cluster. *See Chapter 7.*

Template file does not exist	Server	The designer server task is trying to update the design of a data-base based on a Notes template that cannot be located. *See Chapters 8 and 12.*
The Address Book does not contain a cross certificate capable of validating the public key	Security	*See Chapter 12.*
The Address Book does not contain any cross certificates capable of validating the signature.	Misc	*See Chapter 12.*
The full text index needs to be rebuilt	Server	The full text index may be corrupt and needs to be rebuilt. *See Chapters 8 and 12.*
The ID file is a safe copy and cannot be used for that purpose	Security	*See Chapters 8 and 12.*
The Notes server is not a known TCP/IP host	Comm	The Notes server name cannot be resolved into a TCP/IP address. Check the connection record, local HOST file on the server, or DNS. *See Chapters 3 and 6.*
The remote TCP/IP host is not running the Notes server, or the server is busy.	Comm	The remote server cannot be reached via the TCP/IP network. Check network connectivity and make sure the target Notes server is running. *See Chapter 3.*
The server's Address Book does not contain any cross certificates capable of authenticating you	Security	*See Chapters 8 and 12.*
The server you are currently connected todoes not support passthru and cannot route us to the designated target server	Security	*See Chapter 11.*

The specified ID file may only be used inside of North America.	Security	A North American ID file is trying to be used with an International version of Notes.
This is a non-hierarchically named server anddoes not support passthru routing to remote servers	Security	*See Chapter 11.*
This recipient's public key could not be found in the Address book	Mail	Check the person document of the person. *See Chapters 6 and 12.*
Unable to fixup database <Database Name>	Server	The fixup server task was unable to fixup the database. *See Chapter 12.*
Unable to replicate with server <Server Name>	Replica	The Notes server was unable to replicate with the target Notes server. *See Chapter 10.*
Unable to replicate <Database Name>	Replica	The Notes server was unable to replicate the database with the target Notes server. *See Chapter 10.*
Warning, database <Database Name> has exceeded its warning size threshold	Misc	*See Chapter 8.*
WARNING: Both <Template File> and <Template File> claim to be Design Template '<Template Name>'	Misc	A database and a template both claim to be the template for a database. Under database properties, deselect one database within design properties.
Wrong Password. (Passwords are case sensitive - be sure to use correct upper and lower case.)	Security	An incorrect password was entered for a Notes ID file.
You are not authorized to access that database	Misc	The ACL of a database is set not to allow access. *See Chapter 12.*

You are not authorized to create new databases on this server	Misc	The field within the server document of the Notes server is set not to allow you access to create new databases. See *Chapters 6 and 12.*
You are not authorized to create new replica databases on this server	Misc	The field within the server document of the Notes server is set not to allow you access to create new databases. See *Chapters 6 and 12.*
You are not authorized to delete that database	Misc	You need manager ACL access to a database in order to delete a database. See *Chapter 12.*
You are not authorized to perform that operation	Misc	The proper security equivalencies have not been granted to perform that function. See *Chapter 12.*
You are not authorized to use the remote console on this server	Server	You are not listed as an administrator for the Notes server within the Notes server document. See *Chapter 6.*
You are not authorized to use the server	Server	You are not allowed access to theNotes server within the Restrictions section of the server document. See *Chapter 6.*
Your certificate has expired	Security	Your certificate has expired and you must be recertified. See *Chapter 8.*

Index

A

B

C

S

T

U

W

X

About the Authors

Scott L. Thomas currently is a Senior Network Specialist at Paranet Incorporated, specializing in Lotus Notes and Windows NT architectures. He has his Master's degree in Computer Telecommunications from DePaul University and holds certifications as a Certified Lotus Professional (CLP), Certified Microsoft Systems Engineer (MCSE), and a Certified NetWare Administrator (CNA). He has been designing and configuring enterprise Lotus Notes and Windows NT networks since 1991 for numerous Fortune 1000 organizations.

Before Paranet Incorporated, Scott was a Senior Network Consultant for Price Waterhouse LLC's Management Consulting Services where he specialized in Lotus Notes and Windows NT network design and analysis. While at Price Waterhouse, he also performed several presentations at Price Waterhouse conferences on Lotus Notes and other networking technology topics. He is also co-author of *The Lotus Notes Certification Guide: Application Development and System Administration* and a technical reviewer of *Windows NT Security* by Charlie B. Rutstein. Both books are also published by McGraw-Hill. Scott can be reached at *slthomas@earthlink.net*.

Brad J. Hoyt is the Knowledge Systems Manager for USWeb Corporation, with specific expertise in architecting and deploying community-based knowledge management systems. He has a broad range of experience in collaborative computing technologies, and has been a user (and abuser) of Lotus Notes since before its initial release in 1990. Brad has architected enterprise Notes systems and consulted with many organizations on their Notes deployments. His experience also includes responsibility for multiple in-depth Notes system security reviews in Fortune 500 companies, as well as the development of a methodology for conducting Notes security reviews. He has developed and deployed numerous Notes applications, including the first application used to publicly publish content to subscribers, an application still in use today.

Prior to joining USWeb Corporation, he was the West Region Manager for grapeVINE Technologies LLC. Brad also spent six and one half years at Price Waterhouse LLP, most recently as a Manager and technical architect in the Technology Knowledge Organization. He was also a manager in the Tax Technology Group. He has spoken extensively on technology and Notes issues at conferences and seminars, and has been quoted in periodicals such as *InfoWorld* and *PCWeek*. Brad can be reached at *hoyt@acm.org*.